INSIGHT GUIDES

NORTH aMeRiCan & aLaSKan CRUiSeS

Discovery
CHANNEL

APA PUBLICATIONS
Part of the Langenscheidt Publishing Group
L

INSIGHT GUIDE
NORTH AMERICAN & ALASKAN CRUISES

Editorial
Project Editor
Hanna Rubin
Managing Editor
Lesley Gordon
Editorial Director
Brian Bell

Distribution

United States
Langenscheidt Publishers, Inc.
46–35 54th Road, Maspeth, NY 11378
Fax: 1 (718) 784 0640

Canada
Thomas Allen & Son Ltd
390 Steelcase Road East
Markham, Ontario L3R 1G2
Fax: (1) 905 475 6747

UK & Ireland
GeoCenter International Ltd
The Viables Centre, Harrow Way
Basingstoke, Hants RG22 4BJ
Fax: (44) 1256 817988

Australia
Universal Publishers
1 Waterloo Road
Macquarie Park, NSW 2113
Fax: (61) 2 9888 9074

New Zealand
Hema Maps New Zealand Ltd (HNZ)
Unit D, 24 Ra ORA Drive
East Tamaki, Auckland
Fax: (64) 9 273 6479

Worldwide
**Apa Publications GmbH & Co.
Verlag KG (Singapore branch)**
38 Joo Koon Road, Singapore 628990
Tel: (65) 6865 1600. Fax: (65) 6861 6438

Printing

Insight Print Services (Pte) Ltd
38 Joo Koon Road, Singapore 628990
Tel: (65) 6865 1600. Fax: (65) 6861 6438

©2004 Apa Publications GmbH & Co.
Verlag KG (Singapore branch)
All Rights Reserved

First Edition 2004

CONTACTING THE EDITORS
We would appreciate it if readers
would alert us to errors or out-
dated information by writing to:
**Insight Guides, P.O. Box 7910,
London SE1 1WE, England.
Fax: (44) 20 7403 0290.
insight@apaguide.co.uk**

www.insightguides.com

ABOUT THIS BOOK

This guidebook combines the interests and enthusiasms of two of the world's best-known information providers: Insight Guides, whose titles have set the standard for visual travel guides since 1970, and Discovery Channel, the world's premier source of nonfiction television programming.

The editors of Insight Guides provide practical advice and a general understanding about a place's history, culture, institutions and people. Discovery Channel and its website, www.discovery.com, help millions of viewers explore the world from the comfort of their home and encourage them to explore it firsthand.

This book is structured to guide readers planning to take a cruise in North America.

◆ The **Features** section, with a yellow bar at the top of each page, covers natural and cultural history in a series of informative essays.

◆ The **Places** section, indicated by a blue bar, is a complete guide to all the sights and areas worth visiting. Places of special interest are coordinated by number with the maps.

◆ The **Travel Tips** listings section, with an orange bar, provides a handy point of reference for cruise information on what to see on dry land, hotels, shops, restaurants and much more.

The contributors

This book was produced by **Lesley Gordon**, editor of *Insight Guide Caribbean Cruises*. Gordon collaborated with New York editor and writer, **Hanna Rubin**, who project edited this guide. Rubin, former executive editor

of *Travel Holiday*, recruited a team of talented US writers, such as travel writer and boating expert **Michael A. Smith** who wrote the introduction, *The Wonder of Water*, *A Land Built by Water*, and *Hawaiian History*.

Sherri Eisenberg, a former cruising editor for *Travel Holiday*, wrote *Life on a Cruise Ship*, *What You Need to Know Before Booking*, *Topical Talks*, *The West Coast*, *Napa and Sonoma*, *Wine Country Cruises* and *Pacific Cruises Around Hawaii*.

Christine Ryan, former editor of *European Travel and Life* and *Travel Holiday*, wrote the Alaska introduction, *Environmental Concerns*, *Your Own Private Alaska*, *Native Alaskans* and on the region's wildlife and parks.

Matt Hannafin, a columnist for the *Boston Herald* and a travel guide editor, wrote *Unspoiled Alaska*, *The Impact of Tourism*, *Big Ships versus Small*, and *Homeporting*.

Travel writer **Heidi Sarna** contributed *New England and Eastern Canada: Yesterday and Today*, *Big Ships versus Small* and *Cruising the East Coast*. **Carolyn Spencer Brown** contributed *Southern and Eastern Coastal Ports*, *The Seeds of Discontent*, *New York to Florida* and features on the St Lawrence Seaway.

River cruise expert and author **Theodore W. Scull** supplied the text for *America's Waterways*, *Steamboat Legacy*, *The Coastal and River Cruise Lines*, *The US Army Corps*, *The Upper Mississippi* and *Lower Mississippi Ports*, *The Atchafalaya Basin*, *To the Pacific Northwest*, *Columbia and Snake River Ports* and additional material on the Ohio River.

San Diego Union Tribune columnist and travel book author, **Maribeth Mellin** wrote *Cruising the Baja Peninsula* and *Exploring the Sea of Cortéz*. Editor-in-Chief of cruisecritic.com, **Sharon Dodd**, wrote *Family Cruising* and *Sailing the Great Lakes*.

Leigh Newman contributed *An Introduction to Cajun and Creole Country* and *Cajun and Creole Food*. **M.T. Schwartzman** wrote two features about the Ohio, Tennessee and Cumberland Rivers and their ports and also provided text for *Your Own Private Alaska*.

Steve Wilson compiled the invaluable practical cruise information for Travel Tips. **Pam Barrett** and **Sylvia Suddes** helped to edit the text, while **Roger Williams** and **Hilary Genin** assembled the striking photography. Thanks go to all the cruise lines and tourism offices that provided assistance.

Map Legend

▬ ▬ ▪ ▪	International Boundary
─ ─ ─ ─	State/Province Boundary
⊖	Border Crossing
▪ ─ ▪ ─	National Park/Reserve
─ ─ ─ ─	Ferry Route
Ⓜ	Subway/Metro
✈ ✈	Airport: International/Regional
🚌	Bus Station
❶	Tourist Information
✉	Post Office
✝ ✝ ✝	Church/Ruins
✝	Monastery
☪	Mosque
✡	Synagogue
🏰 🏚	Castle/Ruins
🏠	Mansion/Stately home
∴	Archaeological Site
∩	Cave
🗿	Statue/Monument
★	Place of Interest

The main places of interest in the Places section are coordinated by number with a full-colour map (e.g. ❶), and a symbol at the top of every right-hand page tells you where to find the map.

INSIGHT GUIDE
NORTH AMERICAN
& ALASKAN
CRUISES

CONTENTS

Inside front cover:
North American Cruise Area
Inside back cover:
North American States
and Provinces

Introduction

History

Features

Canadian Empress passes Boldt Castle, St Lawrence River.

Travel Tips

Places

THE WONDER OF WATER

America's pioneers took to the water to explore the New World,

and traveling by ship today provides a fresh perspective

Why travel North America by ship, when there's an excellent highway system, plenty of inexpensive motels and restaurants, and the world's greatest selection of unusual roadside attractions? Because water – oceans, rivers, and lakes – is crucial to this continent, and the view from the deck of a ship is pleasantly different from that through a windshield. Since 1492, explorers, pirates, entrepreneurs, and immigrants have all relied upon water to achieve their goals; in the process, they created the New World. Traveling by water allows contemporary visitors to relive, albeit a lot more comfortably, the experiences of sea-borne folks who came before.

The oceans served as allies in the American War of Independence and, later, in the War of 1812, when a fledgling United States was defended by brave seamen in stout frigates. Great rivers carried produce from the heart of the continent to seaports and the rest of the world; when the keelboats, barges, and steamboats returned upriver, they brought the manufactured goods pioneers needed to tame the wilderness. Ships carried would-be gold millionaires around Cape Horn to California and, later, Alaska; merchant captains from Salem, Massachusetts, sailed to the Far East, earning fortunes in the China trade; whalers from New Bedford and Nantucket provided oil for lighting cities, and baleen for ladies' corsets.

Arriving by sea

Sure, flying is faster, and driving lets you haul more stuff than you need, but nothing beats reaching your destination by sea. Gradually, you'll see traces of the land ahead, before you see the land itself: maybe a smudge of pollution on the horizon (let's not pretend it isn't the 21st century), or the glow of city lights if you approach at night. On an inland passage you'll see other ships, or their red, green, and white lights, some nearing port alongside you, others heading out on new adventures. Look over the side and you might see leaping dolphins, or, at night, their phosphorescent trails as they frolic under the water; a band of eerie light, as wide as an interstate, just beneath the surface means a vast school of fish.

Perhaps the most impressive landfall on the planet, and one that started the new lives of millions of immigrants, is New York City. At night you'll see the glow of the city before you see the buildings themselves; any time of day the graceful Verrazano Narrows Bridge swoops across the Narrows, the "door" to the harbor, and then the golden-torched Statue of Liberty comes into view. How can there be that many lightbulbs all in one place? Landing at JFK or driving in on Interstate 95 just doesn't cut it against making landfall from the Atlantic. ❑

PRECEDING PAGES: approaching New York's impressive landfall; sail past icebergs as big as ships in Alaska; the power of the paddlewheel on the steamboat *Natchez*.
LEFT: *Canadian Empress* sails past the St Lawrence River lighthouse.

A LAND BUILT BY WATER

In the early days of America's history, exploration, trade, and settlement were all made possible by the rivers running through the continent

From the Vikings to modern-day travelers, a journey by water has an enduring fascination, and although the land has changed, the sea is the same as it's always been. What better way to discover a land than to see it unfold as you make a watery approach. Sailing in to New York City offers an unforgettable

experience, when you catch sight of the Statue of Liberty and next to her the restored buildings on Ellis Island. This view has unparalleled significance, since it was the first stop for so many people who were soon to become Americans. In fact, every port has a story to tell about the people and the events that helped shaped a nation.

The Vikings are disappointed

When Viking explorers from Greenland sailed to farthest-north Newfoundland c.1000–1015, they didn't have quite the same experience as modern sailors. The Norsemen found limitless tundra and hordes of unwelcoming natives they called *skraelings* (Norse for "wretches"), prob-

ably the ancestors of the Beothuk Native Americans who met later European explorers. Unfortunately for the Vikings there was no pot of gold at the base of the glacier: After deadly battles with *skraelings*, while finding nothing they didn't have at home, the Norsemen returned to Greenland, where their colony survived until late in the 15th century.

Undoubtedly, during their Canadian adventure, the Vikings explored southward from their settlement at L'Anse aux Meadows, where the remains of buildings and many artifacts have been excavated; unfortunately, reliable evidence of where they voyaged has yet to be discovered. Chances are, they sailed up the St Lawrence River, and maybe as far south as New England. But who knows for sure? Nevertheless, almost 500 years before Columbus, there was a brief, Scandinavian-led sea trade between Europe and North America. Intriguingly, many of the officers and crew of modern cruise ships are Scandinavian.

The Siberians find the land bridge

Because the Vikings went home early, Christopher Columbus gets credit for "discovering" America in 1492, at least as far as the Eurocentric world is concerned. But the earliest humans arrived on foot from northern Asia, according to modern anthropological theory. About 18,000 years ago, during the last Ice Age, the first intrepid Siberians crossed a land bridge between modern-day Russia and Alaska. DNA evidence suggests that over the next few thousand years descendants of these explorers continued migrating south, across the Isthmus of Panama and deep into South America.

When the Ice Age ended and sea levels rose, about 11,000 years ago, the land bridge was engulfed; today it lies under the Bering Strait. Everyone who arrived in North America after that, until the age of aviation, came by boat, including a second wave of Asians around 8,000 years ago. Seagoing accommodations back then weren't as plush as you'll enjoy today, but chances are those adventurers "ooh-ed" and "aah-ed" as much as modern travelers do as they sailed along Alaska's Inside Passage.

The Spaniards find treasure

Columbus's arrival started the real age of American exploration: his account of gold, silver, and jewels in the hands of relatively defenseless natives was bait the *conquistadors* could not resist – and they had the ships, men, and money to mount voyages of discovery and exploitation. For the first half century after Columbus, New World exploration was primarily a Spanish endeavor, in the Caribbean, Mexico (and what is today southern California) and South America.

Montréal. Starting in 1603, another Frenchman, Samuel de Champlain, pushed even farther into the continent, reaching Lake Huron in 1613. He also mapped the Maine coast, and sailed as far south as Martha's Vineyard. Guided by Huron Native Americans, he was the first European to visit Lake Champlain, now a popular tourist destination on the New York/Vermont border, and home to Champ, America's answer to the Loch Ness Monster. The French presence in Canada today results from Champlain's explorations, and the St Lawrence River is still a vital thoroughfare for seaborne trade. Is it different today, if you take a cruise along the St

Eventually other countries joined in, for a combination of commercial and religious purposes. France funded major expeditions, primarily to the northern reaches of the continent, resulting in land claims. On three voyages in the 1530s and 1540s, Jacques Cartier explored Newfoundland and the St Lawrence River, which stretches 750 miles (1,200 km) into the heart of southern Canada. He anchored his ships near what is today Québec City, then took small boats upriver to the site of present-day

Lawrence? Sure, but the basic geography is the same as Cartier and Champlain found.

Plunder and piracy

Precious metals and enslaved African men and women were the first commodities traded in the New World, although "trading" might be overstating the case when it comes to *conquistadors*. Every year, Spanish fleets sailed home with millions of dollars worth of plundered gold and silver, embarking from Havana and following the Gulf Stream past Florida and the Carolinas before veering east. Rich cargoes combined with predictable routes and constricted sea lanes between Florida and

LEFT: Jewish refugees arrive in New York Harbor.
ABOVE: a Silversea vessel sails past the Statue of Liberty on Ellis Island, New York.

Sir Francis Drake

Sir Francis Drake was the classic English sea-dog, a privateer and adventurer who, in the service of Queen Elizabeth I, harassed the Spanish and plundered their treasure on both sides of the Atlantic. Drake's actions before and during the Spanish Armada's assault on England in 1588 contributed greatly to its humiliating defeat, and to England becoming the world's most powerful seafaring nation. But few realize that Drake was also an explorer, and the first Englishman to sail around the world. In the last quarter of the 16th

century, his was the only serious English challenge to Spanish power in North America.

Born around 1540 in Tavistock, Devon, in his early teens Drake was apprenticed to a ship's captain, and learned his skills trading among English and European ports. When his master died, he left the ship to Drake, who sold it and took up with a relative, John Hawkins, another famed English seafarer, in the slave trade to the New World. Maybe trafficking in human beings was distasteful to Drake, maybe the lure of Spanish treasure was too strong – whatever the reason, in 1572 he sailed on the first of several profitable privateering expeditions, attacking the Spanish in the Caribbean and Central America.

Drake's second voyage, begun in 1577, involved passage through the Straits of Magellan at the southern tip of South America, then the long sail up the west coast of that continent. When he captured a Spanish galleon in the Pacific off Costa Rica in 1579, Drake found two pilots aboard, men who guided the treasure ships from Acapulco to Manila. They knew much more about sailing conditions in the Pacific than any English captain at that time. From them, Drake learned that he needed to explore farther along the west coast of North America than any European before him. Some experts think he sailed as far north as the Olympic Peninsula in Washington state, while others suggest he never passed the California–Oregon border.

In any case, he claimed all of what is now the Pacific Northwest for England, then spent a month repairing his ships in a sheltered bay north of San Francisco, possibly Bodega Bay on the Sonoma Coast. During his stay, Drake explored inland, discovering a land rich with precious metals, game and welcoming Miwok Indians. When he left California, he set out on a trip across the Pacific and around the world, arriving back in England in September, 1580.

In 1586, on his way home from a third privateering expedition in the Caribbean, Drake sailed north along the Florida and Carolina coasts, plundering the Spanish colony at St Augustine. He stopped at Roanoke Island to evacuate the English colonists before a rumored Spanish assault materialized – actually, his attack on St Augustine had convinced the Spanish not to venture farther north, but to concentrate on protecting the colonies they already had. (A second Roanoke Colony, founded in 1587, wasn't so fortunate: Its colonists disappeared, but most likely not at the hands of the Spanish.) Without Drake, by the time the English arrived in the New World to stay, at Jamestown, Virginia, in 1607, they might have found a Spanish welcoming committee.

After his glorious adventure against the Spanish Armada, Drake made a final expedition to the New World, once again in company with Hawkins. But he fell ill with dysentery, and died while anchored off Nombre de Dios, near Portobello, Panama, in 1596. Ironically, he had sacked the town on his first voyage, in 1572, and captured it again, just a month before he died. He was buried at sea in a lead-lined coffin. ❏

LEFT: a portrait of Sir Francis Drake (*circa* 1540–96), English privateer and seafarer.

the Bahamas made the treasure fleets perfect quarry for pirates and privateers.

As exploration gradually changed to colonization, each group arriving in the New World had different goals, almost all involving financial profit, legal or otherwise. The English essentially ignored the New World until 1584, when the obscure Amadas-Barlowe expedition explored North Carolina's Outer Banks. A year later Richard Grenville led a second voyage to the area, establishing the first Roanoke Island colony. Grenville thought it would provide a good base for further exploration, stop the Spanish in Florida from moving farther north

Tobacco and iron

In 1588 the English navy defeated the Armada, and the war with Spain soon ended; with the threat of invasion gone, settlement of the New World – and exploitation of its vast resources – became a higher priority for England. In 1607 an expedition established the Jamestown colony, at the southern end of Chesapeake Bay. The colony's leaders intended to export to England a variety of crops and salted fish, along with timber and naval stores (tar, turpentine, pitch, and hemp for ropemaking) culled from the abundant forests. But their balance sheet wasn't impressive until, in 1612, John Rolfe

(the Jesuits had established a mission in what is now southern Virginia and another in North Carolina), and, most important, create a seaport from which English privateers could raid the Spanish treasure fleets sailing along the coast – England was at war with Spain at the time. Unfortunately Grenville's original Roanoke Colony came under threat of Spanish attack and had to be abandoned, the colonists rescued by Sir Francis Drake. A subsequent colony on the same site simply disappeared.

ABOVE: Frenchman Jacques Cartier explored along the St Lawrence River in the 16th century.
RIGHT: a 16th-century Spanish galleon.

played a hunch and sent a load of tobacco back home. Almost immediately, tobacco became as trendy as coffee in London, and the colonists planted every square foot of land they could find – in 10 years, tobacco made up 75 percent of the value of the colony's exports.

More and more colonist-planters spread out on both shores of Chesapeake Bay, whose many bays, inlets, and rivers were ideal for exporting goods. Plantations were chosen to include deep-water frontage, a wharf was built, and ships could sail literally up to the back door, load cargo and transport it directly to England. Chesapeake Bay settlers shipped another cargo back home, as valuable to England then as crude oil is to the US today: iron. Iron ore was discovered in many sites around the bay, and mining and smelting operations flourished – ships sailed from the bay loaded with pig iron, and returned with manufactured goods that made plantation ladies as fashionable as those in London. The Chesapeake Bay colonies were the beginning of England's presence in the New World, and water and ships made it happen.

The Dutch find furs

At about the same time the English were building Jamestown, Henry Hudson was skirting the coast a few hundred miles north. An English-

for wampum (beads made from polished shells used as currency), wampum for furs.

The English get the upper hand

The colony spread north along the Hudson River and east into Connecticut and onto Long Island; its expansion was limited only by English colonists spreading south from Massachusetts Bay. When the two groups met, friction followed. In 1664, after war in Europe weakened Holland and the West India Company, an English force let by the Duke of York took New Amsterdam by force; he renamed the bustling trading village after himself – New York.

man sailing for Holland (the Netherlands), in 1609 Hudson anchored in today's New York Harbor, traded with the Lenape Native Americans for furs, then followed the river that now carries his name as far north as present-day Albany in search of the elusive Northwest Passage. Reaching the limit of navigable waters, he sailed back south, past an island the native peoples called Manna-Hatta, and returned to Holland. Furs were for the Dutch what tobacco was for the English and gold for the Spanish: a lure too strong to resist. Soon, the West India Company sent a party to build a trading post, New Amsterdam, on Manna-Hatta. The Dutch prospered, swapping European goods or trinkets

The Pilgrim Fathers

Not everyone came to the New World primarily in search of lucre: the Pilgrims – Puritans who had broken away from the Church of England – wanted to join a community where they could practice their religion without persecution. They believed that life should be lived based on a strict interpretation of the Bible. This philosophy ran counter to both the Church and the State, and the Pilgrims were driven out of England in 1608, lived in Holland until that social climate became intolerable too, and in 1620 decided to try the New World. Planning to join a extant colony farther south, the Pilgrims fetched up instead on the tip of Cape

Cod. Because it was late in the year, they moved a short distance to a more hospitable harbor in today's Plymouth, Massachusetts, and elected to create their own colony. After enduring a miserable winter which caused the deaths of many of their party, the Pilgrims met the wary but tolerant Wampanoag Native Americans, who taught them how to plant native crops. The Pilgrims learned well: Over the next few years they supported themselves by trading corn for furs, which they exported to England. The Plymouth Colony was gradually absorbed by the Massachusetts Bay colonies, and officially terminated in 1692.

land isn't as plentiful, and the earth is often more rocks than soil, many men of ambition turned to the sea. No New England seaport was more successful than Salem, Massachusetts.

Better known as the site of the 1692 Witch Trials, Salem was founded in 1626 by fishermen from the nearby colony of Cape Ann. Naturally, they continued fishing, as did many of the Puritan settlers who arrived in the next decade. Soon the Salem folks were building ships, and adding to their fishing income by trading in the Caribbean for sugar and molasses to make into rum; some captains traded the rum for African slaves to sell to the sugar planters in

Natural wealth

North America is blessed with fabulous natural resources. The fertile farmlands of the mid-Atlantic and south helped turn many cotton, rice, and tobacco farmers into landed aristocracy. The rich soil of the Great Plains will grow almost any crop, and farms there are measured not in acres, but in square miles. If crops won't grow, livestock will, and the cattle baron became as much a part of Western legend as the cowboy. But in New England, where arable

FAR LEFT: Pilgrims give thanks for their safe landing.
LEFT: English settlers receive the keys to Manhattan.
ABOVE: a Dutch-Native American trade deal.

the West Indies, but most Salemites, still Puritan at the core, chose to avoid that leg of the Triangular Trade. They prospered nevertheless, trading goods, not people, with England, France, and Spain – wealthy shipowners of Salem were called "codfish aristocrats," since their medium of exchange was often that fish. By 1790, Salem was the new United States' sixth largest city, and the richest, per capita. Virtually all of its wealth came by sea, much of it from the newly opened trade with China. By 1799, Salem's sailors had brought back enough souvenirs from India, China, and the East Indies to open a museum – and it's still open: the Peabody Essex Museum is the oldest in the US (see page 333).

Coastlines and rivers

But not all waterborne commerce in North America involves the ocean. A spiderweb of inland waterways, anchored by the Mississippi, Missouri and Ohio rivers, provides access to the heartland (in the days of the dinosaurs, itself a vast inland sea). Before railroads and super-highways, traveling overland was arduous, dangerous, and slow, and transporting goods in volume almost impossible. But the rivers let people living 1,000 miles (1,600 km) from the nearest seaport trade with the rest of the world. Even today, powerful towboats push rafts of massive barges to and fro on the rivers. Without

North America enjoys all kinds of coastline, from Alaskan glaciers to the cobalt Caribbean; from rock-girded New England to rugged Baja; from the inland seas that are the Great Lakes to the languid-flowing Mississippi to the steamy bayous along the Gulf of Mexico; the continent begs to be enjoyed by sea, river, and lake, by cruise ship and canoe. Water helped build the New World, but nowadays most Americans see the rivers that crisscross the subcontinent and the seas that surround it as playgrounds, not job sites: for kids paddling canoes at camp to wealthy yachtsmen sailing from port to port to urbanites strapping kayaks to the tops of their

the rivers, the interior of North America would be as barren as the Outback of Australia.

Rivers were so important to North America in the 18th and 19th centuries that some of the earliest government projects involved water: in 1825, funded by New York State, the newly completed Erie Canal linked the Hudson River with Lake Erie, making it possible to ship goods by water from New York City as far west as Detroit. The wealth generated by the canal helped give New York its nickname: the Empire State. It's possible to cruise along the old canal today, but in small boats, not ships: Even in its heyday, the canal was deep enough only for a loaded barge, often towed by a mule.

cars, water is fun, not work. According to the National Marine Manufacturers' Association, a US-based boating-industry group, an estimated 71.6 million people participated in recreational boating in 2002 – that's about 25 percent of the population of the United States. The Cruise Line International Association says more than 8 million North Americans enjoyed a cruise of two days or more in 2002, with another 1.9 million shipping out in the first quarter of 2003. They share the same waters sailed by the Vikings and the *conquistadors*; the same rivers paddled and poled by Lewis and Clark on their way to the Pacific; the same oceans braved by so many new Americans in search of freedom. ❑

Lewis and Clark

In 1804, Meriwether Lewis and William Clark set out to explore the newly purchased Louisiana Territory, partly in hopes of discovering a river route across America to the Pacific Ocean: the long-sought Northwest Passage. They thought the Missouri River, or one of its tributaries, might link with the Columbia River, which runs for more than 1,000 miles (1,610 km) from its source in British Columbia to its mouth near present-day Astoria, Oregon. At the same time, President Thomas Jefferson charged the two ex-army officers with exploring the mostly unknown territory, while maintaining friendly relations with the Native Americans and generally avoiding trouble. Lewis had been Jefferson's private secretary; Clark was an expert at small-boat handling and skilled in both map-making and illustration. Both were Virginians, as was Jefferson.

Lewis and Clark's expedition was one of the most daring voyages ever attempted, on land or on sea. Bought from France in 1803, the Louisiana Purchase comprised 828,000 sq miles (2.14 million sq km), about the size of the United States at the time. Running roughly northwest from St Louis through the territory's mid-section, the Missouri River had been explored by white men only about as far as Omaha, Nebraska. It was up to Lewis and Clark to sail, row and pole their boats upriver as far as possible until, with luck, the Missouri joined the Columbia and led to the Pacific Ocean.

Lewis, Clark and the other members of the Corps of Discovery set off from St Louis on May 21, 1804. Their fleet consisted of a keelboat – a barge-like vessel propelled mostly by oars, but able to sail if the wind was in the right direction – and a pair of canoe-like pirogues. The passage upriver, against the current, was slow and difficult: It took two months to reach the mouth of the Platte River, near today's Omaha, Nebraska, where they met members of the Otoe and Missouri tribes. Another three months brought the group to a native Mandan settlement near present-day Bismarck, North Dakota, where they spent the winter of 1804–5. In the spring, Lewis loaded the keelboat with vegetable specimens, pelts, creatures live and dead, and sent it back to St Louis. The rest of the trip would be by pirogue, canoe, horse and foot.

It was in the Mandan camp that a young Shoshone woman, Sacagawea, joined the expedition, along with her husband, French fur trapper Toussaint Charbonneau; their child was born in February, 1805, and also joined Lewis and Clark, probably the youngest explorer in history. Sacagawea spoke both Shoshone and Hidatsa, a Plains Indian language; Charbonneau spoke Hidatsa and French; one of the expedition's soldiers spoke French and English – so conversations between Lewis, Clark, and the Shoshone who guided them across the Rocky Mountains passed through several mouths en route.

In the spring of 1805, the expedition pressed on upriver, sighting the Rocky Mountains on May 26,

ultimately leaving the river to take to horse and foot, and crossing the Continental Divide in August. The grueling 160-mile (257-km) march overland to the Clearwater River took 11 days; food ran short, and they had to eat some of the horses. But the party launched their canoes and paddled downstream to the Snake and Columbia rivers. On November 7, 1805, they reached the Pacific Ocean, having covered over 4,192 miles (6,746 km). After spending the winter on the shores of the Pacific, they headed home, arriving in St Louis on September 23, 1806. They hadn't discovered a river passage to the Pacific, but their explorations inspired others to explore further, and to settle the new territory, which today makes up all, or part, of 13 states. ❏

LEFT: Americans believe coastal waters are for fun.
RIGHT: painting by N.C. Wyeth of teenage guide Sacagawea leading Lewis and Clark.

LIFE ABOARD A CRUISE SHIP

A cruise ship can be a fantasy world, where amusement and pleasure are the main objectives – but it's wise to remember that we all have different fantasies

Cruise lines are in the business of turning seafaring history and promises of romance at sea and adventure in port into dream vacations. Most cruise companies add a heavy dose of glitz to the mix – even the paddle wheelers aim to create a fantasy of long-lost 19th-century swank. While subtlety can often slip out the porthole – the bigger the ship, the more likely things will be overdone – other lines manage to stick to the brass railings and dark wood that have always signified a nautical brand of elegance.

Fantasy worlds

Rather like a Las Vegas resort, a cruise ship creates its own universe. Don't expect, just because your ship spends every summer in, say, Alaska, that you'll find Inuit art and native carvings onboard. Cruise ship design is an extension of contemporary resort design. Of course it may be a bit of a jolt to walk into a Western-style saloon when you're docked in Manhattan. As a rule of thumb, the more exclusive the cruise line, the more plush and yacht-like the ambiance – the luxury lines, such as Seabourn and Silversea, feel like private vessels rather than theme parks.

Dining onboard

Until recently, cruise ships adhered to a traditional dining approach that followed a formula – and many still do. Passengers return from a day on shore, and shower and dress in the set style – casual (country-club attire), informal (suits and cocktail dresses), and formal (black tie and ball gowns). Older couples and families with children often choose the early seating (about 6.30pm) so that they can get to bed early. Younger people usually choose the late seating (about 8.30pm) so as not to have to rush around after a long day on land.

Often, there are separate pre-dinner cocktail hours, and then couples head arm-in-arm into the dining room. They sit at "their" table and are served by "their waiters," who, after a few days, know their preferences, such as whether they follow a low-salt diet, and how they take their coffee.

If you are not happy with your seating arrangements, or want to specify who you sit

with, make sure you speak to the maître d' on the first day, when he may be able to make changes – after that, it will be more difficult.

Recently, however, things have begun to change. Some ships – including almost all the luxury lines and many premium ones, too – retain these dining traditions even today. But several years ago Norwegian Cruise Line launched "freestyle" dining, a more casual policy of open, restaurant-style seating and most of the contemporary, and even some of the premium, lines followed in their footsteps. Smaller ships, such as sailboats and yachts carrying fewer than 100 passengers tend to have just one seating where all the passengers dine together.

LEFT: a balcony view on *Golden Princess*.
ABOVE: watching the world go by from the deck.

Most lines design rotating menus highlighting continental cuisine – beef Wellington and Dover sole, for example – then add a few dishes each night that nod to the itinerary's ports. Most dishes are easily recognizable, and almost all lines now incorporate vegetarian selections and healthy options such as grilled chicken breasts and steamed vegetables.

Alternative onboard restaurants are a different story. All the larger ships have at least one, most have two, and some have as many as a dozen. There's usually an Italian trattoria, perhaps a French bistro, and increasingly an Asian venue. In addition, large ships have buffet restaurants, poolside grills, ice cream bars, and often coffee shops, too. These venues usually come with a per-person fee, as well as à la carte charges for certain extras and tips. Small ships tend to stick to just the one main dining room, which is more intimate but can be monotonous on long trips if the menus aren't varied.

Keeping passengers happy

Entertainment and amenities depend on the ship's category, size, and style. Amenities on smaller ships may be limited to lounges and perhaps a small library. Large ships, on the other hand, try to outdo each other to see who

TROUBLED WATERS

Many cruise passengers overlook the extraordinary floating world they are on. The occasional "fly on the wall" documentary claims to present life behind the scenes of a cruise ship, but tends to sacrifice truth to sensationalism: Rampant environmental issues, aggressive outbursts between passengers and even crew members, and sinking ships make better television than social harmony at sea.

The reality is that the crew, as diverse as a United Nations delegation, spend up to eight months at sea. During most voyages, shipboard life runs like clockwork, from the delivery of thousands of meals to a dazzling array of entertainments and activities.

There is one issue to remember though: if you board your ship in a US port, that doesn't mean US laws apply when you are at sea; International Maritime Law governs most voyages. For example, the rules for ship casinos and spas are not as stringent on the water as they would be on US soil. The moral is, as always, "buyer beware."

Also, the official line is that timely departure allows the ship to reach the next port on schedule, but the reality is related to ship revenues. The casino and onboard shops can only open once the ship is at sea. Commercialism aside, if the ship is the prime destination for passengers, then they are happy to spend nearly all their time there.

has the most activities. Typical offerings may include a movie theater (sometimes with first-run films), a card room for bridge players, and a library, with books, DVDs, and CDs that passengers can borrow.

The "gentleman host," also known as the dance host, is a feature on the more traditional cruise lines, including Crystal, Silversea, and Holland America. The role is a throwback to the old-fashioned era of ocean liner cruising. Personable single men in their fifties and sixties are employed to

SHIP STUDIES

Some of the bigger ships have instructional rooms with keyboards for passengers who want to take piano lessons, or wheels and supplies of clay for aspiring potters.

Activities by night and day

Many passengers fill their sea days with traditional ship activities, marking down the ones they want to attend on the daily roster. Offerings vary from galley tours to art auctions, bingo to napkin-folding lessons, and ballroom dancing. Shuffleboard may be out of fashion these days, but the group games continue to thrive with all age groups.

After dinner, travelers can find plenty more options – which is just as well, because ships

act as hosts to unaccompanied older women, or those whose husbands just hate dancing. More single women cruise than their male counterparts, and so the practice is a pragmatic one.

Most large ships now have Internet access. Some charge by the minute, some charge a set fee for a certain number of minutes, others bill passengers by megabytes uploaded, plus a start-up fee. It's often expensive, so it is advisable to find Internet cafés on land instead if you are going to use the facility a great deal.

LEFT: New England fare served with a smile on an ACCL ship.
ABOVE: dancing aboard Crystal Cruises.

tend to sail out of ports at sunset which means passengers do not have the option of spending time enjoying any particular city's night scene. The standard ship's evening entertainment, which could be a stand-up comedian, a cabaret singer or a splashy Broadway-style show, includes two performances every night, timed to begin right after each dinner seating. To entertain passengers later on, many ships have cigar lounges, martini bars, and sports bars, as well – all ready and willing to sell you a drink. There are often comedians and singers appearing in the bars or smaller public areas and even strolling a cappella groups, too, all designed to make sure nobody is bored.

Musical choices

As for music, the cruise lines face the difficult challenge of pleasing impossibly varied tastes. Given the mixed age groups in the discos and nightclubs, the resident DJs have a pretty tough job, too. On the whole, they have to play safe, so you should expect to hear quite a lot of old favorites – the kind of music that everyone knows and no one is likely to object to. Elsewhere on the ship, the cruise director matches the right mood music to specific venues. There is nearly always a discreet piano bar where a quintet plays mellow background music that is also made up of standards and favorites.

> **FITNESS AT SEA**
>
> Royal Caribbean, which likes to be considered the king of fitness at sea, offers rock-climbing walls and ice skating on some of its newer ships.

Different moods

No cruise company throws a party more enthusiastically than Carnival Cruise Line, with its crowded nightclubs and irrepressible spirit. In the disco, you can watch dozens of women, decked out in old bridesmaid and prom dresses, getting down to popular dance music.

On Celebrity and Princess lines, you're more likely to sip a cocktail in a relaxed and subdued lounge. And the upscale luxury lines tend to be even quieter. Classical concerts and recitals stay in the more sophisticated vein, and some practically shut down right after the evening's show. With everyone getting up early each morning for sightseeing, its no surprise that these practical cruise passengers go to bed early.

Sports facilities

When the weather is warm, the pool deck is always the place to be on sea days. The whole contingent of passengers turns out to battle it out over lounge chairs and tables by the grill. Many large ships have two or three pools to cater for the crowds, and some have built large water slides and surrounded the pools with hot tubs or covered the pool area so that it can still be used in the cold weather of, say, Alaska.

On the top deck, you will often find a fitness center. These gyms can vary in their amenities, from a few stair-climbing machines in a

CARING FOR PATIENTS AT SEA

Given that a typical cruise passenger roster includes anyone from the newly-wed to the nearly dead, the ship's medical officers are kept busy. Most medical emergencies are linked to elderly passengers who have pre-existing conditions or who are simply frail, but most of the time, doctors deal with seasickness and 'flu.

Their medicine cabinets are stocked with much the same medications that a doctor on land has, and these fully licensed physicians are capable of prescribing whatever they don't have. Generally, however, cruise ships do not accept health insurance and you will have to pay upfront for all services. Naturally, doctors are reluctant to reveal that deaths occur on board, but on cruises with a high proportion of vulnerable passengers, one or two deaths are not exceptional. And while you'd be hard pressed to find numbers on just how many cruise ship passengers die in a given year, remember that some of these ships have age demographics that are comparable to a retirement home, and that all ships have morgues.

Helicopter transfers to airlift a passenger off a ship are rare, but the captain, advised by the doctor, is empowered to do whatever is in the best interests of the patient. On ships without heli-pads, the swimming pool acts as a substitute and has to be cleared and drained in haste.

mirrored room to sophisticated facilities. You'll get weight training circuits and rows of the latest cardio machines (sometimes with cardio-theater to make the time go faster), and aerobics rooms for yoga, step, pilates, and kickboxing. Usually, access to these classes is included in the cruise price, but some of the more athletic-oriented ships have started charging fees for more popular ones in order both to prevent them getting too crowded and to increase their profits. In addition to the main fitness facilities, many of the larger ships also have paddle tennis courts, miniature golf, running tracks that circle right round the ship's deck and even climbing walls.

In addition to the typical facials and massages and thalassotherapy baths, you may also find some unusual treatments that aren't on your home-town spa's menu. Ionotherapy, for example, is a treatment that claims to "promote weight loss" by soaking the body in mineral infused waters and seaweed. And then there are the tiled razul rooms, which allow couples to slather each other in mud and then rinse off with steam and water that rain down from the ceiling.

Onboard salons offer all the typical options, from manicures and pedicures to make-overs for the ship's formal night and hair color touch

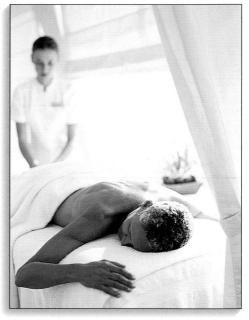

Health and beauty

The spa and salon are often connected to the gym. Fees aren't much higher than you would pay on land, but the quality of treatments can vary. For example, some facials may not even include steam or extractions, and some spas push their employees to hard sell their products, even during what is supposed to be a relaxing massage. Be sure to ask a lot of questions before you book, and if you are not interested in purchasing any products, say so at once.

LEFT: jogging with Radisson Seven Seas.
ABOVE: Crystal Cruises offers opportunities for yoga or a relaxing massage.

ups. Again, prices are not much more than you would pay at home, but the quality may not be consistent with what you are used to receiving. Book well ahead on sea days, as this is obviously when demand is highest.

Casinos

Gambling is a signature feature on most large ships. Typically, passengers appreciate the chance to lay bets in the safe, welcoming, and festive environment that is a casino at sea. Most casinos provide gaming lessons to novices, as well as offering slot machines for those who like to bet less or just don't enjoy craps, blackjack, or poker. Games also tend to be friendlier as passengers compete with their table mates and bingo buddies.

Compared to Vegas, the games move at a slower pace and the rules may be looser – generally, though, the rules follow those established in Las Vegas and Atlantic City. In some cases, the shipboard casinos are even run by the same companies that dominate The Boardwalk and The Strip.

Shore excursions and going solo

When you're ready to get off the ship in port, cruise ships don't just drop you off to fend for yourself. All cruise lines (except for the small

ones, which tend to include excursions as part of the package) will offer a full roster of ship-sponsored shore activities. They often include city tours by coach, walking tours of historic areas, transfers from the port to other regional points of interest, and sports activities such as hiking and kayaking when appropriate. These excursions are usually convenient and well run – and they are popular, so book in advance by checking the cruise line's website or calling your travel agent.

Shore excursions do tend to be a bit more expensive – sometimes a lot more expensive – than if you made the same arrangements on your own. However, there are several reasons why they can be a better option. First of all, if inclement weather or a delay in the schedule change the ship's itinerary, it's the line's job to rearrange the shore excursions, not yours. And if the tour overruns, the ship will wait for excursion passengers to return. If you're traveling alone and you return late, you will probably see the ship sailing off in the distance and be forced to make your own way to the next port – at your own expense.

However, if you don't see what you want on the tour roster when you book your cruise, try to plan in advance. Once onboard, the ship's staff will offer you very little information about the ports and their attractions. The official explanation is that it's for legal reasons, but as they are selling shore excursions it doesn't make much business sense for them to assist travelers to make their own sightseeing arrangements.

If you would prefer a private tour, call the local tourism board in advance and arrange for a guide to be waiting when you walk down the gangway. This way, you won't waste half the day trying to figure out where you are going and the best way to get there.

For cruise ship passengers who want to strike out completely on their own, it is often possible to do so. The major sights in most port cities tend to be concentrated in a relatively small area, so it's easy enough to take a taxi to the hub and sightsee on foot. Visitors' centers will be able to provide information and maps. In order to visit a national park or winery, for example, you may need to rent a car. Again, visitors' centers will be able to point you in the right direction – there are usually rental agencies not far from the docks – but bear in mind that you may not get as much on-the-spot information as if you went on an organized tour – and never forget to check and double check that you will be back in time for your sailing.

There are many advantages of a cruise, but the biggest disadvantage may be the limited time you get in port. Many, such as Montreal, Seattle, and New York, have more to see than you could ever get to in one day. Read up on a destination in advance so that you don't miss out on the highlights in each port of call.   ❑

LEFT: an adrenalin-packed shore excursion: rafters at Endaiveil Falls, Keystone Canyon, Alaska.
RIGHT: P&O's *Aurora*.

WHAT YOU NEED TO KNOW BEFORE BOOKING YOUR CRUISE

In order to get the most out of your cruise, it helps to have done some background research. This chapter provides a few pointers

More than 8 million North Americans take a cruise each year – that's double the number who did so a decade ago. And the word is spreading: almost a million British people now choose a cruise as their main holiday. There is really no such thing as a typical North American cruise, but, as in other parts of the world, cruising is a great introduction to a new destination.

Choosing your cabin

First of all, think about how you envisage spending your time during the cruise. If you prefer to spend every possible minute seeing the sites, then you may not need to spend too much money on an expensive cabin with lots of space and a balcony. But if you think you're going to spend sea days (and maybe plenty of other days) eating, reading, and napping in the privacy of your cabin or relaxing on your balcony, then you must pick a room that's not going to make you feel claustrophobic.

Cabins vary widely in size and amenities, depending on the line and the individual ship. On large ships, the cabins that you get at the lowest rates tend to be windowless, interior ones. You'll need to read the brochure carefully to see how much it will cost to upgrade to an outside cabin with a balcony, then decide if you think it's worth it.

Sailboats, and even small cruising yachts, lean toward tiny, serviceable staterooms. Older, larger ships also tend to have small, balcony-less cabins that encourage guests to spend their time out and about on the ship. You may find you have a mere porthole rather than a window, and not even enough space to store your suitcases in the room. Fortunately, you will always have a private bathroom and twin beds that can usually be pushed together and made up as doubles for couples.

LEFT: the *Golden Princess* has a three-deck atrium.
RIGHT: Seabourn cabins offer comfort and space.

Book a cruise on a newer ship and you'll probably get more room than you could possibly need. The top cabins often come with stocked mini-bars, double sinks, and separate showers and bath tubs. Increasingly, the lines are adding in-room data ports for laptops, and CD and DVD players. Luxury lines also seem to be competing to see who can offer the best toiletries, and the nicest towels and bathrobes. Silversea, for example, offers green tea-scented Bulgari products, Seabourn uses the more masculine Molton Brown, and Crystal provides musky Aveda amenities.

Tallying up the cost

Don't expect the price of your cruise to cover everything. For years cruise lines touted their products as all-inclusive. Maybe that was once true, but not any more. Today, your booking price covers your cabin and your food in the main dining room – but there are plenty of extra costs. It's difficult to spend less than $200 per person extra for a week-long cruise.

Let's start with the port charges, which can range from $100 to $250 per person per week. Then there are the tips for your cabin steward, waiter, assistant waiter, and butler, if you have one. These can add up to as much as $12 per person per day. Figure in an extra 15 percent for bartender tips for any alcoholic drinks that you order onboard, too. Many cruise lines will give you suggested tipping amounts, which tend to be fair, and offer you an envelope for cash. Increasingly, lines are letting passengers

bill tips to their charge cards – always a convenient option for those who don't like to carry a lot of cash when they travel.

There are also the shore excursions – these can really add up. Per person rates range from about $35 for a city tour all the way up to a couple of hundred dollars for activities such as flight-seeing and glacier hiking.

If you purchase anything on board, from a logo T-shirt or evening dress to some casino chips, those charges will be added to your bill, too. And on most ships passengers pay for soft drinks as well as ice cream. Spa and beauty treatments are extra, of course, and

HOMEPORTING

A few years ago, cruise ships sailed almost exclusively from Miami and Fort Lauderdale when offering Caribbean cruises, or from New York when sailing to Bermuda and eastern Canada. But over the past few years the paradigm has shifted entirely, leading cruise lines to disperse their fleets among dozens of home ports around the US, within easy reach of the populations they serve.

The trend began slowly around 1999, but it took the events of 9/11 to push it into high gear. Suddenly, Americans didn't want to fly any more, and cruise lines couldn't simply wait for traveler confidence to return. Ships scheduled to sail in Europe, Asia, and especially the Middle East were hastily

pulled back to US shores, and often scheduled to sail from under-used ports along the eastern seaboard.

People reacted positively: instead of having to fly to their port of embarkation, they could drive. And since ships offer so many onboard activities and entertainment venues, few minded if their itineraries included an extra day or two at sea, getting to and from their destination. Today, cruise lines see the growth of home ports as a tremendous opportunity to attract first-time cruisers. You can depart from Boston, New York, Philadelphia, or Baltimore. On the west coast, ships sail from San Diego, Los Angeles, and San Francisco for visits to Mexico, and from San Francisco and Seattle north to Alaska.

some lines charge for aerobics classes, while others include them in the price. Try to think of your booking price as just the beginning and your bill won't be such a surprise at the end of your trip.

Get the most out of your cruise

If you want specific shore excursions or a table for two, don't leave it till the last minute. Some shore excursions are very popular, especially the smaller, more exclusive ones, and can fill up before you even embark. Sign up for those you know you'll want when you book your cruise. Some lines even let you register online for excursions, so check that option.

And if you want to dine alone, rather than get to know a table full of strangers every night, be sure to request a private table before you get onboard. Likewise with dinner seatings – some cruise passengers prefer to eat early, others late, and once you've been included in one time slot it can be difficult to change. If you're cruising on a ship that doesn't offer open seating at dinner, you should put in your request as early as possible *(see page 23)*.

Spa treatments are a different story. You can't book these before you board, but if you know you will need a manicure on formal night or that you'll want a massage after lunch on the first sea day, book those as soon as you board. The most popular time slots fill up quickly, and frequent cruisers make sure they act fast so that they get the treatments they want and don't miss out on the already limited time in port.

Picking the right ship

Knowing your own taste matters as much as knowing where you want to go on your cruise. Much of the cruise experience is determined by the size of the ship – some are like small inns, with libraries, wood-paneled bars, and intimate dining rooms; others are big, Vegas-style resorts, with themed restaurants and glitzy show lounges. There's a ship for every age, taste, and budget – you just have to pick the right one for you. And that's especially true in North America, one of the few parts of the world where small ships are almost as plentiful as large ones.

LEFT: passing the time by the pool on the *Dawn Princess* in Alaska.
RIGHT: getting away from it all on a Silversea cruise.

Large ships

Of course, even within the "large" group there are different types of ships: Contemporary, Premium, and Luxury. Contemporary ships are aimed at the mass market (and priced accordingly), while Premium-rated ships are higher priced, carry fewer passengers, and offer a touch more class. Luxury ships are even smaller, with the highest level of food and service.

You'll know if you're cruising on a Luxury ship because you'll be paying $500 to $1,000 per day. A quick way to discover whether the ship you're considering is Premium or Contemporary is to divide its tonnage by its pas-

senger capacity to get the Passenger Space Ratio (PSR). This is a good indication of how crowded life will be onboard. For example, the 101,509-ton/2,758-passenger Contemporary ship *Carnival Victory* has a PSR of 36.8, while the 108,806-ton/2,600-passenger Premium ship *Golden Princess* has a PSR of 41.8. The higher the PSR, the less likely it is that you will feel hemmed in by your fellow passengers, or spend a long time waiting for elevators and meal times, or lining up to disembark.

No matter which you choose, these leviathans are very much like miniature cities. With literally acres of space onboard, they offer around-the-clock action and plenty of nightlife.

Choosing a Cruise

First of all, don't assume that you need to pay the prices listed in cruise line company brochures – if you shop around you can usually save money. This is especially true in competitive markets, such as Alaska, where almost all of the major cruise lines (and many smaller players) have at least one ship.

Do your research. Some cruise companies now have flexible pricing systems (like the low-cost airlines), where the price of a cruise varies according to availability when you book.

Book online. Travel websites, such as www. expedia. com, www.orbitz.com, and www.travelocity. com, all offer cruise bargains these days in addition to their well-known flight and hotel deals. There are also many cruise-specific websites worth viewing, such as www.cruisebrothers.com and www.cruise411.com, that can offer information about discounted rates.

Also, consider reading some of the ship reviews at www.cruisecritic.com and www.cruisemates.com – both are editorial websites that compare and rate all types of cruises.

Another major source of information is the cruise line's own website. Most have extensive information about their ships, their routes, and onboard services, as well as specials such as free flights and two-for-one deals, and big discounts during slow travel periods.

Some cruise line websites offer e-mailed newsletters you can sign up for and which notify you of promotional rates, and freebies such as flights and onboard credit. If nothing else, visiting a line's website can give you a better sense of the company's personality and focus.

Get the right help. Unlike airlines and hotels, many cruise lines don't allow passengers to book through in-house reservations agents. Instead you call a toll-free number and they send brochures and put you in touch with a local travel agent.

If you don't already have dealings with a travel agent who is a cruise specialist, consider choosing one who directs a lot of business to a specific cruise line. They often get the best deals and have the most knowledge about the cruises. The cruise line can give you a list of your area's biggest sellers.

Trust the experts. If you don't know which line might be best for you, CLIA – the Cruise Line Industry Association – can give you a list of agents who specialize in cruising. Click on www.cruising.org and use CLIA's online search engine to find a qualified agent in your area.

Find out what you get for your money. Many travelers choose their cruise based on price, but the reality is that although cruise lines may sound similar in their advertisements, they offer very different vacation experiences. Some specialize in great food, while others pay more attention to funky shipboard amenities, such as rock-climbing walls and pottery studios. Be sure to thoroughly research a company's strengths and weaknesses, rather than just their rates, before making your final decision.

Know your ships. Even when you've decided on a particular cruise line that you think suits your requirements, remember that not all ships in a fleet are the same. Newer ones tend to be more expensive, but come with the latest features and more cabins with balconies. So read up on the individual ship you are attracted to before you pay out any hard-earned money. It would be disappointing to book a Royal Caribbean cruise for their retro diners, roller blading circuits, and ice skating rinks only to find that you've chosen an older ship that doesn't offer these activities. A top source of information is the annual *Berlitz Ocean Cruising and Cruise Ships*, which provides exhaustive reviews of more than 250 vessels.   ❏

LEFT: if putting your feet up on your own private balcony is important, be sure to choose carefully.

Pulsating discos vie for attention with intimate piano bars. You can prepare for dinner with a visit to a champagne bar, and round it off with a cappuccino at a café or perhaps a cigar in a wood-paneled lounge before a show. Alternatively, you can opt for a casual meal in a pizza parlor or enjoy an evening pint with fish and chips at an English-style pub, even if you're nowhere near the United Kingdom.

During the day choose to swim, jog, visit the golf driving range, work out in the gym with a personal trainer, or play a game of deck tennis or basketball on a full-scale court. If you prefer sheer indulgence, visit a spa for a massage or wallow in a steam room. And if you feel like shopping, the boutiques on board sell everything from sunscreen to designer gowns.

Best of all, if you're traveling with children, these ships offer extensive facilities for kids, with all-day supervision and activities geared to different age groups, including arts and crafts sessions and pool games. Some even provide children-only galley tours with cookie decorating, as well as child-focused shore excursions (see pages 40–41).

There is one caveat: on some large ships, the relentless "fun, fun, fun" atmosphere of pool games, fashion shows and loud announcements can be overwhelming if you're trying to relax.

Cabins, meals and options

Big ships offer a wide range of accommodations, from small, inside, single cabins to spacious suites with Jacuzzis, bidets, flat-screen TVs, and roomy balconies. Cabins, whatever their size, are furnished to a high standard and all provide en suite bathrooms – with a shower in the lower grade accommodations, a bathtub plus shower in higher grades, and a shower and separate bath in the top cabins.

Meals, by and large, are casual, chain restaurant standard rather than haute cuisine, but the food is varied and, as a rule, it is nicely presented and plentiful. Those so inclined can eat and drink all day, starting with early bird coffee at 6am and finishing with the Midnight Buffet – taking in breakfast, lunch, tea, and dinner as they go, of course.

The most recently built ships have made room for specialty restaurants where passengers can celebrate a special occasion, indulge their gourmet tastes, or simply take a break from the main dining rooms and try something different. There is usually a surcharge of between $8 and $15 per person.

Multiple facilities mean that you will rarely encounter hordes of people in one place at a time, but on sea days (when the ship does not visit a port), sunbathing on deck can be rather a cheek-by-jowl affair, as can the buffet breakfast. Be prepared to wait in line, and don't be surprised to see that many passengers come up on deck early in the morning to reserve deck chairs for later that afternoon.

Disembarking in ports of call

To win over first-time cruise passengers, the big-ship lines also tend to cram their itineraries full of port calls. This is great, as you get a taste of lots of different places, but it does have disadvantages. With so many people on board, the process of disembarking and getting passengers off on tours is a major production. Some ships organize it better than others, but if you have picked a ship that doesn't do it so well, the constant sound of passengers being summoned ashore makes sleeping in quite out of the question. As a rule, the bigger the ship, the longer the wait to disembark, and the sheer size of these vessels means they often have to

RIGHT: cruise ship passengers can eat and drink all day long if they have the inclination.

anchor off some ports and ferry passengers to the shore by tender. However, if you feel seasick in small boats, or have mobility problems, large ships have real advantages.

Contemporary and Premium ships also are well equipped, lively, and offer excellent value. Their comfortable cabins and plentiful facilities can make sea days as interesting and enjoyable as port days. Families, young sporty types, and sociable travelers will love these ships. They're also good for single people and for those who've never cruised before and are worried that they may go stir crazy if they don't have enough to do.

Luxury ships, which tend to be smaller, are a slightly different matter. Here, the extra money you're paying buys you better food and service, more space and attention, and an opportunity to enjoy fabulous amenities without the crowds.

Small ships

In general, the main difference between the experience you will get on a large ship or a small one is not directly to do with the number of passengers, but the amount of public spaces and amenities, and the atmosphere. Small ships offer comfortable lounges and libraries for conversation and reading rather than discos and

THE ROLE OF THE MAÎTRE D'HÔTEL

The ship's maître d'hôtel needs to be a master of diplomacy and tact and an assiduous meeter and greeter. He has an unenviable role, particularly at the start of cruises when he is often inundated with requests for changes to seating arrangements. If you've requested a table for two or a table by the window, he's the one who makes those decisions. Once onboard, you should visit him early to confirm that he received your requests. If you wait until dinner time, it may be too late. You can't just bribe your way to a table for two but, if you act quickly, it may forestall any problems. And, since so many ships have open-seating dining rooms, "assigned tables" are becoming less of an issue each year.

The less glamorous side of this challenging job involves making the dining room run smoothly. If most passengers come back late from an excursion, the staff must allow leeway for mealtimes.

The maître d' is also one of the key figures involved in assuring standards of cleanliness. Hygiene on board needs to be stringent since any virus tends to be transmitted rapidly through the air-conditioning system. Every night, the restaurant may be sprayed with disinfectants to kill bacteria and insects. The dining staff may even be called upon to stay up all night to give the restaurant a total spring cleaning – then they treat themselves to a pre-dawn feast.

sports and martini bars. And while large ships can have cabins as big as your bedroom at home, small ships (except for the truly luxurious ones) usually don't.

In fact, it's the focus that defines a small ship – a focus on education rather than gambling, opportunities for quiet conversation rather than onboard mini-malls with shops and arcades, and extensive lectures rather than dancing and partying. Although smart, luxury ships may technically carry as few as 200 passengers, we're grouping them with the large ships in the following section because of their similarities in style and offerings.

The following sections gives profiles and websites for the major cruise lines that travel the waters of North America. For contact information, see the Travel Tips section *(page 324)*.

Contemporary ships

Carnival Cruise Line (www.carnival.com). Several of Carnival Line's behemoths spend their summers in Alaska, carrying approximately 2,000 passengers per voyage to the major ports of the Inside Passage. You can also choose from less frequent itineraries in Hawaii and Baja, and fall foliage cruises to New England and Canada.

In North America, small ships ply both the coastlines and the inland waterways. And, of course, there are several different kinds of small ship lines. Some, such as Lindblad and Cruise West, can cruise both in the open ocean and in narrow rivers; others, including the *Delta Queen* steamboat (which is a traditional paddle wheeler), remain on the mighty Mississippi all year round. If a cruise on a small ship suits your personality, taste and budget, you'll have plenty of options.

LEFT: view spectacular Alaska from a Cruise West ship.
ABOVE: the *Queen of the West*, a classic paddle steamer sails the Columbia River.

The onboard style is bold, brash and fun. The decor may be kitsch and over-the-top, but the extensive children's facilities are excellent. There are amusements for all ages, including video games for teenagers and flashy casinos for adults.

Carnival ships are perfect for party lovers, for young families, and for singles looking for nightlife, but they are not for those in search of tranquility, or those who dislike crowds, waiting in line, or mass-market food.

Norwegian Cruise Line (www.ncl.com). These ships are known for their excellent bargain offers. They cruise the Hawaiian Islands year-round and Alaska in the summer. NCL also run so-called "leaf-peeping cruises" in Canada and New England in the fall *(see page 115)*.

The onboard style is relaxed and friendly, with full-scale Broadway shows and more dining venues than any other line. All the lines have Italian restaurants, but NCL also offer Indian food, *sushi*, *tapas*, and much more. NCL pioneered the concept of "freestyle cruising" – with open-seating in all dining rooms and relaxed dress codes every night. These ships are ideal for families and couples in search of good value for money, but they are not for travelers who like formality or are seeking a traditional ship-board experience.

Royal Caribbean International (www.royal caribbean.com). Royal Caribbean has some of the biggest ships in the world. They accommodate as many as 3,000 passengers (sometimes more) on cruises to Alaska, Canada and New England, Baja, or Hawaii.

The emphasis is on fun, with a lively atmosphere and sporty amenities, such as rock-climbing walls, ice rinks, miniature golf ranges, and roller blading. This makes the ships perfect for families and athletic types. They do not suit the less-mobile, who may find moving around huge ships a challenge, or those in search of peace and quiet, or anyone who dislikes crowds, waiting in line and eating mass-produced food.

Premium

Celebrity Cruises (www.celebrity.com). Some of Celebrity's ships, which carry 2,000 (sometimes fewer) passengers, spend the summer in Alaska. Others go to Hawaii, or make fall-foliage tours of New England and Canada.

The onboard style is a mainstream brand of elegance served up for big-ship lovers. Their new vessels are larger than the older ones, with lovely, top-grade suites and beautifully designed health spas, while the older, smaller ships are less well equipped but cozier. Their many fans claim that they offer luxury-style travel at a lower rate.

These cruises are perfect for young(ish) high achievers who want to let their hair down, but are not for serious drinkers (unless they can afford the high prices); or for lovers of good entertainment – the shows are unimaginative.

Holland America Line (www.hollandamerica. com). HAL ships each carry approximately 1,800 passengers to Alaska, Hawaii, the Pacific Northwest, or Canada and New England.

The style on these low-key vessels is as subdued as the Premium lines get. Expect to find the old-fashioned late- and early-dinner seatings, fresh flowers, and nautical touches. HAL offers a vintage brand of mainstream cruising at a time when other lines are modernizing as quickly as possible – and their devotees love them for it. They are perfect for older travelers and for traditionalists – sometimes, but not always, the same thing. They are certainly not for people who want a floating party or for families (except during school holidays).

Princess Cruises (www.princesscruises. com). Princess ships carry approximately 2,600 passengers on cruises to Alaska, Hawaii, and New England and Canada.

The newer boats concentrate on fun amenities, such as pottery-throwing classes and New Orleans-style restaurants, complete with Mardi Gras beads and oysters. Military-type precision makes disembarking stress-free, despite the number of passengers. These well run ships also have plenty of balcony cabins. They are great for families and couples but unlikely to please hard-core traditionalists.

Luxury

Crystal Cruises (www.crystalcruises.com). The 940-passenger *Harmony* cruises Alaska in summer, and her sister ship, the *Symphony*, spends the fall in New England and Canada.

The onboard style is elegant, with polished service and exquisite cuisine. You'll find a Wolfgang Puck bistro onboard, and *sushi* bars that serve wild Pacific salmon *sashimi* in Alaska. Passengers also have access to state-of-the-art technology, such as in-room DVD and CD players. Here, everyone has their own tuxedo for formal nights. This makes them perfect for the Ritz-Carlton or Four Seasons hotel customer who's looking for a comparable cruise ship – with some of the best dining to be had at sea. Crystal ships are certainly not designed for the budget-conscious or families (outside school holidays).

Voyager, has a Cordon Bleu-sponsored restaurant that offers cooking classes for guests and hosts celebrity chefs. If having a large cabin is a high priority, these ships are perfect for you, but not for budget-conscious travelers or families with children.

Yachts of Seabourn (www.seabourn.com). Seabourn yachts cruise to New England and Canada with a mere 200 passengers aboard.

These delightfully decadent ships are older than those owned by the other luxury lines, but Seabourn keeps things fresh with pool-deck massages and dancing under the stars. Exclusive tour excursions offer private, small-group

Radisson Seven Seas Cruises (www.rssc.com). These smart, 500- to 700- passenger ships travel to ports in Alaska, as well as New England and Canada.

Their onboard style is proof that, when it comes to staterooms, bigger is better. These enormous, deluxe cabins come with large balconies and marble bathrooms. Because there's no chance of cabin-claustrophobia, the rest of the ship tends to be quieter, and the public rooms feel spacious, too. The newest ship, the

LEFT: Radisson cabins have lots of space and large balconies.
ABOVE: Seabourn is suitable for adult families.

visits to historic sights and trips to the market with the chef. They are perfect for mature - couples and adult families, but not for the budget-conscious or those with young children.

Silversea Cruises (www.silversea.com). These 400-passenger ships travel to New England and Canada or Alaska.

Onboard, it's the large cabins that impress – and the unlimited supply of champagne, all included in the cost, as are all alcoholic drinks. You'll sleep on Frette linens, bathe with Bulgari products, and nap on your own teak veranda. A tuxedo is in every male passenger's luggage. Mature, well-heeled couples and adult families make up the passenger list. ❑

Family Cruising

Children, from babies to teenagers, can find their own special activities and public rooms onboard the large cruise ships. Newer ships have the biggest, most elaborate children's centers where activities are supervised by trained staff. These are complimentary and are divided into age groups. Activities vary by age, but most lines include a variety of arts and crafts programming along with videos, games, and free play.

Seek out ships that offer dedicated deck space when traveling with children between the ages of

three and 13. This space often includes a wading pool, water slides, mini-basketball hoops, and a playground. Inside the large children's playroom you'll find computers with Internet access (for an extra fee), science labs, and video games. Most children's programs restrict swimming to those aged nine or over and need signed permission from parents.

It's important to realize that not all itineraries are child-friendly. Depending on the itinerary, cruise lines may impose age restrictions, or offer very limited children's programming and staff. There are particular regions, including Alaska, Hawaii, and the Baja Peninsula to the Mexican Riviera that are established family routes, while river cruises, and small ship adventures are considered adults'

only. If you are interested in giving your children the best chance to find others of their age onboard, go during school breaks. Shorter cruises attract more families than cruises of 10 days or longer.

Cruise lines that offer a flexible dining program are often the best suited for families with children. The casual buffet will be a hit on long shore days where the family can return to ship and go directly to eat in shorts. Otherwise, select the early seating option. Waiting until 8.45pm for dinner could ruin an otherwise wonderful day.

If you have more than two children traveling with you, we suggest you look for either a family suite or connecting cabins. Children's rates and deals on second/connecting cabins are often available. Every ship that accepts children has cribs available, and some lines stock strollers (for a fee). Be sure to request your crib as soon as you book. It's important to note that diapers (nappies) and formula milk are not usually available onboard, so pack what you need for the entire trip. Bring your own first-aid kit in case of emergency. While all ships have medical staff, there is an additional fee for medical care. Families should consider purchasing travel insurance with medical evacuation coverage just in case someone needs to be flown home or evacuated from the ship.

Most cruise lines that offer children's programming also have babysitting available by reservation for an additional fee per child. Check for the hours of operation, booking requirements, and age limits as soon as you get onboard.

Here are the basics about family travel on the most popular family-friendly cruise lines:

Carnival Cruise Lines (www.carnival.com). Best itineraries for families are Alaska, Hawaii and Baja/Mexican Riviera. All ships offer children's programming. However, the newer the ship the larger and more elaborate the facilities are. All Carnival ships offer strollers for rent. Waterslides are available on all ships. Carnival requires children to be at least four months old to cruise and parents must pay a flat rate for a third or fourth guest in a cabin, regardless of age. Camp Carnival is divided into four categories: Toddlers (2–5), Juniors (6–8), Intermediate (9–11) and Teens (12–15). All counselors are CPR and First Aid certified. Children of 2–8 years old must be signed in at all times (and can only be picked up by the parent who signed them in). All children aged 9 and over are permitted to sign themselves in and out of the program. Carnival heats the pools onboard in Alaska and tailors activities onboard for the Alaskan region, including shore excursions targeted for teens. Children's menus are available in the dining room. The Fountain Fun Card allows for unlimited soft drinks during the cruise for a fixed rate.

Holland America (www.hollandamerica.com). The best itinerary for families is Alaska. Traditionally a favorite of cruisers aged 55 and over, the line has made great strides in attracting families in Alaska. The Club HAL KidZone facility for children and teenagers offers programming for ages 5 and over. They break down the program into groups of 5–8, Tweens 9–12 and Teens 13–17. Children's menus are available in the dining room. Babysitting by front desk staff is available for an additional fee per child. Holland America will supply diapers, baby food, and formula by requests made through Ship Services for an additional fee. Onshore Adventures are specially designed tours for kids and teens.

Norwegian Cruise Line (www.ncl.com). Best itineraries for families are Alaska and Hawaii. The "Kids' Crew" program is divided into four age groups: Junior Sailors (2–5); First Mates (6–8); Navigators (9–12) and Teens (13–17). Staff members do not change diapers; if your child is not potty-trained, a pager will be provided so staff can notify you if your child needs to be changed. Group babysitting for ages 2–12 is available from 10pm–1am, and on port days, from 9am–5pm for an additional fee per child per hour. Freestyle cruising with flexible casual dining options is perfect for families. A soda package for unlimited soft drinks is available for an additional fee.

Princess Cruises (www.princess.com). Best itineraries for families are Alaska and Baja/Mexican Riviera. The children's program features complimentary in-port activities. Age groups are Princess Pelicans (3–7), Princess Pirateers (8–12) and the Off Limits teen centers (13–17). A full schedule of activities runs from 9am–10pm, with two-hour breaks for lunch and dinner, on sea days. During port days the program runs from 8am–5pm and from 7–10pm. Group babysitting for children aged 3–12 is offered from 10pm–1am for a fee per hour per child. Children's menus are available in the dining room and the 24-hour restaurant. Personal Choice Dining is recommended for families who want flexible dining schedules in the main dining room. A highlight in Alaska is the Junior Ranger program for children 6–12 and a Teen Explorer for

13 and over. A partnership between Princess and the National Park Service encourages children to explore Glacier Bay through fun interactive projects. Princess also offers programs in conjunction with the California Science Center and the National Wildlife Federation in other regions.

Royal Caribbean Cruise Line (www.royalcaribbean. com). Best itineraries for families are Alaska, Canada/New England, and Baja/Mexican Riviera. The Adventure Ocean program divides kids into five age groups: Aquanauts (3–5, no diapers), Explorers (6–8), Voyagers (9–11), Navigators (12–14) and Teens (15–17). The newest ships have the most elaborate facilities. All ships will soon have rock-

climbing walls. The program operates from 10am–10pm. Teens have a separate center with lounge and state-of-the-art dance floor and lighting. Sodas are complimentary in the dining room. RCI's Fountain Soda Package is available for adults and children, for a fee.

Royal Caribbean is one of the few lines that still offer in-cabin babysitting for children of 6 months and over, from 8am–2am for an additional fee. This service is limited and must be booked at the front desk at least 24 hours in advance. Group babysitting for ages 3 and over (no diapers), is available from 10pm–1am for a fee per child per hour. There are some family staterooms and suites; request cribs at the time of booking. ❑

LEFT: larger ships have activities for older children.
RIGHT: look out for children's programs that cater to all ages, from toddlers to teens.

ALASKA

Alaska is a land whose natural riches – furs, gold, fish, lumber,
and oil – have all been exploited during its eventful history

A landmass nearly three times the size of France, straddling the Arctic Circle and resting precariously at the northwestern edge of the North American tectonic plate. Some 375 million acres (150 million hectares) of mountains and evergreens and tundra. Summers that last a few bright weeks, and winters that are long and cold and dark. A few thousand polar bears, 8,000 wolves, 40,000 grizzlies, 150,000 moose, and nearly a million caribou. A population of just 640,000 people, half of whom are huddled in one urban area. A place in which those who would make their fortunes vied with those who would preserve its natural beauty; where newcomers either hoped to open the vast region to peaceful commerce, or use it to defeat their enemies. This is Alaska.

If you squint at a map of the state, you'll see that it roughly resembles the head of an elephant as seen from the side (it's facing Russia). The state's southeasternmost section consists of a thin strip of land, running between British Columbia and the Pacific Ocean, composed of fjords, rainforests, and the Coast Mountains. Follow those mountains north into the Alaska mainland, and they morph into the St Elias, Chugach, and Kenai ranges, which make up Alaska's south-central coast. In the state's interior rises a still higher set of peaks, the Alaska Range – the tip of the Rockies and home to 20,320-ft (6,195-meter) Mount McKinley, the highest point in North America. Farther north, past the Arctic Circle, lies the barren Brooks Range. The Alaska Range continues down the Alaskan Peninsula – the "trunk" of the elephant – and trails off, becoming the Aleutian Island chain, which stretches 1,000 miles (1,600 km) toward Siberia.

The first Americans

Scientists still debate whether the first Americans migrated from Siberia through Alaska down into the rest of the continent, and even those researchers who believe they did, disagree on exactly when it might have happened: estimates range from 30,000 to 12,000 years ago. What is reasonably certain is that a land bridge did exist, a vast plain bared by the Pleistocene Ice Age only to be swamped again as the ice sheets started melting, and that today's Native Alaskans – whether or not their ancestors went on to populate the rest of North America – do share key genetic markers with indigenous Siberians. There seems to be no doubt that they are definitely related.

Whenever those early Alaskans actually arrived, some of them migrated into the forests of the interior and the southeast, evolving into the hunter-gatherer Athabascan and Tlingit tribes. Meanwhile, the Aleut, Inupiat, and Yup'ik peoples – more Asiatic in appearance – spread throughout the Aleutian Islands and up the Arctic coast, living off the sea.

The Russians arrive

Existence as the Alaska Natives knew it continued undisturbed until the mid-18th century, when the Russian czar, Peter the Great, started to wonder just what his European rivals were up to in America. Not convinced that the new continent's western reaches didn't, in fact, overlap with Siberia, in 1728 he sent an expedition, led by the Danish explorer Vitus Bering, to find out if the two continents were joined. Bering was able to confirm the existence of the strait that now bears his name. More importantly, on a subsequent expedition, in 1741, his ships returned home bringing news of treasure – huge colonies of sea otters and fur seals in the Aleutians. Bering himself was shipwrecked and died on the island of Avtacha, now Bering Island. So began Alaska's first free-for-all. Soon, countless

Besides, the Crimean War (1854–56) that Russia was fighting against the British and the French, was straining the country's resources, and making it difficult for Russia to defend its overseas possessions.

The art of the deal

As early as 1857 representatives of Czar Alexander II were talking about selling "Russian America," but the United States was too distracted by its own internal rumblings to respond to overtures. After the Civil War ended, however, Secretary of State William Seward made the deal. He was ridiculed by many for

Russian hunters arrived, enslaving thousands of Aleuts. One outfit, the Russian-American Company, was eventually granted an imperial monopoly on pelts; based in what's now Sitka, its managers ruled the region as a semi-private fiefdom well into the 19th century.

By the 1840s, though, the Russian era was nearing an end. Fur hunters of all nationalities had harried the otters almost to extinction.

PRECEDING PAGES: water sports at Misty Fjords; cruising past stellar sea lions at Prince William Sound; a husky races by Mendenhall Glacier, Juneau.
LEFT: Captain James Cook.
ABOVE: trading for oil.

spending $7.2 million on what was called "Seward's Folly." After all, his critics reasoned, the region's otters and seals, and the wealth they produced, were almost gone. No one yet suspected the mineral riches that might be locked in its soil.

So why did Seward do it? For the same reason that Peter the Great had looked eastward a century earlier: national security. Seward figured that whoever controlled Alaska controlled the Pacific. In his eyes, two cents an acre – for that's what the purchase price worked out at – wasn't too high a price to pay.

Of course, the new US district (as it was officially classified) could hardly be called Russian

America. After taking possession in late 1867, though, and renaming it Alaska (Aleut for "great land"), Washington left its purchase alone for the next decade or so.

All that glisters

Then it happened. In November 1880, Joe Juneau and Richard Harris paddled into Sitka, the district's capital, loaded down with half a ton of gold-bearing quartz that they'd mined on a site where the city of Juneau now sits. This discovery launched the first in a series of gold rushes in Alaska and the Canadian Yukon, elsewhere in the Inside Passage, along the

Fishing

The last major gold strike occurred in 1902, in the Fairbanks area, but other profitable industries were appearing, the most important being commercial fishing, especially after canning was introduced. Alaska's rivers and bays were aswim with five different kinds of salmon – not to mention halibut and king crab. In 1878 the first two canneries were built, at Klawock and Sitka, and the Arctic Pack Company established one in 1883 in Nushagak Bay, where salmon runs were greatest. By the early 1900s, dozens of canneries were operating along Alaska's southern coast.

Yukon River, and, most importantly, in the Klondike in 1896. The Klondike fields were a long way inland. The easiest way to get to them was by ship to Skagway in southeast Alaska, from where would-be prospectors had to trudge over the Coastal Range, braving the dangers of White Pass or the Chilkoot Trail to get to them; or else take an expensive steamboat trip all the way up the Yukon River.

Most of the thousands who braved these trails returned with nothing. However, these hopefuls left behind an infrastructure of towns, toll roads, railroads, and suppliers that had evolved to serve (or fleece) them, and it was this infrastructure that opened the interior to permanent settlers.

Logging

Forestry, too, periodically promised to take off, although the industry's growth was repeatedly thwarted by logging companies in the Pacific Northwest jealously guarding their market.

None of this activity had escaped Washington's attention. By 1906, Alaska had a non-voting representative in the House, and in 1912, the district was promoted to the status of territory. This new status conferred the right to elect a territorial legislature and to be considered for statehood – the first statehood bill was put before Congress, and defeated, in 1916. Change was in the air, sometimes literally. The first telegraph lines were strung at the turn of the 20th century; the Alaska Railroad, which linked the port of Seward with Fairbanks, was completed in 1923; and by the 1930s, bush pilots were keeping everyone else connected.

States of war, wars of state

With war looming, plans to build the first road linking Alaska to the Lower 48 picked up speed. For strategic reasons, Canada and the US had decided to build a series of military bases near the Arctic. After the attack on Pearl Harbor brought the US into World War II, the Army realized it had to find a submarine-proof route for transporting the construction equipment. Nine months and $138 million later, the 1,500-mile (2,400-km) Alaska Highway – or at least a gravelly rough draft – was completed.

That wasn't the extent of Alaska's role in the conflict. To divert attention from his assault on Midway, Japan's Admiral Isoroku Yamamoto sent two aircraft carriers north to the Aleutians, where the US had a base. Midway didn't work all that well for Yamamoto, but his diversionary tactic netted him two small islands in Alaska: Attu and Kiska. Unfortunately for Japan, holding on to them did more than divert the Americans' attention: for months, it tied up men and material that the Emperor sorely needed elsewhere.

By the time World War II ended, it had altered Alaska profoundly. Some 300,000 members of the military had been stationed in the territory. Most of the soldiers and support staff left after being demobilized, but some stayed and others brought their families back to settle down. Between 1940 and 1950, the civilian population of Alaska grew from 60,000 to nearly 130,000. And the military didn't close down its bases – in fact, soon they were being expanded in preparation for a new war. A cold one.

Alarmed by the threat Soviet long-range bombers posed to the Pacific Northwest, the Air Force set up a Distant Early Warning Line. By 1957, 50 radar stations were spread along an imaginary 3,000-mile (4,830-km) line running east to west, above the Arctic Circle. The data was fed directly back to North American Air Defense Command headquarters in Colorado,

but a presence was needed in Alaska to scramble into the air should the alert be sounded.

Meanwhile, Alaskans were getting more serious about statehood. President Harry Truman was in favor of it, as was 58 percent of the territorial population and an even higher percentage of the US public. Those opposed to it, inside Alaska and out, had many reasons: the cost of maintaining a state government; fears, on the part of non-Alaskan investors in the territory, of increased regulations imposed by such a government; concern, on the part of Republicans, of losing their slim hold on the Senate if Alaska's seats went Democratic.

There were even worries, on the part of Southerners, that the new state might support civil-rights legislation.

In 1956, Alaskans themselves forced the issue, voting to approve a state constitution and then sending three "members of Congress" to Washington. They were not allowed to take their seats (which didn't exist, of course), but this ploy prompted a fresh round of negotiations. The most important change was the US government's promise to grant the state 161,500 sq miles (418,200 sq km) of federal land, more than a quarter of Alaska's total area. For the time being, the Feds hung onto their remaining property – nearly 72 percent of the

LEFT: specially constructed domed railcars of cruise trains offer fine views.
RIGHT: oil pipelines cut through the Alaskan landscape.

real estate within the state's borders. The question of Native land claims remained unanswered. On January 3, 1959, Alaska became the 49th state in the Union.

What lies beneath

Alaska Natives living along Cook Inlet and on the North Slope had long noticed a black, sticky substance percolating up through the ground. But even after Pennsylvanian oil wells spawned the modern petroleum industry, no one believed that Alaska had deposits big enough to warrant the expense of extraction. True, the federal government had set aside 23 million acres (9.3

million hectares) of the North Slope as a National Petroleum Reserve in 1923, but no test wells had ever been drilled. A minor oil rush on the Kenai Peninsula 30 years later only proved, to the companies involved, that not even a field that eventually produced 220,000 barrels a day could recoup the immense investment needed.

For that, you would need a major strike, a 10-billion-barrel strike – in fact, the kind of strike that Atlantic Richfield made in 1968 on the shores of Prudhoe Bay, on the North Slope. It also just happened to take place on land now owned by the state of Alaska. A year later, the state's Department of Natural Resources auc-

tioned off the rest of its North Slope leases for $900 million.

One problem remained: transporting the oil to refineries in California. The general consensus was for an 800-mile (1,300-km) pipeline from Prudhoe Bay to ice-free Prince William Sound, where tanker ships could be loaded, but one major roadblock stood in its way: the as-yet-unresolved Native property claims. After they were sorted out – President Richard Nixon signed the Alaska Native Claims Settlement Act in 1971 – Congress agreed the pipeline in 1973.

By 1977 the pipeline was completed, at a total cost of $8 billion. Realizing the oil reserves wouldn't last forever, the governor, legislature, and voters decided, by constitutional amendment, to set aside – and invest for the future – at least 25 percent of everything the state was paid by the oil companies. This pot of money became the Permanent Fund. Partly to make sure legislators wouldn't dare loot the fund to pay the state's bills (should times get rough), a dividend program was set up, distributing part of the fund's earnings every year to the residents of Alaska, Anglo and Native alike. In 1982, each one received a check for $1,000.

Changing fortunes

More recently, two of Alaska's other main industries – fishing and forestry – have experienced troubled times. In the 1990s, king crabs were nearly fished out, and salmon catches dropped sharply, particularly in western Alaskan waters. The rise of farmed salmon in other parts of the world has lowered prices significantly. Meanwhile, pulp mills in Sitka and Ketchikan closed, hitting Alaskan loggers hard.

Luckily, a new industry has been thriving – tourism. Not so new, actually – for generations, intrepid or well-heeled travelers like naturalist John Muir or railroad barons E.H. Harriman and Henry Villard had been making expeditions to see Alaska's landscape and wildlife. But thanks to the opening of the Alaska Highway, the launch of the Marine Highway ferry system, the arrival of the cruise industry, and the recent boom in soft-adventure travel, a trip to Alaska has become a possibility – even a priority – for the average American vacationer. More than a million average vacationers each summer, in fact. ❑

LEFT: crab fishing in Haines, Alaska.

Native Alaskans

Few visitors will be surprised to learn that not all Alaska Natives wear polar-bear parkas, live in igloos, or rub noses to say hello. Although hunters from the Inupiat and Yup'ik tribes, who lived along the Arctic coast, did occasionally build igloos for temporary shelter, their home villages tended to be collections of sod-covered, wood-frame dwellings. The Athabascans, who inhabited Alaska's interior, resembled Native Americans more than they did the stereotypical Inuit. They used bows and arrows for hunting, and wore deerskin clothing. The Tlingit, who lived in the southeast along with the Haida (a late-arriving tribe originally from British Columbia), shared large, communal cedar-plank houses; they also caught fish, carved totem poles, and held potlatches – feasts in which a clan would give away all its possessions.

No one knows exactly how many Natives were living in Alaska when the first Russian hunters landed in the late 1740s – about 80,000, some researchers believe – but it's been estimated that tens of thousands were killed by the newcomers. Later waves of European-Americans – miners, mostly – brought drink and disease deep into the backcountry, debilitating still more Native people. Although various US laws over the years promised that Native tribes would be left alone on their lands, none provided ways for the tribes to actually take possession of property. (Alaska Natives were, at least, granted citizenship in 1924.) Finally, in 1966, the state's tribes came together to form the Alaska Federation of Natives. Thanks to its lobbying – and to pressure from oil companies, who wanted the mess resolved so their pipeline could be built – the Alaskan Native Claims Settlement Act (ANCSA) was passed in 1971.

ANCSA ordered that nearly a billion dollars and 44 million acres (18 million hectares) of federal land be divided among regional, urban, and village "native corporations" representing 76,000 shareholders (US citizens who were at least one-quarter Native), in exchange for giving up their aboriginal rights to the land.

These corporations now manage various businesses as well as investments on behalf of their tribal members. By 2001, the Arctic Slope Regional Corporation, for one, was turning over

RIGHT: Inuit Umingmaktok women of the Northwest Territories make a fire so that they can boil tea.

$1.1 billion in petroleum refining, civil engineering, and the like; Cook Inlet Region Inc. (known by the acronym CIRI) owns a small empire of hotels and sightseeing companies.

Facing the future

Money hasn't solved everything, of course. Although the vast majority of the state's 100,000 Natives do still live in Native villages and follow traditional ways, snowmobiles and motorboats have largely – to the regret of some traditionalists – replaced dogsleds and kayaks. However, these modern conveniences have undoubtedly made life a lot easier for the Natives. They struggle to main-

tain a balance, retaining their own culture while taking advantage of what 21st-century society has to offer. In 1992, the Alaska Native Tourism Council was formed to promote rural tourism. It has not brought the communities the economic benefits that some people had hoped for but, on the other hand, the villages have not been overwhelmed with tourists.

Modern society can also prove an attraction for young people, luring them away from traditional communities and ways of life. Alcoholism, too, remains a serious problem, and a number of villages have voted to stay dry. But compared to how Native American claims were treated in the Lower 48 states, ANCSA was a huge step forward. ❑

ENVIRONMENTAL CONCERNS

Alaska is the last wilderness, which is what draws many visitors here. Fortunately, measures are now being taken to protect the wildlife and the habitat

For those who believe that the North American landscape is an economic resource to be developed, Alaska is the last frontier – to let it lie fallow would be foolhardy. For those who believe that the North American landscape is a natural treasure to be protected, Alaska is the last wilderness – one final chance

to get it right. The collision of these two doctrines has left its marks on the history of the state, and will ultimately shape its future.

Usually – though not always – it has been Alaskans themselves in the first camp, and outsiders such as the federal government and zealous conservationists in the latter. (After all, most people who migrated this far north did so hoping to make their fortune, not just gaze at the scenery, no matter how spectacular.) Feelings have run particularly high, though, because the US government owns so much of Alaska's land – nearly two-thirds of the entire state – and hasn't been shy about throwing its weight around.

Protecting natural treasures

Throughout its history, Alaska has been regarded, basically, as a cold-storage locker filled with potentially valuable stuff: furs, gold, copper, fish, fossil fuels. Early on, even environmentalists were more interested in preserving particular animals than the "container" as a whole. For them, the first crisis was the overhunting of seals and otters. The Russians eventually had the sense to suspend operations until the seal population started to recover, but the slaughter resumed when the USA took over.

It wasn't till 1911 that an international tribunal hammered out a treaty protecting both species. Just in time, too – it has been estimated that only 2,000 sea otters remained. Now, there are some 70,000.

As the 20th century rolled on, many parks and refuges created by the US government continued to display a game-preserve mindset. Although Mount McKinley National Park contained the tallest mountain in North America, it was created to protect its Dall sheep and other wildlife. In 1941, Franklin Delano Roosevelt set aside a preserve on Kodiak Island for grizzlies and another on the Kenai Peninsula for moose. And in 1957 a much larger preserve was proposed, one destined to become a land-use battleground into the next century.

The Arctic National Wildlife Range was intended as a sanctuary for the North Slope's vast herds of caribou, as well as for polar bears and migratory birds. Although the man behind the range, George Collins, was employed by the Park Service, he didn't favor bringing the land into the park system. Alaska Natives might not be able to hunt on it, as they had done for generations, and the ecosystem was too fragile for the usual National Park infrastructure. No, better to turn the 8.9 million acres (3.6 million hectares) into a wildlife range under the Bureau of Land Management. (Twenty years later, it was expanded and renamed the Arctic National Wildlife Refuge.) True, doing so left the habitat open to limited gas and oil exploration, but in all it has been a successful compromise – so far.

Oil ups the ante

By the end of the 1960s, another kind of grand project was on the horizon. The discovery of oil in Prudhoe Bay meant a trans-Alaska pipeline was needed. Environmentalists, mostly from out of state, worried about the effects of the heated pipe on the permafrost, the disruption of caribou migration, and, of course, leaks. Unfortunately for them, they had no leverage over Alaska's congressmen. Alaska Native groups did, however, and at first they joined conservation groups in fighting the pipeline. But it was a marriage of convenience – what the Natives cared most about was getting their land claims addressed. Once that happened, the tribes dropped their opposition, clearing the way for the oil companies to build their pipeline (and employ a good number of Native workers). However, the whole process took five years, giving engineers plenty of time to resolve some of the ecological concerns. The fight, though ultimately fruitless, did make the pipeline safer for a vulnerable landscape.

Oil catastrophe

Some 15 years later, environmentalists' worst fears were realized. The 1989 *Exxon Valdez* spill in Prince William Sound was blamed on a negligent captain, but other factors helped turn it into a full-scale catastrophe. The *Valdez*, like most tankers, was single-hulled, not double-hulled; to save money, the pipeline authority had disbanded an emergency team dedicated specifically to spills; the port's clean-up barge was being repaired. A focus on short-term gains left the door wide open for 250,000 barrels' worth of long-term damage. It also, ironically, gave environmentalists the weapons they'd need for battles to come: heartbreaking images of oil-soaked birds and dying otters. The arguments against the pipeline were based on theory, but arguments against future projects would be based on all-too-vividly-illustrated facts.

Tourism enters the fray

Even in a comparatively benign industry like tourism, the interaction of commerce and environment can be complex. Ever since the post-

war launch of the Alaska Marine Highway – a ferry service linking Washington State, the Inside Passage, and points north – the easiest way for visitors to tour the state has been on the water. For the past 15 years, cruise lines have been offering a more luxurious alternative to the ferries, and there's been an enormous jump in the number of passengers visiting the small, historic ports that are so popular as shore excursions.

In 2000, the town of Ketchikan (population 7,922) had twice as many visitors – 565,000 – as it had in 1990. No matter how scrupulously cruise lines now obey regulations banning

waste dumping (their track records haven't been stellar), dozens of ships carrying hundreds of thousands of visitors will inevitably leave their mark. However, unlike extractive industries such as mining, fishing, and logging, tourism does depend upon Alaska remaining Alaska – which bodes well for the future.

Animals in their natural habitat

For most of us, the high point of any Alaska trip is seeing our first grizzly. Or bald eagle. Or moose. Or humpback whale. Or all of the above. You'll see plenty of wildlife on most Alaska cruises, but you may want to add on a day or two at one end of your trip if there's

---

LEFT: cleaning up after an oil spill.
RIGHT: environmentalists campaign to protect Alaska's wilderness from big business interests.

something you've set your heart on seeing and that's most likely found far from the coast.

Bears. Alaska has three kinds: grizzly (or brown) bears, black bears, and polar bears. Grizzly bears are found all over the state; a sure place to see them is in Katmai National Park, where – thanks to a steady supply of salmon – they can weigh as much as 1,400 lbs (635 kg). Compared to grizzlies, black bears are small – the male doesn't grow much beyond 220 lbs (100 kg). Not surprisingly, most black bears are black, but some have lighter-colored, grizzly-like coats. The best way to identify a bear is to look at its back: a grizzly will have a

Quasimodo-like hump. Polar bears, of course, are white and live in the Arctic; they're closely related to grizzlies and almost as large. Bears of all types are omnivorous, eating everything from plants and berries to unlucky caribou calves. Should you spot a bear, whether it's a small black bear raiding a campground dumpster or a grizzly lumbering along a Denali stream, steer respectfully clear.

Eagles. Anyone gazing at the bald eagle's iconic profile might find it hard to believe that back in 1917 the birds were considered such a nuisance that a bounty was posted on them. By 1953, when the bounty was lifted, an estimated 100,000 had been killed. Today, Alaska has

some 30,000 bald eagles, more than any other state in the Union, but habitat loss is still a threat. Fortunately, pesticides were never as big a problem in Alaska as they were down south. Since bald eagles feed on fish, they nest near the water, usually choosing the tallest tree around – as do loggers. These raptors can be spotted all along the coast, but your best bet is the Chilkat Bald Eagle Preserve near Haines, in southeastern Alaska.

Golden eagles are roughly the same size as, and often confused with, immature bald eagles, whose white head and tail feathers haven't yet grown in. Both species are protected. However, golden eagles live farther inland, feeding on small animals and birds instead of fish.

Caribou. Nearly a million caribou range throughout northern Alaska – and as far south as Denali, where you're likely to see them in huge, migratory herds, feeding on grass, mushrooms, and lichen. The only members of the deer family in which both the males and females grow antlers, caribou usually grow to the height of a small pony and have shaggy beige coats.

Moose. With their gawky legs, droopy noses, and mitten-like antlers, moose can look disarmingly goofy, but be careful. More people are injured each year by irritated moose than by bears, partly because they're big (up to 7 ft/ 2 meters tall at the shoulder) and also because they're everywhere: along hiking trails, on highway medians, even in Anchorage backyards. Still, like moose in the Lower 48 states, they prefer to browse in shallow ponds or recently logged patches of forest, where they can find tender young shoots.

Dall sheep and mountain goats. Those tiny white specks on distant ridges barely visible from the Denali shuttle bus are most likely to be Dall sheep, which resemble bighorn sheep. Extremely wary, they rarely descend below the treeline. Mountain goats prefer similar terrain, but their range doesn't extend much farther north than the Chugach mountains, and their horns aren't spiral-shaped but short and spiky, like a cartoon Martian's. There isn't much likelihood you'll see either of these species up close, but look up any time you drive or hike along a mountain range, and you could get lucky.

Seals. Of the five species of "true seals" in Alaska, harbor seals are the ones visitors are mostly likely to see, especially in Kenai Fjords National Park and at the Alaska SeaLife Center in Seward. The others – ribbon seals, ring seals, spotted seals, and bearded seals – keep to the lonely ice packs of the Bering and Beaufort seas. Incidentally, the northern fur seal, whose pelts first lured Russian traders across the Bering Strait, isn't actually a true seal – it's an "eared seal," and as such is a close relative of the Steller sea lion (also found in Alaskan waters – and at the SeaLife Center).

Sea otters. Part of the weasel family, sea otters are much heftier than their landlubber cousins – males can reach the size of a

movie *Free Willy*. They're not particularly cuddly in real life, and they kill seals, sea lions, and even other whales. If you take a cruise around Kenai Fjords National Park, you will have a good chance of meeting up with at least some of these cetaceans. And as you drive along Turnagain Arm, near Anchorage, keep an eye out for the smaller, pale beluga whales (they have distinctive bulging foreheads and beak-like noses).

Salmon. All Alaskan salmon – cohos, chinooks, chums, sockeyes, and pinks – hatch in freshwater lakes or rivers, make their arduous journey to the sea, and eventually

Rottweiler. Like harbor seals, they stick close to shore; unlike seals, they have no fat to keep them warm – just the air trapped in their thick, fine fur. The way in which oil spills kill otters is that their fur gets slicked down and they die of hypothermia.

Whales. The whales most often spotted from day-tour boats include barnacle-covered grays; humpbacks (the ones that slap the water with their tail flukes as they dive); and orcas, familiar to most people from Sea World or the

return to their birthplace to spawn and die. Chinooks (the official state fish) and cohos are most prized by sport fishermen; pinks and sockeyes are more important to the commercial fishing industry. One good place to watch salmon spawn (after mid-August) is the viewing platform on the Williwaw Nature Trail, near the Begich, Boggs Visitor Center off the Seward Highway.

Mammals. You probably won't catch a glimpse of such shy creatures as the lynx or the gray wolf – and to meet a wild muskox you'll have to go deep into the backcountry – but there should be plenty of marmots, squirrels, and foxes to make up for them.   ❏

Left: a caribou in the tundra.
Above: a humpback whale makes an impressive splash in Alaska's waters.

THE IMPACT OF TOURISM

Tourism contributes a great deal to Alaska's economy, but can also be harmful. State authorities, conservationists, and cruise lines are trying to get the balance right

To gain an appreciation of the impact of cruise tourism on Alaska, consider that Ketchikan, the state's sixth-largest city, has a population of around 7,925, yet on any given summer day visiting cruise ships can easily disgorge 6,000 or more passengers into the town's tourist-friendly harbor area. Ditto for state capital, Juneau, which, though larger, is actually more affected by ship traffic since its docks are located right in its downtown core.

Between pedestrians, tour buses, souvenir hawkers, and flightseeing helicopters buzzing overhead, both these ports can sometimes seem like Times Square on an overcast day. Which begs the question: Where's all that quiet, pristine Alaskan wilderness you were supposed to see?

That's the Zen koan that exercises the minds of both the cruise industry and Alaska's government and citizens: how to preserve Alaskans' quality of life while still promoting tourism, which contributes so mightily to the state's economy? And how to create the necessary tourist infrastructure while retaining Alaska's essential wilderness character – which is, of course, the reason people come in the first place?

Preserving towns

There's no question tourism has changed Alaska, both for better and worse. On the plus side, there are whole communities that wouldn't even exist were it not for tourist dollars, among them cruise favorite port of Skagway. This is a town whose initial economic viability lasted all of two years, during the celebrated Klondike Gold Rush of 1897–98.

When the stampeders stopped coming, the town's population dropped from more than 15,000 to 500, but those few remaining citizens had the foresight to create a historic district full of Gold Rush-era buildings, a decision whose contribution to the town's current prosperity cannot be overestimated.

LEFT: a cruise ship dominates the harbor and the mountain landscape in Juneau.
RIGHT: totem poles at Ketchikan Heritage Center.

Causing problems

On the other side of the coin is Juneau, whose citizens have spent the last decade arguing about tourism's impact, their pro and con letters filling the pages of the daily *Juneau Empire*. In 1999, voters passed an initiative that imposed a $5 per head charge on all cruise passengers dis-

embarking at the port, to cover the costs of tourism-related services and infrastructure and mitigate the impact on the town. One year later, concerns over how ship emissions were affecting local air quality led Princess Cruises (one of the dominant lines in Alaska, along with Holland America) to agree to switch off ships' engines while in port, drawing necessary power instead from a hookup with the Alaska Electric Power and Light Company.

The effect on marine life

Such environmental concerns extend to the region's marine environment, where the effects of cruise ships on water quality and wildlife have been a source of controversy for more than two decades.

In 1979, the US National Marine Fisheries Service (now called the National Oceanic and Atmospheric Administration) concluded that uncontrolled vessel traffic in Glacier Bay had probably caused humpback whales to leave its waters over the previous two years. As a result of this and later studies, cruise lines' access to the popular bay was severely restricted, and today only two large cruise ships and three tour vessels (the designation under which small-ship lines operate) are permitted in the park per day. Even so, there have been problems: in 1998,

marine life also remain the subject of ongoing debate, with a 2002 study by the Alaska Fisheries Science Center suggesting that ships may be harming harbor seal populations in Yakutat Bay, site of the popular Hubbard Glacier.

Thankfully, though, the news isn't all doom and gloom. In December 2002, an Alaska Department of Environmental Conservation study found that state and federal regulations have been largely effective in curbing harmful discharge of waste water from cruise ships.

According to the agency's science advisory panel, a properly maintained and well-managed modern ship, operating in compliance

Holland America Line was slapped with a $2-million fine for discharging oily bilge water into the pristine bay and nearby Icy Strait, in violation of the federal Prevention of Pollution from Ships Act. Less than a month later, Royal Caribbean received an even larger fine for dumping waste water in the nearby Pacific. As a result of these incidents, both the state and the industry created new and more stringent rules to curb cruise ship pollution. Still, problems persist. In May 2003, Norwegian Cruise Line's *Norwegian Sun* accidentally released 40 tons of raw sewage into Washington State's Strait of Juan de Fuca while en route from Alaska to Seattle. Cruise ships' effects on

with the regulations, will not release measurably harmful amounts of chemicals or bacteria. Air pollution is also being addressed through engineering, with many new vessels (including Celebrity's Millennium-class ships and Princess's *Coral Princess* and *Island Princess*) being powered by more environmentally friendly gas-turbine engines.

Actively encouraging cruise ships

Meanwhile, many small towns in Alaska and British Columbia are going all-out to attract cruise lines to their docks – sometimes by building new docks, as is the case with BC's Prince Rupert, which trumpets its small-town feel and nearby natural attractions as an anti-dote to "congestion issues" in Alaska. Other towns – significantly the Alaska Native towns of Hoonah (on Chichagof Island, west of Juneau) and Metlakatla (on Annette Island, just south of Ketchikan) – are marketing their rich northwest culture in an effort to draw cruise ship passengers.

In both these cases, tourism is providing a lifeline to areas where revenues from tradi-tional timber and fishing industries have fallen steadily over the past decade. While Metla-katla's enterprise is small-scale, centered around its Tribal Longhouse/cultural center

For the project's initial season in 2004, a deal with Royal Caribbean and Celebrity Cruises will bring in more than 60,000 visi-tors, creating about 300 jobs and accounting for $3.5 million in wages, with wider employ-ment seen in subsequent years – a significant boost to a town in serious need. And if they get it right, cruise passengers will benefit, too, as it will provide a vastly superior experience to shuffling through the nondescript jewelry stores and gift shops that invaded the larger port towns when Alaska cruising first took off, and which still tend to dominate storefronts in the bigger ports.

and attracting only small ships, Hoonah has constructed an entire, purpose-built cruise des-tination called Port Icy Strait at the site of the once abandoned Hoonah Cannery, about a mile from town itself. In addition to restoring the cannery's old belt-driven machinery and designing whale-watching and bear-watching tours, the town has built a totem-carving hut, a museum, a restaurant and retail space, as well as a cultural center at which a Tlingit dance troupe will perform.

LEFT: a cruise ship stands at the end of busy Main Street in Skagway.
ABOVE: a Tlingit Native Alaskan carves a canoe.

A warm welcome

Like most things in the human experience, tourism in Alaska is neither angel nor devil. And lest you're thinking you'll step off your ship and be pelted with rotten eggs, don't worry. You won't. Even in Juneau, hotbed of agitation, the locals still stop their cars to let you cross the street, the bartenders at the Alaskan Bar still pour a friendly beer, and Native interpreters at the top of the Mount Roberts Tramway are still happy to discuss their culture. And a 2002 study found that 40 percent of Juneau residents thought tourism had a positive effect on their community, up from 29 percent in 1998. Things are looking up. ❏

THE SIZE FACTOR: BIG SHIPS VERSUS SMALL

Take a little while to assess what you really want from a cruise, because the experience you will get varies considerably with the size of the ship

Choosing a ship is a lot like buying a car, with many of the same criteria: should it be big or small? Classic or modern? Luxurious or functional? It all comes down to assessing your personal preferences, being

realistic about your budget and deciding on the best vehicle to suit your needs.

Mega-ship or intimate cruise?

The difference between so-called "big ships" and "small ships" could hardly be more stark, and it isn't simply a matter of tonnage or floor space, but what they have to offer. These days, large mainstream ships tend to be very big indeed, carrying 2,000 passengers or more, soaring 14 stories above the water, and stretching to lengths of nearly 1,000 ft (300 meters). These are the so-called mega-ships, a term that came into fashion when "mega" meant ships of 75,000 gross tons or above.

Today, the current largest of the bunch – Cunard's *Queen Mary 2* – is fully twice that size, too big to cross from the Atlantic through the Panama Canal and thus unlikely ever to visit Alaska. The "big ship" designation also includes mainstream and luxury vessels in the 50,000-ton range, carrying between 900 and 1,200 passengers.

By contrast, small ships in Alaska tend to be very small, measuring in the neighborhood of 100 ft (30 meters) in length and carrying between 12 and 140 passengers. Some are closer to yachts in size and appearance, others have the utilitarian feel of expedition ships, and still others look like the miniaturized cruise ships that they are.

A choice of entertainment

In examining whether a big or small ship would best suit your needs, you need to consider three main variables: the onboard experience you should expect during the course of your cruise, the kinds of itineraries and ports of call offered by each, and the cost.

By design, most big ships are busy places, with activities, entertainment, and meals programmed so that, if you cared to, you could be occupied during every waking moment you were on board. As such, they're ideal for families, allowing parents and children to pursue their own interests and stay out of each other's hair. They're also the better choice for people who, although they want to see the natural wonders of the 49th state, don't expect that glaciers, whales, and mountains will be able to hold their interest every minute of the day.

These people want a show in the evening, multiple restaurants for dinner, sports options (of both the active and couch-potato varieties), maybe a casino, and they might even like to take a dip in the ship's pool – if only for the kick of doing so within sight of an iceberg. For these people, Royal Caribbean, NCL, and Carnival are the top choices.

Those looking for a slightly more refined version of this same experience should check out tradition-minded Holland America or stylish Celebrity line, while those with the money to go with their refinement should opt for the luxury lines Crystal and Radisson, which feature much enhanced service, cuisine, and accommodations.

Accommodations and eating

Among the mainstream lines, accommodations run the gamut from smallish inside cabins to the ever-more-prevalent outside ones with private balconies, to absolutely palatial suites

restaurant with two seatings and a buffet option at breakfast and lunch, today's mega-ships are being built with multiple main dining rooms, casual options for every meal, specialty coffee-and-pastry cafés, and multiple, reservations-only restaurants serving Asian, Italian, French, steakhouse, and other menus, at an extra cost of around $5 to $25 per person per meal. NCL's *Norwegian Star* is the dining-option king in Alaska, as it has no fewer than 10 different restaurants.

And if you want to work off the calories you are likely to pack away at those restaurants, the mega-ships all have sprawling gym complexes,

with personal butler service. Balcony cabins offer the pleasant option of landscape- and wildlife-viewing in the privacy of your own room, but if you're just as happy watching from public areas you can save quite a bit on your fare by opting for an inside cabin (if you're not claustrophobic) or a low-end exterior one with a small window.

Dining is another area of great choice on the big ships. Whereas a decade ago the most you could expect to find would have been a main

LEFT: cruise passengers enjoy a spell in a Jacuzzi with views of glaciers and mountains, College Fjord.
ABOVE: Holland America Line offer a traditional cruise.

jogging tracks, and varying sports amenities, from the almost ubiquitous golf-driving nets and basketball/volleyball courts to Royal Caribbean's trademark rock-climbing walls. In essence, sailing aboard a mega-ship in Alaskan waters is like checking into a smart, big-city hotel and then taking that hotel with you to the wilderness.

Small ships for watching wildlife

Across the board, small ships offer exactly the opposite kind of experience, with onboard dining, activities, and entertainment taking a backseat to the natural world outside. All meals are served in a single, simple dining room (with a small buffet also set out in a lounge at lunch and dinner times), while the only entertainment you might expect is, perhaps, a crew talent show or an informal lecture by the ship's onboard naturalist on subjects such as Native art or wildlife.

Instead of such inside-oriented activities, passengers spend their time out on deck with binoculars scanning for whales, bears, sea otters, and other wildlife – which they're much more likely to see from these ships than from the big ones, since small vessels are less obtrusive, can therefore sail closer to shore, and have passenger decks that begin only a few yards

above the waterline. These same factors also mean you get a more intimate experience of Alaska, which is the main reason people choose this type of cruise. Typically, the range of accommodations on these vessels is limited, tending toward cozy outside cabins with few amenities. Most don't even have televisions.

Ports of call

Itinerary-wise, ships both large and small tend to visit the popular Alaska ports of Juneau, Ketchikan, and Skagway, where all passengers get exactly the same experience, although big ships tend to offer a wider range of shore-excursion options. One advantage small ships

do have here is that, with fewer passengers, it takes less time to get on and off the ship, so you have more time in port and less frustrating waiting time. Small ships also have the advantage when it comes to visiting smaller port towns like Petersburg and Metlakatla and sailing narrow wilderness passages like Misty Fjords National Monument – places from which the big ships are barred by their sheer bulk.

Cruise West, Clipper, and American West Steamboat Company tend to mix visits to small towns and wild areas with stops at the larger ports, while more adventure-oriented Glacier Bay Cruises, Lindblad Expeditions, and American Safari Cruises (plus Cruise West's Wilderness Waterways itineraries) stick mainly to wild areas and small ports and offer greater opportunities for hiking and kayaking.

Counting the cost

And now we come to what's bound to be the deciding factor for most people: cost. Counterintuitive as it may seem, the small-ship lines are far more expensive than the big mainstream lines. In 2003, you could get a full seven-night cruise aboard any of the mainstream ships for the same price as one night with Lindblad or American Safari (in the $500 per person range, as opposed to upwards of $3,500 – about the same price you pay aboard luxury lines like Radisson and Crystal). Costs for the other small-ship lines tend to fall into the $2,500 to $3,000 per week range. Mostly, the disparity is due to the higher costs of operating small ships, which, among other things, are US flagged and therefore must employ all American staff.

The bottom line, though, isn't really the bottom line. What really matters is getting the most out of your visit, because for many people it's a once-in-a-lifetime experience. Consider your priorities and your budget. For the same amount of money, you could sail with a mainstream line and take all the best optional shore excursions (helicopter glacier treks, sport fishing, dog sledding); sail with a luxury line and follow our suggestions of things to do on your own in port (see page 93); or sail with a small-ship adventure line, where most off-ship wilderness activities are included in the cost. When it comes down to it, it's all a matter of what you want your money to buy. ❑

LEFT: Tufted puffins are rare Alaskan birdlife.

Topical Talks

While Caribbean cruises tend to come down to port briefings and the occasional lecture on coral reefs, on North American itineraries most give a nod to the regional culture. And many North American cruises – especially the river cruises and Alaska trips – go several steps further, with lectures and narration by experts.

"Port Talks," commonly held a day or two before the ship docks in a specific destination, are a traditional part of the cruising experience. At their best, they don't push passengers into booking pricey shore excursions, but simply introduce the ports of call. Cultural information is leavened with personal anecdotes and key points of interest. On culturally-oriented small ships, shopping advice is secondary to a more in-depth look at the port. However, if learning about the destinations is important to you, get a book from the ship's library or bring your own. Port talks have become increasingly commercial – with sign-up sheets for tour excursions passed out at the end – and it's best not to depend on them for all your information.

Lecturers and their specialties

Small ships are especially good at incorporating academic-style lectures on natural and historical topics. Lecturers may focus on a specific aspect of the flora, fauna, and history of the area. You can learn about sea otters, glaciers, and bald eagles on Alaska's Inside Passage cruises; or westward expansion, lighthouses, and native tribes on the Columbia River. In certain destinations – such as Alaska – all cruise lines make a point of bringing on science experts to offer "deck talks." These running dialogues are broadcast on the public decks so that the expert can point out and explain, for example, why whales breach.

The quality of the talks, both on deck and at the podium, varies tremendously from line to line, and often even from sailing to sailing. Lecturers tend to offer their services only for short periods, which is why the summer sailings in Alaska are a perfect fit for academics. Lindblad, perhaps the best at offering an in-depth look at destinations, recruits a highly-trained, full-time expedition staff. The tiny, 70-passenger *Sea Lion* and *Sea Bird*, for example, travel with four experts at all times. Cruise West

RIGHT: a deck talk with Cruise West can help understand the immediate environment.

and Clipper always offer an expedition leader and assistant, but guides' specialties may differ from ship to ship and season to season.

If an in-depth approach is important to you, do some research before making your choice. Though bigger budgets can lure bigger names, the best guest lecturers are not restricted to the most exclusive lines. Cruise lines promote their visiting speakers and on-staff teams in their brochures, as well as on their web sites. If you can't find the relevant information, call the line. You probably don't plan to do an itinerary twice, so make sure you have the experience you want the first time around.

Some of the most interesting lecturers appear

on theme cruises, which have grown in popularity over the years. They may discuss topics from antiques to calligraphy or comedy, finance or film-making, maritime history or music. It is not unusual to find guest lecturers covering such subjects as gambling or graphology, body language or beauty, or how to cope with divorce or bereavement.

Some lines manage to work their themes around major events and holidays. The *Delta Queen*, for example, makes it to New Orleans for Mardi Gras and to Louisville for the Kentucky Derby. A cruise is a memorable way to take part in these annual events – if nothing else, you avoid the hassle of booking a hotel room months in advance, and you'll have the ship's staff to hold your hand. ❑

UNSPOILED ALASKA

*Alaska remains the most rugged, unspoiled state in the Union.
Cruises from Seattle or Vancouver offer a beguiling mixture of
natural wonders and man-made attractions*

Map
on page
90–1

It's a cliché, but it's true: the central myth of US life is the frontier, and in the 21st century, with highways crisscrossing the Lower 48 states and a McDonald's on every corner, Alaska remains the last great unspoiled place, where caribou outnumber people and glaciers still carve the primordial landscape. People come here seeking something totally different from their everyday lives, something bigger and more grand. They come to see mountains so high they create their own weather, and forests as tall and majestic as cathedrals. They come to see 50-ft (15-meter) humpback whales leap from the water like dancers, while bald eagles soar overhead and brown bears tread through cold mountain streams, the original salmon fishers.

But there's more even than nature. In Southeast, Alaska's main cruising area, the powerful Tlingit, Haida, and Tsimshian Native tribes once ruled, crossing the waters of the Inside Passage to hunt and trade. Today, their cultures are alive and strong still, influencing most facets of Alaskan life from business to the arts. Dotted around the landscape, their totem poles still rise into the sky, carved by new generation artists to tell the stories of their tribes.

The white man first arrived here in 1741 in the person of Danish explorer Vitus Bering, then in 1867 US Secretary of State William Seward bought the territory from Czar Alexander II for US$7.2 million. "Seward's Folly" they called it – at least until gold was discovered in 1898, leading to the great Klondike Gold Rush. Thousands poured in, seeking instant wealth and establishing some of the towns, railways, and even businesses you still see today. But it wasn't only gold-seekers who came. In 1879, naturalist John Muir made the first of his three trips to Southeast, and while viewing the great glaciers noted that here, in Alaska, "one learns that the world, though made, is yet being made; that this is still the morning of creation; that mountains long conceived are now being born, channels traced for coming rivers, basins hollowed for lakes."

In the early years of the 21st century, Alaska is still thus: complete and grand beyond imagination, but always in a state of change.

LEFT: the waterfall at Mendenhall Glacier.
BELOW: Native Alaskans maintain their traditions.

Alaska cruise routes

The following section details all the significant ports and wilderness areas included on Alaska cruises, although each itinerary will vary, and none will visit all the destinations. There are many variations, but just two basic routes: either round-trip from Vancouver or Seattle or north- or southbound between one of those cities and one of Anchorage's two port towns, Seward or Whittier. Some small ships also operate from Juneau and Ketchikan.

Jimi Hendrix was born in Seattle.

BELOW:
the Seattle city skyline and the Space Needle at night.

Seattle, Washington

Once a minor player as an Alaska home port, Seattle has come into its own in recent years, with up to seven mega-ships and a number of smaller vessels sailing from its waterfront.

The city was first settled on November 13, 1851, when the Denny party – a dozen pioneers who had traveled the Oregon Trail from the Midwest with their children – landed at Alki Point aboard the schooner *Exact*. The following spring, most of the party relocated across Elliott Bay to the site now known as Pioneer Square, naming their new city after Chief Sealth of the Duwamish and Suquamish tribes, who helped the settlers establish themselves. Their community grew quickly, and by 1910 Seattle's population had increased to 237,000, helped substantially by its prominence as an outfitting stop for stampeders headed north on the Klondike Gold Rush.

Pioneer Square Ⓐ, centered on Yesler Way a few blocks from the waterfront, is now a historic district showcasing buildings constructed in the early 1890s to replace losses from the Great Fire of 1889, which leveled more than 30 city blocks. Tree-lined and cobblestoned, it is a center of art galleries and nightlife, with numerous bars, antiques shops, restaurants, and clubs. Bibliophiles should head to the **Elliott Bay Book Company**, a legendary independent bookstore on Main Street. On First Avenue, the 1½-hour **Underground Tour** (tel: 206-682 4646 for schedules) takes visitors below street level into the remains of pre-Great Fire of Seattle, preserved due to hasty reconstruction. The **waterfront area**, along Alaskan Way between Yesler Way and Bell Street, is the center of the Seattle tourist area. Visit **Ye Olde Curiosity Shop Ⓑ** (closed Sun) at Pier 54 to see mummies, shrunken heads, a three-tailed pig, and other oddities.

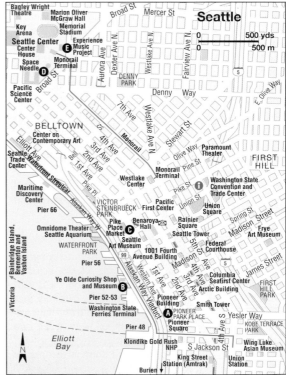

Map on page 68

Inland from the waterfront, head to the intersection of Pike and Western for Seattle's 9-acre (4-hectare) **Pike Place Market** ⊙ (open daily). Begun as a farmers' market almost a century ago, it's expanded over the past few decades and is now home to some of the city's best restaurants as well as hundreds of crafts and specialty stores, selling everything from top-of-the-range kitchenware to Egyptian art. Street performers entertain throughout the day.

Farther west, **Seattle Center** began as a civic complex in 1927 and was drastically rebuilt as the 74-acre (30-hectare) site of the 1962 World's Fair. That's when the **Space Needle** ⊙ went up, that iconic 605-ft (184-meter) observation tower. Nearby, on 5th Avenue, the **Experience Music Project** ⊙ (closed Sun) is a different kind of modern. Housed in a typically impressive Frank Gehry building, the project was originally planned as a tribute to the music of Seattle-born guitarist Jimi Hendrix, but expanded before its opening to include all phases of American popular music, from country to hip-hop and beyond. In addition to displays of music memorabilia, the place is serious about the "experience" part of its name, featuring interactive music rooms and space for live performances.

Streetcars are a familiar sight on Seattle's waterfront.

Vancouver, British Columbia

Located on the mainland just north of the US–Canada border, **Vancouver** is the main southern terminus for Alaska cruises, with lines offering both round-trip itineraries and one-way, north- or southbound cruises between Vancouver and Anchorage/Seward/Wrangell.

Vancouver's European history began in 1792 when George Vancouver sailed up the Burrard Inlet, claimed the land as British territory, and began charting its waters. The settlement began to burgeon through the entrepreneurial efforts of

BELOW: cycling by the Stanley Park sea wall, Vancouver.

one "Gassy Jack" Deighton, a steamboat captain who in 1867 built a saloon in the then-tiny settlement, which was given the unofficial name "Gassy's Town" or simply Gastown. When the town was incorporated in 1869, the residents changed its name to Granville, after British colonial secretary, Lord Granville. It was only later, when the Canadian-Pacific Railway agreed to build its western terminus here, that the name was changed to Vancouver. Today, **Gastown Ⓐ**, just east of the Canada Place cruise ship docks, is a historic neighborhood whose cobblestone streets are lined with restaurants, bars, fashion boutiques, and antiques shops, and galleries. Many of the buildings date from the late 1880s, built after the fire of 1886 wiped out the whole city. The area was renovated in the 1970s after decades as the city's skid row, but even today you are likely to be panhandled. A **statue of Gassy Jack** stands in Maple Tree Square, at the junction of Water and Carrall Streets.

Dr Sun Yat-Sen Classical Chinese Garden was built by Chinese master-craftsmen.

Canada Place Ⓑ itself was built as the Canada Pavilion for Expo '86, the last World's Fair held to date in North America, and was later converted into a convention center and cruise port. You can't miss the place, which was designed to resemble an enormous sailing ship, its roof resembling five white sails rising behind the silvery bulk of the Pan Pacific Hotel. The pier offers restaurants, shopping, a promenade with great views and displays on Vancouver history, and an IMAX theater showing a variety of films.

BELOW:
the Aquabus
runs between
Downtown and
North Vancouver.

Just south of Gastown on Carrall Street, Vancouver's Chinatown neighborhood is home to restaurants, markets, and the **Dr Sun Yat-Sen Classical Chinese Garden Ⓒ** (open daily), the first full-sized classical Chinese garden built outside China. It was laid out in 1985–86 by master gardeners and craftsmen from Suzhou, using techniques from the original Ming dynasty gardens, in

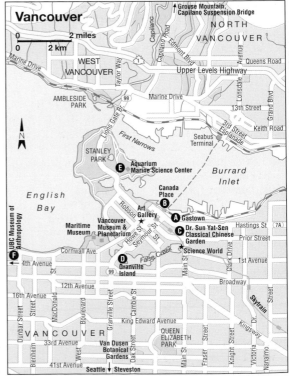

which plant selection and arrangement are intended to create different moods and mimic natural seasonal change year-round. The garden was named for the doctor and revolutionary who overthrew China's Qing dynasty in 1911 and subsequently became the country's first democratic president.

Southeast of Chinatown, the former industrial district of **Granville Island** ⓓ is now a self-contained, idealized city, its factories and warehouses converted into farmers' markets, stores, museums, artists spaces and galleries, restaurants, bars, and a micro-brewery. Street performers do their thing amid throngs of locals, visitors, and workers from the few remaining industries.

Farther north, is Stanley Park's **Vancouver Aquarium Marine Science Centre** ⓔ (open daily), one of the largest and finest aquariums in North America, home to regional sea life such as orca, beluga whales, dolphins, and sea lions.

Those interested in Pacific Northwest Native culture should trek 20 minutes west of downtown to the University of BC's **Museum of Anthropology** ⓕ (open daily), which displays one of the world's best collections of Native art. An extensive totem pole collection, contemporary wood sculptures by Haida artist Bill Reid, a pottery gallery, and more than 13,000 other pieces are housed in a building whose design was based on traditional post and beam architecture.

Victoria, British Columbia

If the Alaskan ports of Sitka and Petersburg are, respectively, the Little Russia and Little Norway of an Alaska cruise, **Victoria** is the Little Britain, a thoroughly proper English presence perched on the southern tip of Vancouver Island.

Native peoples lived on Vancouver Island for thousands of years before Captain James Cook showed up at Nootka Sound in 1778. The transformation of the region didn't really begin, though, until March 1843, when representatives of the Hudson's Bay Company constructed a trading post and fort at a location the Natives called Camosack (Rush of Water). On June 10 of that year it was officially named Fort Victoria after the British queen. The name was continued when the town site was laid out, beginning in 1852.

Like most other towns in the region, Victoria boomed with the gold fever of 1858, when its population exploded from 450 to about 20,000, but the development of Vancouver and other mainland towns eventually left it behind. Nevertheless, when British Columbia became the sixth province in the new Dominion of Canada, Victoria was named its capital city, a distinction it holds to this day.

Ships dock at the Ogden Point terminal, about a mile (1.6 km) southwest of the **Inner Harbour** and the **Downtown/Old Town** area, where much of Victoria's notable shopping, restaurants, and in-town attractions are located. This is where the city began, and though Fort Victoria was torn down nearly 150 years ago, you can still see its shape in a line of light-colored bricks at Government and Fort streets. The names inscribed are those of early Victoria settlers.

Farther south on Government Street, the **Empress Hotel** is one of the icons of the city, the crown of the Inner Harbour. Opened in 1908, it was designed by Francis Rattenbury in the grand Edwardian style, and

Maps:
Area 90–1
City 70

TIP

Aquabus water taxis run on several routes from their base on Granville Island. There are also sightseeing tours. For more information call: 604-689 5858 or visit: www.aquabus.bc.ca

BELOW: totem poles stand tall in Stanley Park.

TIP

For full details of **opening hours** and contact information for the sites and museums mentioned in this chapter, *see Travel Tips page 328.*

still carries the feel of that era both inside and out. Its elegant lobby is the location for the famous **High Tea**, served in three sittings daily. If you want to go, call two weeks ahead for reservations (tel: 250-384 8111) and dress appropriately: no tank tops, sleeveless shirts, very short shorts, or cut-offs.

A stone's throw away sit BC's **Parliament Buildings** (otherwise known as the Provincial Legislature) also designed by Rattenbury, and completed 10 years before the Empress. Surrounded by wide lawns and fountains, the buildings themselves are appropriately dignified, all heavy stone and multiple copper domes. A regal statue of Queen Victoria stands at the head of the grounds, gazing out at the Inner Harbour.

Just to the east, the **Royal British Columbia Museum** (open daily) is considered one of the finest in North America, with galleries concentrating on the natural and human history of BC. Its First Peoples' Gallery showcases the arts and history of the region's native peoples, as does the tribal longhouse and totem pole collection in adjacent **Thunderbird Park** (open access; free). Other galleries offer dioramas of the Ice Age and coastal BC and historical artifacts.

Also in the neighborhood, on Douglas Street, the **Crystal Garden Conservation Centre** (open daily) is filled with tropical plants, birds, butterflies, and monkeys – some 65 species in all. Victoria's most famous gardens, though, are located some 15 miles (24 km) north of the city in Brentwood Bay. **Butchart Gardens** (open daily) began in 1904 when Jennie Butchart began to beautify a worked-out quarry site abandoned by her husband's cement-making operation. That quarry became known as the Sunken Garden, and the well-traveled Butcharts gradually expanded their enterprise to include a Japanese Garden, an Italian Garden, and a Rose Garden, the latter replacing their kitchen vegetable patch in 1929. Now 55 acres (22 hectares) in total, the gardens have attracted visitors since the 1920s, including many cruise ship passengers who arrive via organized shore tours.

BELOW: the Parliament Building, Victoria.

Prince Rupert, British Columbia

Located on mainland British Columbia about 40 miles (64 km) south of the US/ Canada border is **Prince Rupert ❶**. Unlike most of the region's cities, which grew from trading posts and small settlements, Prince Rupert came into being more or less at the behest of one man, Charles Hays, who dreamed of creating a second Vancouver here as the western terminus of his Grand Trunk Pacific Railway. He built the railroad, but then booked passage on a new ship when returning from a finance-gathering trip in England. That ship was the RMS *Titanic*. Hays's dreams for Prince Rupert died with him, and subsequent lack of business on the railroad forced the Grand Trunk into bankruptcy. It was incorporated into the Canadian National Railway system in 1919. Since then, Prince Rupert has depended for its livelihood on a number of different industries: fishing, forestry, and more recently container shipping, sport fishing, and tourism.

Despite its idyllic spot amid gorgeous BC mountains and forests, Prince Rupert was until recently a minor player among Alaska and BC cruise ports. In 2003, however, the town announced plans to build a

new multi-million-dollar pier capable of accommodating the largest of today's mega-ships, scheduled to open in time for the summer 2004 season. The new pier adjoins the current Atlin Cruise Dock.

Adjacent to the piers, the neighborhood of **Cow Bay** maintains Prince Rupert's waterfront character spiced up with restaurants and gift shops. It's one of the oldest parts of town, with many of its wood-frame buildings constructed on pilings over the harbor. On the waterfront in the nearby Downtown area, the **Museum of Northern British Columbia** (open daily) is housed in a reproduction longhouse and displays a collection of Native art as well as pieces illustrating northern BC history from the time of the fur trade to the present day. Its **Carving Shed** provides work space for Native artists working in wood, metals, and the local argillite, a soft black slate carved exclusively by members of the Haida tribe. You can sometimes see carvers working on totem poles, then go out to see the finished product displayed in one of the small parks around town.

Metlakatka

Metlakatla **❷**, on Annette Island just north of the US–Canada border, Alaska's only federal Indian reservation, is a stop for some small ships. Founded in 1867 by Scottish missionary William Duncan and 800 members of the Tsimshian nation, today it's a relatively poor community that's nevertheless home to an active Native arts community, with music and dance troupes performing regularly at its **Tribal Longhouse**, giving visitors a window onto the richness of Southeast Native culture.

Ketchikan

Over 100 years old, **Ketchikan ❸** has evolved from a fish cannery and mining-supply center into one of the busiest tourist hubs in Alaska, visited by almost 700,000 travelers annually. It's the first Alaskan stop for ships sailing north from Vancouver or Seattle, and to passengers disembarking at its docks on the Tongass Narrows it seems to be one long stretch of shopping – which it is, up to a point. Local merchants are certainly happy to see visitors.

Old Ketchikan and new Ketchikan meet on boardwalked **Creek Street**, the former red-light district, built on stilts above Ketchikan Creek, where during the summer run you can look down and see salmon crowded fin to fin, heading upstream to spawn. The area's loggers and fishermen crowded into Creek Street up till 1953, when a grand jury vice investigation forced the bordellos out of business. Today, the street's 30 or more wood-frame houses are tenanted by gift shops, art galleries, and bookstores, plus the touristy **Dolly's House** (open daily), a former bordello that was turned into a museum not long after its proprietor's death in 1975. Feather-hatted "ladies" beckon from the doorway, then tour you around the house's antique interior, which looks much as it did when Dolly first opened her doors in 1919.

After poking around, take the funicular from the boardwalk up 130 ft (40 meters) to the **West Coast Cape Fox Lodge** for a view of the town spread out

Map on page 90–1

Native art such as this jewelry can be found at Metlakatla.

BELOW: Creek Street, Ketchikan.

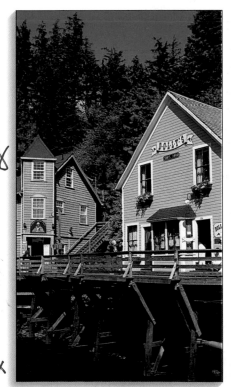

below. After walking through the lobby and checking out the six totem poles in the courtyard, follow the signs to the **Married Men's Trail**, reputedly one of the discreet routes husbands used to reach the bawdy houses below. Watch your step: Ketchikan receives about 160 ins (405 cms) of rainfall annually (that's almost a half an inch every day), so the trail and boardwalks can be slippery.

Back at Creek Street, take Park Avenue about ½ mile (1 km) to the **Totem Heritage Center** (open daily) on Deermount Street. Established in 1976, the center houses a collection of 33 antique totem poles rescued from abandoned Tlingit and Haida villages in the area. Totems are not intended to last forever, and because of Southeast's wet climate, they don't. Most begin to fade and rot within 75 years. By contrast, some of these are well over a century old, and are displayed without restoration, just as they were found. Newer poles are also on display, along with other Native artifacts.

In the heart of town, you can see Native pole-carvers at work at the **Southeast Alaska Discovery Center** (open daily) on Main Street. Half a visitors' advice service, half museum, the center houses displays of Native art plus extensive dioramas that detail the interaction of human beings and nature in Southeast. It's well worth a stop.

The cruise lines offer several good shore excursions from Ketchikan, foremost among them the seaplane trips and short cruises to nearby **Misty Fjords National Monument** (detailed below). **Saxman Native Village**, 2½ miles (4 km) south of Ketchikan, offers further opportunities for learning about Native Tlingit culture, with totem carvers, storytellers, and dancers. Ten miles (16 km) north of town, **Totem Bight State Historical Park** displays carved poles that were begun in 1938 as part of a US Forest Service program in which skilled carvers restored or recreated older poles, and taught their skills to the younger generation. The park is often visited in conjunction with a town tour.

BELOW: MV *Spirit of Endeavour* sails Misty Fjords.

Misty Fjords

One of the perks of the US presidency is the ability to designate areas of public land as National Monuments, and that's exactly what Jimmy Carter did to **Misty Fjords ❹**, east of Ketchikan, on December 1, 1978, setting aside 2.3 million acres (930,000 hectares) as protected land, for the enjoyment of all.

Misty Fjords is one of the quietest places you're likely to encounter on an Alaska cruise – if you can get there. Due to the narrowness of the **Behm Canal** (the primary way in) and the numerous fjords, only small ships can enter. This inaccessibility means the place has retained a primordial feel, encased in dense spruce and hemlock forests, with cliffs rising up to 3,000 ft (900 meters) straight from the waterline and continuing down another 400 ft (120 meters) below your keel. Above the timber line, high ridges are covered with alpine grass, and in places along the shore petrified lava flows testify to the area's volcanic past. Add the almost constant mist and you almost expect to see dinosaurs tramping through. Not only are there no dinosaurs, you may not even see the more standard Alaskan wildlife, but that doesn't worry most people as it's the landscape that's the real draw here.

Places of particular beauty include **Punchbowl Cove**, with the highest cliffs in the monument, and secluded **Rudyerd Bay**. Small ships take on a pair of kayaking Forest Service rangers in this area to provide background history and interpretation. Passengers on large ships who want to visit Misty can do so on shore excursions from Ketchikan, either by seaplane (make sure it will land on one of the lakes, so you can appreciate the grandeur of the cliffs) or by a combined seaplane-float trip, flying to the monument and then boarding a small tour boat for exploration and the trip back.

Map on page 90–1

Wrangell and Petersburg

North of Ketchikan, Wrangell and Petersburg never wanted to be cruise ports, and for the most part they've got their wish. They are visited principally by small ships and otherwise maintain their quiet Alaskan character, with economies built on fishing, logging, and government work.

In **Wrangell ❺**, **Petroglyph Beach State Historic Park** has more than 40 images of unknown age carved into the rocks, some in geometric patterns and some representing animals like the killer whale. Probably the work of pre-Tlingit peoples, they represent the largest concentration of petroglyphs in Southeast. At the opposite end of town, tiny **Chief Shakes Island** (hours vary; tel: 907-874 2023) holds a collection of totem poles and a Tlingit clan house, both constructed by Native craftsmen as a Civilian Conservation Corps project in the 1930s.

In **Petersburg ❻**, settled by Norwegian immigrants around the turn of the 19th century, children still perform Norwegian folk dances for visitors at the **Sons of Norway Hall**. A quiet town, its principal attraction is that it doesn't really have any: this is no tourist trap. Rather, visitors wander along Nordic Drive,

BELOW:
Tsimshian women welcome a visitor.

following the walking trails detailed in the *Viking Visitor Guide,* stopping at local stores like the Hammer & Wikan hardware and general store (good for distinctive baseball caps), or marveling at the number of eagles at **Eagle's Roost Park**. No real marvel when you think about it, as the town's main cannery is next door.

Frederick Sound

The Little Norway Festival, is held every May in Petersburg.

North of Petersburg, **Frederick Sound** is known as one of the best whale-watching spots in Southeast because of the abundance of herring and krill that thrive in its waters. In a typical summer, the Sound will see at least 500 humpback whales. If you're very lucky, you'll see a group bubble-feeding, a process in which several whales circle a school of fish from below, blow out columns of bubbles that concentrate their prey, then surface with their huge mouths wide open. A humpback can take in up to 500 gallons (1,893 liters) of water in one of these maneuvers, straining out the fish through fringed mouth strips made of baleen, a keratin protein similar to human fingernails and hair. On an average summer day, a humpback will eat between 1 and 8 tons of food.

BELOW: sea lions are known for their cacophonous honking.

Other sea life seen in the area includes orcas (part of Southeast's year-round population), harbor seals, Dall's porpoises, and Steller sea lions. The latter can weigh up to 1,250 lbs (570 kg), and on land move like overweight businessmen in a sack race, bounding out of the sea on tiny, inadequate flippers and lolling around in huge groups called "haul outs." Sea lion haul-outs are common around the **Brothers Islands**, in the north of the sound. You'll hear their cacophonous honking as you get close, and that's your signal to grab the binoculars, since it's far more interesting if you can see their faces. Just hope you're downwind, as their fishy smell can be overpowering.

Map on page 90–1

Tracy Arm

A long, narrow, deep-water passage into the coastal mountains about 45 miles (72 km) south of Juneau, **Tracy Arm Fjord** affords cruise ships two of the best glacier-viewing opportunities in Southeast, at **South Sawyer** and **North Sawyer Glaciers**. On the passage in, you'll cruise between mile-high mountain walls jutting straight up from the water, with icy waterfalls snaking down their sides. One of these, known as **Hole-in-the-Wall Falls**, crashes straight down into water so deep that small ships can inch their bows right into the tumbling stream, soaking the crewmen who are usually sent out as guinea pigs. Spruce and hemlock grow up the sides of the less vertical slopes, providing protection for resident brown and black bear, mountain goats, Sitka black-tailed deer, and bald eagles.

As your ship gets closer to the head of the fjord, look at the amount of ice clogging the passage for an indication of recent calving activity at these two glacial walls, which are actually two forks of the same glacier, dead-ending in different valleys. South Sawyer is the wider and more spectacular, and either one may calve off a house-sized chunk of ice as you watch, forcing your captain to turn the ship's bow toward the point of impact and ride the wave it produces. The fjord is part of the **Tracy Arm-Fords Terror Wilderness**, a federally protected 1,021-sq mile (2,643-sq km) area that also includes **Endicott Arm** just to the south, with **Dawes Glacier** at its head.

Glaciers lose their ice mass through calving, which is when large pieces of ice break away from the glacier's terminus.

Sitka

One of Southeast's prettiest cities, **Sitka** ❼ is not visited as frequently as Juneau, Skagway, and Ketchikan because it lacks pier facilities for mega-ships. The fact that it lies on the opposite side of Baranof Island from the Inside Passage doesn't help either, as large ships are required to make a long, open-ocean detour. Small ships have an easier time, as they're able to navigate in through narrow Peril Strait and use the dock on Harbor Drive. The town retains a resolutely non-touristy feel, and since all attractions are within walking distance, you won't need to sign up for organized shore excursions. Just walk around and enjoy the town.

Originally called Novoarkhangelsk (New Archangel), Sitka was the capital of Russian Alaska from 1799 until the US purchase in 1867, and still retains a distinctly Russian feel. At its center is cross-shaped, onion-domed **St Michael's Cathedral**. The original cathedral was built between 1844 and 1848 as the first Russian Orthodox cathedral in the new world, but it burned down in 1966. Some 95 percent of its contents, including ornate icons and a 300-lb (136-kg) chandelier (lifted from its hook by one man standing on stacked benches), were saved by 100 volunteers forming a human chain. The current cathedral is an exact replica, built of fire-retardant materials.

Interestingly, more than 90 percent of the church's congregation is of Native heritage, the local Tlingits having been evangelized in the 19th century by the cathedral's designer, Bishop (now Saint) Innocent Veniaminov, a veritable Renaissance man who translated liturgical texts into Tlingit and Aleut by adapting the Russian Cyrillic alphabet.

BELOW: St Michael's Cathedral, Sitka.

Bishop Innocent's home, straightforwardly called the **Russian Bishop's House,** is about a ¼ mile (0.4 km) east of the cathedral on Lincoln Street. It's a fascinating place, showcasing the interesting life of the bishop. Today, the upper floor of his restored house contains several pieces of furniture made by his own hand, as well as his personal chapel. Downstairs is a museum, the highlight of which is a "Possession Plaque," one of some 20 buried along Alaska's coast around 1799 to formally mark the Russian claim. It was unearthed in Sitka in 1934–5, and is the only one yet discovered.

Farther down Lincoln Street, on the campus of Sheldon Jackson College, the **Sheldon Jackson Museum** was established in 1887 by its namesake, a Presbyterian missionary and the first US General Agent for Education in Alaska. Approximately 5,000 pieces of Native art, acquired by Jackson between 1888 and 1900, form the core of the museum's extensive collection, which includes Inuit masks, full-size kayaks, traditional clothing, argillite carvings from the Queen Charlotte Islands, and Tlingit, Inuit, Aleut, and Athabascan baskets. The museum's octagonal home was constructed in 1895.

Continuing up Lincoln, you'll come to **Sitka National Historic Park** (open daily), one of the most historically significant and beautiful pieces of real estate in town. In 1799, Alexander Baranof, manager of the fur-trading Russian-American Company, decided to move his base from Yakutat Bay (site of Hubbard Glacier) to Sitka, whose harbor is ice-free year-round. Since the current town site was occupied by the Tlingit tribe, who had built a fort on what is now known as Castle Hill, the Russians constructed their own fort at Redoubt St Michael, approximately 7 miles (11 km) to the north. Three years later, probably through the instigation of American fur traders, musket-armed Tlingits from

BELOW: Tongass National Forest and Mendenhall Glacier in the summer.

JUNEAU HIKING TRAILS

The most memorable thing about Juneau for many people is the rich variety of hiking trails that can be reached easily from the dockside and city center. Starting points are clearly marked and you can get information about routes and the degree of skill and stamina needed from the US Forest Service volunteers at 8465 Old Dairy Road (open Mon–Fri; tel: 907-586 8800).

Among the best-known trails are Mount Roberts, Perseverance, and Mount Juneau. Mount Roberts takes off from a trailhead at the north end of Sixth Street. It's a steep climb, but a good one, with alpine ground cover above the treeline, and splendid views. If you want to cheat, you can hop on the Mount Roberts Tramway *(see page 81)*, which takes you from South Franklin Street, near the dockside, up to the treeline, to commence your hike. The starting point for the more gentle and most popular trail, the Perseverance Mine Trail, is a few blocks further north, on Basin Road. On this route you can explore the ruins of some of the early mining sites, including the Silver Bowl Basin Mine and the Glory Hole. Or you can continue along Granite Creek Trail as far as the creek basin. Experienced and fit hikers can link up with the steep Mount Juneau Trail, which provides the best view to be had with two feet on the ground.

Maps:
Area 90–1
Town 80

several villages attacked and destroyed this fort, forcing the Russians to flee north. Baranof counter-attacked in September 1804, but the Tlingit were ready, and at the beginning of October waged a battle for the town from their new fort about a mile to the east. They won, but the Russians laid siege for six days, with the frigate *Neva* laying down a bombardment that finally forced the Tlingit to abandon the fort, ceding control of their town. The site of this conflict is now a peaceful beachside forest, with a wide, winding trail lined with totem poles leading to the fort site, now an empty meadow. Outside the visitors' center, which has a display of Native art and a studio for working artists, a recently carved totem tells the story of Tlingit history, while another marks the battle site, honoring Chief Katlian and the other Tlingit who fought there. Back in the center of town, off Lincoln Street and up a flight of steps, historic **Castle Hill** is just a hill these days, but offers the best view in the city.

For wildlife enthusiasts, Sitka's **Alaska Raptor Center** (open daily), on Sawmill Creek Road, not far from the Battle Site, is a hospital and recovery center for birds of prey, including American bald eagles. Each year, about 200 injured birds from around the country arrive here for treatment. Those that can no longer survive in the wild are kept on as raptors in residence. Visitors can tour the facility, learning about its programs and dropping in on bald and golden eagles, hawks, falcons, and owls, some of them in cages and some on open perches. Standing 4 ft (1.2 meters) from a bald eagle is a rare experience.

Juneau

At first sight, **Juneau** ❽, Alaska's capital city seems anything but grand. Only about a mile long and not half as wide, its central area can easily be walked in 15 minutes or so, and the governor's mansion is just another (albeit larger) home on Calhoun Avenue. It's when you step back and raise your eyes above the low buildings that you see Juneau has one of the most magnificent locations imaginable, sitting like a patch of moss on the edge of the Gastineau Channel, with massive Mount Juneau and Mount Roberts behind it, soaring over 3,500 ft (1,070 meters) toward the sky.

Juneau was founded in October 1880 by gold prospectors Joe Juneau and Richard Harris after they were led to the site by Tlingit chief Kowee, who traded his information for 100 Hudson's Bay blankets and a promise of work for his tribe. By Christmas, 30 miners and a small naval detachment had moved in, and by the following spring the town had 600 residents, a monthly steamboat service, and several stores and saloons. Large-scale mining followed, and in June 1900 Juneau supplanted Sitka as the seat of territorial government.

It is, of course, not a good place for a state capital. Risk of avalanches prevents the city growing any farther up the mountains (a fact attested to by the many bare avalanche paths on their forested slopes) and the 1,500-sq mile (3,900-sq km) Juneau Icefield, which lies beyond those mountain peaks and surrounds the town, means that construction of roads to the outside world is impossible. The only way in or out is by air or sea.

BELOW: a view of Juneau from Mount Roberts Tramway.

Downtown Juneau fairly bustles when the cruise ships dock.

Despite this, Juneau's small downtown area bustles, with four large ships in port on almost any summer day, its passengers filling the stores along Marine Way and Franklin Street. The city's 30,000 residents go about most of their business in the other 3,247 sq miles (8,410 sq km) officially encompassed within the city limits, much of it water and wilderness.

Several attractions are located downtown. On Whittier Street, off Egan Drive, the **Alaska State Museum** Ⓐ (open daily) is the official repository of the state's history, with galleries devoted to Alaska's Native peoples, natural history, and Russian and American involvement. It's a good place for putting everything in perspective. A children's gallery/playroom features a scale model of Captain George Vancouver's ship *Discovery* where kids can climb around. At the corner of Franklin and Marine Way, the **Red Dog Saloon** Ⓑ dates to Gold Rush days, though this isn't its original location. Always bustling, its floors are covered in sawdust and its walls and high ceiling are decked with memorabilia. The atmosphere is very touristy. Across the street, in the back of the Gold Rush-era Alaskan Hotel, the Victorian **Alaskan Bar** is quite a bit more authentic. Real ale lovers should head 3½ miles (6 km) north of town to the **Alaskan Brewing Company** for a tour of the brewery and a sampling of their award-winning beers.

If you're more keen on dogs than beer, stay in town and look for the bronze **Statue of Patsy Ann**, a beady-eyed bull terrier who was Juneau's "official greeter" in the 1930s and 1940s, always managing to sense when a ship was coming in before anyone else did. She's located right on the docks, at the berth closest to town, looking out toward the water. Behind her, on the top floor of the parking garage, Juneau's Public Library offers free internet access. You'll save money by checking your e-mail here, since ships charge by the minute.

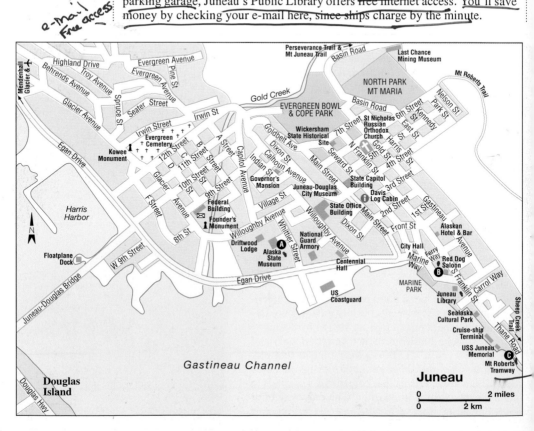

Midway down the docks, the **Mount Roberts Tramway**  whisks visitors to an interpretive center 1,800 ft (550 meters) above the city, with spectacular views of Juneau, Admiralty Island, the Chilkat Mountains, and the Glacier Bay area – as long as you're there on a clear day. On the way up, look to the right to see the ruins of the **Alaska-Juneau (AJ) Mine**, once one of the richest. At the top there's a worthwhile film on Tlingit culture, plus a gift shop and restaurant, but outside is where the real goodies are. The tramway's Tlingit owners have blazed a network of alpine trails ranging from an easy jaunt to a 6-mile (10-km) summit hike. It can be slippery going if it's wet, but don't miss this if you're surefooted, since the scenery is mind-bogglingly beautiful.

The **Mendenhall Glacier** is Juneau's other major attraction, located 13 miles (21 km) north of town, snaking another 12 miles (19 km) back into the mountains, and stretching 1½ miles (2 km) across the head of the Mendenhall Valley. Like all glaciers, it's constantly on the move, flowing downhill at a rate of 77 yds (70 meters) a year – in other words, it takes the ice about 250 years from its birth in the Juneau Icefield till it calves into the waters of Mendenhall Lake. For all that, though, the glacier is still receding: in 1750, it stretched 2 miles (3 km) farther down the valley. You can view the glacier from the visitors' center or take one of six trails (from ⅓ to 6¾ miles/0.5 to 11 km) designed to bring you closer to the glacier face.

You can get to Mendenhall by city bus from downtown (take the Lemon Creek/Mendenhall Valley blue line), but shore excursions simplify the matter, and usually include a visit to another Juneau activity – either a city tour; an outdoor all-you-can-eat salmon bake in a rustic setting; a visit to the **Macaulay Salmon Hatchery**, where you learn about salmon life and view spawning

Map on page 80

BELOW: a wolf and Mendenhall Glacier.

Modern-day gold prospectors pan for fun these days.

fish in season (June–Sept); a wildlife-viewing cruise by high-speed catamaran; or a float trip down the Mendenhall River. By far the best option, however, is one of the various helicopter trips that allow you to soar up over the mile-wide glacier and then land on its surface for a walk around. Impressive as they may be from ground- or ship-level, you won't grasp the true enormity of a glacier until you see it from above, stretching as far as the eye can see. Prices are high (typically US$200–300), but this is an experience you'll never forget.

Skagway

In 1887, Canadian government surveyor William Moore arrived in **Skagway 9** this spot, took a walk through the mountain pass that leads into the Yukon territory, and thought it would make a wonderful wagon road if gold were ever discovered. Thinking long-term, Moore and his son soon established a homestead in the valley, built a wharf and a sawmill, blazed the first trail through the pass, then sat and waited for their first customers to show up. The Tlingits thought they were insane to settle in a place where the winter winds are so ferocious they had earned it the name Skagua, "home of the north wind."

Gold Rush town

BELOW:
nostalgia and
youth in Skagway.

In 1896, prospectors discovered gold in a tributary of the Klondike River, and within a year the Klondike Gold Rush was on, turning Moore's homestead into a frontier boom town whose population soon exceeded 15,000. Lawlessness, prostitution, and drunkenness followed, and at its peak the town supported more than 70 saloons and was controlled by a gang of criminals led by the notorious Jefferson "Soapy" Smith.

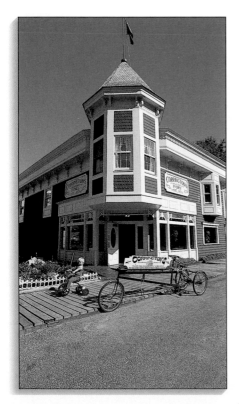

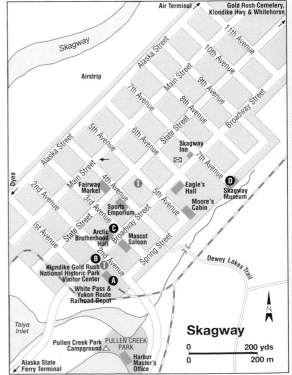

Skagway

Those were the good days. Soon a massive, two-year building project succeeded in putting a narrow-gauge railroad through the mountains from Skagway to Lake Bennett, in British Columbia. The town began to take shape, laid out in a straight line four and a half blocks wide, running straight up the valley from the water's edge. Then, as quickly as it started, the rush was over, the prospectors driven off by bad luck, bad weather, and just plain discouragement. Within a few years, the town's remaining residents had turned to tourism to make ends meet, and by the mid-1930s Skagway was in the throes of a full-fledged preservation movement, which we can thank for the pristine state of the town today.

Because Skagway really *does* look like a Gold Rush town, with original frame houses and stores lining the wide expanse of Broadway, almost all of them dating from the Gold Rush or the years immediately afterwards. But it's a bit of an illusion: many of these buildings were originally located elsewhere in town, and moved to this seven-block stretch in the early 20th century specifically to give tourists the full stampeder treatment. Today, nearly every one of them houses a gift shop, with 1890s-themed bars, theaters, museums, and even a Starbucks sprinkled throughout. Since the town's piers can accommodate four cruise ships, the town can become so busy it looks like Disney World.

Coming into town from the docks, one of the first things you'll see is the large **White Pass and Yukon Route Railroad ⓐ** depot, near which is parked one of the line's old rotary snow-plowing engines. The train ride through the White Pass and back is a very popular excursion, with antique engines and cars crossing impossibly high trestles and giving glimpses of stunning views, but be warned – if it's a foggy day, you won't see anything more than the occasional marmot scurrying away from the noise. The depot itself was built in 1898 and is well worth a visit even if you're not taking a ride.

The visitors' center for **Klondike Gold Rush National Historic Park ⓑ** (open daily) – which is downtown Skagway itself, a designated historic site since 1962 – is located here, and those wishing to get out of the shopping melee can pick up a free trail map with routes heading off both east and west of town. Hikes range from 1–10 miles (1.6–16 km) and are rated by difficulty, all but the easiest involving some moderately strenuous uphills. A free guide to the historic buildings is also available.

Streetcar Tours are available as excursions, but they're extremely theatrical and touristy. Go only if you don't want to walk. Otherwise, head up Broadway past the **Arctic Brotherhood Hall ⓒ**, established in 1899 and with a facade covered in driftwood.

From there, follow your town map from the visitors' center and check out the other historic buildings, including the **Golden North Hotel**, the **Moore Cabin**, built by William himself in the 1880s, and the **Mascot Saloon**, which is fitted out with mannequins in typical 1890s drinker poses.

At 6th Avenue, the Fraternal Order of Eagles Hall has hosted the *Days of '98* show since 1927, featuring can-can girls, a reading of Robert Service poetry, actors playing "Soapy" Smith, and the like. Ships generally sell an excursion that links the show with a motorcoach tour of town. On 7th Avenue, make a right-hand turn

Maps:
Area 90–1
Town 82

BELOW:
a horse-and-buggy
tour of Skagway.

A Chilkat dancer performs in Haines.

and walk one block to the old Town Hall, which now houses the **Skagway Museum ⓓ**, a very professional display featuring Gold Rush artifacts and other bits of town history. Continue walking 1½ miles (2 km) through town, up State Street, to visit the old **Gold Rush Cemetery**, the final resting place of "Soapy" Smith and of Frank Reid, the man who finally did him in, and died in the process.

Back at 2nd Avenue, stop for refreshment at the **Red Onion Saloon**, restored in 1898 style and featuring an interesting brothel museum upstairs. Costumed guides lead tours that are heavy on innuendo but also informative, giving a real taste of what life was like for the working girls of the north.

For an excursion out of town, you can rent bikes (or sign up for the ship's bike tour) and head west about 9 miles (14 km) to visit Skagway's former sister-town, **Dyea**, completely abandoned just after the Gold Rush. It's a hilly ride, but well worth it. Many ships also offer a White Pass mountain-bike excursion, going up by van and down by bike.

Haines

About 15 miles (24 km) southwest of Skagway, **Haines ❿** might as well be a thousand miles distant, so different is it from its bustling neighbor. Big ships pass right by on their way up the Lynn Canal, but the town's Port Chilkoot Dock is able to accommodate smaller vessels. This is real small-town Alaska, with about 2,500 resident humans but at least as many American bald eagles – one of the largest concentrations on earth.

The town's principal tourist feature is **Fort William H. Seward**, constructed in 1904 as Alaska's first military base. Don't expect anything remotely military-looking. Instead, the fort is a lovely group of white clapboard houses and barracks, all laid out around a parade ground one block from the dock. Decommissioned after World War II, the fort was purchased by a group of army veterans for use as a co-operative community. Today, the officers' quarters are private homes, while other buildings house a hotel, a bed-and-breakfast, the **Chilkat Center for the Arts** (a respected performance space), and **Alaska Indian Arts** (closed Sat–Sun; free), a non-profit enterprise that operates a workshop, apprentice program, and gallery-cum-store dedicated to perpetuating Native arts, including totem carving. Out on the parade ground sits a re-creation **Tlingit tribal house** where in summer the famous Chilkat Dancers host a storytelling theater.

Near the small-boat harbor, the **Sheldon Museum and Cultural Center** (open daily) presents displays about Tlingit culture and the history of white settlement in Haines. The collection is based around pieces originally acquired and displayed by Haines storekeepers Steve and Bess Sheldon, beginning in 1925.

In the same neighborhood, on Main Street, you'll find Dave and Carol Pahl's **Hammer Museum** (closed Sat–Sun) with displays of more than 1,200 fine hammers of all kinds, from long-handled models used to hang barn posters to ones used for paving cobblestoned streets. There's even a Tlingit stone hammer unearthed while the basement was being dug. Not to be missed by anyone who loves quirky museums.

Outside town, the 48,000-acre (19,400-hectare) **Chilkat Bald Eagle Preserve** (open daily) is one of the area's prime attractions, usually visited on an organized shore excursion, either by jet boat or inflatable raft. We recommend the latter, an entirely appropriate way to appreciate the quiet river and vast Chilkat Mountain vistas. A guide accompanies (and rows) each boat to acquaint you with the area's natural history and help spot moose, bear, and some of the preserve's 200–400 resident eagles. Ships that are too big to dock in Haines often offer excursions here from Skagway via high-speed ferry, including trips to the Eagle Preserve.

Glacier Bay

In 1879, as naturalist John Muir was sailing around Southeast, one of his Native guides told him about "a large bay full of ice" nearby. Days later, Muir became the first white man to record his impressions of what we now know as **Glacier Bay ⑪**.

Just 100 years earlier, he couldn't have done so. In 1794, Captain George Vancouver of the exploration ship HMS *Discovery* sailed into the mouth of the bay and described it as "a compact sheet of ice as far as the eye could distinguish." The farthest ships could penetrate before hitting ice was 5 miles (8 km). Today, the bay extends more than 60 miles (100 km). One of the most popular natural wonders in Alaska, Glacier Bay is a living museum where the Ice Age is a recent memory – so recent that some of the land is still rising an inch and a half every year, after being compacted for millennia by ice up to 4,000 ft (1,200 meters) thick. As the ice retreated, life began to move back in: young forests near the bay's mouth, where the land has been free longest, and newer, smaller vegetation the farther north you travel. Mountain goat and brown bear tread the peaks above, while beneath the waters swim minke, orca, and humpback whales. It was to protect these latter that in 1979 the Park Service began limiting the number of vessels permitted to enter the bay. Today, only two cruise ships can sail here per day, plus a restricted number of small cruisers, tour boats, and private boats. Each cruise ship takes aboard a park ranger who explains the park and its history.

Even without explanation, though, this is a stunning place. Snow-capped mountains rise on all sides to heights of 15,000 ft (4,570 meters), while the shores are pocked with coves, deep fjords, and 12 tidewater glaciers that calve ice into the cold water. At the north end of the bay's western arm, **Johns Hopkins Glacier** calves so much that it's rarely possible to approach closer than 2 miles (3 km), but cruise ships can usually approach to within a quarter mile (0.4 km) of nearby **Reid**, **Lamplugh**, **Margerie**, and **Grand Pacific glaciers**. Despite all the calving, some of these glaciers are actually making a net advance, regaining some of the ground they've lost over the past two centuries. In the bay's east arm, all the glaciers are in retreat.

Hubbard Glacier

A regular stop on cruises doing the Vancouver–Anchorage route, **Hubbard Glacier** is the longest tidewater glacier in Alaska, stretching some 76 miles (122 km) to the sea at Yakutat Bay. And that distance gets a little longer every day, since Hubbard has been

Map on page 90–1

The Glacier Bay National Park and Preserve not only has snow-capped mountains but also deep fjords, tidewater glaciers and freshwater lakes. Glacier Bay Visitor Center is open daily noon to 8.45pm from the end of May to early Sept.

BELOW: sailing through Glacier Bay National Park and Preserve.

Seals take a break from the ice cold water.

advancing rapidly for the past century. In 2003 alone, the glacier's exceptionally wide, 6-mile (10-km) face advanced some 450 ft (137 meters) in only four months. Scientists believe this movement will eventually block access to adjacent Russell Fjord and create the largest glacier-dammed lake in North America. It almost got there in 1986 and again in 2002, when the trapped waters rose to 200 ft (61 meters) above sea level before the glacier retreated once again.

Prince William Sound and College Fjord

Infamy came to **Prince William Sound** ⑫ on March 24, 1989, when the tanker *Exxon Valdez* ran aground on Bligh Reef, spilling 11 million gallons (41 million liters) of oil. The results were catastrophic, fouling some 1,300 miles (2,100 km) of coastline, destroying ecosystems and economies, and taking the lives of millions of marine fauna. Time and a multi-billion-dollar clean-up operation have undone much of the damage, and today Prince William Sound is once again a vastly appealing natural area, home to whales, sea lions, eagles, and Alaska's other iconic critters.

The sound is surrounded to the east, west, and north by the **Chugach Mountains**, out of whose heights came the glaciers that carved the coastal plateau, creating fjords, islands, and the sound's craggy shores. For all its beauty, though, Prince William is a sparsely populated place, with only 10,000 people spread among the isolated communities of Whittier, Valdez, Cordova, and the Native villages of Tatitlek and Chenega. At the extreme northeast of the sound, **College Fjord** is a collection of 16 glaciers, mostly named after the Ivy League schools that funded an expedition here in 1899. While not as spectacular as Glacier Bay or Hubbard Glacier, it's a tremendously scenic spot.

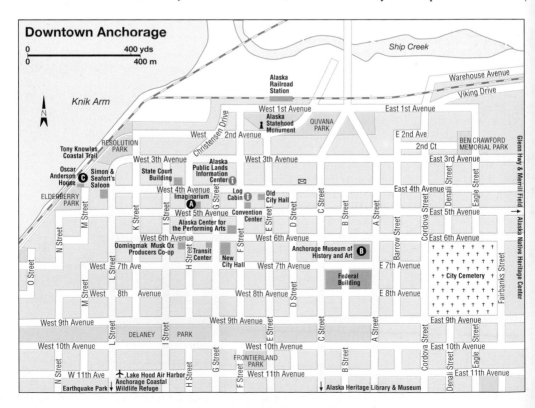

Downtown Anchorage

Anchorage, Seward and Whittier

On the northern side of the Kenai Peninsula, with the Chugach Mountains between it and the Gulf of Alaska, **Anchorage** ⓭ is Alaska's largest city, with some 40 percent of its population. It's the northern terminus for cruises sailing the Inside Passage-Gulf route from Vancouver, but because navigating around the peninsula would eat up a full day, ships actually dock in the small southern Kenai ports of Seward and Whittier, and ferry passengers to and from Anchorage by bus.

Though Captain Cook first charted this part of Southcentral Alaska in 1778, history didn't really begin here till 1915, when President Woodrow Wilson selected Ship Creek Landing as the construction headquarters for the Alaska Railroad. A typical tent city sprang up overnight, and Anchorage was formally incorporated five years later, in 1920. World War II prompted another boom, as troops arrived to counter the Japanese (who occupied the Aleutian islands of Kiska and Attu for more than a year), and Cold War tensions with nearby Russia brought a huge investment in infrastructure throughout the 1950s.

The city today, though still remarkably young, has survived a period of haphazard growth and begun accumulating the diverse businesses, restaurants, and cultural institutions of a modern metropolis. Surrounded by mountains and wilderness, it's spread out like a small Los Angeles, but does have a downtown core at **Ship Creek**, where the first development started. There, a scenic overlook lets on to views of the railroad headquarters, depot, and rail yards, as well as a bit of the city port.

Down D Street at the corner of 4th Avenue, the bright building with the conical corner roof is the **Wendler Building**, Anchorage's first grocery store. Look out front for the **statue of Balto**, the legendary sled dog who in 1925 led his team 53

Maps:
Area 90–1
Town 86

BELOW: the restored Old City Hall, Anchorage.

Maps:
Area 90–1
Town 86

*Native Alaskan art is
on display at the
Anchorage Museum.*

BELOW: the Iditarod
Trail Sled Dog Race.

miles (85 km) through a raging blizzard and –50°F (–46°C) temperatures to deliver diphtheria vaccine to Nome. The spot marks the traditional starting point of the annual **Iditarod Trail Sled Dog Race**, which commemorates the event.

Those with children may want to head down D to 5th Avenue for the **Imaginarium Science Discovery Center Ⓐ** (open daily), a hands-on exploratorium with various labs and touch tanks, a planetarium, exhibits, and demonstrations. Otherwise, go over to 7th Avenue, where the **Anchorage Museum of History and Art Ⓑ** (open daily) occupies the blocks between C and A streets. It's the state's largest, with almost 20,000 objects and artifacts and 350,000 photos illustrating state history.

Back at Ship Creek, you can pick up the **Tony Knowles Coastal Trail**, named for a recent state governor. The trail leads down the coast a little more than 10 miles (16 km) to Kincaid Park, offering scenic views over the waters of Knik Arm and the possibility of spotting wildlife – maybe even the occasional moose. At Elderberry Park, the small **Oscar Anderson House Ⓒ** (closed Sun) was the first wood-frame family home in Anchorage, and offers presentations on early city life. Several miles farther along, **Earthquake Park** commemorates and interprets the 1964 earthquake that devastated Anchorage, flattening whole neighborhoods in this part of town.

About 15 minutes northeast of downtown, the **Alaska Native Heritage Center** (open daily) should not be missed. The 26-acre (11-hectare) facility provides a fantastic introduction to the cultures and traditions of all Alaska's main Native groups, from the Tlingits, Haida, Tsimshian, and Eyak of Southeast to the Athabascans of the Interior, the Yup'ik and Cup'ik of Southcentral, the Aleut and Alutiiq of the Aleutians, and the Inupiaq and St Lawrence Island Yup'ik of the far north. As such, it's a valuable stop even if you've visited or are planning to visit Native sites throughout Southeast. The Welcome House holds displays of Native art, a workshop for Native craftsmen, and a theater where traditional music, dance, and storytelling are presented throughout the day. Outside, examples of five regional Native homes are arranged around Lake Tiulana, with Native guides available to explain them to visitors.

Most people don't linger in the port towns of Seward and Whittier, but anyone with an interest in ocean life could spend a couple hours at Seward's **Alaska SeaLife Center** (open daily), a research facility and education center-cum-aquarium built with settlement money from the *Exxon Valdez* oil spill. The highway between Seward and Anchorage also offers attractions. If your cruise visits Glacier Bay, Hubbard Glacier, and/or Tracy Arm you can safely skip smallish **Portage Glacier**, which has receded so far that you can't even see it from the visitors' center. Do stop, though, at **Girdwood**, a funky little town a little farther along. There, the **Mount Alyeska Tram** lifts visitors 2,300 ft (700 meters) above the valley floor to the alpine tundra, where you can walk around and take in stupendous views of the mountain scenery, including seven glaciers. From here, the route back to Anchorage skirts the inlet known as **Turnagain Arm**, a beautiful drive amid mountains and forest. ❑

Whale Watching

Alaska is prime whale-watching country, with 17 different species in residence, including humpbacks, orcas, and gray whales. Many Southeast cruises include an opportunity to get up close to these fascinating creatures, especially the humpbacks, as they feed on the herring and krill in Frederick Sound. The **humpbacks** are, in any case, the stars of the show, both for their visibility and their behavior. Measuring 40–50 ft (13–16 meters) in length, they are seasonal residents, feeding here from June through September and then heading south to winter around Hawaii or Mexico. They're easy to recognize by their huge, mottled tails, tell-tale hump, and enormous flukes, which can grow as long as 14 ft (5 meters).

You'll generally see humpbacks gliding through the water, then arching their backs and giving a wave of their flukes before making a deep sounding dive. If you're lucky, you will also see them *breaching*, jumping straight up out of the water and then crashing down on their sides – an amazing display, considering that humpbacks typically weigh between 25 and 35 tons. Scientists have so far been unable to explain why they do this, and many speculate that they're just having fun.

Orcas, otherwise known as killer whales, are year-round Alaska residents and one of the animals featured most prominently in Native mythology and art, along with the raven, eagle, and bear. They are known for their panda-like, black-and-white coloration, their very tall dorsal fins, and their speed, as well as their ferocity as hunters, but they are also very family-oriented, traveling in pods of up to 50 males, females, and calves, with the females in charge of the group.

Orcas can grow up to 32 ft (10 meters) in length and weigh as much as 10 tons. Since their hunts take them far afield, they can be seen almost anywhere in Southeast and up the coast into Prince William Sound, either swimming with their dorsal fins slicing through the surface or leaping like dolphins in graceful arcs above the water.

RIGHT: an Orca breaching. Whales can be seen from Southeast to Prince William Sound.

Gray whales are a bit less common, since they summer farther north, in the Chukchi and Bering seas, but if you're on a Gulf of Alaska cruise in early May or late September you may have a chance.

Like humpbacks, grays are baleen whales, consuming huge amounts of tiny schooling fish, but they can be easily distinguished from their cousins by their short flukes and lack of dorsal fins. Males can grow to about 39 ft (13 meters) long and weigh up to 34 tons. At their winter home around California and Mexico's Baja Peninsula they're known to be exceedingly friendly, often swimming right up to whale-watching boats and letting people pat their heads.

Other whales commonly seen in Alaskan waters include the **minke**, at 26 ft (8 meters), a smaller, more torpedo-shaped blackish-gray version of the humpback, with shorter fins and no hump. The minke is the smallest of the baleen whales and is believed to have a distinctive song. The **beluga**, a very small (16-ft/5-meter), pudgy, white whale with a rounded beak can also be found here. ❏

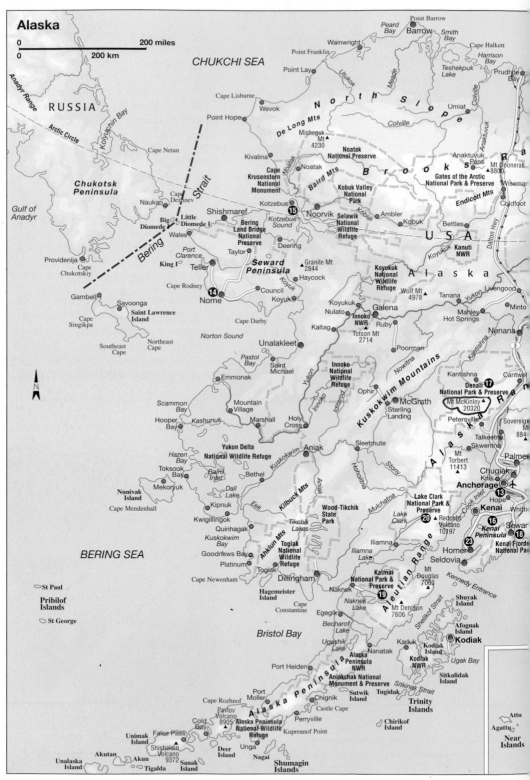

Alaska

0 — 200 miles
0 — 200 km

CHUKCHI SEA

RUSSIA

Anadyr Range

Arctic Circle

Gulf of Anadyr

Chukotsk Peninsula

Naukan
Cape Dezhnev
Cape Netan
Providenija
Cape Chukotskiy

Big Diomede
Little Diomede I
Wales

King I
Teller
Cape Rodney
14 Nome
Council
Koyuk
Cape Darby

Gambell
Savoonga
Saint Lawrence Island
Cape Singikpa
Southeast Cape
Northeast Cape

Peard Bay
Point Barrow
Barrow
Smith Bay
Cape Halkett
Harrison Bay
Prudhoe Bay

Wainwright
Point Franklin
Teshekpuk Lake

Point Lay
Meade
North Slope

Cape Lisburne
Wevok
De Long Mts
Utukok
Colville
Umiat
Colville

Point Hope
Misheguk Mt 4230
Noatak National Preserve
Anaktuvuk Pass
Anaktuvuk
Mt Doonerak 8800

Kivalina
Noatak
Baird Mts
B r o o k s   **R a**
Wiseman
Gates of the Arctic National Park & Preserve
Endicott Mts
Coldfoot

Cape Krusenstern National Monument
15
Kotzebue
Noorvik
Kobuk Valley National Park
Ambler
Kobuk
Bettles
U S A

Shishmaref
Kotzebue Sound
Selawik National Wildlife Refuge
Kobuk
Dalton Hwy

Bering Land Bridge National Preserve
Deering

Bering Strait

Port Clarence
Taylor
Seward Peninsula
Granite Mt 2844
Haycock

Koyukuk National Wildlife Refuge
Kanuti NWR
Koyukuk

Wolf Mt 4978
Tanana
Manley Hot Springs
Livengood
Minto
Nenana
3

A l a s k a

Koyukuk
Nulato
Innoko NWR
Ruby
Galena
Poorman
Kaltag
Totson Mt 2714
Yukon

Norton Sound
Unalakleet

Pastol Bay
Saint Michael
Emmonak

Scammon Bay
Mountain Village
Marshall
Holy Cross

Hooper Bay
Kashunuk
Innoko National Wildlife Refuge
Ophir
McGrath
Sterling Landing

Hazen Bay
Yukon Delta National Wildlife Refuge
Baird Inlet
Dall Lake
Aniak
Sleetmute

Toksook Bay
Bethel
Eek
Kilbuck Mts
Aniak
Kuskokwim Mountains

Mekoryuk
Nunivak Island
Cape Mendenhall
Kwigillingok
Kipnuk
Quinhagak
Ahklun Mts
Tikchik Lakes
Wood-Tikchik State Park
Hoholitna
Stony

Kuskokwim Bay
Goodnews Bay
Togiak National Wildlife Refuge
Platinum
Togiak
Dillingham

BERING SEA

Cape Newenham
Hagemeister Island
Cape Constantine
Naknek
Egegik

St Paul
Pribilof Islands
St George

Bristol Bay
Becharof Lake
Ugashik Lake
Nanatak
Port Heiden
Alaska Peninsula NWR
Aniakchak National Monument & Preserve

Cape Rozhnof
Port Moller
Chignik
Castle Cape
Perryville
Kupreanof Point
Alaska Peninsula National Wildlife Refuge
Pavlov Volcano 8905
Cold Bay
Unimak Island
False Pass
Shishaldin Volcano 9372
Deer Island
Unga
Nagai
Shumagin Islands
Akutan
Akun
Tigalda
Unalaska Island
Sanak Island

Denali National Park & Preserve **17**
Kantishna
Cantwell
Mt McKinley 20320
Petersville
Sovereign Mt 884
A l a s k a   R a n
Talkeetna
Skwentna
Palmer
Mt Torbert 11413
Chugiak
Knik
Anchorage
13
Hope
Kenai Whittier
Cook Inlet
Sterling
Lake Clark National Park & Preserve **20**
Redoubt Volcano 10197
Iliamna
16
Kenai Peninsula
18 Seward
Iliamna Lake
Homer
23
Seldovia
Kenai Fjords National Pa

Mt Douglas 7063
Katmai National Park & Preserve
19
Mt Denison 7606
Aleutian Range
Kennedy Entrance

Naknek Lake

Shuyak Island
Afognak Island
Karluk
Kodiak Island
Kodiak NWR
Kodiak
Ugak Bay
Sutwik Island
Tugidak
Sitkinak Strait
Sitkalidak Island
Shelikof Strait

Cape Newenham
Chirikof Island
Trinity Islands

Attu
Agattu
Near Islands

N

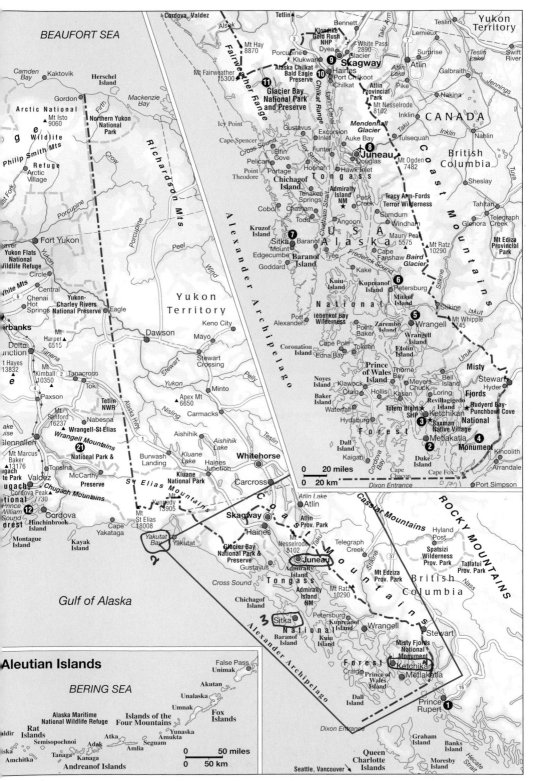

YOUR OWN PRIVATE ALASKA

A cruise is a good introduction to Alaska, but to see more of the wildlife and the rugged far north, you could opt for a cruise-tour, or a tailor-made tour which gives you more time on land

Map on page 90–1

Do you take a simple Alaska cruise, exploring the coastline solely by ship, or do you leave additional time for an inland tour as well? This is the fundamental choice facing Alaska-bound travelers. While a seven-day cruise provides an opportunity to see many of Alaska's spectacular natural attractions, it omits the more rugged landscape found farther north – including the unforgettable sight of Mount McKinley. At 20,320 ft (6,194 meters), it's the tallest peak in North America and visible from Anchorage – 125 miles (200 km) to the south on a clear day. You can see Alaska by land and sea in a combination package known as a cruise-tour. Most Alaska-bound cruise lines offer this option, which may include travel by bus, private railcar, or a specially designed day boat. Accommodations may be in luxury high-rise hotels or sometimes in wilderness lodges built specifically for cruise passengers.

Alternatively there is the option of traveling independently on your own tailor-made tour. Customizing your itinerary to suit yourself means that you are free to dawdle, to sightsee along the way, even to explore the historic port of Seward – where most cruises pick up or drop off their Alaska-bound passengers. A few ships use tiny Whittier as an alternative terminus. So, whether you take an organized tour or an independent pre- or post-cruise expedition to some of the key sights – the choice is yours.

LEFT: a hiker at Bridalveil Falls, Keystone Canyon. **BELOW:** kayaking near Kenai Fjords National Park.

The lay of the land

In order to understand how tour patterns are constructed, it's important to understand Alaskan geography. Alaska's two largest cities, Anchorage and Fairbanks, are linked by the Alaska Railroad and the George Parks Highway (via the Glenn Highway). In between lies Denali National Park, home to a number of wild things, including grizzlies, Dall sheep, and moose. Virtually every land tour includes this main corridor, which runs north–south through the center of the state.

Increasingly, cruise operators are offering multiple-night stays in the Denali area, so passengers can take advantage of the many outdoor activities in the region without straying too far from the main transportation network. These outings may include hiking, river rafting, flightseeing, and other soft-adventure activities, which may be included in the package or sold as excursions by the cruise lines.

Keep in mind, though, that Alaska is a big place – more than twice the size of Texas and six times the size of the UK – and sometimes it's more intriguing to venture beyond the well-traveled path to Denali. It's not an either/or situation, though. In order to see the more outlying parts of the state, you will have to add them on to the basic Anchorage-Denali-Fairbanks

corridor. This usually results in a longer and therefore more expensive trip. In some cases, it may be possible to add just a single component to your cruise. However, these options vary considerably and you'll have to check the individual cruise line brochures to see what's available.

Cruise-tours farther afield

Anyone interested in the history of North America will revel in the ghost town of **Kennecott**, once a thriving copper mill on the border of Wrangell-St Elias National Park, the largest national park in the United States *(see page 99)*. A little-known chapter of gold-rush history lives on in **Nome** ⑭, a Bering coast town of about 3,500 residents, where they still pan for nuggets on the beach. A visit to Nome is usually combined with a stopover in **Kotzebue** ⑮, an Inuit community 26 miles (42 km) above the Arctic Circle that is the headquarters for one of the regional Native corporations established in 1971. A true escape to the top of the world lies at the end of the Dalton Highway, which leads through Alaska's caribou country and on to the oil fields of Prudhoe Bay.

At the height of the summer season, travelers – and not just cruise passengers – converge on Anchorage, Denali, and Fairbanks, so the further you venture from the main tourism corridor, the farther you'll be from the crowds. An option for passengers passing through Seattle or Vancouver is to head inland to the Canadian Rockies, stopping in picturesque locations like Banff, Jasper, Calgary, and Kamloops. And passengers sailing from Seattle or Vancouver can choose a local tour, which may include hotel accommodations and sightseeing to attractions such as Seattle's Space Needle *(see page 69)* or Vancouver's Chinatown and the historic Gastown district *(see pages 70–71)*.

A river-rafting trip on Nenana River, Denali National Park.

BELOW: a variety of tour options at the waterfront.

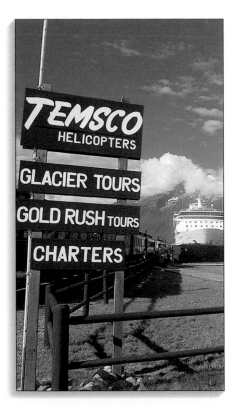

BOOKING A CRUISE-TOUR

Experienced travelers recommend taking the land segment of a trip before the cruise, because touring tends to be tiring – rising early to get the luggage ready and then boarding a bus or train or plane to the next destination. Cruising, on the other hand, is more leisurely, so it's nice to segue the land adventure with a relaxing week aboard ship. Cruises that follow this pattern – tour then cruise – typically travel in a southbound direction, while vacations that cruise then tour usually travel in a northbound direction, which may be more desirable for those with a historical mind-set, since this is the traditional route to Alaska taken by the early explorers and later the Gold Rush prospectors.

Booking a land tour with a cruise line offers a number of advantages. As the state's largest tour operators, the lines have buying power. Typically, they book huge blocks of the best hotel rooms during the peak summer months, leaving little available for the independent traveler. In some cases, they own the properties – as well as the buses and day-boats – so travelers are ensured a consistent level of quality and a seamless transition from ship to shore. Although it is possible to book the tour and cruise segments separately it is not recommended, since sailing schedules are co-ordinated with tour departures.

Map on page 90–1

Alaska and the Canadian Yukon

If you're interested in Alaska and the adjacent Canadian Yukon – two regions separated by politics but linked by a common history and rugged landscape – Holland America Westours is your best choice. Several of the company's 25 tours highlight a portion of the 1,500-mile (2,400-km) Alaska Highway (sometimes known as the "Al-Can"), built as a supply route during World War II, and/or **Kluane National Park** – the Canadian equivalent of Denali that is home to five of the seven tallest mountain peaks in North America.

The Alaska–Yukon route is paired with a three- or four-night cruise of the Inside Passage, sailing to or from Vancouver. These packages meet the ship in Skagway. As a result, they feature the towns of Canada's Yukon Territory during the land portion of the trip. The entire vacation may be done in as little as 10 days, and part may be spent traveling the Yukon River aboard the line's private day boat, the *Yukon Queen II*, which motors between Eagle, Alaska, and Dawson City in the Yukon Territory. These packages include travel on the Alaska Railroad as well as aboard private, glass-domed railcars that are hooked to the back of the train. For overnight accommodations, the company has its own chain of Westmark Hotels. Some, such as the properties in Skagway and Dawson City, have a colorful Gold Rush motif. Others, like those in Anchorage and Fairbanks, are mid- or high-rise hotels.

The Alaskan wilderness

For an extended stay in the Alaskan wilderness, you can try Princess Tours, which operate five riverside lodges and custom built hotels for cruise-tour guests. These properties include a hotel in Fairbanks and two lodges in the Denali area. One lies just a mile from the park entrance, the other has unobstructed views of Mount McKinley just 41 miles (66 km) away. Not far from the main tourism corridor lies the company's lodge on the **Kenai Peninsula ⑯**, an area south of Anchorage brimming with glaciers, moose, and some of the best sportfishing in Alaska. For something more remote, the company has more accommodations beside the Copper River just outside Wrangell-St Elias National Park, about 200 miles (320 km) northeast of Anchorage.

All provide a comfortable base for exploring the surrounding wilderness. Each lodge has a restaurant, which offers an opportunity to sample Alaskan cuisine, such as an elk burger or reindeer chili. Outdoor decks or patios provide a place for evening cocktails and watching the sun set. Like Westours *(above)* the company operates its own glass-domed, private railcars, which are hooked to the back of the public cars of the Alaska Railroad along the train's mainline route between Anchorage and Fairbanks via Denali. Travel on the railroad is typically part of the operator's wilderness lodge itineraries, which also include a seven-day Gulf of Alaska cruise.

Do-it-yourself Denali

Denali National Park and Preserve ⑰ permanently occupies the top slot in Alaska's greatest-hits line-up, and justifiably so – not only for the mountain itself but also for the wildlife living on and around it.

BELOW: an Alaska wilderness.

John Corbett as
"Chris" in Northern
Exposure, *a US TV*
series set in the
fictional town of
Cicely, said to be
based on Talkeetna.

BELOW:
a Native Alaskan
at a cabin near
the Chena River.

Arranging your own visit to Denali gives you the chance to spend a few nights deep inside the park, which increases the odds that you'll actually *see* the peak (often swathed in clouds) as well as the grizzlies and the Dall sheep.

The 126-mile (203-km) drive from Seward to Anchorage takes from three to four hours non-stop, and for the first 80 miles (128 km), there's little to stop for. Long stretches remain unblemished by so much as a pay phone. The views, however, are stunning: The highway swoops through the **Kenai Range**, and its astonishingly green mountains seem, at times, to lift the road into the air.

Just as the Seward Highway meets the **Turnagain Arm** (a tidal basin branching off Cook Inlet), you'll see at the 78-mile (125-km) marker a turnoff for the Portage Glacier Access Road; about 5 miles (8 km) down that road lies the Forest Service's Begich, Boggs Visitor's Center, whose displays go above and beyond the usual dioramas. Locals entertain with stories and you can sit in a life-size kayak and even see a dish of snow crawling with little black ice worms – algae-eating, glacier-dwelling cousins of the common earthworm.

Considering the city's population is 269,000, downtown Anchorage seems small: a handful of squat, glass-box office buildings and one indoor mall. To be fair, about 30 city blocks were destroyed in 1964's Good Friday earthquake – at 9.2 on the Richter scale, it's still the most powerful US quake recorded. The town does, however, have some sophisticated hotels and restaurants (for seafood, try Simon and Seafort's). In summer, the high season, lodging is expensive; a good option is downtown's relatively reasonably priced Voyager Hotel, which is also in a good location.

Continue north on the Glenn Highway 35 miles (56 km) to the Parks Highway. You'll follow that road (named not for Denali but for George Parks, one of Alaska's territorial governors) another 70 miles (113 km) toward Talkeetna. The scenery along the way isn't spectacular – spruces and more spruces – but if the weather co-operates, you may, starting at mile marker 78, glimpse snowy Denali in the distance.

In **Talkeetna**, you can get a better view of the mountain by taking an air-taxi tour circling Denali's peak. A handful of outfits offer a 90-minute tour for around $200 per person. Try it only if the weather is clear; if not, you could stop in Talkeetna anyway for lunch. First settled in the 1890s by gold prospectors, the village – a collection of old and new wooden buildings scattered among the trees – is now a staging area for climbing parties. It's also rumored to have been the inspiration for the town of Cicely on television's *Northern Exposure*.

From Talkeetna it is 130 miles (210 km) to the park entrance, around which several hotels cluster, such as the Denali Crow's Nest Hotel. Most visitors experience the park on a six- to eight-hour guided wildlife drive on the park's one road. On the tour you'll see the same grizzly bears, elk, and Dall sheep on your way in and out, but you don't have to do the whole trip in a single day. Instead, you can overnight at Kantishna Roadhouse, a former mining camp located in the very heart of the park. The cost of the tour includes accommodations, transport, all meals, and guided hiking and mountain-biking forays into the wilderness.

Map on page 90–1

Fully escorted tours

For a fully-escorted tour, Royal Celebrity Tours has the greatest number of options: all the company's cruise-tours include a tour director, who travels with your group during the land segment. Although Royal Celebrity is limited in terms of its destinations, concentrating mostly on the main Anchorage-Denali-Fairbanks corridor, the company also takes travelers off the beaten path to secluded towns like Homer *(see page 102)*, a picturesque fishing village on the Kenai Peninsula south of Anchorage. Extended time may be provided in **Seward ⑱**, which serves as the transfer point for seven-day Gulf of Alaska cruises linked to all the company's cruise-tour packages.

Seward sits at the northern tip of ice-free **Resurrection Bay**, and thanks to the Alaska Railroad, it's the most convenient deep-water port for Anchorage. These days, most people come to Seward to leave it – either on a cruise or venturing into the surrounding Kenai Fjords National Park. However, the town has an early-1900s shopping district that makes for a pleasant hour of wandering around and regaining your land legs. On the waterfront, and worth a visit, is the multi-million-dollar **Alaska SeaLife Center** (open daily) – much of it paid for by Exxon – where you can watch seals gambol and sea lions roar (the hands-on "discovery pool" is great for children).

Small-ship cruise-tour options

Cruise West, the largest of Alaska's small-ship operators, has a wide variety of land programs. In keeping with the small-ship experience, which emphasizes an up-close and more personal view of nature, the land accommodations provided by Cruise West tend to be more remote and rustic, albeit with all the comforts

BELOW: binoculars are an essential tool while touring Kenai Fjords National Park.

passengers have come to expect. In Denali, for example, groups are limited to just six to 12 people at Camp Denali and the North Face Lodge. Another lodge, Kantishna Roadhouse, began as a gold-miners' tent camp and is set nearly 100 miles (160 km) inside the park at the end of the only road.

Crossed oars at Sitka, Alaska.

Fishing in the backcountry

Say the word "Alaska" to some people, and a dreamy, far-off look comes into their eyes as they picture a remote fishing lodge, rustic but comfortable, without a cell-phone tower or a convenience store in sight. If you're one of those people, and believe that going to Alaska by ship means you've abandoned any hope of living that backwoods fantasy, take heart. It's true that many lodges require week-long stays that rival in cost the most luxurious of cruises. It's also true that none of the major cruise lines offers any multi-day, add-on fishing trips. But setting up your own two- or three-night stay at a fly-in lodge can be a snap.

All of the cruises that wind up at Seward or Whittier provide bus and/or train transfers to Anchorage (about $65 per person), where most fly-in lodges arrange to pick up their guests. One of the oldest of these outfits, Brooks Lodge – founded in 1950, before Alaska even became a state – is also one of the most popular, despite its remote location in **Katmai National Park ⓳**, about 290 roadless miles (467 km) down the Alaska Peninsula from Anchorage. (In the elephant's head that is Alaska, Katmai forms the base of the trunk.)

BELOW: fly-fishing on the Kenai Peninsula.

In recent years, Brooks Lodge has become even better known for grizzly-watching than for the still-excellent sockeye-salmon runs – studies show that more than 2,000 bears roam Katmai and the adjacent preserve. Throw in tours of the park's famous Valley of 10,000 Smokes – the once-steaming ruins of a

massive 1912 volcanic eruption – and you've got the ingredients of a stellar get-away for everyone in the family, anglers and non-anglers alike. A two-night Land of Katmai package, which covers lodging, airfare from Anchorage and back, and the Valley tour, costs around $1,100 per person (2004 rates). This doesn't include meals or a fishing guide, for which you should budget an additional $135 per half day. This may seem expensive, but it's low-priced as far as fly-in lodges go.

If everybody in your party will be putting on waders, however, a three-night fishing package to **Lake Clark National Park** ⑳, a wilderness-locked preserve on the Alaska Peninsula, 160 miles (257 km) from the city lights, is a wiser choice. The $2,735 per-person price (2004 rates) includes everything: lodging in a cabin for two at Lake Clark Inn, all-inclusive, the air transfer between Anchorage and Lake Clark National Park and two full days of "fly-out" fishing. A pilot/guide will take you out in search of the perfect fishing hole, even if it means landing in two or three different places to discover what's biting. The inn itself sits on the edge of 50-mile (80-km) glacier-carved Lake Clark, which is full of Arctic char, rainbow trout, grayling, and Pacific salmon. The innkeepers will freeze and pack your catch for you before you head back to Anchorage.

Ghosts in Copper Country

Wrangell-St Elias ㉑ is Alaska's – and the country's – largest National Park. Within its borders lie nine of the country's 16 tallest peaks, and its glaciers are big enough to cover entire states. But the park isn't just for outdoors types – history enthusiasts can tour the ghostly remains of Kennecott, an abandoned mining town that is tended by the Park Service. Princess is the sole cruise line

Map on page 90–1

BELOW: brown bears don't need a rod for fishing.

offering add-on trips to Wrangell-St Elias National Park, flying guests into the park, to spend their nights in a Princess lodge. If you want to organize your own excursion to the national park after disembarking at Seward or Whittier, hop on your cruise line's bus or train for the five-hour trip to Anchorage and once there, drive east of Anchorage on the Glenn Highway. Beyond Palmer, the highway begins to retrace the Matanuska River's descent between the stony, snow-capped **Chugach Mountains** to the south and the equally stony, snowcapped **Talkeetna Mountains** to the north. After you pass King and Pinnacle mountains, about 100 miles (160 km) from Anchorage, signs for Glacier Park Resort will start appearing. This is a privately owned attraction that, for a small fee, provides you with the opportunity to walk on 18,000-year-old **Matanuska Glacier**. Anyone who's visited Kenai Fjords National Park's Exit Glacier – where the rangers sternly chase off daredevils trying to scramble on the ice – may wonder if it's wise to do so here. Be careful; the glacier's edges are often covered with earth, so you can be well out on the ice before realizing what you're walking on.

Flights to Wrangell-St Elias National Park leave from Glennallen, 187 miles (300 km) and about five hours' drive from Anchorage. McCarthy Air can fly you into the park. Theoretically, you could drive there, but the road turns into rutted, rocky gravel so rough that car rental companies make it off limits.

Back in 1900, copper was discovered in the Wrangells by two prospectors who were lucky enough to hit what soon became the single richest strike in America. **Kennecott** was the company town; the ore mills, the administrative offices, housing for the 500 workers – even a skating rink – were all here. But the place emptied out after the mine closed for good in 1938. Apart from a hotel, built nearly 20 years ago to mimic the original mine structures, Kennecott has become a ghost town.

BELOW: panning for gold at the El Dorado Gold Mine near Fairbanks.

In the good old days, all Kennecott lacked was a red-light district, but that was okay – an entire red-light town waited 4 miles (6 km) back down the road to civilization. **McCarthy** was where the bars and the brothels set up shop, and even now the area's few full-time residents prefer to live there. Follow the locals' lead and base yourself in McCarthy, not Kennecott. Ma Johnson's Hotel is truly historic, not a mere simulacrum. Visitors can take guided tours of the original Kennecott buildings, hike or mountain-bike up to the Bonanza or Jumbo mineheads, or raft down the Kennicott River (yes, it *is* spelled differently). You can even take ice-climbing lessons.

Over the line

Remember those mysterious markings on your classroom globe – the Tropic of Capricorn, the Equator, the Tropic of Cancer? In real life, of course, there's no dotted line on the tundra to indicate the Arctic Circle. Just the same, crossing it will transport you into a whole new world. Where else can you watch polar bears prowl the permafrost, hitch a ride on a mail plane as it hops between Native villages, or just enjoy the midnight sun? One thing you probably won't do – in summer, at least – is see the Northern Lights. For them, you'll have to wait for winter's long nights.

From Seward or Whittier use your cruise-line

transfer to Anchorage, where you can catch the Alaska Railroad's *Denali Star*, bound for Fairbanks. Operated by the state, this train is notably less expensive than its cruise-line competitors; the fare from Anchorage to Fairbanks in high season is $175 (2004 prices), compared to the $225 you'd pay to ride Princess's train. And the *Star* also has tour guides, two rolling cafés, and duplex dome cars, so you won't miss a thing if the reticent Denali decides to make an appearance through the clouds. It's an all-day journey, after stopping briefly at the park, crossing endless birch forests, and threading through Nenana, the riverside town that hosts the annual "Ice Classic," in which people from all over the state bet on when the ice will break up.

Map on page 90–1

Fairbanks ㉒ itself is a small but sprawling city whose downtown holds little of interest to visitors, but it does make a great home base for ventures to all points north. You could take a five-hour flightseeing tour out over the Arctic Circle, 150 miles (240 km) away, with Northern Alaska Tour Company, or for the same price (around $250), the plane will land at Prospect Creek, on the Dalton Highway 20 miles (32 km) north of the Circle, where a van will meet you and drive you back across the line, stopping for dinner on the banks of the Yukon River.

More adventurous trips include mail-plane junkets, in which visitors ride along with postal pilots making their appointed rounds to 28 remote villages in Alaska's backcountry. A three-stop jaunt can last from two to four hours, and there are longer visits to Native villages. One joint operation – between Fairbanks-based Warbelow's Air Venture and Alaska Yukon Tours – takes you north of the Circle to a log-cabin, Athabascan village called **Fort Yukon**, which was founded as a Hudson's Bay Company trading post in 1847, and is now home to about 600 people. And, instead of trekking all the way back down to Anchorage

BELOW: the northern lights above Fairbanks.

Map on page 90–1

at the end of your trip, you can probably get a flight straight home from Fairbanks International Airport.

There are plenty of chain hotels in Fairbanks, usually filled with tour groups paying top rates in the summer months. If you are using the town as a base you could avoid these and settle into the suburban Seven Gables Inn, near the Chena River, between the university and the airport.

Motor Homer

Motor Homers... an RV is good way to enjoy sights off the beaten path.

BELOW: a view of the Alaska Range.
RIGHT: ice climbers in the Alaska Range.

If you want to immerse yourself in all the eccentricity, neighborliness, and dramatic scenery that adds up to Alaska, you could rent an RV. Although major tourist hubs like Denali are well supplied with places to stay, elsewhere in the state, good lodgings can be hard to find. Take, for example, the fishing village of **Homer** ㉓, which isn't (yet) on the mega-ships' itineraries. Located on the tip of the Kenai Peninsula, Homer has a handful of motels and B&Bs, but the real social scene is out on the Spit, the 4-mile (7-km) gravel jetty that serves as a combination fishing and cargo port and general recreation area, complete with campsites.

Although there are no RV rental agencies in Seward itself, Anchorage-based Alaska Dream RV Rental will arrange to meet arriving cruise-ship passengers with a fully-equipped motorhome. After the obligatory orientation, you're set loose to head north on the Seward Highway. Go as far as the Sterling Highway turnoff, at milepost 90, then west on the Sterling Highway, along the spine of the Kenai Peninsula. As you reach the town of Cooper Landing, look to the left to see the green waters of **Kenai Lake** – the luminous hue is caused by sunlight reflecting off finely-ground glacier silt. After Soldotna, continue south along scenic **Cook Inlet**. Those white-topped volcanic peaks across the inlet, seeming to keep pace with you, are mounts Redoubt, Iliamna, and Spurr, all in or near Lake Clark National Park.

The drive from Seward takes about five hours, so you should reach Homer by nightfall. Two or three days in Homer will be enough time to try your hand at deep-sea halibut fishing, to take a natural-history motorboat tour around **Kachemak Bay**, or to explore the town's art galleries. Although Homer was founded in 1896 by the usual gold-seeking drifters, enough counter-culture dropouts washed up there over the generations to earn it a reputation as a Bohemian enclave. Think of it as the Taos of Alaska.

On the way back to Anchorage you can overnight at the Williwaw Forest Service campground, off the Portage Glacier exit; there's nowhere to stay but the campground. Continue past the Begich, Boggs Visitor's Center to the Anton Anderson Memorial Tunnel (toll charged), which punches through **Maynard Mountain** to **Whittier**, a former Army base set on the shore of beautiful, if not quite pristine, **Prince William Sound**. Ever since the tunnel was opened to passenger vehicles in 2000, adventure outfitters have been sprouting here, taking advantage of Whittier's relative closeness to Anchorage – getting to Valdez, the other outdoor-sports hub on the Sound, takes at least twice as long. A three-hour kayaking trip with Alaska Sea Kayakers including equipment and instruction, can cost less than $100 per person.   ❑

NEW ENGLAND AND EASTERN CANADA: YESTERDAY AND TODAY

The history of this region is one of rivalry and exploitation, but the importance of the ocean has been a constant factor throughout the centuries

The beauty of the New England and the eastern Canada coast, all rocky inlets and carved-out bays, rivers and straits, is largely the result of a powerful glacier that retreated some 10,000 years ago from as far south as Long Island, New York, the terminal moraine of the icy mass.

Today, the landscape, roughly between New York and Montréal, makes for a gorgeous place to cruise. From the shores of New England to the Bay of Fundy, St Lawrence Seaway and Saguenay River, the scenery is spectacular, especially if you travel on a ship that is small enough to hug the coastline.

Along the way, whale sightings are not uncommon on New England and eastern Canada itineraries, especially around Cape Cod Bay, Massachusetts, one of the world's prime whale-watching spots.

The bounty of the sea

As long as there have been humans living in the region, there's been a connection to the sea. Cod, swordfish, lobsters, whales, and many other ocean creatures helped sustain Native American tribes for thousands of years, from the Wabanaki tribe of coastal Maine to the Pequot and Wampanoag in Massachusetts and Connecticut, and the Mi'kmaqs of Prince Edward Island, Nova Scotia, and New Brunswick in Canada.

These Native American groups had lived in the region since the last Ice Age, and when the white man finally arrived, it was the indigenous peoples who taught them such things as how to grow corn by using fish as fertilizer – no small tip considering that the hilly terrain and rocky soil of the coastal areas was far from ideal for farming.

PRECEDING PAGES: Schoodic Peninsula, Maine.
LEFT: USS *Constitution* (Old Ironsides) and Bunker Hill National Monument from the waterside.
RIGHT: on parade in Canada.

The white man arrives

But the co-operation between the newcomers and the native population wouldn't last for long. The year 1492, when Columbus and his cohorts sailed across the ocean blue, was the

beginning of the end for the Native Americans. Bent on finding a shorter western sea route to Asia (shorter, for example, than the four years it took Marco Polo to travel overland from Italy to China in the 13th century), England, France, and Spain wound up making landfall on the eastern coast of North America, "the New World," by mistake.

It hardly mattered that none of them were actually successful in ever making it to Asia. Their poor sense of direction turned out to be extremely fruitful; for the Europeans that is. Following in the footsteps of Columbus, between the late 15th and early 17th centuries explorers such as John Cabot, Giovanni da

Verrazano, Jacques Cartier, Henry Hudson, and Samuel de Champlain all mounted expeditions to the New World, where they discovered great riches. Treasures included animals that could be killed for their furs, abundant forests, fast-flowing rivers, huge hauls of fish, valuable minerals, and, above all else, plenty of land they could simply grab from the Native peoples.

The Europeans mined the minerals, traded furs, and cut down the forests, so they could use the lumber to build ships, waterproofing them with tar obtained from pine trees. They prospered at the expense of the Native Americans, most of whom would be dead by the

They called their new colony Acadia. At the same time, English settlers were arriving, too. The Pilgrim Fathers, Puritans who were fleeing religious persecution back home, came in 1620 to what they called "New England." They settled farther south than the French in what is now Massachusetts, at a place they named Plymouth, after their port of departure. This formed the second permanent European settlement in North America, after Jamestown, Virginia, founded in 1607.

Soon after, Britain sent Scottish settlers to present-day Nova Scotia, which is Latin for New Scotland. By the 18th century, British

1700s, either killed outright or by diseases brought over by the European settlers.

The French and the English

Between the mid-1600s and mid-1700s, both England and France fought for dominance in North America and sent for people to come and build communities. The battling culminated in the French and Indian War of 1754–63, which had the French and Native peoples fighting on one side against the English colonists on the other.

In the early 1600s, France began sending settlers to the present-day provinces of Québec, Nova Scotia, and New Brunswick to trade furs.

strongholds included major cities like Philadelphia, Boston, New York, and Halifax.

While the French got along with the Native population for the most part and had no great interest in displacing them, the settlers from England and Scotland had other aspirations. They were intent on appropriating land, cutting down the forests, using the lumber for shipbuilding, and putting up fences, whether the Native Americans liked it or not. Since the rocky coastal soil wasn't great for farming, many of the English and Scots diversified, becoming fishermen and whalers, using whale oil for fuel and exporting dried cod to Europe and the West Indies.

British domination

In the end, it was the British who gained the upper hand. In 1713 the Treaty of Utrecht, at the end of the War of the Spanish Succession, ceded Nova Scotia and New Brunswick to them. By 1755, the British were expelling the rebellious Acadians from both provinces. Now displaced, many went to Louisiana, another French colony, where they became known as Cajuns, believed to originate from a mispronunciation of the word Acadians.

In 1763, the Treaty of Paris (at the end of the Seven Years' War in Europe), formally ended the French and Indian War as well, giving the

(the American War of Independence), England was forced to give up control of the 13 American colonies and formally recognize their independence. By 1783, thousands of Loyalists – Americans loyal to Britain – fled north to New Brunswick, many settling in Saint John.

Some eight decades later, on July 1, 1867, Britain finally gave home rule to Canada, via the British North America Act. What were known in England as the North American Colonies – Québec, Ontario, Nova Scotia, and New Brunswick – joined together to become the Dominion of Canada, which other provinces eventually joined to form the present-day country. The new

English control of all of Canada, including Québec, and the land east of the Mississippi River. Québec's French-speaking citizens still harbor resentment over the dominance of the English, as can be seen in the repeated attempts over the years by Québec's French-speaking citizens to secede from Canada.

Independence

Some 20 years later, England suffered a serious setback. Under the Treaty of Versailles, signed in 1783, at the end of the bitter Revolutionary War

LEFT: whalers pursued their quarry for months.
ABOVE: Cambridge colleges in 1743.

dominion had a governor-general, appointed by the British Crown, and its own parliament. The date, now called Canada Day, is celebrated nationwide with fireworks and parades.

The legacy of the settlers

Nowadays, many immigrant groups are represented in the region, including the Irish, large numbers of whom emigrated in the mid-1800s and settled in and around Boston, to escape starvation when a failure of the potato crop led to devastating famine in Ireland. The Irish also formed settlements in Eastern Canada, particularly in Newfoundland. However, the legacy left by the British is definitely considered to be the most influential. Along with their language, there remains a democratic form of government, the Protestant religion, and a love of learning. Both Harvard and Yale universities, among the most prestigious in the country, were founded by Puritans in New England more than 300 years ago.

Much less of the French legacy remains, but you'll see it in Québec, New Brunswick, Prince Edward Island, Nova Scotia, and parts of Ontario, where French is still spoken, elements of the home country's cuisine have been retained, and Roman Catholicism, which the French largely introduced to Canada, remains the dominant religion.

an important form of transport up until the 1930s. For decades there were popular overnight steamer services, including the New Bedford Line and the Fall River Line, between New York City and towns in Connecticut, Rhode Island, and Massachusetts. After the work day ended, Wall-Street employees and businessmen, among others, would board the giant steam boats along with 1,000 to 1,500 fellow passengers, and cruise home to towns like New Haven, Hartford, Stonnington, New London, Newport, Fall River, New Bedford, and Boston.

Today, passenger ferries are still in service between the north shore of Long Island and

An affinity with the ocean

What has continued through the centuries, more strongly than language, religion, or culture, is a connection to the sea. Places like Nantucket, Fall River, and New Bedford, Massachusetts, were huge whaling hubs in the 17th and 18th centuries, while to this day, Maine and New Brunswick remain important centers for lobster fishing.

Throughout the centuries, the sea has not only been an important food source for New Englanders and eastern Canadians, but has served as a mode of transportation, too. Although there have been railroad lines along parts of the New England coast since the middle of the 19th century, travel by sea was also

Connecticut, and also from the mainland of Massachusetts, Rhode Island, and Connecticut to off-shore islands like Martha's Vineyard, Nantucket, and Block Island. Further north, Prince Edward Island and Cape Breton Island are connected to the mainland, the former by the 8-mile (13-km) Confederation Bridge, opened in 1997, the latter by a causeway. For speed and convenience, most local people drive there these days, but some, when they have time to do so, still like to travel the old-fashioned way – by sea. ❏

ABOVE: the steamboat *Quaker City* on the East River, New York, in the 1890s.

Fish, Whales, and Wealth

New England's waters once teemed with fish, and any man who could scrape together the cash to buy a small boat had his start in the fishing industry. Profits from hard work in small boats led to bigger boats, able to sail farther offshore – as far as the Georges Banks east of Cape Cod and the Grand Banks southeast of Newfoundland, where money swam in the shape of codfish. A bank, by the way, is an area of seabed substantially shallower than the surrounding waters, and often more fertile; larger fish gather on banks to eat smaller ones.

If you've read *Captains Courageous*, by Rudyard Kipling, or seen the classic 1937 film of the same name starring Spencer Tracy, you know about banks fishing in its heyday: tough crews sailing graceful schooners far offshore, returning to port only when the holds were filled with cod. A few of the old schooners, or modern replicas, are still sailing today, taking passengers on trips into the late 19th century.

But it wasn't codfish that built the great mansions in Sag Harbor, Nantucket and New Bedford – it was whales. From the time of the Pilgrims until the 1950s, whales weren't seen as the gentle leviathans we love to watch today: They were a swimming tank of valuable oil, bone and ambergris. In early colonial days, whales often cruised near enough to shore to be hunted from boats launched off the beach. If the whalers were successful, they towed the carcass back to shore and "tried out" the oil in cannibal-sized iron pots on the sand. "Trying out" involved boiling blubber to reduce it to fat, which was skimmed off, and oil.

Whale oil was used both as a lubricant and as fuel; whalebone found its way into buggy whips and ladies' corsets; ambergris, a waxy substance sometimes found in the intestinal tracts only of sperm whales, was used in perfumes, and thought to be an aphrodisiac. Pound for pound, it was the most valuable product of the whale, and one reason sperm whales are rare today.

As longshore whales became scarce, men built specialized ships to hunt the large creatures at

sea, first in the North Atlantic, then off the Brazilian coast, and finally across the vast Pacific. As one area was "whaled-out," ships sailed farther, looking for new, fertile grounds. At the height of the whale-fishing boom, the 1850s, Yankee whaleships cruised every corner of the world, including the Arctic Ocean. When a ship returned from its voyage, which lasted three or, sometimes, four years, the valuable oil was sold, the crew paid off, and the captain and owner raked in the profits. It could take only a few successful cruises to turn a whaling captain into a stay-ashore shipowner; a few more could set him up for life.

If you stroll down the main street of any old

whaling port in New England, you can still see many of the shipowners' mansions and marvel at the riches created by this uncontrolled industry. There are also fascinating whaling museums in Sag Harbor, on eastern Long Island, NY, in New Bedford, and on Nantucket Island, Massachusetts. The last surviving whale ship, the *Charles W. Morgan*, is located at Mystic Seaport in Connecticut. It's worth reading Herman Melville's 1851 masterpiece *Moby Dick* before you go, to get an inkling of what it was like. On the other hand, if you prefer live whales to dead ones, whale-watching cruises from Boston will take you to the Stellwagen Bank, where nowadays whales frolic, unhassled by harpoons. ❑

RIGHT: an artist's impression of Herman Melville's Moby Dick.

THE SIZE FACTOR: BIG SHIPS VERSUS SMALL

Where ships are concerned, size does matter, because it dictates the kind of cruising experience that can be offered

Your cruise experience will depend greatly on whether you choose a big ship carrying thousands of passengers or a smaller one carrying just a few hundred. The vibe on each category is worlds apart, and so is the price tag.

Small ships will typically cost you two or three times as much as bigger ones, which are as glitzy as Las Vegas and attract a broad swathe of people looking for a bargain as much as for an exciting vacation and a couple of interesting ports. On a small vessel, the mood is mellower and focused on the history and natural features of the areas visited en route.

Big and busy

As any veteran cruiser knows, big ships are bursting at the bulkheads with things to do, places to eat, and spaces to shop, shop, shop. The largest ones have 12 to 15 decks of restaurants, bars, lounges, boutiques, and cabins of all shapes and sizes, many with private balconies. You'll find swimming pools, a casino, a sprawling spa, gym, children's playroom and video arcade, Internet centers, and four or five restaurants, from casual to semi-formal.

Like the ships themselves, everything is large, including the size of tour groups in port, lines to get on and off the ship, and the queue at the pizza counter. By the time you're finished with a round of bingo, a wine tasting, and a spinning class, there's scant time to get out on deck to see where the ship's sailing. Then again, there's not much to see, as big ships can't hug the coastline like their smaller sisters.

Royal Caribbean's 142,000-ton, 3,114-passenger *Voyager of the Seas*, which made her debut run to New England and Canada in 2004, has a rock-climbing wall built right on to the funnel, plus an indoor ice skating rink, miniature golf course, in-line skating track, basketball court and at least a dozen dining and entertainment venues.

While you won't get bored on a ship like this, you might be distracted from what's outside it. And that's just perfect if you're not nuts about history, geography, or nature. A big ship is also a good idea for anyone with a propensity for seasickness (the bigger the ship the less likely you'll feel it rock and pitch) and anyone looking for a good bargain (you can often snap up a cabin on a big ship for $100 a day, or less).

The biggest cruise ships in the world, those of the Royal Caribbean, Carnival, Norwegian, Princess and Holland America lines, stick to the major ports with deep-water harbors and developed tourism infrastructures, built to handle the large numbers of passengers. The port cities of Halifax, Nova Scotia; Saint John, New Brunswick; Newport, Rhode Island; and Boston, Massachusetts are popular calls for the mega ships. If a port doesn't have docking facilities to accommodate huge ship like these, then they must anchor off shore and shuttle passengers in via tender boats.

Small and sane

The smallest ships headed to the New England and Canada coast seem in tune with the rhythm of the region's sleepy fishing villages and historic sights. In their club-like chatty atmosphere conversation among fellow passengers and crew takes center stage, along with the scenery and places visited along the way. You can usually visit the captain on the bridge whenever the mood strikes you – there's little formality.

Of the small ships spending time along the New England and Eastern Canada coast, there are two kinds. One is the very smallest expedition-style vessel, carrying fewer than 150 passengers and offering a low-frills, ultra-casual setting, from compact but comfortable cabins to family-style dining and plainish decor. They typically have just one casual restaurant where clothes like jeans and khakis are perfectly acceptable. You'll find one or two bars, and an all-purpose lounge where passengers congregate to chat, read, and listen to presentations about the destination. Evening entertainment is along the lines of someone playing the piano before dinner and a movie shown before bed. But just because these ships aren't fancy, doesn't mean they're cheap. Expect to pay about $200 to $300 per person a day.

Where these small ships shine brightest is in the great lengths they go to to acquaint passengers with the culture and history of the region in which they're sailing. Popular historians sail aboard to provide passengers with background about a region. They give informal talks, chat with passengers and dine with them each evening. They may accompany tours on shore, or even guide them.

To enjoy these small ships – which include the 49- to 138-passenger ships of Clipper, American Canadian Caribbean Line (ACCL), and American Cruise Lines (ACL), plus the 42-passenger, three-masted schooner *Arabella* – you've also got to enjoy the cozy, meet-everyone-on-the-first-day kind of intimacy that comes with them. If you need a lot of privacy, these ships aren't for you.

Each has its own personality. ACL and the *Arabella* offer the most comfortable amenities; Clipper is the most "big-ship like" with officers

always in dress whites; and ACCL the most budget-oriented, but maybe the friendliest.

These ships can hug the coastline, so you can actually see what's on shore without squinting through binoculars. It's not unusual for the captain to cut the engine or double back if a pod of whales is spotted. You'll generally be in port with only other small ships and the sound of binoculars coming out of cases and cameras advancing is about as loud as it gets.

If you like the idea of a smaller ship, but want something plusher and not quite as focused on education and the itinerary, then the 200- to 700-passenger ultra-luxury ships of

Seabourn, Silversea and Radisson Seven Seas are the answer. They are the most costly of the lot, so expect to pay at least $300 to $500 a day. You'll get a suite (most have balconies) and all wines and spirits included. Waiters are as professional as they are in a Fifth Avenue hotel, and dining is a formal affair. These ships have spas, workout rooms, entertainment lounges, and pursuits like wine-tastings, dancing lessons and seminars on topics from health issues to handwriting analysis. Most feature onboard lecturers as well, and because they're able to navigate into more remote waterways, passengers are brought a lot closer to the real New England and Canada. ❏

LEFT: passengers and crew mingle on small ships.
RIGHT: nautical details from the USS *Constitution* at Charlestown Navy Yard.

CRUISING THE EAST COAST

There's a lot to see on a New England cruise, from vibrant New York to historic Boston and rural Canada, from affluent islands to craggy coastlines, from sleepy ports to scenic rivers

Maps:
Area 118
City 116

Cruising the Hudson to or from New York City is one of the most spectacular river journeys you'll ever experience. Many ships make a New England and Eastern Canada round trip, others go one-way from the Big Apple. Against the backdrop of the city's famous jagged skyline, ships pass by the Statue of Liberty and Ellis Island, and glide under the dramatic span of the Verrazano Narrows Bridge. Ships docked in **New York City ❶** land passengers smack dab in Midtown between West 48th and 50th streets (at the New York City Passenger Ship Terminal), and within easy walking distance of some of the city's most famous landmarks and sights, including one of the world's major cross streets, 42nd Street.

New York, New York

Unless you've got more than a day before or after your cruise, it's a good idea to focus on exploring just one or two parts of the city, especially if you're walking, in order to make the most of your time. If you want to see the heart of the city, first check out the towering **Empire State Building ❶** (open daily) at 34th Street and Fifth Avenue and take the elevator up the 86 floors to the panoramic rooftop. Then head north on Fifth Avenue to walk past the pair of marble lions guarding the beaux arts **New York City Public Library ❶** at 42nd Street and Fifth. The lions were named Patience and Fortitude during the Depression. Continue on to **St Patrick's Cathedral, Sak's Fifth Avenue** department store and the **Rockefeller Center ❶** at 50th Street (NBC studios tours offered daily; tel: 212-664 3700 for more information).

LEFT: South Street Seaport.
BELOW: the Statue of Liberty.

Continuing north through the 50s, browse the city's **highbrow boutiques** from Gucci to Prada and Harry Winston. All the diamonds, crystal, and silver (and little blue boxes) you could ever want can be found at **Tiffany & Co**, located at 57th and Fifth. Next, either head east on 57th Street and back to the ship, or, if time allows, continue north two blocks to FAO Schwarz, the toy store featured in *Big*, the 1988 movie starring Tom Hanks; and the grand **Plaza Hotel**, at the southeast corner of Central Park. If you've got time, hop into a horse-drawn carriage for a spin through **Central Park ❶** (not cheap, at $35 for the first 20 minutes, but fun); or head to 61st Street and Fifth Avenue for an elegant high tea in the muraled, marble rotunda at the **Pierre Hotel** (daily 3–5.30pm; no reservations required).

Uptown on 112th Street and Amsterdam Avenue is the cavernous **Cathedral of St John the Divine**; nearby is **Columbia University**'s ❶ gorgeous campus (notice the Italian Renaissance design of the domed St Paul's Chapel). A pleasant afternoon spent

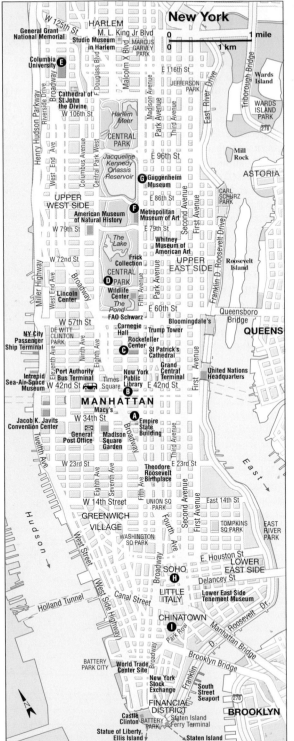

in the **Metropolitan Museum of Art** (closed Mon) among Egyptian ruins is another good option (Fifth Avenue and 82nd Street); other museums in the area include a New York classic, the **Solomon R. Guggenheim Museum** (closed Thur) at 89th Street and Fifth Avenue, a beautiful, sinuous building housing a splendid collection of modern art and sculpture. Or head downtown to the boutique-lined streets of cool **SoHo** , especially Spring Street, or wander through the narrow alleyways of **Chinatown** , where the sights and smells of the Orient are the closest thing you'll get to being there.

Although the ambience is not much better than a gas station, the **New Green Bo** restaurant (66 Bayard Street) is one of the best spots in the neighborhood for authentic Shanghai food like *kao fu* (a delicious wheat dish), scallion pancakes, and steamed soup dumplings.

Getting around town

Walking is the best way to see New York's fascinating cityscape en route to the official attractions. If you're fit, you can walk from the piers to anywhere between about 72th and 14th streets within four or five hours (about 20 blocks equals a mile).

If so much walking doesn't appeal, you can hail one of the ubiquitous yellow taxis (fares start at $2 and rarely exceed $15) or hop on the red, double-decker Gray Line tour buses that crisscross the city. They're a great way to see it all (Uptown, Downtown, and Brooklyn), without a lot of effort; you can join the tour loop at the Circle Line terminal just a few steps south of the cruise ship piers and get on and off as you like. Prices start at around $35.

If you're worried about personal safety, try not to be. Remember that there is safety in numbers. Take sensible precautions, as you would in any major city, like keeping your wallet in your front pocket and your purse strapped across your body.

New London, Connecticut

A little pocket of history conveniently located within a 20-minute drive of some of Connecticut's best attractions, including

Maps:
Area 118
City 116

Mystic Seaport and the Mohegan Sun and Foxwoods casinos, the small town of **New London ❷** is a mile up the Thames River from Long Island Sound. New London is not a major port on the New England/Canada route, but things are picking up, with the debut call of Holland America's 1,266-passenger *Maasdam* in 2004. The smaller 50- to 100-passenger ships of lines like American Cruise Lines and American Canadian Caribbean Line are New London's main business. Large ships dock at the drab State Pier and smaller ones dock at the much more attractive City Pier a few blocks away, where the waterfront area has recently been redeveloped.

The city was founded in 1646, and many 18th- and 19th-century buildings have survived, as well as a handful of 17th-century homes, many open to visitors. To see them, pick up a map of self-guided walking tours from one of the information kiosks in town (you'll find one on the corner of Golden Street and Eugene O'Neill Drive, just a few blocks from the cruise ship piers).

The ships' organized excursions are always a convenient option, but you can easily tour alone by taking a taxi (if there are no taxis at the pier, call Yellow Cab, tel: 860-443 4321 or Port City Taxi, tel: 869-444 9222). At Union Station, next to the City Pier, you can hop on the train for a lovely 15-minute ocean-view ride to historic and attractive **Mystic Seaport** (open daily), a 17-acre (7-hectare) living museum of replicas and antique vessels you can visit and/or sail on. They are on the site of a once-thriving shipyard that built clipper ships and packets up until the early 20th century.

Other more esoteric attractions nearby include the **Nautilus Museum** (closed Tues am; free) in Groton (just across the Thames River from New London), where you can explore the first nuclear submarine; the playwright **Eugene**

The Solomon R. Guggenheim Museum was built to a design by Frank Lloyd Wright.

BELOW: fast-paced Broadway in New York City.

TIP

For full details of **opening hours** and contact information for the sites and museums mentioned in this chapter, *see Travel Tips page 331.*

O'Neill's summer home, which is open for tours; and the **Mashantucket Pequot Museum**, (open daily) the largest Native American museum in the world, located at the Foxwoods casino.

Block Island, Connecticut

A port of call for ships carrying fewer than 100 passengers, like those of American Canadian Caribbean Line and American Cruise Lines, the 11-sq mile (28-sq km) **Block Island**, 12 miles (19 km) off the Rhode Island coast, is a favorite summer retreat for mainland residents. It's also a breath of fresh air for visitors, with no shortage of rustic stone walls, picturesque ponds and 17 miles (27 km) of beach. It was first inhabited by the native Narragansett, who called it "Manisses," the "Island of the Little God." The current name comes from the Dutch explorer, Adrian Block, who sailed here in 1614.

When in port in this rural hamlet, with a population of just 800 year-round residents, there's no better pastime than a day at the beach or a trek to the Mohegan Bluffs, a mile from downtown. From the top of these 200-ft (60-meter) cliffs, you'll get a bird's-eye view of the brick-built, Victorian-style Southeast Lighthouse, dating from 1873. Other outdoor activities include bicycling and hiking along the island's 32 miles (50 km) of rural trails.

Newport, Rhode Island

A living museum of America's great industrial-era wealth, and for centuries before that a thriving center of trade and whaling for Native Americans and later colonialists, **Newport** ❸ remains a symbol of opulence and of sailing. The summer seaside retreat for the USA's turn-of-the-20th-century rich and

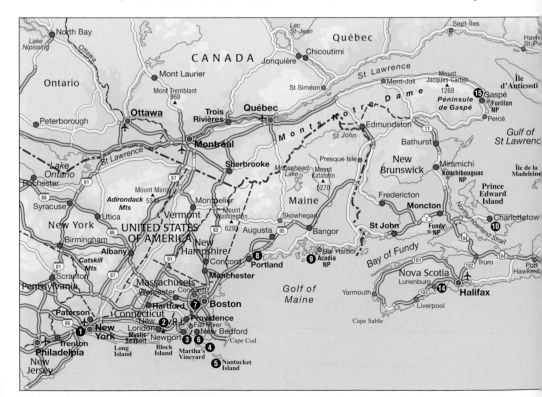

famous, from the Vanderbilts to the Astors, Newport is a great place to see how the other half lived – and some still do live.

Perched on the southern tip of the largest island, **Aquidneck**, in Narragansett Bay, it's no surprise that Newport appealed those who had their pick of the most gorgeous settings money could buy. It has all the right ingredients, from dramatic windswept bluffs and cliffs, to lonely lighthouses and picturesque beaches. What's more, downtown Newport has classic cobblestoned streets lined with cafés, stores, and shady trees. Its harbor is supremely photogenic, with hundreds of private pleasure yachts bobbing in the water, and even a handful of 36-ft (12-meter) America's Cup racing yachts moored here; for 70 years, Newport was the home of this famous race.

Ships of all sizes call at Newport these days, including the largest, like the 2,600-passenger *Grand Princess*. They all anchor just offshore and whisk passengers right into town on a 10-minute tender ride. The tender pier is just a block from the information center (23 America's Cup Avenue) and a kiosk is often set up on the pier, as well. All Newport's most popular sights are within a short walk or drive of the downtown area.

There are 11 summer "cottages," inspired by European palaces and run by the Newport Preservation Society, that are open for viewing, including the most famous, the 70-room **The Breakers** (hours vary; tel: 401-847 1000), commissioned in 1893 by Cornelius Vanderbilt, who made his fortune in steamships and railroads. The marble, Italian-Renaissance-style mansion was designed by Richard Morris Hunt, the beaux-arts master who also designed the Metropolitan Museum of Art in New York City. Many of the mansions are on Bellevue Avenue, where **The Elms** and **Marble House** offer self-guided audio tours,

Map on page 118

New England lobster is legendary, and is served in many guises.

BELOW: an artist paints on the Cliff Walk, Newport.

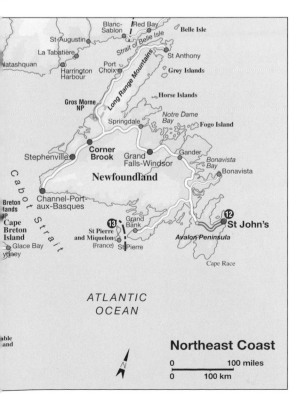

Northeast Coast

0   100 miles

0   100 km

while the others have tour guides on site who lead a new tour every 10–15 minutes. For something truly different, call ahead (tel: 401-847 0478) and reserve a spot on the Rooftop and Behind-the-Scenes Tours at The Elms, to get a fascinating glimpse of how the staff lived and worked at this French château-style mansion, built by Pennsylvania coal magnate Edward Berwind.

Getting around

To see the mansions, you can go with the organized bus tour your cruise ship will offer, or for a more independent trip, hop on the No. 67 vintage-style, trackless trolley-bus that runs past many of the mansions and other important attractions (all-day passes available). On the way to the mansions, stops include the Gothic church of **St Mary's** (where JFK and Jackie Bouvier married), the **Tourno Synagogue** (the country's oldest continually-operating synagogue, built in 1763), the **International Tennis Hall of Fame** (open daily) and the entrance to the Cliff Walk *(see below)*. There's a handy map that highlights these attractions as well as detailing the bus route.

Other worthwhile sights within walking distance of the tender pier include some impressive **colonial homes** downtown. Following your map, head to Third, Spring and School streets, as well as to Queen Anne Square, to see some of the best examples. Many of them are owned by the Doris Duke-founded Newport Restoration Foundation (visit www.newportrestorationfoundation.com or www.newporthistorial.org for details before you go). Another worthwhile and rewarding experience is the 3½-mile (5-km) **Cliff Walk**, which enables you to stroll along Newport's jagged coastline for views of the shoreline on one side and, on the other, many of the town's Gilded Age mansion estates.

BELOW:

an aerial view of the colonial homes on Cliff Walk.

Martha's Vineyard, Massachusetts

Martha's Vineyard ❹, known simply as "the Vineyard," is New England's largest island. It's a small-ship port, although every now and then a big ship will call here. Ships anchor offshore and tender passengers into Oak Bluffs, a town of brightly-painted Victorian cottages. The island's two other main towns, Vineyard Haven (a center of wooden-boat building) and Edgartown, are equally classic New England communities. Islanders revel in their home and in being separate from the mainland. Martha's Vineyard is 100 percent original; you won't find a single traffic light or a McDonald's. It's no surprise that a fair share of celebrities and notables have been attracted to the setting.

Besides its handsome old towns, Martha's Vineyard is a haven for nature lovers, with great **beaches** (though many are private, there are three public ones in Oak Bluffs and four in Edgartown, including one of the best, East Beach) and dramatic **cliffs** and **meadows** that make for great long walks and bicycle rides. If your ship doesn't rent bikes, venture off on your own with a good map – there are many rentals shops in Oak Bluffs, including Vineyard Bike & Moped, tel: 508-639 4498, and DeBettencourt's, tel: 508-693 0011.

It was the Native American Wampanoags who were the island's first inhabitants, and they retain part of their original homeland in the rural southwest. In the 19th century, whaling and fishing were the Vineyard's main source of income and successful mariners built beautiful homes with their newly-acquired wealth, many of them in **Edgartown**. Here, vestiges of the island's past can be seen at the **Old Whaling Church** on Main Street, and at the **Vineyard Museum** (closed Sun–Mon) on the corner of Cooke and School streets. What really put the island on the map, though, were the Methodist summer camp meetings held

Map on page 118

A pretty cottage in Oak Bluffs, Martha's Vineyard.

BELOW: everything made with local blueberries.

The Blueberry Hut

Blueberry Pie $10.00
    By the slice 2.50
Blueberry Bread ... 4.75
    By the slice 1.00
Blueberry Buckle 8.00
    By the slice 1.75
Blueberry Muffins .. 1.00
    Pkg. of six 4.51
Jam 4.00
Blueberry Cookies .. .75
Beverages .... .75
    coffee milk
    tea iced tea
    apple juice

at Wesleyan Grove, in Oak Bluffs during the mid-19th century; thousands attended these popular gathering, then went back home and spread the word of the island's beauty.

Nantucket, Massachusetts

The town's Chamber of Commerce is a good place to go for visitor information.

A port of call for a number of small ships that anchor offshore, **Nantucket Island ❺** is everyone's idea of classic New England. This small island, 30 miles (48 km) south of Cape Cod, was the world's top whaling port from the 17th century up until the early 19th century, when New Bedford, on the mainland, supplanted it. Before the English arrived in 1641, the Wampanoag tribe populated the island. Although it is a popular tourism destination, the island still manages to keep much of its low-key charm. It's known for the great **beaches** that wrap around its coast – these are public, unlike those on Martha's Vineyard which are mostly private.

The two main towns, **Siasconset** and **Nantucket Town** (the latter is just called "Town" by local people), are cobblestoned and lined with grand elms and elegant old houses built by whaling merchants. Stroll the streets of Town, especially Main Street, to soak up the appealing maritime flavor. Many historic homes are open for viewing within a several block radius, such as the grand, Greek Revival **Hadwen House** (tours for groups of 15 or more) at 96 Main Street, built in 1845. When it reopens, you should also try to pop into the **Whaling Museum** (closed in 2004 for renovation) at 13 Broad Street, where you'll see the skeleton of a 40-ft (12-meter) finback whale. If there's time, finish your day in port by ending up at one of the island's wonderful beaches, like the Jetties or Surfside (you can get a beach shuttle bus from Nantucket Town).

BELOW:
fishermen on
Nantucket Island.

New Bedford, Massachusetts

New Bedford ❻, a port of call only for small ships like those of American Cruise Lines, was the whaling capital of the world in the 19th century and remains a major Atlantic deep-sea fishing port. An hour south of Boston and 30 minutes east of Newport, the town's **Whaling Museum** (open daily) is the big draw and this is where you should spend your time in port. The museum is part of the 34-acre (14-hectare) New Bedford Whaling National Historical Park, which was created in 1996 and is spread over 13 city blocks; it also includes a visitors' center, the Seamen's Bethel, and the schooner *Ernestina*. You'll learn some fascinating insights about whales here; for instance, while the eye of a blue whale is the size of a teacup and it's ear the size of the tip of a pencil, the giant mammal's tongue weighs more than a VW beetle.

Exhibits include ship replicas – *The Lagoda* is claimed to be the largest model ship in the world – navigation instruments, whale skeletons, including one of a rare, juvenile blue whale, nicknamed Kobo – and paintings, glasswork, and scrimshaw (carved whalebone or whale ivory).

At the Boston Tea Party Ship and Museum.

Cuttyhunk, a tiny island off the coast of New Bedford, is also included on a few small-ship itineraries. It's the last link in the Elizabeth Islands chain that reaches westward from the elbow of Cape Cod. Experiences on this serene island, just 2 sq miles (5 sq km) are all about beaches, sailing and quiet walks among the rolling hills of bayberry bushes and willowy grasses.

Fall River, Massachusetts

Located in the northern reaches of Narragansett Bay, about 20 miles (32 km) north of Newport, Rhode Island, **Fall River** is accessible only to the smallest vessels belonging to companies like American Cruise Lines. Visitors can enjoy a trip on some historic boats, including the battleship USS *Massachusetts*, submarine *Lionfish*, and other veterans of World War II. What is more, at the **Marine Museum** (open daily) at Fall River, there are artifacts from the *Titanic* and a replica of the famous liner. At the **Lizzie Borden Museum** (May– June Sat–Sun; July–Aug daily) there are guided tours highlighting 1890s Fall River and that famous, unsolved murder mystery.

BELOW: the Boston Tea Party Ship, a replica of the original, is docked by the waterfront.

Boston, Massachusetts

The hub of North America's early colonial history, **Boston** ❼ was founded in 1630 along the Charles River. A port of call on many itineraries that sail from New York, and also an embarkation port for a handful of cruises that sail between Boston and Montréal or Québec City, Boston is a great catch. You can easily spend your entire day exploring the historical sights, from the USS *Constitution* (otherwise known as *Old Ironsides*) to the Paul Revere House. There are gorgeous pockets of Victorian-era townhouses in the stylish **Back Bay** ❹ and **Beacon Hill** ❺ neighborhoods, and just across the river in Cambridge is Harvard, founded in 1636. Boston is also a great place for pursuits like window shopping, pub-crawling (the *Cheers* bar, whose facade featured in the opening credits of that once-beloved sitcom, is actually called the Bull &

Maps:
Area 118
City 124

Finch and it's on Beacon Street) and eating in fun places like Faneuil Hall, Quincy Market, and Newbury Street, Boston's version of Fifth Avenue.

Your ship's city bus tour will take you to the top sights, and ensure you see the best of Boston, but if you want more freedom (and fewer crowds), it's easy to explore on your own. Grab the free *Where* magazine available in the terminal, and use its map to walk the **Freedom Trail** or join a trolley tour. Brush Hill Tours' Red Bean Town Trolley service has narrated two-hour loops on vintage-style trolleys through Boston's historic districts; you can hop on and off all day, and stops include the Shaw Memorial across from the State House, where you can buy tickets. The 3-mile (5-km) marked trail wends between Boston Common, the country's oldest public park, and the 18th-century *Old Ironsides* battleship, passing 16 historical places, including the site of the first public school in the Colonies (c.1635) and the **Old State House** ⊙ (open daily), dating from 1712, which is where the Declaration of Independence was first read in public. Also on the route are the **site of the Boston Massacre**, **Paul Revere House** ⊙ (open daily),

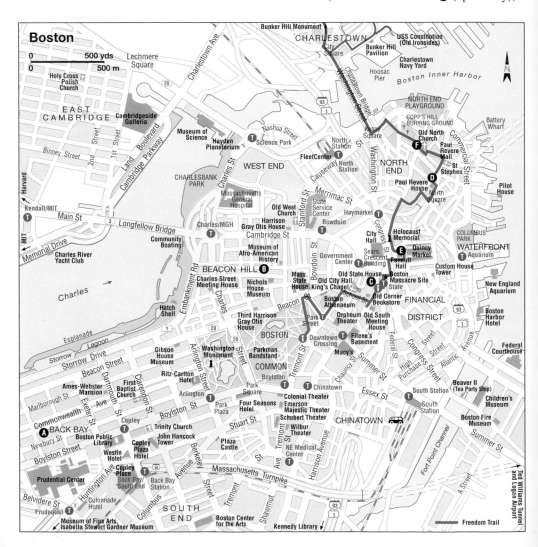

the oldest 17th-century structure in Boston, **Faneuil Hall ⑤** (open daily), where speakers from John Hancock to Susan B. Anthony and John F. Kennedy have taken to the stump, and **Old North Church ⑥**, from where the famous lanterns signaled Paul Revere's midnight ride. The historic heart of Boston is walkable, though you can't do it from the Black Falcon terminal. The good news is that it's only a 4-mile (6-km) taxi ride to Boston Common. Metered taxis are available at the pier. Once in town, Boston's efficient subway system (MBTA), called the "T" for short, stops at points throughout the city.

Maps:
Area 118
City 124

A treasure chest of history at this Beacon Hill antiques shop.

Just beyond Boston

While there's enough in Boston itself to keep you busy for several days, if you've seen the city before, there are a number of great tour options to places outside Boston that are best explored on an organized ship's tour. About an hour's drive south of Boston is **Plymouth**, where the *Mayflower* landed and the USA took root. Here you can see a replica of that famous ship, and in nearby Fall River visitors can enjoy a trip on some other historic boats *(see page 123)*. Whale-watching tours also depart from Boston; a 30-minute motorboat ride gets you to Stellwagen in Cape Cod Bay, the best place for whale spotting. Inland, anyone interested in the Revolutionary War may want to sign up for a tour of **Lexington** and **Concord**, where the American Revolution was born (about a 50-minute drive from pier).

Portland, Maine

Maine's largest city, **Portland ⓪**, is set on a peninsula in pretty **Casco Bay**. A few ships include Portland on their itineraries, though Bar Harbor to the north, with its more natural setting, sees many more cruise ship calls. In Portland, vessels dock

BELOW:
Harvard Square.

BELOW: the Portland
Headlight on the
rocky Maine coast.

at (or near) Old Port, the city's revitalized waterfront. Formerly the city's warehouse district, its red-brick buildings have been transformed into stores, galleries, pubs, and restaurants and they're all within walking distance of the pier.

Just outside the city, over the Casco Bay bridge, along a stretch of Maine's rocky coast in Cape Elizabeth, is the extremely photogenic **Portland Headlight** (open Sat–Sun). Built in 1791, it is said to be the oldest lighthouse in continuous use. From its hurricane deck, you will have great views of the 200-plus islands in Casco Bay. There's a good museum in the former quarters of the lighthouse keeper. In town, many 19th-century buildings and homes are open for tours. Don't miss **Victoria Mansion** (109 Danforth Street), a fine example of Victorian architecture, with etched and stained glass, frescoes, and ornate woodwork. Join your ship's organized tour, or stop by the visitors' center near the docks at 245 Commercial Street for self-guided walking-tour maps, as well as tickets for guided walking and bus tours of Portland's historic sites.

If you prefer to skip the history in favor of a little shopping you can head out to nearby **Freeport**, a shopping mecca where factory outlets abound. Most cruise lines provide transport to Freeport, otherwise make the short trip by taxi.

Bar Harbor, Maine

Located in the lush Acadia National Park on **Mount Desert Island**, an expanse of gorgeous forest, lakes, and rugged nature, **Bar Harbor** is just a short bridge span away from the mainland. It has much to the visitor, starting with the stunning approach to port, which is about as scenic as you can get, with Cadillac Mountain just beyond the jagged coastline. Ships pull alongside the docks at Harbor Place or Town Pier, right in the center of town. To see the **Acadia**

National Park ❾, take a guided hike or a drive along the 27-mile (43-km) **Park Loop Road**, which wends around **Cadillac Mountain** (cross your fingers and hope it's not a foggy day) and affords views of spectacular natural sights like **Thunder Hole**, where ocean surf crashes dramatically against granite cliffs.

There are some 55 miles (90 km) of car-free carriage trails that wind through the park, with great scenery and a chance to spot wildlife, from the occasional moose, to beavers, foxes, eagles, hawks, and the peregrine falcon. You can also appreciate the region's wildlife (such as seals and puffins) from the water, by signing up for a kayaking excursion or a whale-watching trip – the best time to spot the great mammals is between April and October, when humpbacks, finbacks, minkes, and dolphins gather in the waters off the island to fill their bellies after a long winter.

If you don't feel like nature tours and don't want to go far, take a stroll along Bar Harbor's Victorian-era streets. Don't pass up the opportunity to eat a freshly-caught Maine lobster at one of the many restaurants along the waterfront area (like the Pier Restaurant at 55 West Street). The crustaceans have been the mainstay of this region for centuries. In town, there is also the worthwhile and interesting **Maine Lobster Museum and Hatchery** (open daily), at the Mount Desert Oceanarium, and the **Abee Museum** (open daily), featuring Native American exhibits.

Prince Edward Island, Canada

The small-ship lines often include a call at **Prince Edward Island** (P.E.I.), Canada's smallest province. It is known as the birthplace of Canada, because an 1867 conference in **Charlottetown** ⑩ established Canada as a new nation. Explore **Province House**, a neoclassical stone structure which was the province's first public building, now a National Historic Site, and **Founders Hall**, a waterfront pavilion from where you can enjoy walking tours, shopping and exhibits. The first European to set foot on the island was Frenchman, Jacques Cartier, in 1534 *(see page 15)*. P.E.I. was first claimed by France and later by England, and consequently settled by French-Acadian farmers as well as immigrants from Ireland, Scotland, and England. For centuries before Cartier landed on its shores, the Mi'kmaq (also spelled Micmac) tribe populated the area. An interesting way to spend the day is to stroll through the old section of Charlottetown, where you'll find historic monuments, old mansions, museums, churches, and parks.

As much as its historic appeal, Prince Edward Island, about 40 miles (64 km) at its widest and 140 miles (225 km) long, is on the tourist map because of its natural beauty, from its dramatic sandstone cliffs to its red soil, rocky coves and lovely white beaches, sand dunes, fishing villages, and rolling hills. A great pastime is simply driving along one of the island's scenic highways, including Lady Slipper Drive, Blue Heron Drive, and The Kings Byway.

Sydney, Cape Breton Island, Nova Scotia

Head for the hills when you debark in industrial **Sydney** ⑪ (referred to as Steel City). The **Cape Breton Highlands** are a gorgeous sea of lakes, dramatic cliffs, panoramic vistas (like that from atop Cape Smokey), and rocky coastline. You

Map on page 118

In Cavendish, on the northwestern side of P.E.I., is the house of Lucy Maud Montgomery, who wrote the classic novel Anne of Green Gables, *about life on Prince Edward Island in the late 19th and early 20th century.*

BELOW: on parade at the Fortress of Louisbourg, Cape Breton Island.

The Cabot Trail in Cape Breton is named for the explorer John Cabot and is one of the most scenic drives in North America.

BELOW: wild poppies in Newfoundland.

can see why waves of Scottish settlers in the early 19th century were reminded of home. The island is a rich blend of Celtic, Gaelic, and French traditions, evident in the architecture and music, and the lyrical names of many of the island's towns and regions. Eastern Europeans also settled here at the turn of the 20th century to work in the coalmines and steel plants.

There's no better way to spend a day in port than a drive along one of the highway trails that cut through the island's breathtaking landscape. The 184-mile (296-km) long **Cabot Trail**, for instance, traverses the northern shore of Cape Breton and runs into the **Cape Breton Highlands National Park**, where it's not uncommon to spot moose, bald eagles, and puffins, and humpback whales in the waters of the Gulf of St Lawrence. The National Park begins a few miles north of Chéticamp, extending from the Gulf to the Atlantic and is bordered on three sides by the Cabot Trail. Day-long guided bus tours of the trail are offered by most cruise lines calling here; you can also rent a car and go solo, some local car rental companies, such as Enterprise Rent-a-car on Grand Lake Road, will pick you up at the pier. Along the Cabot Trail is the village of **Ingonish**, which is occasionally used as a port of call and an access point to the Trail.

Other sights to see on Cape Breton include the **Alexander Graham Bell National Historic Site** (open daily) including his lovely estate, Beinn Bhreagh (Gaelic for Beautiful Mountain), on the shores of Bras d'Or Lake in Baddeck, about an hour from Sydney, where Bell spent many years of his life. A modern museum building here is dedicated to the great man. The **Fortress of Louisbourg National Historic Site** (open daily; *see page 127*), painstakingly restored, is on the southeast coast of Cape Breton, on the Fleur de Lis Trail.

St John's, Newfoundland

Since it's farther north than most ships have time to reach on typical seven-night or shorter itineraries, only one or two small-ship lines with offbeat itineraries visit **St John's ⓬**, the capital of Newfoundland and the oldest city in Canada, founded in 1582. Situated at the easternmost point in North America (the exact point is Cape Spear), St John's is a busy commercial port that receives ships from around the world. Newfoundland is an extremely picturesque place, and excursions offered by ships often include a full day's drive with stops at a puffin colony and seabird reserve, as well as a drive to Petty Harbour for a walking tour of Cape Spear.

St Pierre and Miquelon

An occasional port of call made by only the smallest cruise ships, the French enclave of **St Pierre and Miquelon ⓭** belongs to a group of small islands off the southern coast of Newfoundland. Here you can experience the last vestige of France's overseas empire through French-speaking, beret-wearing residents (many descended from Acadians and Basques), French restaurants, with great wines, cheese, and seafood, and other aspects of French culture. For centuries, the isles were a popular stopover for sailors coming in from fishing expeditions to the Grand Banks.

Lunenburg, Nova Scotia

A handful of small ships call at **Lunenburg** ⑭, perched on a steep hillside some 57 miles (88 km) southwest of Halifax. Long known as Nova Scotia's major fishing port, the area offshore is also known for whale sightings, especially around La Have Bank, where the sea is full of the plankton and other nutrients that attract humpback, fin, minke, and right whales (the rarest of all the great whales). Established in 1753 as a British colonial settlement, Lunenburg attracted settlers from Germany, Switzerland, and France. Today, quite a few 19th-century buildings survive, from the 1829-built Stephen Finck house, to the Victorian neo-Gothic Zion Evangelical Lutheran Church, built in 1891. In 1995, the town was added to the prestigious UNESCO World Heritage List.

A replica of the *Bluenose II* racing schooner is sometimes in port, when not in Halifax. Its predecesssor, *Bluenose I*, never lost an international race and is immortalized on the Canadian dime. Lunenburg also has connection to the cinema. It was a location for movies, including *Simon Birch* and *Dolores Claiborne*, and home of the shipyard that built the tall ship *The Bounty*, featured in the 1962 version of *Mutiny on the Bounty*, starring Marlon Brando and Trevor Howard.

Herons gather on the sandbar on the Gaspé Peninsula.

Gaspé Peninsula, Québec

The small towns along the beautiful **Gaspé Peninsula**, which forms the southern leg of the St Lawrence River, are included on a few small-ship itineraries. While the towns themselves aren't especially attractive, the region is physically inspiring and rich in wildlife, especially its bird species and whales, namely finback and belugas. The historic village of **Gaspé** ⑮ (meaning "end of land" in the Mi'kmaq language), like Prince Edward Island, was first claimed by Jacques Cartier in 1534. He made landfall there, and stayed just 11 days, while searching for a sea route to the Orient. Excursions here are usually centered on nature, and often include a day at **Forillon National Park**, a 92-sq mile (238-sq km) stretch nestled between the St Lawrence and Gaspé Bay, that includes some nine different climatic variations. Thousands of seabirds nest on the cliffs here, and a variety of plants have survived since the Ice Age.

South of Gaspé is the town of **Percé**, where a craggy, 264-ft (88-meter) rock, the **Rocher Percé**, with a large hole in the center, bursts from the sea just off shore. During low tide, you can walk out to it via a sand spit and check out the many fossils. Even if your ship is not anchoring offshore, sailing anywhere near the Rock allows you to take a great photo.

Not far off shore from Percé is tiny **Bonaventure Island**, which was settled by Basque and Breton fishermen in the early 16th century. Today it's populated by thousands of birds. The island's cliffs, beaches, and trails harbor the world's largest natural bird sanctuary, including a gannet colony and many other species of birds such as puffins, cormorants, and murres. The island also has numerous scenic trails alongside cliffs, crevasses, and beaches.

If your cruise continues to Montréal and Québec City, see the chapter on the St Lawrence Seaway, *page 313*, for more information. ❏

BELOW: catch of the day.

New York–Florida–Bahamas Sailings

In the past couple of years, some lines have launched itineraries along the east coast that are almost entirely US-based. Originating from New York, these sailings, which can be year-round or summer season only, call at major tourist destinations such as Miami and Orlando, before a brief stop in the Bahamas. These itineraries owe their Caribbean stopovers to a quirk in US law. Just about every major cruise line flies foreign flags rather than those of the United States of America. Usually, this is because other nations levy fewer taxes and have less stringent regulations. In an effort to penalize this practice, the Jones Act requires foreign-flagged cruise lines that want to call at American ports to stop in at least one international destination, or pay a huge fine. This has discouraged many lines from focusing primarily on US-based routes.

These days, however, there's more demand than ever before to cruise on itineraries that focus on East Coast port of calls. Certainly, New England/Canada trips have been a staple of cruise lines. But now they're looking south – and major companies, ranging from Norwegian Cruise Line to Carnival Cruises, are launching New York to South Florida voyages. Key stops, depending, of course, on the individual trip, include Orlando (via Port Canaveral) and Miami, and, in all cases, passengers can count on a little side trip to one of the Bahamian islands – which is, of course, a nod to fulfilling the rules of the US Jones Act.

New York City: It all starts here, where cruise ships line the ancient piers on the West Side's Hudson River. Beyond the city itself, the magnetic attraction for sailing from New York is the marvelous vistas of the most famous skyline in the world, from the Chrysler Building and the Empire State Building to the Statue of Liberty and Ellis Island.

From the cruise ship terminal, it's a quick cab ride to the theaters of Broadway and the effervescence, night, day and in-between, of Times Square. But there's more. Visiting the city's museums alone could take days, and the Metropolitan Museum of Art, the Museum of Modern Art, the Museum of Natural History, the Whitney Museum of American Art, and the Solomon R. Guggenheim Museum are just the big-name attractions. New York's architecture offers opportunities to see many panoramic views – a trip to the top (well nearly the top) of the Empire State Building offers a gorgeous one. The Statue of Liberty is another option; take the Liberty Ferry from the Battery to see this 305-ft (93-meter) statue, a gift from France, unveiled in 1886.

Experienced New York visitors also recommend a tour of some of the city's fascinating neighborhoods, which include Chinatown, Little Italy, and the Lower East Side for ethnic atmosphere, and SoHo and TriBeCa for hip-and-trendy fun. And when it seems that New York has exhausted the visitor, it's time to head for Central Park for some rest and relaxation. In particular, highlights include Strawberry Fields, created in John Lennon's memory, the lovely Bethesda Fountain, imposing Belvedere Castle and, finally, the

Sheep Meadow for roller-blading and cycling. For visitors wishing to honor the victims of the terrorist attack on September 11, 2001, the site of the World Trade Center is easily reached by subway.

Port Canaveral: The gateway to Orlando, Port Canaveral offers access to America's great collection of amusement parks and entertainment centers. Disney World, Universal Studios, SeaWorld and the many other attractions in Orlando are an hour's drive directly west of Port Canaveral, accessible by bus or car. One note of caution, however: on this type of New York to Florida itinerary, passengers have only a day in port – and because Orlando itself is an hour away, it's important to keep track of time. One positive on this itinerary is that cruise lines generally provide a longer-than-usual day in port (sometimes 16 hours) to offer extra time.

For those who want to stay closer to the ship, nearby Cape Canaveral, home of the John F. Kennedy Space Center, offers a chance to step back in time to the beginning of the nation's space program in the 1950s. One exhibit is the control center used during the early space missions. There are replicas of the rockets used to send space capsules into orbit, including a huge hangar that houses a Saturn launcher lying on its side. There is also a life-sized space shuttle and other vehicles. A bus tour will take you past the launch pads used by the space shuttles, where, when the program resumes in 2005, you may see a shuttle sitting atop its booster rocket as its being prepared for a mission.

And there's more; some 6 miles (10 km) west is the US Astronaut Hall of Fame. It was founded by astronauts who flew *Mercury* and *Gemini* missions, and features displays of their experiences.

Miami: The port of Miami, one of the busiest cruise ship ports in the world, spills across a five-lane bridge into this vibrant city that combines the many cultures of the region. What that means is that it's basically a hop and a skip from the heart of this eclectic city and the only challenge is choosing among the many options. Trendy travelers will head to the famous beaches and restaurants of South Beach, with its art deco historic district. Families will aim for Key Biscayne, an island connected by a causeway, that's home to the Miami Seaquarium; the Miami Metro Zoo, another child-friendly stop, is near the Miami International Airport. And foodies won't want to miss sampling great Cuban food in Little Havana or Haitian cuisine in Little Haiti.

Bahamas: On this route, ships typically call at Nassau on New Providence Island, that key call at a foreign port. Nassau's virtues include beaches, duty-free shopping and the over-the-top Atlantis Resort on Paradise Island. Among the resort's open-to-the-public attractions (you pay a fee as a day visitor) are tours of its archeological sites (known as "The Dig"), lagoon, and aquarium. The Atlantis's gargantuan casino and its plethora of restaurants also welcome cruise visitors. Back in Nassau, worthwhile stops include the Pirates of Nassau Museum, Fort Charlotte Castle, and Government House. ❏

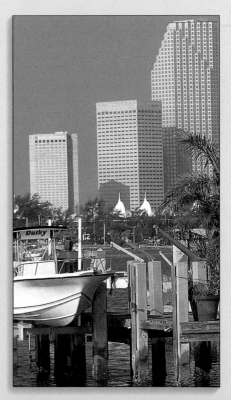

LEFT: children on a Hudson River ferry looking over to Manhattan, New York.
RIGHT: a view of the Miami skyline from Venetia Causeway, Florida.

THE FALL AND RISE OF THE SOUTH

From the early colonial settlements to eventual independence,
the southern states have played a pivotal role in the nation's development

The establishment of colonies in the New World was initially inspired by the commercial interests of the British crown. What evolved, however, was something far more potent: the birth of democracy and the development of a new nation. Many of the events that marked the development of

NOVA BRITANNIA.

OFFRING MOST

Excellent fruites by Planting in
VIRGINIA.

Exciting all such as be well affected
to further the same.

LONDON
Printed for SAMVEL MACHAM, and are to be sold at
his Shop in Pauls Church-yard, at the
Signe of the Bul-head.
1609.

colonial North America began in New England. Ultimately, however, many of the events that defined the new United States of America unfolded in the South. Indeed, five southern states were part of the original 13 colonies formed under British rule in the early 18th century. The coastal states of Virginia, Maryland, North Carolina, South Carolina, and Georgia played vital roles in the young nation's early economy.

Today, the southern and Atlantic coasts of the United States are rich with historic sites that commemorate America's early heritage. At the same time, each has carved out its own culture and distinct identity.

Early attempts at settlement

The earliest European settlement was established on the shores of what is now South Carolina in 1526. The Spanish explorer Lucas Vázquez de Ayllón led two ships to the mouth of the Peedee River and tried to establish San Miguel de Guadalupe. However, the initial experiment failed within a year, and those who survived returned to Hispaniola, which is now Haiti and the Dominican Republic. Still, the Spanish and French influence between 1513 and 1763 remained a potent force in the region thanks to arriving sailors, soldiers, missionaries, and colonists from the Florida Keys in the extreme south and from as far north as Virginia and as far west as Alabama.

England shows an interest

English colonial interest in the New World had begun by the early 1600s with the formation of two private companies to settle the Atlantic Coast: the London Company in the southern Virginia territory and the Plymouth Company in northern Virginia. The former sponsored a group of 105 settlers who were the first to land, in 1607. This was the group that founded Jamestown on the James River, in honor of King James I.

The settlers' first few years were marred by harsh winters, short supplies, and consequent starvation. Many of the survivors wanted to return home by the end of their second winter, but they were prevented from doing so by Lord Thomas de la Warr, who had arrived from England with new supplies and more settlers. The state of Delaware was later named after Lord Thomas. His presence marked a turning point, and the colonists began to prosper after they entered agreements with local Native American tribes and learned from them how to grow crops.

This was also the time of Captain John Smith (1580–1631), one of the original settlers who remained committed to life in the New World. Smith, who had fought for England both in France and in Hungary, where he had been captured by the Turks, is credited with discovering much of the region as he sailed up the Chesapeake Bay. His accounts of his travels, and the maps he drew, were to prove helpful to later settlers. In the New World, he made contact with Chief Powhatan, who provided the colonists with much of their food in that first difficult year.

One of Powhatan's daughters was Pocahontas, but despite a tendency to romanticize her story in children's narratives, she was never became involved with John Smith. Instead, she married John Rolfe, the colonist credited with cultivating Virginia's first commercial tobacco crops, which helped the colony become profitable. Tobacco growing was a labor-intensive exercise, however, and one of the first group of African slaves arrived in Jamestown in 1619 aboard a Dutch ship, to work the crop.

Colonial ambitions

Other enterprising businessmen sought to establish colonial ventures. In 1632, King Charles I granted a charter for Maryland to George Calvert, better known as Lord Baltimore. Baltimore very much wanted to see the colony become a reality. In 1633 the first group of settlers, led by Leonard Calvert, Baltimore's youngest son, set sail for Maryland to establish a colony. The Calverts eventually became involved in a border dispute with the Penns of Pennsylvania that would not be resolved for nearly a century.

After numerous attempts to resolve the matter, the Royal Astronomer in England appointed Charles Mason and Jeremiah Dixon to survey the area, in 1763. It took four years, but Mason and Dixon finally established a 244-mile (393-km) boundary that settled matters. Mr Mason and Mr Dixon's efforts remain visible today, as Americans commonly refer to southern states as lying below the "Mason Dixon Line."

Southern expansion

In 1653 colonists from Virginia began to expand southward into what is now the Carolinas. Ten years later, King Charles II created the colony of Carolina, which was then about the size of what

are now North and South Carolina and Georgia. However, this created friction with the Virginians who had settled in Albemarle Sound in the northern part of the region, and who resented being part of the Carolina Charter. Hostilities were eased in 1691 when the crown began recognizing the area as "North Carolina." It officially became a colony when it received a Royal Charter from Charles II in 1729.

South Carolina was already an agricultural success story, with plantations growing indigo, rice, and cotton. Charleston (originally named Charles Town, after the King) was founded in 1670 by a group of 200 colonists from the

English-ruled island of Barbados. They were led by Sir John Yeamans, a powerful plantation owner on the island.

Georgia became a separate colony in 1752, about 20 years after King George II granted the territory to General James Oglethorpe. With Fort King George, established in 1721, Georgia protected the northern colonies from the Spanish and French, occupying the Florida territories to the south. Oglethorpe reinforced his reputation when he led a large military force against the Spanish. When the Spanish sought revenge by sailing into Georgia, Oglethorpe and his troops were there again to drive them back south into Florida. Oglethorpe would later

PRECEDING PAGES: a view of East Battery at sunrise, South Carolina.
LEFT: encouraging investment in the New World.
RIGHT: Chief Powhatan smoking in his hut above a settlement on the shore of Chesapeake Bay, 1686.

show his prowess for city planning when he came up with a grid design that made Savannah one of the most beautiful and best-laid out cities in the US, as it remains today.

The Revolutionary War

The events that led to the Revolutionary War built slowly. The colonists demanded the same rights granted to Englishmen, including representation in Parliament. But there were a number of other contributing factors that eventually led to war. The French and Indian War began in 1754 and grew into a conflict that ended French rule in Canada and brought George Washington

to prominence. (Its counterpart in Europe was the Seven Years' War, of 1756–63.) Washington's military career got off to a miserable start when he was forced to surrender Fort Necessity in the Ohio Valley. In 1755, after French and Indian forces resisted an English attempt to take Fort Duquesne, Washington was sent in to lead British and Colonial forces to safety. William Pitt (Pittsburgh is named after him) eventually took over leadership of the British effort in 1758. By giving colonists more independence he also gave them reason to be more supportive of the war, and this helped turn the tide. By February 1763, the Treaty of Paris had been

COLONIAL BEGINNINGS

Two sites in Virginia offer the opportunity to step back into early Colonial times. Jamestown, on an island in the James River, 60 miles (100 km) upriver from Chesapeake Bay, is the site of the first permanent English colony in America, established in 1607 by a group of men sent by the Virginia Company to search for gold and a route to the Orient. Archeological digs have located a number of the original structures, including the original James Fort.

Williamsburg was started after three English ships, the *Susan Constant, Godspeed*, and *Discovery* weighed anchor in 1607 near the banks of the James River, about 7 miles (11 km) from Jamestown. It served as the capital of Virginia

for over 80 years before Thomas Jefferson, then governor, made Richmond the capital in 1780. Williamsburg played an important role in the Civil War during the Peninsula Campaign of 1862, when Confederate troops delayed the advances of Union General George McClellan.

In the early 20th century, Colonial Williamsburg was restored and today reflects the life of the Colonists. There are reenactments, from the daily routine of slaves, who made up nearly half of the city's population, to that of the men who operated local stores and businesses. Here too is where George Washington secured his first military commissions, and where Thomas Jefferson was educated.

signed. Among other things, it granted British control of all territories east of the Mississippi.

Victory for the British

But victory had left a debt of £140 million sterling, and this led to a number of controversial efforts to raise revenue in the colonies. There was the American Revenue Act of 1764, better known as the Sugar Act. A year later, Prime Minister George Grenville urged Parliament to impose more measures. The Quartering Act required citizens to provide food and shelter to British troops; and the Stamp Act of 1765 imposed taxes on any legal document, from marriage licenses to newspapers.

By 1766, the Colonists had begun demonstrating their opposition. By this time King George III was in power and Charles Townshend had become Chancellor of the Exchequor. He convinced Parliament to approve the Townshend Acts, which imposed even more taxes on such vital imports as lead, paint, tea, paper, and glass. It also included a further step to ensure that governors and judges did what the Crown wanted by having them paid directly from England. Colonial opposition to the Townshend Acts grew into a boycott covering the import of any British goods.

England responded by sending in troops to quell disturbances. In March 1770, tensions were highlighted by the Boston Massacre, when protesters surrounded British sentries. The troops opened fire and left five people dead, including former slave, Crispus Attucks.

Most of the taxes imposed under the Townshend Acts were repealed by the end of 1770, except the levy on tea. British legislators wanted to make a statement about maintaining power. This soon backfired, and the Boston Tea Party took place in 1773 when a band of rebels boarded a British ship and dumped its cargo of tea into Boston Harbor.

The British response was fairly swift. In 1774 Parliament passed the Coercive Acts, known in the colonies as the "Intolerable Acts." Among other things, the port of Boston was ordered closed until the East India Company was compensated for the goods dumped in the Boston Harbor. But in Philadelphia, the First Conti-

nental Congress began meeting to deal with the Coercive Acts. Members felt that the British had no right to impose taxes. It approved a measure that all Colonists stop drinking tea imported by the East India Company, but initially it didn't go along with the demands of more radical members who wanted to begin forming a Continental Army.

Toward a more perfect union

The threads of a nation's fabric started to be woven together during the hot summer of 1776 in Philadelphia, then the American capital. The Declaration of Independence was written and

signed by, among others Benjamin Franklin of Pennsylvania, Thomas Jefferson of Virginia, John Hancock and John Adams of Massachusetts, William Hooper of North Carolina, and Button Gwinnett of Georgia.

The Liberty Bell, which was used to summon citizens for special events, was sounded for people to assemble for the reading of the Declaration on July 8, 1776.

However, by September 1777 the British had gained control of Philadelphia after fending off attacks by Washington and his troops. Washington would eventually set camp 18 miles (30 km) away in Valley Forge, where his troops withstood a harsh and deadly winter. By the

LEFT: the final battle of the War of Independence at Yorktown in 1771. RIGHT: George Washington, first president of the United States (1789–97).

following spring, Washington had his troops pursuing the British back into New York and the tide began to turn.

Hostilities continued until the final battle of the war at Yorktown, Virginia, in 1781. Combined colonial troops under Washington's command took on General Charles Cornwallis and his outnumbered British soldiers. Washington sent Lieutenant Colonel Alexander Hamilton to deliver a letter to Cornwallis, expressing the desire to stop what Washington termed the "useless effusion of blood." Realizing the cause was lost, Cornwallis officially surrendered on October 19, 1781.

tion of American neutrality and meddling in domestic affairs, among other things.

Fort McHenry in Baltimore Harbor offers one of the more inspiring episodes of the War of 1812, the rematch between the US and England. The Battle of Baltimore was waged on September 13–14, 1814. Despite intense British cannon attacks, the star-shaped fort at the mouth of Baltimore Harbor never fell. The flickering image of a huge red-white-and-blue American flag waving in the air over the fort as the "bombs burst in air," inspired Francis Scott Key, who was in custody aboard a British ship at the time of the attack, to pen the words of a

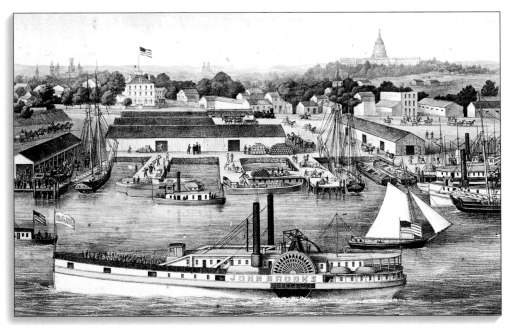

The nation's federal structure was initially determined in the Articles of Confederation. Adopted by the Second Continental in 1777 and ratified by the 13 states in 1781, it served as the first Constitution until 1788. However, certain weaknesses in the original document made it necessary to come up with a stronger version. A Constitutional Convention was convened in Philadelphia in 1787 and a new Constitution became effective on March 4, 1789.

Renewed Anglo–American tension

By the early 1800s, tensions between the States and the former British rulers were again building over what was viewed as Britain's viola-

poem he entitled *In Defense of Fort M'Henry*. The poem eventually became the country's national anthem. *The Star Spangled Banner* paints images of the "rockets red glare," and "the land of the free, and the home of the brave." Key's brother-in-law had the entire poem printed onto handbills, and it was put to the tune of a British drinking song that was popular at the time, *Anacreon in Heaven*.

The war between the states

Although slavery had largely ended in the northern states by the time the new Constitution was drawn up in 1787, the practice was still made part of the document at the insistence of delegates from both the North and South. The incidence of sectionalism grew to a point that a Mississippi senator named Jefferson Davis spoke of his concern about the growing tension between North and South.

By the time of the 1860 election, the Democratic Party was splintered along regional and political lines: southerners backed the pro-slavery candidate, Senator John Breckenridge of Kentucky, while those who believed that the abolition of slavery should be a matter for individual states, not Congress, supported Illinois Senator Stephen Douglas. There was also a third-party candidate, John Bell of Tennessee, standing for the Whigs. The Republican Party nominated Abraham Lincoln, a young congressman from Illinois. Ironically, Lincoln believed that the Constitution prevented the government from taking action against slavery where it already existed, but he was determined to stop it spreading further.

Once Lincoln was sworn in as 16th president in 1861, South Carolina followed through on their threat to secede from the Union if Lincoln were elected. The Civil War, which tore a young nation apart, began with an attack on Fort Sumter in Charleston Harbor.

Ultimately, the North won the war and slavery was abolished. But resulting southern tensions continued to reverberate over the next 100 years and more. Economic realities, again more harshly felt in the South, inspired decades of decline, as a tremendous amount of reconstruction had to be undertaken following the near-total destruction of cities like Atlanta and coastal ports including Charleston, South Carolina, and Savannah, Georgia.

The cradle of democracy

The country's first capital, where George Washington was sworn in as the united nation's first president, was in New York City. It was then moved to Philadelphia on a temporary, 10-year basis in 1791. However, a joint donation of 100 sq miles (258 sq km) of farm- and marsh-land from the neighboring states of Maryland and Virginia inspired the creation of the country's capital city, which lies along the Potomac River.

The establishment of Washington, DC as the capital evolved as a compromise between Alexander Hamilton and the northern states, who wanted the new federal government to cover the debts of the Revolutionary War; and Virginian-born Thomas Jefferson (who was president from 1801–09) and the southern states, who wanted the capital to be in a location that would be friendly to slave-holding agricultural interests.

The design for the new city was the work of Pierre Charles L'Enfant, a Frenchman who served in the Continental Army and was a captain with the US Engineers. L'Enfant envi-

sioned a grid pattern that included broad boulevards and a series of squares and circles where monuments could be placed. Actual development of the city began in 1801. Unfortunately, the first-built capital was captured and burned in 1814 by invading British forces, but the city was quickly rebuilt.

Today, Washington communicates a feeling of the 19th-century South, with landmarks and historic monuments that offer a rich blend of the nation's history. Even before the outcome of the Civil War was decided, former and newly-freed slaves began settling in the area, providing an important historical link for African Americans. ❏

LEFT: Sixth Street Wharf, Washington, in 1863.
RIGHT: the celebrated memorial in Washington DC to Kentucky-born Abraham Lincoln, president at the start of the Civil War, nears completion.

The Seeds of Discontent

No region of the United States is identified more strongly with slavery than the South. Slavery began in the colonies in 1619 when a small group of enslaved Africans was delivered to Jamestown, Virginia, although it was the northern colony of Massachusetts that was the first to legalize the practise, in 1641. Between 1619 and the mid-19th century, it is estimated that some 15 million slaves were brought to the Americas.

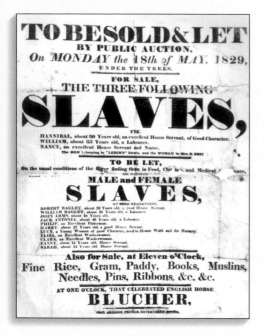

The slavery issue was a major topic in Philadelphia at the Constitutional Convention of 1787. It was enveloped in a divisive debate among representatives from North and South over how slaves should be counted for taxation purposes and representation in the Lower House of Congress. The ultimate compromise was that representation would be based on white inhabitants and three-fifths of the euphemistically-named "other people."

Many of the founding fathers of the nation owned slaves. Generations of Americans, to this day, claim to be descendants of Thomas Jefferson through his relationship with a slave, Sally Hemmings. Jefferson, however, was also vehemently opposed to slavery, and introduced a bill to end the practice. George Washington owned slaves while he was a British citizen, although he began freeing them once the colonies had separated from the mother country. Other founding fathers, such as John Adams, were outspoken critics of slavery.

Reform and opposition

By the end of the 18th century, reforms aimed at ending slavery – most notably the Abolitionist Movement – began in earnest. At that time, Philadelphia was an important abolitionist center. One effort was the Underground Railroad, a secret network of free blacks and whites, and its Philadelphia link featured a group of local Quakers. One of the most daring of its activists was Harriet Tubman, born a slave in Maryland, who had escaped to the North. She risked her life 19 times to cross the Mason-Dixon Line and lead slaves out of the South. Ironically, the entire effort only freed about 1,000 people a year. Other, more visible and more charismatic leaders, included the great black orators Frederick Douglass and William Lloyd Garrison.

Not everyone agreed with moves to abolish slavery. A huge part of the South's socio-economic system was based on enslaved men and women working in the plantations and the cotton fields, staffing the houses, and serving as concubines. It has been estimated that a slave with a strong back was worth about $500 in the early 1800s, rising to around $1,800 by the late 1850s.

John Calhoun, a South Carolina senator who served as the nation's seventh vice-president from 1825–32 under John Quincy Adams and Andrew Jackson, was among the early leaders in the pro-slavery movement. On Capitol Hill he vociferously defended the rights of the "Old South" and spearheaded numerous legislative efforts to preserve and allow slavery in new territories. After a fallout with Jackson, Calhoun returned to the Senate and continued to battle against anti-slavery efforts until his final appearance on the Senate floor, about three weeks before his death in March 1850.

Differences between North and South over slavery even had a theoretical dividing line. The Mason-Dixon Line, originally drawn up in 1767 to settle a land dispute between Maryland and Pennsylvania *(see page 135)*, came to symbolize the line of demarcation between slave and free states some 50 years later with the passage of the Missouri Compromise of 1820.

As America expanded west, slavery remained a background issue until 1854, when Stephen A. Douglas sponsored the Kansas-Nebraska Act. In part, the act allowed settlers in new territories to decide whether or not to own slaves, something Douglas called "popular sovereignty." It started the United States down the slippery slope toward Civil War. Many familiar names supported slavery, including Robert Barnwell Rhett of South Carolina, William Loundes Yancey of Alabama and Robert Augustus Toombs of Georgia. And there were those opposed, like Connecticut abolitionists Henry Ward Beecher, brother of author Harriet Beecher Stowe, who wrote *Uncle Tom's Cabin*, and the violent anti-slave crusader John Brown, who was convicted and hanged for leading a raid on a federal arsenal at Harper's Ferry, Virginia, in a bid to arm slaves. The

Reconstruction, the 10-year effort after the Civil War to rebuild the South, did not mean that all was harmonious. The war may have ended and slavery abolished, but the "Jim Crow" movement to seg-regate blacks from whites also began at that time. Jim Crow was a popular term of the day, taken from a song written by a black minstrel. During these years, many former slaves, unable to deal with the problems that came with freedom, returned to their former masters.

Despite these rough beginnings, momentum was building toward another kind of war – the battle for Civil Rights. This movement crystallized about a century later, in the 1960s, under the charismatic

officer leading the federal troops that captured Brown was Robert E. Lee.

As he accepted his nomination for president, Abraham Lincoln said it would be impossible for the country to survive if it were half enslaved and half free. He declared freedom for slaves in the South in his Emancipation Proclamation, delivered on New Year's Day 1863. Lincoln was assassi-nated in April 1864, so he never lived to see pas-sage of the 13th amendment banning slavery, in December 1865.

leadership of Dr Martin Luther King, Jr, who was assassinated for his beliefs. Today, he is recog-nized as a hero for his efforts to propel the battle for equal rights for all American citizens.

However, despite a greater public awareness and a variety of laws designed to deal with it, from the Civil Rights Act of 1964 to Affirmative Action, racism remains a problem in the 21st century. The Ku Klux Klan, a white supremacist organization, continues to hold rallies. White supremacists still promote the separation of races, and there are constant challenges to the principles of Affirma-tive Action, which was designed to end discrimi-nation based on race, color, gender, or national origin. There is still a long way to go. ❑

LEFT: notice for a slave auction, 1829.
ABOVE: Martin Luther King delivers his historical speech on the steps of the Lincoln Memorial in 1963.

SOUTHERN AND EASTERN COASTAL PORTS

Map on page 146

From sultry Savannah afternoons and Charleston's jazz age to the monuments of Washington and Philadelphia, the ports of the south and east coasts offer a wealth of things to enjoy

A cruise up or down the southern half of the East Coast is rich in history and atmosphere. Itineraries usually start or end in major port cities such as Philadelphia and Charleston, and trips generally last about a week. The peak seasons are spring and fall, as temperatures and humidity soar high enough in summer to make touring less than ideal. Most of the major cruise lines now offer southern coastal itineraries. Some of them emphasize the South's long and varied role in the nation's evolution; others simply offer an enjoyable look at some of the most interesting and significant places in one of the country's most distinct regions.

Exploring Savannah, Georgia

Savannah ❶ was established by James Oglethorpe, an English general who arrived in the colonies in November 1732. After gaining the trust of local Native American leaders, Oglethorpe began designing the plans for the city, based around a series of central squares, rimmed by public buildings, churches, and private homes. Oglethorpe's vision helped make Savannah one of the country's first planned cities and, over the centuries, sultry Savannah has evolved into one of the most elegant cities as well.

Begin your exploration at the Savannah visitor information center on Martin Luther King Jr Boulevard, and then walk through the city's historic section, an area bordered by Montgomery, Bryan, Gordon, and East Broad streets. Monterey Square on Bull and West Gordon streets is the site of Mercer House, which played an important role in the memoir-cum-murder-mystery *Midnight in the Garden of Good and Evil*, which was filmed here. Down West Gordon Street at Albercorn, is Calhoun Square, named for South Carolina Congressman John Calhoun, a combative defender of the Old South. At 329 Albercorn Street is the home of Juliette Gordon Low, who founded the Girl Scouts of America here in 1912. Walk up Bull Street past Madison Square and you'll come to Chippewa Square, which has a statue of General Oglethorpe. Lafayette Square at West Charlton and Albercorn was named for the Marquis de Lafayette, a key French ally during the Revolutionary War. And Pulaski Square, between West Harris and West Charlton streets, was named for Polish patriot Casimir Pulaski, who died during the siege of Savannah in October 1779 while fighting the British.

Savannah's waterfront area is where visitors can find some of the city's best restaurants, bars, and

PRECEDING PAGES: Swann Fountain in Logan Square, Philadelphia. **LEFT:** triplets at the US Capitol Building, Washington DC. **BELOW:** a Midshipman's cap.

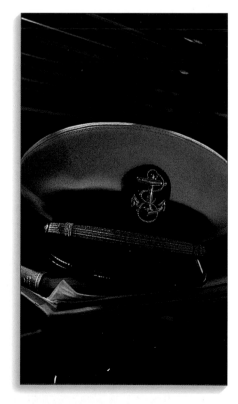

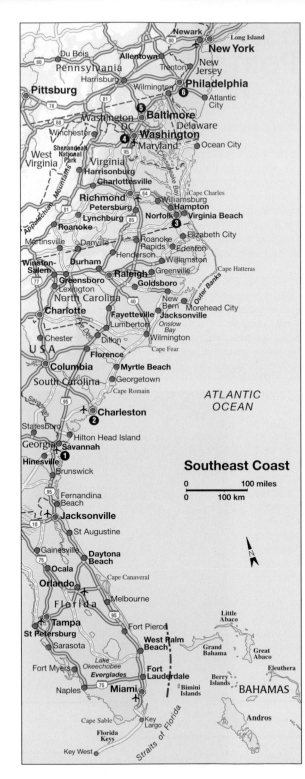

Southeast Coast

0   100 miles
0   100 km

shopping. It is also where the **Waving Girl statue** is located. This honors Florence Martus, a local girl who lived with her brother in a lighthouse at the entrance to Savannah Harbor. Legend has it that she spent years waving at ships while waiting for a sailor with whom she had fallen love but who never returned from a voyage. Another local legend claims Savannah is one of the most haunted cities in the USA. There are a number of books and tours that describe the other-worldly events that earned it this reputation, including one starting from the Wright Square Tourist Depot at the corner of Bull and York streets.

Charleston, South Carolina

Victim of wars, fires, and hurricanes through the centuries, **Charleston ❷**, at the junction of the Ashley and Cooper rivers, has had a tempestuous past. The city, whose history dates back to the late 1600s, was also home to four of the signatories of the US Constitution, which helped bind the 13 original colonies into a new nation. Charleston also played a major role in the Civil War, which divided the young country less than a century later. Today's Charleston presents a more peaceful face, and the flavor of its heritage can be gleaned from its people, its plantations and gardens, and the differing architectural styles of its buildings.

Originally known as Charles Towne, the city was first located farther up the Ashley River. The residents eventually moved closer to the tip of the peninsula where the Ashley and Cooper rivers meet to form Charleston Harbor. The city quickly became an important center of commerce and agriculture, and the many plantations in the area helped make it one of the wealthiest cities in the world. During the Revolutionary War, the British occupied Charleston for two years, from 1780–82. The British presence led to an underground resistance movement, spearheaded by Francis Marion, known as the Swamp Fox. Some 80 years later, shortly after Abraham Lincoln's inauguration, South Carolina was the first state to secede from the Union.

One of the best ways to experience Charleston, and its various historic periods, is to take a walking tour of downtown. The sites are divided into categories, including The Patriots of Charleston, Slavery and Freedom, the Historic Homes Walk, and Wicked Charleston, which offers a view of the city's red-light district, from the French Quarter of the 18th century to Dutch Town of the following century. While the tours your cruise ship offers will include some of the highlights, it may make sense to strike out on your own and take one of the locally advertised tours if you want to spend more time finding out about this city's history.

A good start would be a visit to the **Charleston Museum** (open daily) at 360 Meeting Street. Founded in 1773, the museum's exhibits focus on early Native Americans, the contributions of African-Americans, the plantation system, and the Civil War. Try to leave time to visit the waterfront area known as **Aquarium Wharf**, on the corner of Calhoun and Concord is the state's most visited attraction, the **South Carolina Aquarium** (open daily). Also at Charleston Harbor is the **Fort Sumter Visitor Center** , from here boat trips depart to **Fort Sumter**, which played a prominent role in a major battle of the civil war. The **Citadel Museum** (open daily), near Hampton Park, features military exhibits and artifacts. The **Gibbes Museum of Art** (closed Sun am) at 135 Meeting Street, showcases the city's premier collection of the arts.

The dance that took the name of Charleston, 1926.

For visits to some of the city's historic homes you can buy a Charleston Heritage Passport, which grants admission to six of the city's historic and cultural antebellum landmarks. Highlights include the **Aiken-Rhett House**, the **Nathaniel Russell House** (closed Sun am), and the **Edmonston-Alston House** (closed Sun–Mon am). Across from the Charleston Museum on Meeting Street stands the **Joseph Manigault House** (closed Sun am), once the home of a

BELOW: weavers making baskets from sweetgrass.

Maps:
Area 146
Town 148

TIP

For full details of **opening hours** and contact information for the sites and museums mentioned in this chapter, see Travel Tips page 334.

RIGHT: a schooner sails at sunset.

wealthy rice plantation owner. The **Heyward-Washington House** was home to Thomas Heyward Jr, a signatory of the Declaration of Independence, and it is located in the neighborhood that was used by DuBose Heyward as the setting for his 1925 novel, *Porgy and Bess*, which George Gershwin turned into a folk opera almost a decade later. The **Slave Mart Museum** (closed Sun am) at 6 Chalmers Street presents the African-American experience in a building once used for slave auctions, where the last bidding took place in 1863. At Charleston's **City Market**, African-Americans hand-weave sweetgrass baskets, one of the oldest forms of handicraft brought to Charleston by the enslaved Africans.

Norfolk, Virginia

One of the oldest US cities, **Norfolk** offers visitors a view of the country's naval history. Norfolk harbor is located at the meeting point of Chesapeake Bay and the Atlantic Ocean, about 190 miles (305 km) south of Washington, DC, and has been a key port city since colonial times. It played a major role in the Civil War, and as home port to the Atlantic Fleet at Naval Station Norfolk, is considered the world's largest naval facility. Norfolk's origins can be traced back to 1607, when three ships full of English settlers landed at the mouth of Chesapeake Bay.

Walk the **Cannonball Trail** to gain a glimpse of the city's rich history. It starts at the Freemason Street Reception Center on East Freemason Street, and winds through the city, passing some 40 objects of historic interest, including the towering Martin Luther King Monument at Church Street and Brambleton Avenue.

Norfolk is easy to negotiate on land or water, on foot or by vehicle; it has free transportation aboard electric transit buses. Passengers disembark near the

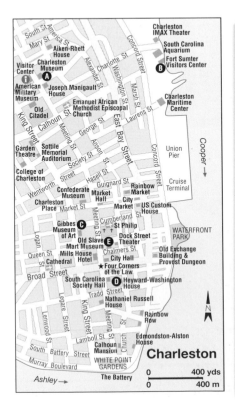

Nauticus National Maritime Center and the Hampton Roads Naval Museum, home to the USS *Wisconsin*. Also close by is the **Tugboat Museum** (open daily), and after a short walk south down South Street you reach **Town Point Park** and the **Armed Forces Memorial**.

Historic **Fort Norfolk**, built under orders from President Washington in 1794, is best known for its role in protecting the city during the War of 1812 and is a short trip north from the pier up South Street.

A relatively new addition to Norfolk's historic attractions is the **General Douglas MacArthur Memorial**. It spans four buildings in the heart of downtown, featuring a museum and special galleries. Nearby is St Paul's Episcopal Church at Market Street and St Paul's Boulevard, the lone survivor of the British destruction of Norfolk on New Year's Day 1776. The **Hunter House Victorian Museum** at 240 W. Freemason Street offers insight into 1890s Norfolk.

While much of the city's high-profile arts institutions are in the heart of town – there's opera, ballet and symphony concerts – there are three distinct, slightly out-of-the-way experiences that merit a detour. The **Chrysler Museum of Art** (closed Mon–Tues and Sun am) is a showplace, featuring permanent exhibitions of American and European masterpieces, along with collections of decorative arts and glass. And don't miss **Historic Ghent**, the neighborhood where the most chic theaters, cafés, and stores are clustered. And finally, those interested in antiques and crafts should not bypass Granby Row.

Norfolk has the distinction of being close to Williamsburg and Jamestown, two of the most important historic sites related to the founding of the United States of America. A worthwhile side trip is a visit to **Historic Colonial Williamsburg**, a living history museum that offers a glimpse of life in the 18th century via more

Map on page 146

BELOW: a carriage ride back in time to historic Williamsburg.

than 500 buildings, homes, workshops, and taverns. The **Jamestown Settlement** and **Yorktown Victory Center** also showcase a living history experience – along with galleries and exhibits – that, in this case, feature life from the first permanent English settlement to the post Revolutionary War victory era.

Washington, DC

The familiar landmarks of **Washington, DC ❹** make it tempting to prolong a visit beyond the time ships spend here when using it as a port of call. From the White House to the Capitol Building, the Washington Monument, the Lincoln Memorial, and the variety of military memorials, to some of the greatest museums in the world – including the Smithsonian Institution – there's enough to see on a trip to Washington to turn it into a case of sensory overload.

The nation's capital, named after the first president, George Washington, was founded in 1791. It's also known as the District of Columbia – in honor of Christopher Columbus – and blends a rich historical past with the pace of a vibrant, modern city. It is very easy to get around Washington, especially as the subway system, the Metro, makes frequent stops near many attractions. The city is divided into four quadrants – Northwest, Southwest, Northeast, and Southeast – and the US Capitol building sits on the spot where they all meet. One of the most pleasing aspects of this southern city is that for the most part, admission to its historic sites, museums, and attractions is free.

Head first to the **National Mall**, which stretches from 3rd Street NW and the Capitol to 14th Street. The grounds include most of the city's major historical attractions, including the **Washington Monument ❹** (open daily; free), which towers 550 ft (168 meters) over the mall; the **Lincoln Memorial ❸** (open

A treetop view of the Thomas Jefferson Memorial in Washington, across the tidal basin.

BELOW: the US Capitol Building.

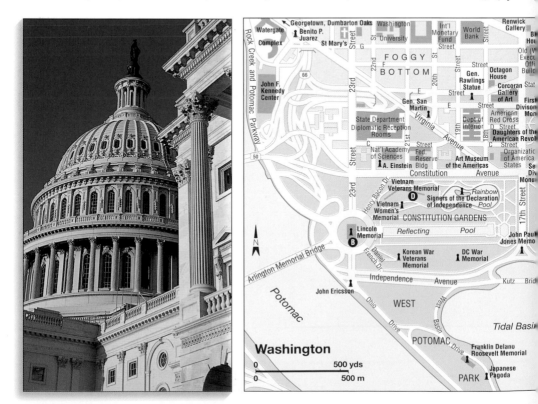

daily; free), honoring America's 16th president, Abraham Lincoln, and the **Thomas Jefferson Memorial Visitor Center** **C** (open daily; free), in honor of the country's third president. Other sites include the **Vietnam Veterans' Memorial** **D** and the **National Gallery of Art** **E** (open daily). Plan to spend some time at the huge **Smithsonian Institution** (open daily), which comprises 14 different museums, ranging from the **National Air and Space Museum** **F** (open daily; free) to the **Hirshhorn Museum** **G** (open daily; free). Guided tours are available at the **US Capitol** **H**.

Maps:
Area 146
City 151

After a long day of sightseeing, visit the chic, lively Georgetown neighborhood. Centered at M Street and Wisconsin Avenue, historic **Georgetown**, which dates back to 1751, is full of stores, pubs, and restaurants. Once sated, take a step back in time by strolling through the leafy side streets, or head over to the nearby C&O Canal, which borders the Potomac River, where there are lovely towpaths for a leisurely walk. Another peaceful option in Georgetown is **Dumbarton Oaks Gardens**, a 10-acre (4-hectare) expanse open to the public.

The rotunda at the Smithsonian National Gallery of Art.

Baltimore, Maryland

The historic city of **Baltimore** **5** is one of the East Coast's most vibrant, offering a combination of classic elegance and quirky character. A city of neighborhoods, each one more distinct in ambiance than the last, it's also the birthplace of *The Star Spangled Banner*, America's national anthem, and was home to writers such as Edgar Allan Poe and H.L. Mencken, and baseball giant Babe Ruth. Much of the action in Baltimore revolves around the city's waterfront, where there are museums, stores, and restaurants.

The area has served as a maritime gateway since the 1600s. Baltimore was

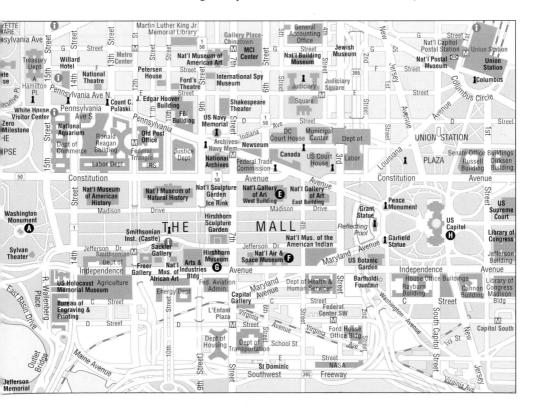

Shooting the breeze at The Wharf Rat, Inner Harbor, Baltimore.

established in 1729 as a port from where farmers transported crops grown in Maryland. The canning industry later became an important part of the local economy. The city was also able to rebuild and thrive following a devastating fire that destroyed much of the business district in 1904. But today's Baltimore really began to shine through the efforts of a municipal, business, and volunteer partnership that began in the 1970s.

Start at the **Harborplace**, a model of urban development when it was launched in the early 1980s. Consisting of 101 stores, 16 restaurants, and 40 foodstands, not to mention street performers and impromptu concerts, this nucleus of the Inner Harbor is also home to some major attractions, such as the **National Aquarium** (open daily), the **Maryland Science Center** (closed Sun pm and Mon), and the restored USS *Constellation*. That vessel, which dates back to 1855 and is docked at Pier One in the heart of the downtown waterfront, was the last all-sail vessel built by the navy. Beyond *Constellation*, which has tours, the Inner Harbor area is home to other maritime-related attractions. There's the **Baltimore Maritime Museum** (open daily), whose centerpiece is the submarine *Torsk*, along with the Coast Guard cutter *Taney* and the **Chesapeake Lightship**. During warm summer months, *Clipper City*, a tall ship, offers day trips.

Adjacent to the Inner Harbor is **Port Discovery**, a huge hands-on activity center and museum geared to families, and the restored **Power Plant**, which now houses everything from the Hard Rock Café to an ESPN Sports Zone bar. For a cultural fix, walk over to the **American Visionary Art Museum** (closed Mon), which celebrates folk art (and has a fabulous restaurant).

One attraction not to be missed is **Fort McHenry** (tel: 410-962 4290 for opening times), 3 miles (5 km) south of the Inner Harbor, which withstood a brutal two-

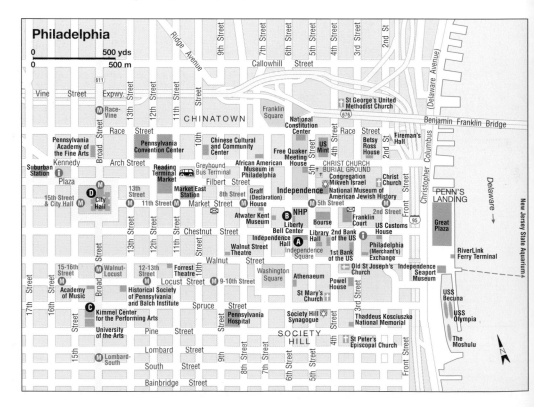

day attack by advancing British forces in September 1814 during the Battle of Baltimore, and inspired Francis Scott Key to write *The Star-Spangled Banner*.

Another lovely neighborhood is **Fell's Point**, the site of the original city. It has historic ambiance, with streets paved in Belgian blocks and 18th- and 19th-century restored row-houses. This waterfront village is home to offbeat pubs like Bertha's, The Cat's Eye, and The Horse You Came In On – classics all. There are also boutique-style stores, selling everything from antiques to fake tattoos.

Just north of the Inner Harbor is the city's most gracious neighborhood. **Mount Vernon** is anchored by its distinguished Washington Monument and residents are proud that it preceded the more famous structure in Washington, DC (it was architect Robert Mills' first effort at an ode to the president). What sets Mount Vernon apart, beyond its beautifully restored townhouses, are its cultural centerpieces, which include the **Walters Art Museum** (closed Mon–Tues), whose collections span medieval to Renaissance and baroque to Asian, and the **Peabody Institute**, one of the nation's foremost music schools.

Baltimoreans are sports fanatics and are proud of **Oriole Park** at Camden Yards, a ballpark built with a nod to the past but with contemporary amenities. Take a two-block side trip to the **Babe Ruth Birthplace** and **Baltimore Orioles Museum** (open daily), at 216 Emory Street. Football fans might also like to visit M&T Bank Stadium, home to the NFL Baltimore Ravens.

Philadelphia, Pennsylvania

As one of the country's first seats of government, **Philadelphia** ⑥ offers visitors the story of the United States' birth. There's Independence Hall, where it all started with the adoption of the Declaration of Independence in 1776, the Liberty

TIP

If you plan to tour Philadelphia's Old Town independently, then a good place to pick up maps and information is the Independence Visitor Center on 6th and Market streets, tel: 215-965 7676.

BELOW: hanging out in Fell's Point, site of the original city of Baltimore.

Map
on page
152

*"Benjamin Franklin"
appears in
18th-century Elfreth's
Alley, number 126
is a museum.*

BELOW:
the Liberty Bell.
RIGHT:
Swann Fountain
and City Hall Tower.

Bell, the National Constitution Center, and Christ Church Burial Ground, where Benjamin Franklin and his wife are buried. Given the city's revolutionary past, there is a true sense of history that literally hangs in the air.

Philadelphia is located at the narrowest point between two rivers, the Delaware and Schuylkill. William Penn chose this as the site of Philadelphia because it offered convenient access via land and water. At the time, the Delaware River was a major component of local commerce. In 18th-century North America, when the roads were unpaved and often so muddy a wagon could be swallowed up to its wheels, transporting goods by water was often a quicker alternative, so the Delaware River could be referred to as the new country's first super-highway.

Today's Philadelphia offers a strong link to its colonial past while also presenting a world-class cultural scene. Much of it is tied together in **Independence National Historic Park** (open daily). Take a ride in a horse-drawn carriage from one of several locations near Independence Hall and get a first-hand view of the historical sites: **Independence Hall Ⓐ**, on Chestnut between 5th and 6th streets, retains a sense that Franklin, Jefferson, and Hancock are still present. The **Liberty Bell Ⓑ**, which was moved in October 2003 to a home closer to Independence Hall, offers a close-up view of a well-known American symbol of freedom. You may also pass by Benjamin Franklin's former home on Market Street.

Cruise lines offer transportation for the short trip from the Philadelphia Cruise Terminal to **Center City**, a 25-block historical area that is ranked among the best areas in the US for walking. The streets are easy to navigate, with north–south ones numbered, and east–west ones named for trees.

A striking cultural attraction is the **Kimmel Center for the Performing Arts Ⓒ** on South Broad Street, home to the Philadelphia Orchestra. The red mahogany of Verizon Hall, the center's main concert hall, is shaped like a cello. **Philadelphia City Hall Ⓓ** (closed Sat–Sun), which has a giant statue of William Penn at its peak, tops the US Capitol Building in Washington, DC, as the nation's largest municipal building in the US.

Philadelphia's neighborhoods

Neighborhood scenes in Philadelphia run the gamut from the quiet elegance of **Rittenhouse Square**, with its variety of restaurants, cafés, and central park area, to **South Street**, where there's an eclectic blend of clubs, restaurants, pizzerias, Italian ice-cream joints, stores, and tattoo parlors. With its 6 acres (2.5 hectares) of green intersected by shaded benches and walkways, Rittenhouse Square is both a geographical and social crossroad that brings together a cross-section of residents. During the May Flower Market, the square is a rainbow-colored sea of petals and pollen. Of course if you prefer a more lively experience you can have fun simply strolling along the main South Street strip, from Front Street to 7th Street.

Then there are the galleries, studios, and stores of Chestnut Hill, North Philly, North East, Old City, University City and South Philly. ❑

THE WEST COAST

From wine country to desert, whale-watching to
walking, cruise lines offer a wide range of West Coast trips

Traditionally, West Coast cruising has been limited to jumping-off points to the Western Caribbean, Hawaii, and Alaska. But there are other, more local options: wine-country cruises are a lovely way of seeing Northern California, and Baja cruises are the best vantage point for whale watching. Because these itineraries may only last for a long weekend, they're a great addition to a longer tour of the West Coast. Travelers in the wine country board a riverboat in San Francisco, cruise out into the bay, then sail around the Napa and Petaluma rivers for three or four nights. Afternoon tours visit wineries, spend time in tasting rooms, and explore the great artwork that collectors have accumulated. Evenings consist of cocktail hours, followed by four-course dinners, and more wine and conversation.

Because of the amount of alcohol involved, this is not a family-oriented vacation. Passenger lists are made up of young urban professionals, empty nesters, and retirees, all with a love of food, wine, and travel – and plenty of disposable income. Most such cruises are on small vessels, from 22-passenger yachts to 100-passenger ships.

Baja cruises, which take marine-life enthusiasts for an up-close look at whales in their natural habitat, are also on small vessels. In the winter months, warm weather draws whales down to Mexico's Sea of Cortéz and California's Baja peninsula. This hilly, cactus-lined desert scenery is the opposite of lush Napa, and these trips attract more active, rugged passengers. Days are filled with kayaking, sailing, hiking, and snorkeling. Passengers can swim with pods of dolphins and watch elephant seals and California sea lions up close. Evenings are filled with *mariachi* bands and margaritas.

These very different itineraries are offered by Cruise West and American Safari Cruises. The latter serves a sophisticated option to equally sophisticated passengers, while the former runs larger boats, at lower rates, and tends to carry slightly older passengers. Read their itineraries carefully before booking: both cruises include all shore excursions in the cost, so there's very little free time to explore; the vineyards on your itineraries may be the only ones you see.

In Baja, there are other options. Lindblad Expeditions runs 14-night cruises, offering a more in-depth look at the region. Larger lines such as Carnival and Royal Caribbean offer Baja as part of California and Mexico itineraries on their 2,000-passenger megaships. It's a totally different experience, with formal nights and plenty of onboard activities that are as much the focus of the cruise as the destination itself. Don't expect to have a similar experience to the one you'll get on a small ship, though – they may sail in the same waters, but they're as different as night and day. ❑

PRECEDING PAGES: a view over San Francisco.
LEFT: the Golden Gate Bridge from Fort Point.

NAPA AND SONOMA

Wine may not be such a rare commodity as the gold that attracted people here in the 19th century, but it's proving to be a valuable crop

Wine may be a way of life in the Napa and Sonoma valleys today, but the original inhabitants utilized this lush region in different ways. Long before the Europeans arrived, Coast Miwok and Wappo Native American tribes lived in the green valleys that lie between Mayacamas Mountains and Vaca

Range, just inland from the Pacific. They hunted in the lush woods, and fished in the Napa and Petaluma rivers and in Lake Berryessa. They shared the land with deer, elk, grizzly bears, and panthers.

Their currency was obsidian, a glass-like, black volcanic rock that was traded and used for tool making. Where we might have spas, the Native Americans built "sweathouses" and dove into the valleys' icy clear streams, including present-day Ritchey Creek and Mill Creek, to cool off. They ate fish and shellfish, as well as game, and they gathered the acorns that fell from the area's many great oak trees, ground them up and baked them into bread.

Religious settlements

The first white settlers arrived in the Sonoma Valley in 1823 from Mexico, when a Spanish priest came to form a mission called New San Francisco, later renamed St Francis of Solano. The San Francisco mission itself had been unsuccessful because of the bay area's damp weather, but the priest was hopeful that the temperate valley would provide a more comfortable home. The mission buildings were constructed out of California redwood, and the Franciscan monks planted their own vineyard with cuttings from home – the first vines ever grown in the valleys. Within a year the redwood buildings burned down, and a new mission was built out of adobe and topped with tiled roofs. It's a signature architectural style that prevails in California even today.

When the Spanish-Mexican government began to administer the mission in 1834, they took control of the day-to-day lives of the Native Americans, and a lot of the protections offered by the church began to fade. In addition, the native population – which had few immunities – lost hundreds of lives to smallpox and other diseases.

The Gold Rush

By the time the United States acquired California in 1848, pioneering North American farmers had already begun arriving in the Napa and Sonoma valleys in droves. They came in search of land to cultivate and on which to build ranches and homes, and a new way of life. In 1849, the quest changed – the California Gold Rush had officially begun, and the Americans who poured into the area had just one thing on their minds: wealth. Miners filled the gold fields, searching for what they were sure was their destiny.

For the majority whose fortunes were not to be made in gold, there was plenty of work in the area's cattle ranches, sawmills, and grist mills. The Napa River sawmill was located near what is now the Krug Winery, and a gristmill stood in present-day Bale Grist Mill State Historic Park – and both were booming during these years.

Wine's beginnings

So how did the local industry change from gold and lumber to wine? In the early 1870s, a San Francisco physician named Charles Hitchcock bought much of what would later become parkland for a country estate. The Hitchcocks and their socialite daughter, Lillie Hitchcock Coit, threw colorful society parties, complete with poker games, and with plenty of bourbon and cigars. These soirées, in addition to a railroad line from the Bay area, helped to elevate the Valley from a home for rough-and-tumble migrant workers to the vacation destination for San Francisco's elite that it remains today.

Another land purchase had an impact, too. The Reverend Theodore Lyman of San Francisco's Trinity Episcopal Church also bought acres of Mill Creek watershed land, and this helped to protect a large portion of Napa from development and preserved the land for later use as vineyards.

Unfortunately, the original grapes the monks had planted were so-called "mission" grapes, which don't produce high-quality table wines. In 1857, Hungarian immigrant and entrepreneur Agoston Haraszthy, now known as the father of the commercial wine business, saw the potential in Napa's Mediterranean-style climate. Haraszthy established the original Buena Vista Winery and began to explore which varieties did best in California. He imported thousands of cuttings and tried out over 300 different varieties, planting some in Sonoma and selling the rest to other Californians for the development of vineyards.

But in the 1890s this fledgling wine business ran into trouble in the form of phylloxera, a small bug that attacks vine roots and feeds off plant juices, and which had been imported accidentally along with some French vines. Eventually, researchers were able to find a rootstock that could withstand the bugs, and by the turn of the 20th century the wineries that European-trained winemakers had developed around Buena Vista had been revived. The next setback was Prohibition. From 1920 to 1933, alcohol consumption was outlawed in the United States, so it became illegal to make wine in California.

Left: bottles and barrels at a winery in Napa Valley.
Right: stained-glass window at the Sebastiani Vineyard, Sonoma.

It wasn't until the mid- to late-1960s that the Napa Valley wine business began to grow once more. It was the renowned 1976 Paris Exposition wine tastings that really put Napa on the map as a wine force and helped to seal its international reputation. It was originally the full-bodied Cabernet Sauvignon that got noticed – these red grapes thrive in the warm sunshine of Napa's eastern hills.

Sonoma

Although Napa has dominated the region in both prestige and number of wineries, Sonoma's wine industry has made increasing

progress since the 1970s and has now built up it's own distinct reputation. Sonoma wineries began by using inexpensive grapes for mass-market "jug" wines, but Sonoma now has a great reputation for its higher quality vintages.

Today winemaking is everything in Napa and Sonoma. Vineyards cover the undulating hills, and just about every other surface. In the fall, during the annual harvest and the crushing that follows, the vines turn from green to golden and scarlet. It's the most popular time of the year to visit, as the summer's heat gives way to pleasantly mild temperatures (in the region of 75–85°F/24–29°C) and the streets and tasting rooms get busy. ❑

WINE COUNTRY CRUISES

Map on page 164

The lush and lovely Napa and Sonoma valleys are America's wine country, and a river cruise to this area can be informative and fun, especially when rounded off with a visit to San Francisco

Napa County is a 30-mile (48-km) thrust of flatland between the pine-forested Mayacamas Mountains and the buff-colored Howell Mountains in Northern California. It lies just northeast of San Francisco, reached on State Highway 29, "The Great Wine Way," and the valley ends in the north at Mount St Helena. Sonoma County lies about one hour's drive from San Francisco on the US 101, the freeway that traverses the north–south length of the county, entering it near the town of Petaluma.

While it is true that a river cruise taking in the smart ports of California's wine country is no less expensive than a driving vacation, the organization, assistance, and access that cruises offer can help you get far more out of your trip. Vintners themselves will often lead wine tours, and crowded tasting rooms can be bypassed for private ones. In exchange, you will give up the opportunity to dine in the region's famous California-cuisine restaurants, play golf, go hot-air ballooning, and seek out those vineyards whose bottles grace your table at home. But, especially for first-time visitors to the region, a wine-country cruise is an opportunity to discover new vintages, and it's a wonderful introduction to Northern California's stunning valleys.

NAPA

Although similar in landscape and scenery to the wine regions of Bordeaux in France and Tuscany in Italy, the Napa Valley is, at the same time, very American. Local people celebrate the industrious spirit that brought this region international acclaim in winemaking, with a pluckiness and entrepreneurial passion that's all their own. You'll notice that they dress casually, and their layers are a practical response to the temperature, which can drop 10–20°F (5.5–11°C) after the sun sets.

The city of **Napa ❶** itself has a population of only 74,100, but the area gets nearly 5 million visitors each year. They tour the wineries – or as many of the 280 that they can fit into a long weekend. This is the world's most densely concentrated winery region, with almost 38,000 acres (15,380 hectares) of vineyards. And while that may sound enormous, once you get off the ship and start touring the area by bus, it will feel just about right. All roads are flanked on both sides, as far as the eye can see, with grapevines, as golden in summer as the ore the old prospectors came here seeking. The fields are studded with clusters of shady oaks, imposing vineyard estate signs, and the occasional winery building.

But when it comes to these buildings, you never know what's just around the bend. While the Mexican

LEFT: Napa country vineyards.
BELOW: the Sattui Winery, Napa Valley.

For grapes to mature on the vine the fruit requires the ideal soil and climate conditions found in California.

hacienda styling of tiled roofs and stucco walls prevails in California, Napa is clearly a place that is interested in individual style. Nowhere is this more obvious than in the architecture. In an homage to French-styled wines, a winery may build its estate to look like a French château from the Loire Valley, while a winery owner of Italian descent may construct buildings reminiscent of Tuscan villas, surrounded by imported cypress trees. It makes for an interesting and varied landscape, and a glimpse into the heart of the vintners' different influences.

Exploring the wineries

However fascinating the architecture, the bulk of any visit to the valley will, of course, be spent in the vineyards and at the wineries. Excursions often include a guided tour of the vines and an informative lecture about the difficulty of cultivating them, before descending into the caves to look at how the wine is stored and barreled. As you walk through the fields, you can eat the grapes straight off the vine and wonder at how something is transformed from ordinary to extraordinary, while you find out about all the work that goes into that process.

Most cruise ship itineraries tend to visit the same vineyards, although some tours focus on the wine, others on the scenery. One of the more popular wineries to visit is **Schramsberg Vineyards ❷** (Schramsberg Road; open daily 10am–4pm; tel: 707-942 2414; www.schramsberg.com). Located on a Napa County hillside just south of the town of Calistoga, Schramsberg sits on a beautifully manicured estate, complete with pools, gardens, and a somewhat unexpected Victorian-style house.

Here, the stunning grounds are as much a draw as the sparkling wines themselves. Visitors can explore the caves and thousands of yards of 19th-century

BELOW:
Hop Kiln Winery.

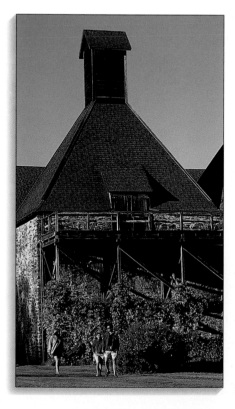

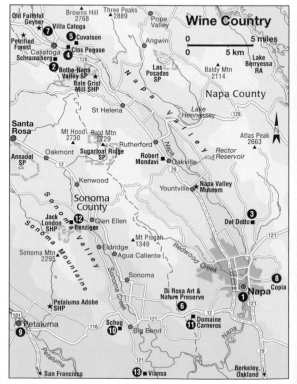

tunnels, which were originally dug by Chinese laborers. Today, you'll find that they're filled with fermenting California champagne – and you will get to taste some before you leave.

Del Dotto Vineyards (1055 Atlas Peak Road; open daily 11am–5pm; tel: 707-256 3332; www.deldottovineyards.com) near St Helena is another popular stop on wine tours. The vineyards here are known for their full-bodied reds, such as Cabernet Sauvignon, Cabernet Franc, Merlot, and Sangiovese, and this visit, too, is as much about the site as it is about the wine itself. The vineyard offers guided tours of the hand-dug caves as well as visits to the 1884 distillery.

Perhaps the highlight of a wine touring cruise day is a private lunch with wine pairings in the caves – that is, matching the appropriate wine to the food. Different lines pick different wineries for this, but Clos Pegase and Cuvaison are two popular choices. **Clos Pegase** ❹ has lovely stone caves (1060 Dunaweal Lane; visitor center open 10.30am–5pm daily; free guided tours at 11am and 2pm; tel: 707-942 4281; www.clospegase.com). **Cuvaison** ❺ (4550 Silverado Trail; open daily 10am–5pm; tel: 707-942 2468; www.cuvaison.com) is famous for its Cabernet and Merlot.

The art of collecting

In Napa, art comes second only to wine, and you shouldn't leave without visiting some of the area's amazing private collections. It's clear evidence that the wine business has been thriving for quite some time here, and plenty of successful artists and art collectors have been inspired enough to make glittering Napa their home.

Some cruises make a point of highlighting the area's obsession with art. The **Di Rosa Art and Nature Preserve** ❻ (5200 Carneros Highway; tel: 707-

Visitors with time to explore the Wine Country can take a trip to Hop Kiln Winery in Sonoma County, northwest of Petaluma. The working winery is also an historic landmark. The tasting room is open daily 10am–5pm, tel: 707-433 6491.

BELOW: cycling through vineyards near Calistoga, Napa Valley.

The valley's wine stores sell wines from the region's vineyards.

226-5991; www.dirosapreserve.org), housing one of the largest regional art collections in the country, with 2,000 works by over 700 artists, is a stop on some itineraries. Vineyards surround the property and the site's 250 acres (100 hectares) of land include a lake, and lawns planted with 150-year-old olive trees. The preserve can only be visited as part of a tour, unless you make special reservations in advance.

You can also take an exclusive art tour of Venetian-style **Villa Catoga** ❼ (3061 Myrtledale Road; private tours only; tel: 707-942 3900; www.catoga.com), muralist Carlo Marchiori's Calistoga estate. Marchiori, born in Rossano, near Venice in 1937, created murals for various hotels and casinos. It's an over-the-top fantasy, with Greco-Roman ruins, Thai stupas, and elaborate fountains outside and plenty of *trompe l'oeil* murals inside.

Many lines are now adding tours of **Copia** ❽ (500 First Street; tel: 707-259 1600; www.copia.org), the American Center for Wine, Food, and Art, to their itineraries. Opened in 2001, this $80-million cultural center is a celebration of Napa's main enthusiasms. If your cruise schedule doesn't include Copia, try to get there in your free time if you can – and check their website for special events, too, as they often engage celebrity chefs for lectures and book signings.

SONOMA

Ranking second only to Napa County in the United States for the number of wineries, Sonoma County has more than 175 wineries. Ships cruise up the Petaluma River toward the drawbridge and dock in Sonoma's Victorian waterfront town, **Petaluma** ❾. This lovely little town has a pedestrian district

BELOW: at the Wine exchange, Sonoma.

WINE TASTINGS

Many cruise itineraries include the following three types of tastings (and pay for the cover charges) so that you will get to sniff, swirl, and sip appreciatively.

● **Wine Bar Tastings**. This is the most common type, and, even for novices, it is very easy to follow. When you walk up to the bar you will see a list of wines you can sample. Some wineries include more expensive "library" and "reserve" wines, and many allow you to put the fee toward your subsequent purchase.

● **Sit Down Tastings**. Instead of being jostled at the bar, you'll sit in an elegant, private room – often with wood-paneling and a cozy fireplace, and learn in more detail the properties of the vintage as the corks are extracted and the wines are poured for you. A similar option is the Walking Tasting, in which a guide leads you around the property, holding sit-down tastings at intervals on different parts of the site.

● **Barrel Tasting**. This most educational tasting is held in a cool, stone underground cellar. A guide places a siphon into a hole in the barrel and extracts wine to taste. Because this type of tasting allows visitors to sample wine that has not completed the aging process, it is often held in conjunction with a tasting from bottles, too.

with antiques and specialty stores, bars, and restaurants along what was once called Main Street.

With its ornate gingerbread-trimmed houses, iron-grilled storefront businesses, and manicured gardens, it's not surprising that Petaluma is on the National Register of Historic Places. The town is such a period piece that it's been used as a backdrop in movies such as *American Graffiti* and *Peggy Sue Got Married*, to depict unspoiled America in the 1950s.

Obviously, none of the vineyards are in town, so the day is spent touring the valley's wineries in the green and golden hills before returning to Petaluma in the early evening. Since a lengthy dinner will be served on the cruise ship or yacht and represents a large part of the evening's entertainment, most passengers take little more than a quick look around town before walking up the gangway in time for cocktails and socializing. After a long day spent sipping and spitting, it's surprising that the cruise ship passengers are able to look at wine again, much less consume more alcohol at dinner, and yet wine-lovers who book these intensive cruises are truly committed, and they always seem to manage.

More wineries

The days you spend docked on Sonoma's Petaluma River are not so dissimilar from the days on the Napa River, except that the wine appreciation is mixed more with shopping than with museums and galleries. And, as in Napa, some of the vineyards cater to connoisseurs with expensive, high-quality vintages, while others specialize in the most standard of table wines.

Many winery visits include a private tour and tasting at the 50-acre (20-hectare)

Map on page 164

The tasting room at the family-run Chateau Potelle Winery, in the Napa Valley, is open daily 11am–6pm from April, tel: 707-255 9440.

BELOW: Potelle Vineyards, Napa Valley.

Passengers can drink and ride on the Napa Valley Wine Train.

Schug Carneros Estate ⑩ (602 Bonneau Road; tasting room open daily 10am–5pm; tel: 800-966 9365; www. schugwinery.com). Vineyards planted with Pinot Noir and Chardonnay grapes surround this winery. The resulting wine is so rich and complex, and ultimately French in character, that as much as one-third of the product is exported to Europe.

You can sip sparkling wines on the lovely stone terrace of a very regal-looking chateau at Tattinger's swanky **Domaine Carneros** ⑪ (1240 Duhig Road; tours and a glass of wine daily 10.15am–4pm; tel: 707-257 0101; www. domaine.com). It's worth trying a glass of their Famous Gate Pinot Noir, which is available only at the winery.

The focus at Glen Ellen's **Benziger Family Vineyards** ⑫ (1883 London Ranch Road; open daily 10am–4.30pm; free tastings; tel: 707-935 3000; www. benziger.com), however, is on the ideal soil and climate of Sonoma Mountain for cultivating grapes, rather than the glamour of a well-bottled champagne. Here, you'll learn how nature and science work together, and tour the crushing and fermentation areas. The best part is a vineyard tour by a tractor-pulled tram. Benziger puts out excellent Cabernet as well as Fumé Blanc and Semillon.

Again, you may be able to lunch at a vineyard. One vineyard that features on many cruise ship itineraries is **Viansa Winery** ⑬ (25200 Arnold Drive; open daily 10am–5pm; free tastings; tel: 707-935 4700; www.viansa.com). This premium grower specializes in rare Italian varieties, and has built a Tuscan-style villa, planted olive trees, and painted frescoes to make the vines feel at home. Here, you can enjoy Italian food and wine pairings that have been designed to highlight the wines at their best. You'll be able to take home practical advice on

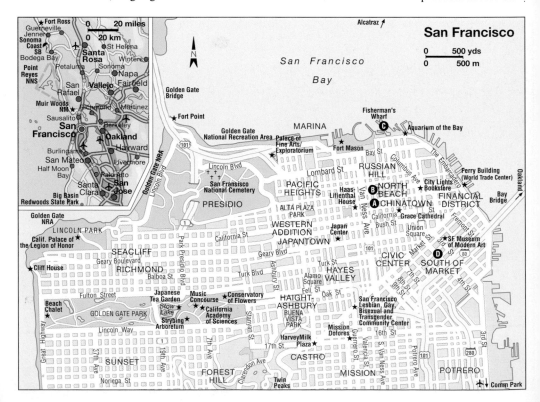

matching antipasti, salads, roast meat, and pastas with Pinot Grigio, Arneis, and Sangiovese at your own table.

Maps:
Area 164
City 168

SAN FRANCISCO

Passengers on wine country cruises sail through the San Francisco Bay on their way to and from the wine valleys, past the Bay Bridge, Alcatraz, and Fisherman's Wharf. On the way out to the valleys, you may sip a glass of champagne on deck while you watch the sun set; on the way back, you will probably sleep until you arrive at the city's port for disembarkation. If you're interested in sending wine home, many of the lines can arrange for shipping from the dock – even if your state has complicated shipping laws *(see box below for more details).* However, at around $50 a case, the expense may mean it is hardly worthwhile.

From the harbor, San Francisco International Airport is approximately 45 minutes away, but instead of getting straight on a plane, many cruise line passengers choose a "cruise and stay" option, giving them plenty of time to see the sights and absorb the atmosphere of this fascinating West Coast hub before moving on. And it would be a great shame not to, for San Francisco is unmissable, with a personality that's both uniquely Californian and completely urban and international.

Every visitor takes a different memory away from San Francisco, whether it is the street dropping away toward the whitecapped bay, the mist drifting through the Golden Gate Bridge, blurring the sparkling lights, the fun of a cable-car ride, gliding up and down the city hills, or a visit to colourful China-town. Spending a few days here before or after your cruise will add immeasurably to the whole experience.

If you are staying on or have more time to explore the Wine Country you can visit the Iron Horse Ranch and Vineyards, northwest of Petaluma in Sebastopol. Tours by appointment Mon–Fri, tel: 707-887 1507.

BELOW: carrying out a visual check on the wine at Iron Horse Vineyard.

A WINE EDUCATION

Exclusive tours and visits to the caves don't protect cruisers from the wine shipping laws in the States. It's easy to buy a bottle or two and pack them in your suitcase, along with information about vintages you'd like to buy once you return home, but for those who hope to buy case upon case, the story is a little more complicated. First of all, the individual laws of the state you're shipping to trap the wineries. Some don't allow individuals to ship in wine at all, others limit the number of bottles. If you're from the USA, be sure to ask lots of questions about your home state's policies; if you're from elsewhere, check your country's customs policy before you leave home.

When you find a wine you like, ask lots of questions about its availability. Some are shipped to wine stores in every city of the world, others (which are only bottled in small amounts) must be purchased at the vineyard. If you find one you like but may never see again, ask the vintner what the tastes and flavors are so you'll be able to ask sommeliers for similar vintages. Wine enthusiasts describe wines using words such as grass and smoke. For example, if a limited-production rich, full-bodied Chardonnay has been described as oaky, buttery, and butterscotchy, then you know that those are flavors you like in a wine.

Map on page 168

Chinatown Ⓐ, not far from central Union Square, is exciting. The biggest outside Asia, its streets are narrow, crowded, and alive with color and movement. Mysterious alleys abound, packed with tiny, cluttered herb stores and hole-in-the-wall stores, where you can buy anything from cheap trinkets to exquisite screens and hand-carved furniture costing thousands of dollars. Dozens of Chinese restaurants can be found, from the fancy and the famous to any number of obscure eateries where you can eat well and inexpensively, especially if you go for *dim sum*, delicious pastries filled with meat, chicken, shrimp, or vegetables.

Chinatown ends where **North Beach Ⓑ** begins. The once tawdry strip has been gentrified and while a few seedy clubs still beckon, critically acclaimed restaurants, nightclubs, and jazzy swing bars entice a different crowd altogether. This area has always been congenial to writers and artists, although it has retained the flavor of an old-fashioned Italian neighborhood. A favorite haunt of writers is the **City Lights** bookstore on Columbus Avenue, launched in 1953 by the poet Lawrence Ferlinghetti, one of the literary luminaries of the 1950s Beat era.

Straight up Columbus Avenue is another of the city's premier attractions, **Fisherman's Wharf Ⓒ**, with its unruly but entertaining resident sea lions. Pier 45 remains the closest to a working site the wharf can offer. Here, fishermen depart each day before dawn and return with sand dabs, scallops, Dungeness crabs, and sea bass. The catch they bring back often determines the "special of the day" at the restaurants clustered around the wharf.

BELOW:
Fisherman's Wharf.
RIGHT: the Palace of Fine Arts by the waterfront.

On the piers, you'll also find Ripley's, Believe It or Not! (tel: 415-771 6188; Entrance fee), and its neighbors the Wax Museum (tel: 800-439 4305; fee) and the Guinness Book of World Records Museum. From the wharf you can take trips around the bay, including one to **Alcatraz** (tel: 415-773 1188). Alcatraz is slowly falling apart. Its steel bars are being eaten away by salt air and its pastel buildings are giving way to the ravages of time. Just over a mile offshore from San Francisco, the island is windswept and scoured by swift tides. After being garrisoned with soldiers in the 1850s, it became a prison that later housed such hardened criminals as Mafia leader Al Capone. The prison was finally closed in 1963.

Two blocks inland from the wharf's Hyde Street Pier is the cable-car turnaround, where the Powell-Hyde car begins its ascent into the wealthy neighborhood of Russian Hill – one of the best ways to see the hill, whose high-rise apartments and mansions have cashed in on the spectacular vistas. The cable cars continue up to Nob Hill, celebrated mostly for the size and elegance of the mansions that encircle the neo-Gothic splendor known as **Grace Cathedral**, said to be a replica of Notre Dame in Paris.

"South of Market," or **SoMa Ⓓ**, as it is known, is today one of the hottest locations in the city, a focal point for art galleries and cafés, nightclubs, and local theaters. The **San Francisco Museum of Modern Art** (tel: 415-357 4000; closed Wed; fee), is a wonderful building displaying works by American and European artists, such as Max Ernst, Picasso, Paul Klee, and the Californian painter Richard Diebenkorn. All in all, there's so much to see and do in San Francisco that you'll probably want to come back for more. ❏

CRUISING THE BAJA PENINSULA

Cave paintings and Spanish mission houses, gray whales and nesting sea turtles are among the delights of a Baja cruise

The Baja California Peninsula is an unusual cruise destination, as its desert shores contain few towns or significant sights. Baja's best attractions lie in the water, in the coves, bays and islands of the Pacific Ocean and the Sea of Cortéz.

Choosing a cruise line

Once you've decided you would like to cruise the Baja Peninsula, you need to choose a cruise line, as they all have something different to offer. Several lines include Los Cabos, a booming resort region at Baja's southernmost tip, as part of their Mexican Riviera itineraries. Most continue on to Mazatlán, Puerto Vallarta, and other ports on mainland Mexico's Pacific Coast. The Sea of Cortéz, also called the Gulf of California, is the favored destination of American Safari Cruises, Lindblad Expeditions, Clipper Cruises, and Cruise West. Their itineraries involve kayaking, snorkeling, bird watching, and other nature-oriented activities, combined with land tours in Los Cabos, La Paz, and Loreto. Baja Expeditions, one of the first companies to offer tours in the area, places the emphasis on intense activity, with scuba diving, kayaking, and nature cruises. Holland America combines more mainstream cruising with stops at several Baja towns.

Some cruise lines include Pacific coast whale-watching excursions in their itineraries; others offer extensions to the breathtaking Copper Canyon on mainland Mexico. Most of the cruises are scheduled in winter, from October to April, to coincide with the migration patterns of birds and whales. The timing guarantees unparalleled wildlife experiences.

Marine life

Binoculars and bathing suits are the preferred accoutrements for passengers on Sea of Cortéz voyages. More than half a dozen species of whales frequent the lagoons and bays along Baja's shores. Most famous are the gray whales, which migrate each winter to Pacific Coast lagoons *(see box, page 174)*. At least six species of whales, including the grays, also frequent the Sea of Cortéz, one of the most biologically diverse bodies of water in the world.

Manta rays leap and splash their wings on the sea's shimmering surface; dolphins dance beside cruise ships and *pangas*, the small skiffs preferred by local fishermen; sea lions grumble from their slippery perches along rocky islands; the aptly named magnificent frigate birds soar in thermal currents in the clear blue sky. Most trips include several stops at deserted islands and plenty of wet landings on pristine beaches, but Baja's incredible topography is not ignored.

The lay of the land

The 860-mile (1,380-km) long peninsula appears brown and barren on first glance. The German Jesuit, Father Johann Jakob Baegert,

LEFT: a pelican flies over the Gulf of California.
RIGHT: a fisherman lands a dorado in Cabo Pumo, Baja, Mexico.

in an account of the topography of the region and the Native American customs and language, published in 1773, described it as "nothing but a pile of stones full of thorns… sticking up between two oceans." But Baegert is known for having a generally poor impression of the land where he had come to establish a mission.

Despite this early pessimistic view, Baja's astonishing variety of plants, animals, and geological formations have since inspired scientists and naturalists, who devote their lives to studying what the writer and environmentalist Joseph Wood Krutch (1893–1970) later called "The Forgotten Peninsula."

A ridge of mountain ranges runs the length of the skinny, finger-shaped peninsula, dividing the two coasts. Over half of Baja's landmass is desert, although grapes flourish in the wine region of northern Baja and fruit orchards cover hillsides in the south. Stalwart cardón cacti rise as high as 60 ft (18 meters) above prickly pear, and cholla cacti on the rocky ground. Date and coconut palms abound, adding a tropical air.

Cave art

Most cruise ships confine their wanderings to the southern portion of the sea between Loreto, once the capital of Baja Sur, and La Paz, the

AMONG THE GREAT GRAY WHALES

Gray whales migrate some 12,000 miles (19,310 km) from the Bering Sea to Baja's Pacific coast lagoons and bays every winter to give birth to their one-ton calves. Watching these mothers and babies at play at Magdalena Bay in the remote southern Pacific is one of Baja's greatest experiences.

A few cruise lines include the gray whales in their itineraries from December to March. Passengers on American Safari cruises start in La Paz and travel by land to the Pacific Coast, then return to La Paz to board their ships. Lindblad and Baja Expedition passengers travel by land from La Paz, board their ships at Magdalena Bay and spend several days with the whales before sailing south around

the tip of Baja into the Sea of Cortéz. At the bay, passengers board zodiacs or other small craft and drift close to the mothers and babies cavorting in shallow waters.

Boats are not allowed to approach the whales, but the whales often swim close to the boats while breaching and spouting. Gray whales were nearly slaughtered to extinction after almost a century of whaling off Baja's coast. The Marine Mammal Protection Act, enacted in 1972, finally ended the massacre, and the whales are returning to Baja's lagoons and bays in greater numbers every year. Floating eye-to-eye with a 30-ton mother whale is an experience you won't forget in a hurry.

current capital. When Hernán Cortés (also called Cortéz; 1485–1547), the conqueror of Mexico, arrived in the bay of La Paz in 1535, this area was sparsely inhabited by members of the Guaycura tribe. Evidence of earlier inhabitants can be found in the extraordinary rock murals in remote mountain caves throughout Baja. Most of the renowned murals, which date back some 7,500 years, are found in central and northern Baja in the Sierra de Guadalupe and Sierra de San Francisco.

Harry Crosby, author of *The Cave Paintings of Baja California*, dubbed the unknown artists simply "The Painters." Their murals, often

Spanish missions

The discovery of pearls in the bay of La Paz caught the interest of early explorers, but the inhospitable land and unfriendly residents discouraged speculators. Spanish missionaries arrived in the mid-1600s and established their first mission at Loreto in 1697. Father Juníper Serra, a Franciscan monk from Mallorca, in the Balearic Islands off the coast of Spain, set out from here in 1752 to establish a chain of missions from San Diego to San Francisco, in the land then known as Alta California (in Spanish, *alta* means upper and *baja* means lower). The Loreto mission church now bears the sign

painted as much as 30 ft (9 meters) high on boulders and in caves, depict giant human figures, deer, bighorn sheep, and many other animals and fish, and are painted in much the same fashion as those found in the caves of Lascaux, France. A few small paintings can be found in the hills outside Loreto, but the most famous ones are far from the cruise ships' routes. However, you can be sure of seeing plenty of reproductions of the paintings in museums, hotels, and stores.

LEFT: a gray whale surfaces at Laguna San Ignacio.
ABOVE: the Loreto Mission is the oldest in the Americas, and has an adjoining museum.

"Head and Mother of the Missions of Lower and Upper California."

Culture clashes

The Guaycura people living in southern Baja when the Spaniards arrived were less than thrilled by the foreigners' intrusion. The *padres* (priests) insisted their reluctant converts wear clothing and practice monogamy, two concepts that were foreign to the Native Americans. Resistance on the part of the indigenous peoples was intense; a tile mural over the entry to the parish church in San José del Cabo depicts the culmination of the conflict between the two cultures, showing the

Native Americans dragging Padre Nicolás Tamaral to a raging fire. Tamaral became Baja's first martyr. The Guaycura and Baja's other indigenous peoples ultimately lost the battle, however, as they gradually succumbed to imported diseases, to which they had no built-up immunity.

Today's residents are a mixed bunch called *bajacalifornios*. Most are descendants of European, Mexican, and American immigrants who settled on the peninsula when they were prospecting for pearls or manning whaling ships in the late 19th century, or working at fish canneries in the 20th century. Immigrants

from around the world are now drawn to southern Baja by the promise of profits. Development is booming around Los Cabos and along both coasts as the region becomes a major tourism destination. Chefs from France, Italy, and Switzerland, hotel owners from Spain, and investors from all over the world are influencing the emerging cultural, social and economic character of southern Baja.

Conserving the area

The rapidly changing landscape is affecting the Sea of Cortéz, which the Nature Conservancy calls "a global conservation priority." Scientists have discovered 31 species of marine

mammals and between 500 and 800 species of fish in the Sea of Cortéz. Its islands and coastlines are home to sea lions, nesting sea turtles, and 210 species of migratory birds.

FONATUR, the Mexican government agency charged with tourism development, has proposed a controversial series of marinas along the coastline in an *Escalera Náutica*, or Nautical Ladder. Environmental groups throughout the world are monitoring such projects with fierce scrutiny.

Much of the northern section of the sea is protected in the Mexican Gulf of California Biosphere Reserve, which covers 3,700 sq miles (9,583 sq km). This section is closed to commercial fishing, sport fishing, and oil drilling. Portions of the southern sea, including the marine reserve off Loreto's shores, are also protected, although enforcement of rules against commercial fishing is uneven.

If those in charge of them behave responsibly, cruise ships sailing in the Sea of Cortéz may have a positive impact on conservation: passengers who experience the extraordinary beauty of Baja know that this region is a natural treasure to be cherished and preserved.

One such passenger wrote eloquently of his explorations in the 1940s. John Steinbeck made several expeditions into the area with marine biologist Ed Ricketts. The author described the wealth of marine life and the harshness of land conditions with characteristic curiosity and insight in *The Log from the Sea of Cortéz*. He summed up the Baja experience with these words: "Nights at anchor in the Gulf are quiet and strange. The water is smooth, almost solid, and the dew is so heavy that the decks are soaked. The little waves rasp on the shell beaches with a hissing sound, and all about in the darkness the fishes jump and splash.... The very air here is miraculous, and outlines of reality change with the moment."

But although he was writing some time ago, Steinbeck was aware even then of the conservation problems, for he also wrote that fishing boats were "bringing up tons of shrimp, rapidly destroying the species so that it may never come back and with the species destroying the ecological balance of the whole region." ❑

LEFT: for watery views of Baja take a zodiac cruise.
RIGHT: pelicans rest on a boat in the Sea of Cortéz, the islands nearby are home to over 200 bird species.

EXPLORING THE SEA OF CORTÉZ

The lovely town of Loreto, islands rich with rare birds and marine life, and an excursion into Copper Canyon are among the many attractions of a Sea of Cortéz cruise

Waves from the Pacific Ocean splash into the more placid Sea of Cortéz at El Arco, the rock arch at Baja's southern tip. Cruise ships on Mexican Riviera itineraries anchor near the arch, while those on Sea of Cortéz cruises rarely even stop at **Los Cabos**, the most Americanized part of Baja. Most of their passengers enter Baja at the Los Cabos airport, however, because of its many convenient flights. The cruise lines then transport passengers by road to La Paz, about four hours north. The trip usually includes a stop in Todos Santos, a burgeoning artists' community where handsome brick and stucco homes have been converted into top-notch restaurants and galleries. A few nights' stay in Los Cabos before or after a cruise is a great way to indulge in creature comforts.

The resort destination is made up of two towns – San José del Cabo and Cabo San Lucas – and the 20-mile (32-km) long Corridor that connects them. The airport is located outside **San José del Cabo ❶**, where early 19th-century stucco houses transformed into chic restaurants and bars are clustered near the jacaranda-shaded **Plaza Mijares**. The spires of **Iglesia San José** rise above the treetops in front of the plaza and the side streets are lined with galleries and stores selling fine folk art and home furnishings. If you find things you like, don't worry about carrying them back with, as you can always ship your purchases home.

The rapidly developing **Corridor** linking the two towns is the most expensive and exclusive destination in Mexico. Elegant resorts are tucked atop cliffs or beside sandy coves far from outsiders' probing eyes. But there are plenty of golf courses in full view, and guests in the Corridor tend to play golf, indulge in spa treatments, dine at gourmet restaurants, and rarely see the rest of Los Cabos.

Cabo San Lucas ❷ is the antithesis of the Corridor. Its raucous, rowdy bars, especially Squid Row and Cabo Wabo, are packed with young Americans fond of tequila shooters and dirty dancing. Streets around the Boulevard Marina waterfront are jam packed with bars, restaurants, and souvenir stores, all competing for attention with loud music and eye-popping signs. **Plaza Amelia Wilkes**, a couple of blocks inland, is a peaceful refuge with a white, wrought-iron gazebo. To avoid the clamor on the waterfront, browse through the stores in the massive **Puerto Paraíso** shopping mall and exit onto the walkway beside the marina. Vendors here hawk fishing trips, boat cruises, and trips to **Lovers' Beach**, a barren beach beneath El Arco. If you prefer margaritas

LEFT: cruising the Sea of Cortéz.
BELOW: Playa los Cerritos.

and grilled fish with your sand, head for **Playa Médano**, where parasailers, kayakers, and reckless drivers on wave-runners compete with swimmers. A parade of restaurants, hotels, and activity stands provide shade, refreshments, and all the beach toys you could desire.

La Paz

A Mayan sculpture on display at the Museo de Antropología, La Paz.

Sunsets are a family event in **La Paz** ❸. Children swing and slide at playgrounds in the sand along the Malecón, a scenic seaside promenade. Couples flirt under the watchful eyes of grandmothers strolling in the sun's golden glow. All pause as a fiery globe sinks beyond the Bahía de la Paz, the Bay of Peace. This city of some 175,000 residents may be the capital of Baja Sur, but it feels like a small town in a time warp.

Although it is the departure point for most Sea of Cortéz cruises, La Paz is poorly served by international airlines, and, as already mentioned, passengers typically fly into Los Cabos and travel four hours north by road to reach their ships. Spending a night or two here is the perfect accompaniment to a cruise focused on marine life. Before heading out to sea, devote a few hours to the **Museo de Antropología** (closed Mon) for an excellent overview of Baja's history and topography. The photos of petroglyphs in remote caves and the ever-expanding collection of fossils and whale skeletons found high in the mountains are especially fascinating.

BELOW: the beach at sunset.

If you have time to explore the city, begin at the **Malecón** then stroll west to **Plaza Constitución**, also called Jardín Velazco. In classic Mexican style, the plaza is a gathering point for men having their shoes shined in the shade, children playing in the kiosk, and downtown workers eating *tacos* and hot dogs

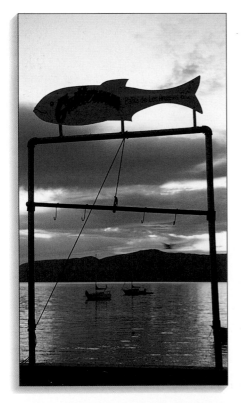

bought from plaza stands. The **Catedral de Nuestra Señora de la Paz** facing the plaza was built in 1861; its simple stone-block towers poke above the jumble of downtown streets packed with department stores, shoe stores, pharmacies, and stationers.

Few downtown stores carry folk art or souvenirs, but there are some excellent shopping opportunities in the area. Collectors regularly stop by the small workshop at Ibarra's Pottery to check out the latest bowls and platters with artist Julio Ibarra's geometric designs and desert-inspired colors. Artesanías la Antigua California on the Malecón carries a good selection of folk art from around Mexico. But the best purchase you can make in La Paz is a plate loaded with *almejas diablo*, fresh clams spiced with hot sauce. This traditional dish is served at seafood shacks on the beach at **Playa Pichilingue**, north of town.

Isla Espíritu Santo and Isla Partida

Sea lions gather by the hundred on the guano-covered rocks at **Isla Espíritu Santo ❹**, raising a ruckus that brings smiles to snorkelers swimming in placid clear coves. The 23,000-acre (9,300-hectare) island is a favorite of cruise ship naturalists and environmental organizations. Its habitat is so precious the Nature Conservancy organization purchased the island in January 2003 to protect its endemic cacti, rabbits, reptiles, and marine life.

Ships cruise around Espíritu Santo, the adjacent **Isla Partida**, and smaller islets of Los Islotes as passengers look for sea lions, blue-footed boobies, and sea turtles. Snorkelers board small zodiacs, kayaks, or skiffs to get closer to underwater caves and sea lions eager to swim with humans. Hiking trails lead along beaches and up hillsides past stately cardón cacti, elephant trees, and

Map on page 180

TIP

For full details of **opening hours** and contact information for the sites and museums mentioned in this chapter, see Travel Tips page 338.

Below: walking along the Malecón at La Paz.

prickly pear cacti dotted with spiny fruit. Boobies, hummingbirds, and the endemic blacktailed jackrabbits are just a few of the species you can spot. In the sea, schools of parrotfish, Cortéz angelfish, and groupers swim along coral reefs, while manta rays glide through clear waters and moray eels hide in crevices, poking their heads out to view the intruders. These island expeditions usually include a picnic, sometimes with a bonfire, on the white sands at Bahía Bonanza, Ensenada Grande, or another remote beach where the sight of whales gliding by never fails to bring a cheer from onlookers.

Loreto

Horse-drawn carriages line the waterfront when cruise ships arrive at **Loreto** ❺, the loveliest seaside town in Baja. The Sierras rise in a jagged ridge behind the mission church's bell tower and palms poke above the simple adobe buildings lining the few streets. This peaceful community of some 13,000 residents was the site of the first European settlement in the Californias and the headquarters for the chain of missions spreading through Baja and Alta California in the 18th century. Today, a new wave of speculators has arrived, seeking their fortune in the rapidly developing resort community of Nopoló, 5 miles (8 km) south of town. Some ships offer excursions to the golf course and tennis center there.

Passengers are tendered to the small harbor beside the promenade called Calle de la Playa. Piles of boulders topped by a concrete sidewalk form a sea wall with wrought-iron benches facing the water. It's the perfect place to watch fishermen come in on *pangas* (small skiffs) followed by seagulls and brown pelicans.

Archways formed from entwined tree branches frame a pedestrian path along Calle Salvatierra from the waterfront to **Plaza Salvatierra**, a tiny park framed

Souvenirs made from coconut shells and sea shells are sold at stands and local markets.

BELOW:
cactus and desert rocks at sunrise.

COPPER CANYON

One of Mexico's most spectacular adventures takes place a few miles from the eastern edge of the Sea of Cortéz, just beyond the port city of Los Mochis. Chihuahua al Pacifico trains climb from sea level up 9,000 ft (2,745 meters) into the Sierras to the edge of the Barranca del Cobre (Copper Canyon), a series of dramatic canyons, gorges, and cliffs. The train travels through tunnels and over suspension bridges from Los Mochis to Chihuahua in Mexico's cowboy country in 12 breathtaking hours. Most riders opt to stop at one of several small towns along the way, spending the night in mountain lodges and restored haciendas. The Tarahumara people, so fleet of foot they can run down their prey, live in caves and small settlements in the Copper Canyon, clinging tenaciously to their traditional way of life. Archeologists have uncovered caves and pottery dating to AD1000.

Although they resist the corruption of their traditions, the Tarahumara interact with tourists by selling their handwoven baskets and woodcarvings at the railroad stops. Clipper Cruises offers a three-night pre-cruise extension to the Copper Canyon, Lindblad has a one-night extension with a stay in Chihuahua, and Cruise West offers a four-night Copper Canyon Adventure.

Map on page 180

by cafés. The plaza fronts **La Misión de Nuestra Señora de Loreto**, the oldest mission in the Californias. Jesuit priest Juan Maria Salvatierra is credited with overseeing the construction of the church in 1699, and building work continued until 1752. The church, with its gilded altar and statue of the Virgin of Loreto, was restored in 1976. Although the main building is unimpressive, the bell tower provides an excellent landmark as you wander through town.

Beside the church, the **Museo de los Misiones** (closed Mon) also called the Museum of Anthropology and History, contains religious relics, tooled leather saddles, and displays of Baja's history. Farming implements are scattered around the shady courtyard. A few 18th-century houses near the mission have been converted into small shops. Check out the silver jewelry and replicas of Baja's cave paintings at El Alacrán, and the sculptures made from dried cardón cacti at La Casa de la Abuela (Grandmother's House), the oldest house in town.

Visitors to Loreto have the rare opportunity to visit a mission village that seems frozen in the 18th century. The road to **Misión San Javier** can be muddy, and rough, but the drive into the mountains past fruit orchards, massive boulders, and towering cacti offers a bit of insight into life in Baja's interior. The mission church was established in 1699 as the center of the Jesuits' original farming community. Today, a few wood, brick, and stucco houses line the street to the church, which was built between 1720 and 1744. One of the best-preserved mission churches in Baja, San Javier has several side altars and a fortress-like bell tower. Ask if the ship's tour includes side trips to cave paintings hidden along unmarked dirt roads near San Javier.

The Sea of Cortéz is Loreto's most valuable natural asset. Scientists and environmentalists say it is one of the most diverse marine nurseries and habitats in the world. Manta rays leap, spin, and splash on the water's surface in the summer as dolphins practice their choreography beside the pangas. Swarms of dorado, tuna, and marlin attract hundreds of anglers to Loreto from June to September. From December to March, blue whales, orcas, finbacks, and sperm whales all migrate around Loreto's shores.

BELOW: boats at Loreto marina.

Loreto's islands

The **Parque Marítimo Nacional Bahía de Loreto** ❻ (Loreto National Marine Park) was established in 1977 to protect the sea and several islands in this area, and commercial fishing is prohibited in the 23-sq mile (60-sq km) park.

Most itineraries include a day or two of cruising around the islands, stopping at various locales when marine life is present. **Isla del Carmen**, just off Loreto's shores, has several limestone caves at shore level and reefs where lobster and tropical fish congregate. Kayaking from Carmen to **Isla Coronado** (another good snorkeling spot inhabited only by sea lions) and **Isla Danzante** (favored by divers) makes a fabulous excursion.

During the winter, blue and finback whales spout and breech all around this area. The blue whales, said to be the largest mammals on earth, are particularly exciting to spot. Captains and crew members are quick to point out sightings. ❏

HAWAIIAN HISTORY IN A COCONUT SHELL

The history of the Hawaiian Islands was shaped by a strong hereditary monarchy, strong-willed missionaries and avaricious sugar barons

The Hawaiian Islands are among the earth's youngest, and are still being formed by active volcanoes. They were also the last major islands to be discovered by Europeans. Located thousands of miles out to sea, about as far north of the Equator as Cuba, Hawaii was uninhabited until around AD200, when explorers from the Marquesas Islands arrived in their seaworthy catamaran-canoes. This was yet another stage in the colonization of the Pacific Islands by seafarers originating in Southeast Asia; over many centuries, their descendants settled most of the islands of Polynesia.

The first immigrants to Hawaii discovered a tropical paradise, teeming with birds and plants found nowhere else. Coconuts, sugar cane, and pineapples came later, transplanted from other lands by later colonists, but historians reckon the Marquesans found 2,200 species of plants, maybe 70 types of birds, and reefs and lagoons teeming with fish. For more than half a millennium, the settlers lived in harmony with the new lands, until they were discovered and dispatched by similarly adventurous Tahitians about 700 years later. After that, the islands lay undisturbed until 1778, when Captain James Cook chanced upon them during an expedition to North America's Pacific Northwest.

Discovery by Europeans

Why weren't the islands found sooner, during the Great Age of Discovery? Well, perhaps they were. The Spanish began trading between Acapulco, on Mexico's western coast, and the Orient early in the 16th century, but their ships relied on trade winds and ocean currents to shorten times of passage between ports. The winds that drove the ships west also pushed them south of the islands, while those that

carried them home were more reliable farther north. Evidence suggests that a few Spanish ships, probably blown off course by storms, stopped off or were wrecked in the islands, perhaps as early as 1527.

Spanish sailing charts from the 1500s show islands that may be Hawaii, and some accounts say that James Cook carried one of these charts on his expedition. When Cook arrived, the Hawaiians knew of and revered iron, which they had no means of producing on their own; the few iron objects they owned were adapted from ship's hardware. He also noted islanders with symptoms of advanced syphilis, a European disease that devastated native cultures all over the New World. During the two centuries before Cook's arrival, nine Spanish ships had gone missing in the Mexico–Orient trade, so it's reasonable to suspect at least one ended up on a Hawaiian reef.

PRECEDING PAGES: hike along the rim of the Waipio Valley, Big Island, for great views. **LEFT:** climbing the rigging of a tall ship. **RIGHT:** the Kauai Akialoas, a native Hawaiian bird, is now extinct.

Nevertheless, Captain Cook and his crew were the first Europeans whose visit to the Hawaiian Islands had a lasting impact. He called them the Sandwich Islands, in honor of the Earl of Sandwich, First Lord of the Admiralty; among foreigners, the name was used throughout the next century, although native peoples always called the islands Hawaii.

In January 1778, Cook landed at Waimea, on the island of Kauai, and was greeted warmly by the natives. On a subsequent visit a year later, however, relations soured, resulting in Cook's death in a fracas at Kaleakekua Bay on the Big Island in February 1779. Cook's crew

water and food stores and allow their crews a few days of shore leave. By the turn of the 19th century, white foreigners – *haoles* in Hawaiian – were common visitors to the islands.

Kapu

Present at the death of Captain Cook was a Hawaiian warrior prince called Kamehameha, whose goal was the unification of the islands under a single king – himself. His campaign started in 1782; by 1795 he was king of almost all the islands, but it took him until 1810 to subdue the most remote, Kauai and Ni'ihau. King Kamehameha I had 21 wives and many

returned to England and reported their discovery of the two islands – and the abundance of fur-bearing animals in the Pacific Northwest. Soon, a flourishing fur trade began between North America and China. Within a decade of Lewis and Clark's 1804–06 voyage of discovery that took them from St Louis, Missouri, to the Pacific Ocean *(see page 21)*, daring entrepreneurs established trading posts on the Pacific Coast. One of them, founded by John Jacob Astor, became the city of Astoria, Oregon.

The Hawaiian Islands were an ideal port of call for ships laden with Oregon furs en route to Canton, on the other side of the Pacific; captains dropped anchor to replenish drinking

children. His favorite wife was Kaahumanu, a remarkable woman by any standards. When Kamehameha died in 1819, he left the throne to his son, Liholiho. But Kaahumanu insisted that the king had wanted her to be joint ruler, and she was named *kuhina nui*, or queen, of Hawaii. Liholiho took the title of Kamehameha II.

Almost immediately, the new king abolished *kapu*, the system of religion-based laws and practices that had regulated every aspect of Hawaiian life for centuries. Abolishing *kapu* (related to the English word taboo) in Hawaii was like outlawing Judaism in Jerusalem, or Islam in Mecca. Penalties for breaking *kapu* were harsh, usually involving death, and many of the practices prescribed by the system were unusual: commoners had to prostrate themselves before chiefs and nobles, for example, and were forbidden from allowing their shadow to fall upon the house of a chief. *Kapu* also applied to eating customs – who could eat what, who could legally dine with whom. Women were forbidden from eating with men, and were not allowed to partake of many tasty foods, like coconuts, bananas, and pork. *Kapu* also encompassed worship of the many Hawaiian gods, and their respective temples. It was a system endemic to Hawaiian life.

Why did Kamehameha II abolish *kapu*? Life in Hawaii was changing rapidly, thanks to the increasing numbers of *haoles* arriving every year – some just passing through aboard ships, but others settling ashore to harvest sandalwood for shipment to China, or to engage in other pursuits. To move ahead, the king realized that things had to change, but it is unlikely that he would have had the courage to end *kapu* without Kaahumanu's prompting. *Kapu* relegated women to second-rate status, something the queen wasn't happy about; she used her position to convince the king that *kapu*'s time had run out. The two of them ended the system in November 1819, by eating together publicly in front of chiefs and influential *haoles*. With this one meal, a tradition of 1,000 years ended literally overnight.

The missionaries

The end of *kapu* opened a void in Hawaiian life – the ancient gods and idols were gone, long standing religious and social practices rendered null and void. This void would be filled, at least for some Hawaiians, by Christianity: The first organized party of Congregationalist missionaries, charged with saving the souls of the "heathens," arrived from New England in 1820, only months after the abolition of *kapu*. Kamehameha II allowed the missionaries to stay and preach for one year, as a trial. One year led to two, to four, and to forever. As is the wont of missionaries, these staid New England Congregationalists first put an end to what they considered the immoral acts of the islanders, drinking and sexual freedom, the *hula*, and even surfing. On the other hand, the mission-

aries built schools as well as churches, developed a written Hawaiian language, which had not existed previously, and began to educate Hawaiians irrespective of social position, while showing them the path to salvation. They also established an American presence in the islands, which would prove very valuable to the United States in later years.

Kamehameha II died in 1824, while on a trip to London; his younger brother, only 10 years old, became Kamehameha III, making Kaahumanu the real ruler for the first eight years of his reign. Kaahumanu was one of the first Christian converts, and instituted civil laws

based on the Ten Commandments and Congregationalist practices. The church, and by association, the missionaries, became even more influential, even though only a small minority of Hawaiians had been accepted into the congregation. Many attended services – some say because they loved the singing – but only a handful had been admitted officially to church membership.

The plantation era

By 1840, the Congregationalists' influence was ebbing, due to Kaahumanu's death in 1832, Kamehameha III's lack of interest in their religion, and the growing acceptance by the

---

LEFT: an artist's impression of Captain Cook's death.
RIGHT: an 1873 engraving of female surfers.

Captain Cook

Captain James Cook was born in 1728 in Yorkshire, England. He went to sea at 18 aboard a coastal trading vessel, volunteered for the Royal Navy, and advanced rapidly; he was named master of his own small ship in 1757, and joined the fleet sailing for Canada to capture Québec from the French. Cook proved to be an excellent surveyor and cartographer, and spent much of the next decade charting the coast of mainland Canada and Newfoundland. But Cook's lasting fame was to be earned on the other side of the world.

Starting in 1768, Cook made three expeditions to the Pacific: The first took him to Tahiti to observe and record a celestial phenomenon called the transit of Venus, occurring in early June, 1769. Following this, he explored the southern Pacific, determining that New Zealand was an island, and not part of a larger landmass. Cook then sailed west to explore and survey the east coast of Australia before sailing back to England, where he arrived in July, 1771.

A year later, Cook sailed on a second expedition deep into southern waters, becoming the first explorer to sail south of the Antarctic Circle. He then explored the Indian Ocean and Polynesia before returning to England in July, 1775. His voyage had lasted three years, but within a year he was off again, this time to explore North America's Pacific Coast in search of the Northwest Passage. En route, he stopped at Tahiti, and while sailing north from there discovered the Hawaiian Islands; he called them the Sandwich Islands in honor of the First Lord of the Admiralty, the Earl of Sandwich. (Although the natives always called the islands Hawaii, well into the 19th century foreigners still called them by Cook's name: in 1866, for instance, Mark Twain wrote affectionately of his visit to the Sandwich Islands.) After a brief stay at the island of Kauai, Cook continued northwards, and spent a year exploring the Pacific Northwest, Alaska, and the Aleutian Islands, sailing through the Bering Strait and beyond the Arctic Circle before returning to Hawaii, this time landing on the Big Island.

Here, a strange twist of fate and timing caused Cook to be welcomed as a god by the natives. His ships anchored in Kealakekua Bay, at the time of the celebration of Lono, a fertility god who, legend said, would return to Hawaii on a floating island. Kealakekua Bay was Lono's sacred harbor, and his symbol was a white sheet of tapa cloth hanging from a crossbeam. Cook's white-sailed ships looked like floating islands to the Hawaiians, who greeted him as Lono returning to his native land. After a month of feasting and celebration which stretched the islanders resources beyond breaking point, Cook weighed anchor and sailed away. But a few days later Cook's ships met a violent storm, and were forced back to Kealakekua Bay for repairs. Since gods' floating islands don't often suffer storm damage, the Hawaiians began to suspect Cook wasn't divine after all.

Friction developed between the Hawaiians and the Europeans, culminating in a ship's boat being stolen by the islanders. On February 14, 1779, Cook's efforts to recover the boat degenerated into violence, and he was killed on the beach at Kealakekua Bay, along with four sailors. The Hawaiians were repulsed by English firearms; many were killed and even more injured, including Kamehameha, who would later become the first king of all Hawaii. Eventually, and in return for numerous gifts, islanders returned parts of Cook's body, mostly charred bones, to his shipmates, who buried the remains at sea in Kealakekua Bay. Today a white obelisk marks the site of Cook's death, on a plot of land that is officially British territory. ❑

LEFT: Captain James Cook explored Polynesia and stumbled upon Hawaii in the 18th century.

Hawaiians of foreigners of all stripes, including Catholics, atheists, and hard-drinking sailors. The latter were especially accepted; without exports, other than a modest trade in sandalwood to China, the islands' economy relied heavily on cash infusions from the crews of passing ships, and on products brought by those ships. Whaling ships started calling at Hawaii in 1820, and by the 1840s, the peak of the whaling industry, hundreds would anchor every year in Honolulu and Lahaina. In 1846, 429 anchored at Lahaina alone. Every sailor who came ashore needed something that he was willing to pay cash for.

Sexual mores

Island women, coming from a very different cultural and religious background from that of Puritan New England, viewed sex without the same inhibitions as the missionaries, and saw the sailors' desires as completely natural – and profitable. Eventually, however, the missionaries managed to enact rules that prevented Hawaiian girls from visiting the ships, but, hard as they tried, they couldn't stop the commerce ashore. It was a classic battleground between morality and mammon, and, as usual, mammon won: Human nature and island tradition prevailed, and not much changed overall. At times the friction between ships' crews and straitlaced missionaries degenerated into violence, once even going as far as to involve a cannonade of one of the minister's homes.

Alternative sources of income

In their zeal to save Hawaii's women, the missionaries found another source of income for the islanders: sugar cane. In 1836 they persuaded the king to lease to the *haole* firm of Ladd & Co., 980 acres (396 hectares) of land on Kauai to establish the Koloa Sugar Plantation. Their idea was that many Hawaiians would be hired to harvest and process the cane, taking some of the economic pressure off the women. Starting pay for a worker on Koloa Plantation was a princely $2 a month.

Sugar cane wasn't native to Hawaii, but had been imported by the earliest settlers; by the time Captain Cook arrived it was growing wild all over the islands. Before 1836 its cultivation

RIGHT: French seamen are entertained at an Oahu hula extravaganza.

had been limited to small plantations, or simply to harvesting wild cane. Hawaiians liked to chew the cane raw, rather than refine it into granular sugar. Traditionally, all the land on the islands was owned by royalty, and common folk worked the fields as heavily-taxed sharecroppers. The main crop was *taro*, a starchy tuber that was as important to Hawaii as the potato was to Ireland; boiled and pounded into a paste, it becomes *poi*, a staple food of the islands even today. Breaking one's back to harvest and process sugar cane, when it was easy to cut off a wild stalk and chew the sweetness out of it, didn't appeal to Hawaiians, and more

young men chose to ship out on whalers or trading vessels than work the sugar plantations. Consequently, lack of labor meant that the Koloa Plantation got off to a slow start, cultivating only a tiny percentage of its land in the first few years. It eventually prospered, however, and was the first plantation in an industry that would change the islands drastically.

In 1848 King Kamehameha III enacted a law that permitted Hawaiian commoners to own land outright for the first time, rather than just work it for a share of its yield. Two years later, he modified the edict to allow foreigners, as well as natives, to buy land, opening the door to foreign investment. Within a few years, enterprising *haoles* had established giant plantations for cultivating and refining sugar, but in order for any of them to be profitable, they needed farmhands to cut and process the cane. The answer was to import labor; the Hawaiian sugar barons turned first to China, then to the Philippines and Japan. Some European laborers arrived, especially from Germany and Portugal. Many laborers worked the cane long enough to get a grubstake, then bought stores and businesses in the towns, which meant that foreign workers could soon be found in all sectors of Hawaii's economy, not just in the fields. The multi-racial Hawaiian culture today is a

Hawaii in 1874, removing import tariffs on sugar. The sugar barons got even richer and more influential: by 1887, the *haole* political machine forced passage of laws disenfranchising anyone owning less than $3,000-worth of land, or with an annual income of less than $600. This deprived virtually all Hawaiians of the right to vote.

The end of the monarchy

While the *haole* planters supplanted native Hawaiians as the power in the islands, there were still monarchs on the Kamehameha throne. After Kamehameha III died childless

result of the intermarriage of these workers with Hawaiians, *haoles*, and each other.

California, whose population was growing rapidly thanks to the Gold Rush, was the first main market for Hawaiian sugar, followed, during the Civil War, by the Northern states, because most American sugar was produced in the Confederacy, primarily in Louisiana. Hawaiian plantations were six or seven times as productive, acre for acre, as those in the US, so after the Civil War ended, in 1865, the United States continued to be Hawaii's best customer. The *haole* planters, who by now essentially owned the islands, persuaded the Senate to confer "favored nation" status on

in 1854, his nephew Alexander Liholiho became king, but he died from asthma at only 29, in 1863. His brother became Kamehameha V, and attempted to regain some power for native Hawaiians and the monarchy. He established literacy and property qualifications for voters, and consequently became unpopular among *haoles*. Fortunately for them, he died, also childless, in 1872 – the last Hawaiian monarch to descend directly from Kamehameha the Great.

After the death of Kamehameha V, Hawaiians began electing their kings. The first, William Lunalilo, died after only a year on the throne; a subsequent election elevated David

Kalakaua, a descendant of high chiefs, in 1874. He was a champion of Hawaiian traditions (he compiled the islands' legends and myths in a book that is still in print), an enthusiastic world traveler, and *bon vivant*. Kalakaua visited the United States in 1874, and negotiated with President Grant the favored-nation treaty which removed sugar tariffs; in return, Kalakaua gave the United States a long-term lease on Pearl Harbor. This agreement cemented the relationship between the United States and Hawaii, which had also been courted over the years by Great Britain and France. It also resulted in more power to the

Queen Liliuokalani, Hawaii's only official queen, tried to regain power, but it was too late: the sugar barons were too strong, with close ties in Washington. When, in 1893, Liliuokalani tried to throw out the Bayonet Constitution and ratify a new, Hawaiian-friendly, substitute, possibly robbing the sugar barons of some of their power, the US minister in Hawaii, John Stevens, called in the Marines – without authorization from Washington.

The forces from the gunship, the USS *Boston*, occupied Honolulu, deposed Liliuokalani and named Sanford Dole leader of the government. Dole, descended from one of the first mission-

planters, and ultimately led to the end of the ruling monarchy.

In 1887, *haoles* formed a political group that forced Kalakaua to accept a new constitution, legend says at the point of a bayonet. The "Bayonet Constitution" included onerous property and income qualifications for voters, and essentially relegated Kalakaua's role to one of figurehead. He died in San Francisco in 1891, having named his sister, Princess Liliuokalani, as his successor.

aries, was a cousin of James Dole, who started Hawaii's first pineapple plantation in 1899.

Annexed by the United States

Eventually, President Grover Cleveland sent an investigator to the islands. He reported the injustice of the whole affair to Congress, but the sugar barons were too strong even for the President, and his protests were ignored. In 1894, Sanford Dole and his cronies set themselves up as leaders of the Republic of Hawaii, repelled a feeble counter-revolution led by Liliuokalani, and sentenced her to jail for five years for treason, although the punishment was never carried out.

FAR LEFT: King Kalakaua V, Hawaii's last king.
LEFT: Queen Liliuokalani, 1893.
RIGHT: US Marines from the USS *Boston.*

Hula

Mentioning "hula" to most *haoles* evokes the image of a girl in a grass skirt and bikini top swinging her hips on Waikiki Beach, while onlookers snap pictures and maybe buy the odd *lei* or two. (Actually, the Waikiki Hula Show closed in September, 2002, after 64 years of dancing.) But to Hawaiians, hula is opera and theater and dance and beauteous grace, wrapped in a tapa-cloth skirt. (No grass skirts in traditional Hawaiian hula – they actually originated in the Gilbert Islands.)

Originally, hula was danced by both women and men, for secular and religious reasons, but by the time Cook arrived in the islands, it was predominantly a female pursuit, performed as entertainment; the men's dance, called hula kui, became a ritualized martial arts exercise based on lua, an ancient Hawaiian self-defense regimen akin to karate or tae kwan do.

Hula is a lot more than simply the hip-swaying dance tourists love: In the centuries before missionaries taught Hawaiians the three Rs, the islanders had no written language. Instead, culture, folklore, and religion were taught orally or visually, using the hula – it was opera under the palms, to the accompaniment of gourd drums and chanting. There were many different dances, taking years to master. Professional hula dancers began studying as children, usually starting as young as four or five years old, and would not be qualified until well into their teens. Once skilled, though, the women (and only the prettiest girls were chosen to study hula) were revered and honored by society, and lived lives similar to today's pop stars or movie idols. But hula was for everybody, not just trained dancers; every Hawaiian danced.

When the missionaries arrived, their misunderstanding of Hawaiian culture led them to believe the hula lascivious. Contemporary illustrations show hula dancers dressed in voluminous tapa cloth skirts, but bare-breasted and tattooed; written accounts suggest they were often naked but for an assortment of fashion accessories: Historian Gavin Daws, in his excellent Hawaiian history, *Shoal of Time*, writes of dancers at the court of Laka, goddess of the hula: "Hundreds of dancers garlanded with green leaves and flowers and adorned with dog-tooth anklets moved to and fro in serried ranks, their bare brown flesh glistening with sweat."

And even worse, the hula also served to beseech the gods for some favor – a rich harvest, bountiful catch of fish, fertility, and so forth. A hula dancer uses every part of her body, not just her hips – the head, hands, arms, legs, and feet also serve to tell the tale. In time the missionaries managed to have the hula outlawed; by the time King Kalakaua revived it, along with other Hawaiian traditions, in the 1870s, many of the traditional dances had been forgotten. A great deal of the tradition was lost forever.

Today, though, traditional hula is back, and getting more popular all the time, as native Hawaiians revive their heritage. And with the male hula now on the increase the dance has become a symbol of rediscovered cultural identity. Once again, hula schools teach the dances to children of both sexes; hula masters are as revered as college football coaches on the mainland, and schools compete in statewide hula championships. The most prestigious and biggest one, the Merrie Monarch Festival, is held in Hilo, on the Big Island, in April in honor of King Kalakaua – it lasts a week, with parades and competitions in both traditional and modern hula. ❑

LEFT: hula is an important Hawaiian cultural tradition that combines storytelling and music.

By 1900, Hawaii had officially been annexed by the United States, against the wishes of most Hawaiians, who were unable to vote as few met the onerous voter requirements devised in 1887 by the forward-thinking *haoles*. Annexation linked Hawaii, politically and economically, to the United States; it was one step short of statehood, which had been proposed many times during the previous half-century but never really taken seriously by the American government.

Today, when they hear the name Dole, most people in the US think of pineapples, not of overthrowing a government. And now, the

his crop in 1901, and by 1906 had established a cannery in Honolulu.

Dole was a genius at marketing pineapples, and by 1922 he'd outgrown his land. His solution was to buy a whole island and turn it into a plantation: he purchased Lanai outright for $1.1 million, or about $12 per acre, cleared 18,000 acres (7,300 hectares) of land for planting, and built a deepwater harbor and a town for his workers. It was, not surprisingly, the largest pineapple plantation in the world, shipping a million a day at the height of its glory. Castle & Cooke bought Dole's operation, changed its name to the Dole Pineapple Com-

Hawaiian Pineapples, District of Wahiawa, Island of Oahu.

pineapple is synonymous with Hawaii, even though the fruit comes from South America, and wasn't introduced to the islands until 1813. The man probably responsible was Don Francisco de Paula Marín, a Spaniard who served as adviser and interpreter for King Kamehameha the Great (he also introduced coffee). Although pineapples grew widely throughout the islands, they weren't harvested commercially until 1899, when Boston entrepreneur James D. Dole planted 60 acres (24 hectares) in central Oahu with the spiny plant. He started the Hawaiian Pineapple Company to market

ABOVE: pineapples and plantation workers, 1910.

pany, and continued satisfying the world's appetite for pineapples. In 1987, thanks to cheaper pineapple production in Asia, the Castle & Cooke management retired most of the fields, built hotels and golf courses, and opened Lanai to tourists.

War in the Pacific

The United States Navy base at Pearl Harbor was opened in December 1911, and immediately became the country's most important military installation in the Pacific. On December 7, 1941, the Japanese Navy attacked the US fleet here, as well as nearby Schofield Barracks, a US Army base. Almost 2,400 service personnel and civilians were killed, and 18 major ships sunk or heavily damaged. Anti-Japanese sentiment erupted: On the mainland, many American citizens of Japanese ancestry were interned for fear they would aid the enemy – but far too many Hawaiians had Japanese blood to make internment feasible here. Instead, the islands as a whole were put under martial law, which replaced civilian law enforcement with military courts and police. The islands became the staging point for all major military campaigns in the Pacific.

Americans of Japanese Ancestry (AJAs) were regarded as suspicious characters by many non-

Asian Americans, and their loyalty was always in question, even though thousands from both Hawaii and the mainland volunteered for military service during World War II. The 100th Infantry Battalion was made up of about 1,500 Hawaiian AJAs – some regular Army personnel, some members of the Hawaiian National Guard, some Army reservists – who had joined up before the Pearl Harbor attack.

In 1943, President Roosevelt allowed other AJAs to volunteer for Army service, and the 442nd Regimental Combat Team was created from 3,000 Hawaiian and 1,500 Mainland AJAs. The 100th saw combat first, and suffered such heavy casualties in the battles in south-

ern Italy that they were nicknamed the Purple Heart Battalion. By the time they joined up with the 442nd, in June 1944, the 100th had lost more than 900 men.

The troops of the combined units, now called simply the 442nd, fought in eight major campaigns in Italy, France, and Germany. In October 1944, the 442nd lost more than 800 men in their dramatic rescue at Biffontaine, France, of the Texas 1st Battalion, trapped in the Vosges Mountains for seven days by German troops. In April 1945, the 442nd discovered the German concentration camp at Dachau and freed the prisoners. By the end of the war, the 442nd Regimental Combat Team had earned more than 18,000 individual decorations, including one Medal of Honor, and eight unit citations.

In June 2000, following a re-examination of wartime records, President Bill Clinton awarded an additional 20 Medals of Honor to veterans of the units, including one to Hawaii's Senator Daniel K. Inouye, who lost an arm in combat. The 442nd was the most highly decorated American unit in the war, and the performance of its Japanese-American troops dispelled any doubts about their loyalty.

Hawaiian statehood

Statehood for the islands of Hawaii was first proposed in the 1850s, when they were still called the Sandwich Islands, and again after the monarchy ended in 1894. During the 20th century, 22 bills proposing Hawaiian statehood died in the US Congress. But after World War II the climate had changed, partly because of increased support and lobbying from islanders, including many AJA veterans who were now in politics, and partly due to economic conditions; Congress changed Hawaii's status as a sugar exporter, and the islands now had to compete with other foreign producers without tariff protection.

The sugar barons, still powerful, decided to get behind statehood, and in March 1959, Congress passed the Hawaii Statehood Bill. It was ratified by Hawaiians by a ratio of 17 to 1, and the islands officially became the 50th state on August 21, 1959. The same year, jet service was inaugurated between California and Hawaii, and the door to tourism opened wide. By 1980, tourism was Hawaii's main industry, and it remains so today.

The racial mix

You'll have to look pretty hard to find a pure-blooded Hawaiian today – thanks to more than two centuries of ethnic intermingling with *haoles* from all over the world, there are only a handful left. Experts estimate there were about 400,000 natives on the islands when Captain Cook arrived. By 1820, the number had dropped to about 140,000, most of the decline due to European diseases; by 1880, there were only 48,000. Today, Hawaii has about 1.2 million residents, only 13 percent of them *kanaka maoli*, having at least some native Hawaiian blood. Like Native Americans on the

radicals calling for the complete return of the islands to people with native Hawaiian blood, because the overthrow of Queen Liliuokalani was illegal, to others wanting billions of dollars in reparations, to conservatives asking for some extra help for the people of Hawaiian heritage who need it.

In 1979 an Office of Hawaiian Affairs was opened to help address the questions of Hawaiian sovereignty, and has worked to help *kanaka maoli* receive various benefits due to them because of their Hawaiian blood. However, the situation is complicated, as are most things involving governments, land disputes,

mainland, *kanaka maoli* suffer social and economic problems way out of proportion to their numbers. Poverty, drug abuse, illegitimacy, crime, and suicide all affect a much higher proportion of *kanaka maoli* than of the population in general.

To combat this, a rising chorus has been calling for changes to give *kanaka maoli* a stronger voice in controlling their own lives. Called the Hawaiian Sovereignty Movement, its members range right across the board, from

LEFT: events at Pearl Harbor in 1941 were later retold in a Hollywood blockbuster.
ABOVE: making *leis* for visitors, Ka'anapali, Maui.

and century-old injustices. With luck, cooler heads will prevail and something realistic will be done to help disadvantaged islanders, and bring a satisfactory outcome to this complex problem.

Looking to the future

More positive, though, is the propensity of many Hawaiians to study and reclaim their ancient traditions and rituals, the Hawaiian language, the *hula*, native arts and crafts, and other aspects of their culture. The Hawaiian Islands have a fascinating heritage and history, worth learning and saving for future generations of *kanaka maoli* and *haoles* alike. Maybe we'll all be dancing the *hula* one day soon. ❑

PACIFIC CRUISES AROUND HAWAII

Map on page 200

Cruise enthusiasts are delighted that legislation has finally added Hawaii to cruise schedules, as the islands, in all their diversity, make ideal destinations

Hawaii receives almost 6½ million visitors a year, so it's surprising that cruises around Hawaii only began fairly recently. Until 2003, the Jones Act, which is also known as the Merchant Marine Act of 1920, forbade foreign-flagged ships from carrying cargo or passengers between US ports without stopping at a foreign port in the process. This meant that cruise lines, which are almost all registered in the Caribbean, could not cruise around Hawaii without also visiting Mexico, Canada, the Republic of Kiribati, or the South Pacific in the same sailing. Since none of these destinations are closer than two days from Hawaii, itineraries grew to as much as two weeks, and lines were forced to spend most of their time outside Hawaii.

However, congress made an arrangement in the spring of 2003 with Norwegian Cruise Line, which exempts them from the Jones Act in exchange for purchasing some US-flagged ships. These ships were originally under construction for American Classic Voyages, the previous US-flagged cruise company, which went out of business in 2001. From July 2004, NCL could cruise around the Hawaiian islands without stopping at foreign ports, and other lines are lobbying for similar rights. While this is an obvious win for NCL, the true winners are passengers who can look forward to sailing around Hawaii's lovely islands without having to brave the Pacific's sometimes rough waters.

This series of islands is lined up in a row, close enough to sail between in a few hours and far enough away that they maintain their individuality. They're also small enough to make it possible to see the highlights of each in an afternoon. It won't be an exhaustive or complete experience, but it will be enough to have swum in the ocean and sunned on the beach.

While Hawaii is a US destination, it is the Pacific that has kept it insulated from change: The stretch of ocean between Hawaii and the mainland has protected the islands from becoming a mere extension of the West Coast. Here, the influence of the Hawaiian Kamehameha dynasty remains strong, and the island style of living prevails.

In fact, you'll notice that Japan – on the other side of the Pacific – has a significant influence on Hawaii as well, especially on Oahu. Here, *sushi* stands sit next to burger joints, and signs printed in Japanese are almost as prevalent as those written in English. Hawaii has a diversity that few other American states can claim – it is truly a melting pot of Eastern and Western influences, and you'll see that from the moment you land on Oahu, the jumping-off point for Hawaiian cruises.

LEFT: a surfer at sunset on Honolulu Bay. **BELOW:** an open-air spa, Big Island.

TIP

For full details of **opening hours** and contact information for the sites and museums mentioned in this chapter, see Travel Tips page 340.

Most cruises to Hawaii offer such an extensive roster of shore excursions that there are few day trips you can't book directly through the cruise line. The one exception is a visit to the beach, which can be organized independently. Whether you book through the cruise line or through an outside tour operator, you should expect to pay a high price for the more extravagant shore excursion. Flightseeing tours by helicopter or prop plane, for example, will cost approximately $160 per person – a price that many visitors are willing to pay for a splurge on this once-in-a-lifetime experience.

From volcanoes that continue to spew lava to frothy seas dotted with surfers, Hawaii's islands have a personality all their own. This individual style is a blend of island-casual and Polynesian influence – you can take home gorgeous silk *aloha* shirts or plumeria-print sundresses. Hawaii has its own sound and flavors, too. After a visit here, you'll never look at pineapple, coffee, or macadamia nuts in the same way again, and you may consider picking up your own ukulele or slack-key guitar before you return home. Even if you don't, the sounds of Hawaii's sweetly nostalgic ukulele music will echo in your head long after you disembark.

OAHU

It isn't the largest of Hawaii's six islands, but **Oahu** ❶ has the largest airport, so it is understandable that many cruises make it the starting or end point of their trip. This means that passengers planning to arrive early or stay on in Hawaii after their cruise will often choose to add extra days in Oahu, rather than returning to one of the other islands.

Oahu is also the most developed island in the chain, and Honolulu, the state capital, feels like a major US city. In fact, it is a business and political center

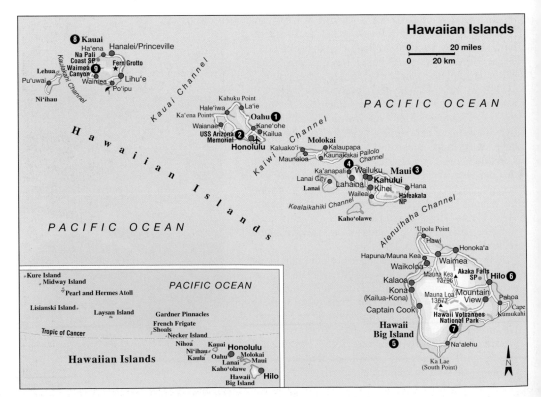

that happens to have a lovely beach, rather than a genuine beach town. It is almost urban in places, especially compared to the sleepy port towns and wide-open coastlines of the other islands. But that's Oahu's strength as well as its weakness. Here, in addition to historical landmarks and significant museums, you'll find sophisticated restaurants, cosmopolitan shopping opportunities, and some of the nicest hotels around.

Waikiki

Kalakaua Avenue Ⓐ is home to several of the island's more upscale hotels, as well as the center of Waikiki's shopping district. Here, in the Royal Hawaiian Shopping Center, you'll find designer boutiques such as Louis Vuitton, Chanel and Fendi, which often sell designs created for the Japanese market, as well as US products. You'll also notice some local designers, including Cinnamon Girl, a Hawaii-based boutique that features floral-patterned slip dresses with delicate, velvet spaghetti straps. You won't be able to avoid a number of kitsch stores along the avenue that sell the inevitable plastic grass skirts and coconut-shell bra tops, and ceramic tiki glasses for *mai tais*. You can find many of these souvenirs at the International Market Place, which is also on Kalakaua. If you're in the mood for more shopping, take a taxi to the enormous Ala Moana shopping center, just a 10-minute ride away.

Just off the avenue is **Waikiki Beach Ⓑ** with the volcanic Diamond Head in the distance. Waikiki is a 2-mile (3-km) long white sand beach that's so nice you might be willing to ignore the crowds. Here, the water is blue and warm, due to the fact that the weather remains in the balmy 70s and 80s Fahrenheit (mid-20s Centigrade) all year round.

Maps:
Area 200
Town 202

Surfing is something of a tradition in Hawaii.

BELOW:
Waikiki Beach.

Chinatown

Honolulu's **Chinatown** ⊙, like that of New York and San Francisco, is loud and bustling and dirty, but full of atmosphere and not to be missed. Here, at **Oahu Market**, street vendors sell brightly colored fresh flower *lei* in the island's signature arrangement, the tiny yellow *ilima*, which looks very much like small hibiscus blossoms and ranges from a pale sunshine yellow to a darker ocher. True, a shell *lei* will make the trip home better, but they don't smell nearly as good, and they're usually made in Vietnam rather than on the island.

You can also buy herbal remedies, live chickens, Vietnamese food, and tropical fruit; the latter makes a nice mid-afternoon snack; the live chicken might be a bit more problematic.

Fresh fragrant fruit can be found at stands in Oahu.

Diamond Head Crater

Farther down the coastline from Waikiki, about a 20-minute drive away, lies **Diamond Head** ⊙ itself. This mountain is nothing more than a 760-ft (232-meter) pile of volcanic ash that forms a tuff cone, but it is impressive just the same, and a great spot to go hiking. Don't expect an easy walk up this 350,000-year-old hill – the dry World War II-era paths are steep and winding, and there isn't much shade. Though the hike takes less than an hour, that hot Hawaiian sun feels fearsome as you climb toward the peak, however, the view of Waikiki and Oahu's south shore is one of the island's best. The crater's interior and exterior slopes are part of the 500-acre (200-hectare) **Diamond Head State Monument**. Inside the crater there's an interesting visitor center, and since the National Guard maintains a lookout post here, there are restrooms and picnic tables for public use.

Diamond Head is a nickname given to the crater in 1825 by British sailors who mistook worthless calcite crystals found on its slopes for diamonds. Its original Hawaiian name was Lae'ahi, which means "brow" *(lae)* of the yellow-fin tuna *('ahi)*. Hawaiian legends say that the fire goddess Hi'iaka, Pele's younger sister, noticed the resemblance between Diamond Head's profile and that of the *'ahi* and named it Lae'ahi, which in later years was shortened by map-

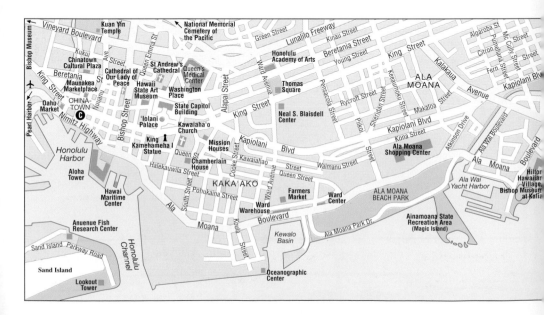

makers to Leahi. The steep slopes were favored for *holua* sliding, a tropical form of tobogganing over dry ground.

Map on page 202

Hanauma Bay Beach Park

Nearby Hanauma Bay is no less crowded than Waikiki, but it's a lovely alternative just the same. Come in the morning before the buses arrive at this protected inlet, which is actually located in the eroded crater of an extinct volcano. At Hanauma (meaning "the curved bay"), you can snorkel in the turquoise-colored water and marvel at the protected but brightly colored fish and sea turtles that swim around the bay's coral reef. The bay also has a useful visitor center (open daily), which shows a film about the area's ecology. There are overlooks at the top of the cliff, where those in a hurry can look down on the natural pool below, take their pictures, and move on.

Fresh leis *on sale at a stand in Honolulu.*

Almost 2 miles (3 km) past Hanauma on Route 72, you'll arrive at **Halona Point**. This unassuming rock formation hides a secret – a naturally formed lava tube blowhole, from which water spouts into the air when the tide comes in. Depending on the tide, the seawater can spray as much as 10 ft (3 meters) high. Scan the coastline for whales, then look down to your right and catch a glimpse of Halona Cove, the site of Deborah Kerr and Burt Lancaster's steamy sex-on-the-beach love scene in *From Here to Eternity* – regarded as extremely daring when the film was made in 1953.

The Bishop Museum

The **Bishop Museum** (open daily), at 1525 Bernice Street, Honolulu, was started in 1889 by Charles Reed Bishop in honor of his late wife, Princess Bernice Pauahi Bishop, who was the last descendant of the royal Kamehameha family. Housed in a former boys' school, the museum is designed to present the history of Hawaii to both local people and visitors, and is generally considered to be the best anthropological museum and research facility in all Polynesia. Inside, you'll find Hawaiian artifacts, including musical instruments, masks, and weapons, and royal heirlooms such as furniture and clothing – don't miss

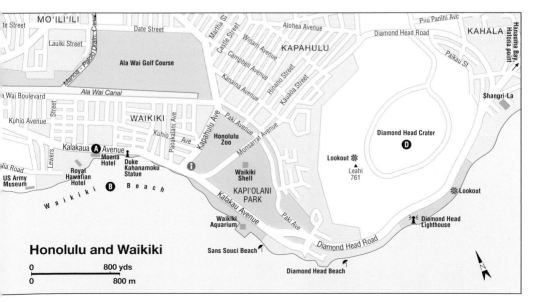

Honolulu and Waikiki

0	800 yds
0	800 m

The USS Arizona Memorial is Hawaii's most visited site.

BELOW: Big Beach in Makena State Park, Maui.

the feathered cloak. The museum also has a large natural history collection, featuring seashells, endemic birds, rare insects, and a 55-ft (17-meter) sperm whale, as well as a planetarium. If you have the choice, go on a weekend so as to avoid the many local school groups who come to soak up their heritage, including the history of the ukulele and the grass skirt.

Pearl Harbor

The site of the 1941 World War II attack by Japan is still an emotional place for Americans and Japanese visitors alike. The USS *Arizona* **Memorial** ❷ (visitors' center open daily), built to commemorate the ship that had the greatest losses in the air strike, is Hawaii's most visited site – and tends to be the most crowded space on the island. It is often a reflective and tearful stop on a trip that's otherwise more about sunshine than sadness, and the memorial is a fitting tribute to that fateful December day – as well as an interesting explanation of the strategic value of Hawaii's statehood. The program starts off with a 23-minute documentary film, followed by a tour of several galleries filled with historical information and an impressively detailed timeline leading up to the attack. Most visitors find they get wrapped up in the strategy of the political players.

The tour finishes with a boat trip to the actual memorial, which is located in the middle of the harbor. Go early if you can – tickets for admission times are handed out on a first-come, first-served basis each day, and sometimes they run out before noon. Also, if you go on your own, rather than with a tour, be sure to ask your taxi driver to take you to the *Arizona* Memorial, rather than Pearl Harbor – the latter remains an active military base, for good reason.

MAUI

Traditionally, it was agriculture and whaling that sustained the island of **Maui** ❸. The fertile volcanic soil was excellent for growing sugar cane and sweet pineapples, and whales proliferated in the nearby waters. Today, tourism has replaced foodstuffs as Maui's bread and butter. Much farmland has been converted to golf courses and resorts.

Still, the same tropical climate that favored pineapples now favors visitors. High rainfall provides gushing waterfalls, stunning rainbows, and bright green grass that contrast sharply with the blue water of the ocean and the blue skies above. Maui draws surfers from around the world to its frothy coastline, and honeymooners, as well as other sun worshipers, flock to its golden beaches. Despite the onslaught of tourism in the past several decades, Maui remains island casual and laid-back, with a sandals and T-shirt dress code that lasts from morning to night. You can leave your suits and cocktail dresses on the ship.

Lahaina

Maui's tourism center, located on the western side of the island, was once the rough-and-tumble whaling capital of the world. On the outskirts of town you can still do some humpback whale-watching during the season, which runs from December through April. That means that all winter long and during the first part of spring, almost 1,000 humpback whales reside here, escaping the frigid waters of the Bering Sea and forming their own community.

At Lahaina's harbor, which opens up onto Front Street, you can still see some references to the town's rugged origins, such as the turn-of-the-20th-century Pioneer Inn, the original prison (there is still a Prison Street), and the remains of the 1830s stone-built whaling fort. But the bulk of the area is made up of tourist stores and pricey restaurants. Don't be surprised by the high cost of normally inexpensive things like chicken and beef dishes: here, almost everything has to be imported, which naturally adds to the cost. Not everything is expensive, though. If you hit some stores that are part of mainland chains, you can sometimes get good deals on sweaters and other warm-weather clothing that (surprise, surprise) don't sell particularly well on the tropical island of Maui.

You can't swim in Lahaina, since it remains a busy commercial port, so you will need to find a taxi to take you to nearby Ka'Anapali if what you really want is a beach.

Map on page 200

Ka'anapali

Just 3 miles (5 km) up the road, the trip to **Ka'anapali** ❹ should be a short one, but congestion and narrow, winding streets mean that it can take as long as 20 minutes to get there. Ka'anapali beach is exactly what most visitors have in mind when they imagine Hawaii's shoreline. White sand stretches along the coast for miles, interrupted only by palm trees and exotic birds, from the Hyatt Regency and the Westin up to the Sheraton Maui. Don't be concerned about trespassing on private property: All beaches on the island are public, and the hotels can't prevent you from swimming in the surf, snorkeling, or lying out on the

BELOW: Bud the birdman in Lahaina.

lounge chairs, using the pools, and other facilities (though they can stop you from using their bathrooms). Anyway, as many of the daytrippers who crowd the beach end up lunching in the hotel restaurants, the hotel managers don't wish to discourage them.

A trip to Haleakala National Park should start with a stop by the visitors' center.

Kahului

Located on the northern, windward side of the island, **Kahului** is too windy and cool for a visit to the beach. However, this commercial center and residential port town is a great launching point for tours around the lush, misty, and flower-filled Iao Valley (known as the "Yosemite of the Pacific") as well as **Haleakala National Park**. The crater at the top of dormant Mount Haleakala volcano, which last erupted in 1790, sits at 11,000 ft (3,350 meters) – the highest point on the island. It's often topped with clouds but, on a clear day, you can see views of Maui's sugar-cane fields, eucalyptus trees, white-sand beaches, and coconut palms when you're at the top, as well as The Big Island and Oahu off in the distance.

The crater is as barren as the rest of the mountainside is fertile. You can drive, hike, or cycle down, passing through several different climates as you descend toward the shore. Many cruise lines offer helicopter rides over the area, which, although not cheap, provide a nice little adventure, and a different vantage point on Haleakala's waterfalls, varied landscape, and even more varied climates.

BELOW: the falls at Haleakala National Park.

Hana Highway

The jungle-covered town of **Hana** lies at the end of a long and harrowing drive from Kahului. This is a trip that's about the journey rather than the destination. The road to Hana itself is an adventure, famous for its steep twists, and there are said to be over 600 turns and 65 bridges. It's only 55 miles (90 km) between the two towns, but it can take as long as two hours to make the trip. This is not a trip to be taken by the faint hearted, but it is a right-of-passage for any first-time visitor to Maui. After this, your cruise will feel like a smooth ride no matter what kind of storms you hit.

THE BIG ISLAND

The **Big Island** ❺ is often just called Hawaii. It's younger than the other Hawaiian islands, but larger than all of them combined. Some cruise ships that come to the Big Island stop at both the ports of Hilo, on the east coast, and Kona on the west, offering cruisers an opportunity to really cover some ground. Others stop in one port or the other and simply bus their passengers around the island.

The Big Island has an incredibly varied landscape, with rainforests that can be seen on horseback, cactus-studded deserts, tropical beaches, and snowy mountains that tower over it all. It's no surprise then that the island grows Kona coffee (the only gourmet American coffee beans) and macadamia nuts, as well as papaya fruit, and is fertile enough to support cattle ranches. If you only have one day, you'll have to make some tough choices about what to see because there just won't be time to take in everything. You can rent a car in advance, or sign up for the ship's shore excursions – either way, you won't want to miss a moment on this fascinating island.

Hilo

With 42,000 residents, **Hilo ❻** is the largest city on The Big Island. It is the commercial center of the sugar-cane industry, and has been wiped out several times in history by tsunamis. Since the tidal waves last washed over the town in 1960, you will have a sense as you drive through that Hilo is a much newer place than it actually is, with the strip malls and modern shopping centers. That said, Hilo doesn't feel cosmopolitan like Honolulu, but rather like the largest version of a small Hawaiian town. While many ships dock here, they merely use the port, which is outside of the city limits anyway, as a jumping-off point to see this part of the island – or the whole island, if the ship isn't stopping in Kona.

There are plenty of stores in Hilo, and some cruise lines offer shore excursions to macadamia nut orchards to learn about and then purchase nature's little nuggets. But, although you may see passengers returning to the ship with large boxes of nuts and raving about the discounts, time in port is limited on a Hawaii cruise, and it would be a shame to miss the natural beauty of this island.

Akaka Falls State Park

The true beauty of the windward coast, however, is found outside of Hilo, in the rural, rolling, orchid-filled countryside. About 15 miles (24 km) north of the city, at Highway 220, Honomu, **Akaka Falls State Park** (free) is a 66-acre (27-hectare) garden sanctuary for rare tropical flowers, and you'll see plenty of wild orchids, philodendron vines, bright pink ginger flowers, and azaleas, as

Map on page 200

Take a horse-and-buggy ride to see some of the sites on The Big Island.

BELOW: the Haleakala Crater, Maui.

Hawaii brims over with bright flora like this poinsetta bush.

well as less-recognizable flora and plenty of birds. Hike the well-maintained half-mile (800-meter) path past the bamboo grove, and past the 100-ft (30-meter) tall Kapuna waterfall that serves as a marker as you make your way up the trail to Akaka itself.

The spectacularly dramatic 420-ft (128-meter) high Akaka waterfall pours its bounty into a steam-eroded gorge lined with leafy ferns. Just be careful on the slippery path: The ancient legend says that the Hawaiian god Akaka, fleeing home after his wife returned unexpectedly and discovered his infidelity, slipped and fell off the ledge and over the falls. On the journey back to Hilo, **Mauna Kea**, the tallest volcano on the island, looms in the distance.

Hawaii Volcanoes National Park

Some 30 miles (48 km) from Hilo, just off Highway 11, **Hawaii Volcanoes National Park ❼** (open daily) is a fascinating place to visit. Established in 1916, the 218,000-acre (88,220-hectare) park centers around Mount Kilauea, the world's most active volcano. Kilauea towers at 13,677 ft (4,170 meters), shadowing the dramatic landscape, which is covered with bubbling lava flows and defined by its black-rock, ashen surface, the appearance often compared, somewhat melodramatically, to the surface of the moon. Just inside the entrance there is a visitors' center with some educational information and a schedule of ranger-led tours of the park. If you've rented a car, you can drive the 11-mile (18-km) loop that encircles the caldera, passing through a desert and some rainforest on the way. You can also drive down the aptly-named Chain of Craters Road, which leads to the coastal area of the park and sometimes to glimpses of active lava flows.

BELOW:
Hawaii Volcanoes National Park, The Big Island.

Waimea

This cattle-ranching town at the base of the Kohala Mountains is home of the *paniolos*, Hawaii's own brand of cowboy. Lest you forget you are in the USA, the cowboy way of life is as strong a presence here as it is in Texas. In 1809, John Palmer Parker herded up cattle across the cactus-lined fields for King Kamehameha I. Eventually, he bought his own herd, established the Parker ranch, and married the king's granddaughter. Over the past two centuries, the ranch has changed the look of the whole area. Many wealthy ranching aficionados have bought land in the valley and started rodeos and opened saddle stores. Today, 175,000-acre (70,820-hectare) Parker Ranch remains a working ranch with 35,000 head of cattle. The original ranch house and a ranch museum (open daily) can be visited. Parker also offers wagon rides, riding lessons, and big-game hunting for Polynesia boar.

KAUAI

Kauai ❽ is the northernmost, and most verdant, of all the Hawaiian islands. It was supposedly settled by a pre-Polynesian tribe called the Menehune, otherwise known as the "Leprechauns of the Pacific," because legend has it that they were only 2 ft (60 cm) tall and worked mostly at night. What remains of them is the stonework and ditches that they created around the island, as well as legend.

Today, you'll still find misty mountainsides and dense Technicolor tropical forests. In fact, it is so lushly green and richly colored with bright, exotic flowers that Hollywood producers often choose to shoot movies here. They come when they are trying to depict jungle scenes, as was the case with *Raiders of the Lost Ark* (1981), or romantic, tropical paradise scenes, as in *South Pacific* (1958).

Map on page 200

BELOW: Kalapaki Beach, Kauai.

*A woodcarver at
Waimea Falls Park.*

Fortunately, the attention has not spoiled the natural, dramatic beauty of Kauai – no building is allowed to be taller than the palm trees, even in the port town of **Nawiliwili**, where most ships stop. Since most of the island's approximately 58,000 residents live along Kauai's shores, the interior of the island is as unspoiled as can be, so it is worth looking for shore excursions that take you away from the beach and into the jungle.

Waimea Canyon

Within **Koke'e State Park** (open access; free), on Highway 550, the ocher-colored **Waimea Canyon** ❾ is the shining star. At 10 miles (16 km) long and about 3,600 ft (1,100 meters) deep, Waimea was described by Mark Twain as the "Grand Canyon of the Pacific." Rings around the canyon display the lasting results of centuries-old volcanic eruptions and lava flows. There are lookouts all along the way, but the best views of Kalalau Valley are from the last two. Before you start out on a hike or a drive around the rim, stop at the Koke'e Natural History Museum for some hiking maps of the area and information on local birds and geological phenomena. If you choose to take a shore excursion here instead, many lines stop at the Spouting Horn blowhole on the way back to the ship.

The Fern Grotto

The only way to reach the **Fern Grotto** is by water. Traveling down the Wailua River in a motor boat or kayak is one of the most popular shore excursion options in Kauai. **Wailua Marina State Park** (open access), on the Kuhio Highway, offers a 1½-hour riverboat tour of the fern-covered cavern. Along the way, hula dancers entertain and guides share folklore about the island, and you can see Opaekaa Falls and the remains of Holo-Holo-Ku, which is a *heiaus,* an ancient Hawaiian temple. The grotto itself is of stone, with a canopy of fern fronds. It can be crowded, and, especially since musicians are usually on hand to play "The Hawaiian Wedding Song" for tourists, it doesn't feel much like a quiet sanctuary. But it's still considered by many to be a must for first-time visitors.

BELOW: Opaekaa
Falls, Kaui.

Po'ipu Beach

Crescent-shaped **Po'ipu Beach** on the island's southern shore is a great place to go if you just want to lie out on the sands and do very little, especially since the nearby Haupu Mountain range blocks Kauai's rain showers and lets the sun shine here more often then elsewhere. In case you are surprised by the showers in other parts of the island, remember that you don't get grass this green without a little rainfall.

But there is much more to do than just sunbathe here. You can rent a horse from nearby stables or a bike, enabling you to ride horseback or cycle along the coastline; or you can snorkel and surf in the clear, blue water. In some places, the beach itself is narrow but the generally calm water is full of colorful fish. Look into shore excursions that arrange these activities for you – most ships do offer active visits to Po'ipu as part of their repertoire, and it's easier than doing it alone.

Menehune Fish Pond

The 240-acre (100-hectare) **Huleia Refuge** at Kilauea was established in the mid-1970s to provide protected wetlands for endangered waterfowl. Here, 31 species of birds reside, including endangered stilt, coot, and moorhens. Not all the species are native to Hawaii. In fact, of the 31 species, 18 have been introduced. The wooded hills of the park itself are closed to the public in order to protect the fragile balance of the ecosystem here, but you can catch a glimpse from the state-created overlook at the **Menehune Fish Pond**. The pond itself, filled with mangroves and rocks, is a registered historic landmark, and was originally dredged in the 1600s on the orders of a Hawaiian chief.

Na Pali Coast State Park

Lined with cliffs that end sharply at the sea, the **Na Pali Coast State Park** (open daily; free) on Kuhio Highway is another dramatic spot on the island of Kauai. It is really a trip for the fit and energetic, and if you're into hiking, you will get the most out of the experience, as the 11-mile (18-km) Kalalau Trail is the only way to access the most beautiful part of this rugged coastline. The trail narrows and widens, crosses streams and valleys, and passes fertile fruit trees and gushing waterfalls before opening up onto the sheer drop. Then, switchback paths lead hikers down to golden **Kalalau Beach**. Because the trek takes the better part of the day, you should remember to check your ship's schedule before setting out to make sure you are not late back for your sailing – there are shorter hikes to choose from if you don't have time for Kalalau, or if you feel it would be too much for you. Either way, be sure to wear good, strong hiking boots and pack plenty of water and sunscreen. ❏

Map on page 200

TIP

The best panoramic views of the Kalalau Valley, the largest valley along the Na Pali Coast, can be found at the edge of Waimea Canyon at Koke'e and the Kalalau Valley Lookout nearby.

LEFT AND BELOW: catching rays on Po'ipu Beach.

AMERICA'S WATERWAYS

A cruise along America's waterways gives an insight that
could not be gained by traveling the highways

An American river journey offers a perspective at a pace that allows travelers to view tangible relics of the past and appreciate how amazingly well the water arteries function today. Highways tend to obliterate geography, while a river is a natural stream flowing through an ever-changing landscape.

Today's steamboat cruises embarking at Pittsburgh set off from a city whose original raison d'être was river commerce, and whose impressive skyline is the direct result of that connection. As the Ohio River twists and turns southwestward, the great city disappears from sight and mind and ahead is 1,935 miles (3,113 km) of river to the Gulf of Mexico. A remarkable odyssey awaits the modern traveler, the chance to view a continuous kaleidoscope of America – its farms, industry, woods, bluffs, small towns, and big cities.

Long stretches of the Mississippi below its junction with the Ohio remain pristine, with few, if any, signs of human interference. As the sun sets, it adds a golden tint to the surface; when the sky is clear, gaze up at the stars as they pop into view as if many tiny lamps have been switched on. An evening on the river makes you want the journey to go on forever without any intervening ports to sever the magic.

The passenger steamboat shares the river with the serious business of waterborne traffic, a steady stream of barges lashed together with a powerful pushboat in charge of guiding today's equivalent of a laden raft en route to its destination. The cargo may be coal, gravel, trap rock, chemicals, fuel oil, or grain, and these bulk commodities move far more cheaply on the river than by train or truck.

But American rivers are not all about commerce, industries, and cities. On the Snake River in Washington, the boat will glide amid natural buttes, with no sign of human habitation and no parallel road to scar the landscape. At night that landscape changes completely, and you wake to the lush forests and waterfalls of the misty Columbia River Gorge. When the boat reaches the Pacific, the ocean swells and cascading breakers call a halt. An onward journey requires a deep-sea ship to cross the 5,000 sea miles (9,300 km) to the Orient.

Once hooked on river journeys, it is satisfying to know that there are thousands of miles of waterways to explore, from the Atchafalaya and Arkansas to the Tennessee and Tombigbee. The Mississippi River system includes a network 12,350 miles (19,875 km) long, and this excludes the 1,173 miles (1,888 km) of the Gulf Intracoastal Waterway paralleling the Gulf of Mexico. There's a lot to explore, and your first journey will only whet your appetite for the rhythm of the river, the sense of leisure, and the land unfolding before you. ❑

PRECEDING PAGES: two mermaids adorn the *Mississippi Queen* riverboat; "Tom Sawyer" fishing on the Mississippi River.
LEFT: the *American Queen*, the world's largest paddlewheel steamer.

AMERICA'S STEAMBOAT LEGACY

The heyday of the steamboat only lasted for about 70 years,
but the impact on the American imagination was considerable

The arrival of the steamboat in 1811 was a huge breakthrough, in that it permitted travel against the current, and transformed the Mississippi into a fully-fledged commercial artery. Upriver travel had not been an option under sail and it was almost impossible using oars or paddles. Consequently, nearly all

river traffic had to go downstream until the first steamboat arrived.

The steamboat era

Appropriately named for its ultimate destination, the *New Orleans*, a sidewheel steamboat, inaugurated a new era when Nicholas and Lydia Roosevelt and their retinue set off from Pittsburgh down the Ohio, a 1,835-mile (2,936-km) journey that took several months. Their steamboat was modeled on a Robert Fulton design that first saw service half a dozen years before on the Hudson River. Four years on, the steamboat *Washington* made the same journey upstream from New Orleans in only 24 days, while a com-

plete downstream run could be made in around 10 days, about what it takes today.

Steamboats were powered by the internal combustion engine, developed in England and the USA at the end of the 18th century. Fuels such as wood, coal and, later, oil, caused burning, or combustion, inside tightly sealed spaces. That energy drove pistons, arms, or rods attached to a means of propulsion such as a paddlewheel and later a screw propeller. Paddlewheels might be placed on the sides of the hull or as a single wheel at the stern, with vessels referred to as side-wheel and stern-wheel steamboats, or simply sidewheelers and sternwheelers. Travel became faster, more frequent, more reliable, more comfortable, and generally less expensive than ever before.

Eventually, the steamboat took its place in popular US culture far from the rivers themselves. Novels such as Mark Twain's *The Adventures of Huckleberry Finn* (1884) featured steamboat races. Later, Edna Ferber's *Show Boat* (1926) brought steamboat heritage to the printed page, and inspired the musical play of the same name that continues to be performed today. Steam showboats came to every US river town that could produce an audience, even well past the heyday of the boats as major carriers. Equally appealing were Currier and Ives prints, which brought dramatic steamboat scenes into people's homes.

During the 19th century, some 11,000 steamboats were built, and their average lifespan was just 18 months. The greatest loss occurred on April 27, 1865, when the *Sultana*, taking Union troops home from the South at the end of the Civil War, exploded just above Memphis. No exact figure is known, but the best estimate is 1,700 killed, burned, or drowned out of about 2,000 aboard a steamboat that had a legal passenger certificate for only 365.

Passage ranged from deck class, which meant sleeping in a hammock, to a berth in a dormitory, to cabins for one to four people. Often upper and lower berths had a door than opened onto a side deck or an interior public lounge. At the start of the steamboat era, there was no electricity, just gas lamps, and not even running water.

Still, some public rooms could be opulent. Here you might find one- and two-deck-high lounges, often topped with skylights, furnished with fancy Victorian couches, stained-glass windows, inlaid wood, and dining saloons with glittering crystal chandeliers, parquet floors, and rich tapestries. The exterior wedding-cake look came from the many decks, tall fluted black stacks, white decorative woodwork, handsome pilot houses, perhaps with an eagle or a pair of antlers attached, and the oversized Union, state, and company flags proudly flying. But the vast majority of steamboats were not at all fancy, in or out, but rather basic workhorses designed to carry as much as possible for the lowest price.

The steamboat helped create Pittsburgh as a powerhouse of US industry and a major transportation hub because of its location at the start of the navigation of the Upper Ohio, a river that flowed 981 miles (1,568 km) to the junction with the Mississippi at a town called Cairo (pronounced Cayrow). From here, the widening river flowed even more easily for another 954 miles (1,528 km) to the Gulf of Mexico.

The iron horse arrives

With the steady expansion of the railroads in the 1850s and following the Civil War, the steamboats' heyday as a means of mass passenger travel was relatively short-lived. By the 1880s, most towns of any note were located on or near a railway line that often paralleled the river. Increasingly the railroads had a powerful effect in turning a town's focus away from the river to an inland depot, even though some steamboat travel between towns could be more direct than by rail, especially when the origin and destination were on opposite banks.

As passenger traffic continued to drop, steamboats became more freight-oriented. The steam engines were then applied more efficiently to powerful towboats that pulled or pushed strings of barges. Today on the Midwestern rivers, the towboat has become almost exclusively an oil-fired diesel pushboat, with lines of barges up ahead, although the word towboat is still used, because a tow means a string of barges.

LEFT: a steamboat on the Mississippi River in the 19th century.
RIGHT: Mark Twain's literature featured steamboats.

Steamboats continued until recently to ply rivers as day excursion boats, from major cities such as Cincinnati or Detroit. Louisville still has its *Belle of Louisville* and New Orleans has the *Natchez*, both true steamboats, and there are numerous diesel-powered vessels, including dozens of gambling boats serving many other river cities.

One of the last scheduled overnight river steamboat services was operated by the California Transportation Co. between San Francisco and Sacramento until the outbreak of World War II. The 1926-built *Delta King* and *Delta Queen* sailed every night at 6pm from

opposite landings, passing at about midnight and arriving the next day at 6am. It was largely a tourist service, carrying passengers' automobiles, yet had men's dormitory accommodations priced just below the cost of a Southern Pacific train ticket. War put an end to the service as the boats were needed to ferry troops and wounded men around the San Francisco Bay area.

After the war, the Cincinnati-based Greene Line of Steamers, dating from 1890, bought the *Delta Queen*, boarded her up for the ocean journey via the Panama Canal, and refitted her for passenger cruise service. She still plys the Mississippi today, as the sole genuine link to the once-abundant voyaging steamer fleets. ❏

The Army that Looks After the Rivers

R iver navigation and flood control are maintained by the US Army Corps of Engineers, a federal government organization founded in 1779. The Army Corps has been responsible for surveying and charting channels, removing snags and sandbars, and building locks and dams. More recent tasks have included managing water resources in an environmentally sound fashion.

The Mississippi (Lower and Upper) and Ohio heavy rainfall. The first recorded floods occurred in 1849 and 1850, and by 1879, the government had taken action to control the river and improve navigation by establishing the Mississippi River Commission. The MRC surveyed the river and its tributaries, relocated and deepened the shipping channels to improve safe and continuous navigation, and constructed levees to control flooding.

Despite this, major floods occurred in 1882, 1912, 1913, and 1927, causing widespread devastation. The Flood of 1927 remains the most notorious, and there are people alive today who can remember the havoc it created. Families with foresight, ingenuity, and plenty of help built rafts for

River system improvements have dealt with the waterways' natural navigational impediments. On the Columbia-Snake, the Corps' additional projects include building hydroelectric plants and providing safe passage around the dams for migrating fish.

The Lower Mississippi

The Lower Mississippi has been altered more than the rest of the Midwestern system to improve navigation and flood control. While there are no locks on the lower river, there are long stretches of levees, embankments built to straighten out the river and to prevent high water from spilling off into the adjoining farmlands and flooding fields and towns, as so often happened in the past in periods of themselves, their employees, pets, and possessions. When everything was piled aboard, the raft was tied up to the strongest pole or tree to wait out the flood, which eventually covered 26,000 sq miles (67,340 sq km). Where levees were breached, it destroyed cities, towns, industries, transportation, and farms. Some 200 people lost their lives and at least 600,000 were displaced.

Additional measures were enacted to control the rivers and extend the protecting levees, and they have largely been effective. In the upper reaches between Cairo and New Madrid, a setback levee was constructed 5 miles (8 km) west of the riverfront levee to act as a floodway at extremely high stages. Because of the levees, river passengers will find that sightlines inland are often blocked, but step ashore and walk atop one for better view.

When you look at a map of the river, notice the numerous lakes either side, often in the shape of an arc. These were once part of the main channel, and when the Army Corps decided to straighten the river by building levees, these winding stretches ended up cut off from the main flow. Nowadays they are popular fishing ponds and an important source of food and recreation for local residents.

The Upper Mississippi

In the river's natural state, navigation by Indian canoe, pirogue, keelboat and, later, river steamer was hazardous because of rapids, submerged rocks, shoals, sandbars, and snags. Water levels rose and fell, creating dangerous fast-flowing surges during spring flooding, and there were often low-water periods later in the year that made continuous navigation impossible. Recognizing the important role the river could play in the economy, in the 1830s the US government began making improvements, designed to remove the most dangerous obstacles. Dynamiting cleared rocks, and secondary channels were closed off to create a main navigation channel with adequate depths. Gradually the minimum channel depth deepened from 4½ ft to 6ft (1.37 meters to 1.83 meters).

When steamboat traffic declined at the end of the 19th century in favor of railroads, the river lost its commercial viability. However, the development of powerful diesel-driven tugs and towboats gave the river highway a new lease on life, and Congress passed legislation providing for a 9-ft (2.75-meter) channel depth and a minimum width of 400 ft (122 meters). The US Army Corps began construction in earnest, mostly between 1930 and 1940, eventually completing 29 locks and dams between St Louis and St Paul that created a series of slack-water pools where the river level could be controlled under most circumstances.

The Ohio River

The Ohio River originally had 50 locks and dams, some the removable wicket type that folded down to allow the boat to pass. These have been replaced by 18 high-lift dams, creating pools to maintain depth for navigation. The lock chambers

LEFT: a string of seaplanes is towed down the Mississippi River during the 1927 flood.
RIGHT: securing the levee with sandbags in Cairo, Illinois, 1937.

to one side allow the river traffic to pass through with the boats being lifted or lowered to the new level. The dams create steps in the river but their purpose is not flood control. The Army Corps has built a series of reservoirs to take excess run-off and to release water as necessary.

The Columbia and Snake rivers

The 465 navigable miles (748 km) along the Columbia and Snake rivers begin at sea level at the mouth of the Columbia near Astoria, Oregon and rise some 738 ft (225 meters) to Lewiston, Idaho. The US Army Corps has been active here since before the turn of the 19th century. Eight

large dams have been built, with the first, the Bonneville Dam, erected in 1937. The dam sites generate a huge amount of hydroelectricity, but because the rivers are a major spawning ground for returning salmon and steelhead fingerlings, fish ladders have been built to provide passage for the fish.

However, the numbers of salmon that make it up to spawn have dropped markedly, and such methods as carrying fish around the dams in tanker trucks have been tried, and fish hatcheries built. Considerable controversy has emerged about the salmons' endangered future. The most drastic measures propose having the dams removed altogether to allow the salmon to migrate freely. Thus far there has been no resolution. ❑

THE COASTAL AND RIVER CRUISE LINES

Coastal and river cruising is entirely different from the open-sea experience, with a distinctive appeal. Here are some tips on what to expect

Coastal and river cruise lines have a great deal in common. While their vessels range in size, they would all be considered small vessels. The maximum passenger capacity is just over 400, but most carry only

about 100. They nearly all fly the US flag and are staffed by US crews. The domestic itineraries, plus Canada, are destination-driven, usually with a port or two every day and some daylight cruising. Coastal boats often tie up at night. None of the vessels has a casino, a spa, a gym, a shopping center, or a lido deck with swimming pool, and they don't stage art auction. With limited or no entertainment, *Delta Queen* being the main exception, the boats mostly attract a crowd of retired Americans, some Canadians, and a few others.

Lindblad Expeditions is renowned for an outstanding enrichment program that appeals to people interested in learning about the culture and natural attributes of the areas through which they are cruising. *Delta Queen*, Cruise West and Clipper come next, with a good standard of interpretation of relevant topics; the rest have some enrichment programs, but only in specialist areas. All the lines have what most of the passengers are looking for: a friendly atmosphere and the chance to see the USA and its scenery.

The amenities, cruising regions, and seasons of each fleet vary, and are outlined below. Full contact details of each are given in the Travel Tips section *(pages 324–5)*.

American Canadian Caribbean

This well-known Rhode Island-based firm (www.accl-smallships.com) reinvented shallow-draft coastal cruising. The three-ship fleet comprises the *Niagara Prince* (with capacity for 84 passengers), *Grande Caribe* (100 passengers) and *Grande Mariner* (100 passengers) that sail the East Coast, St Lawrence Valley, Great Lakes, and Mississippi River system.

The boats provide no-frills accommodations, outside cabins that are tiny and bathrooms that are even more so. *Niagara Prince* has a combination dining room and lounge and the other two have one located above the other. The food is good, hearty US fare, served family-style by a young all-American crew. Atmosphere is very relaxed and sociable, and the entertainment is provided by local storytellers, and perhaps a traveling enrichment lecturer. The strong points of these boats are that they can squeeze under very low railroad bridges that no other operator can manage, hence their cruises along the Illinois waterways and the Erie Canal.

American Cruise Lines

One of the smallest lines in the business, American (www.americancruiselines.com) operates two 49-passenger coastal ships, the *American Eagle* and *American Glory*, covering the eastern seaboard from Maine to Florida.

The on-board style of these two ships offers some of the largest cabins in the coastal cruising industry, with sitting areas, and some with verandahs. The forward observation lounge hosts a complimentary cocktail hour with hot hors d'oeuvres. There is a second midships lounge and a small library. The dining room, located aft, offers some of the best food to be found in these waters, and the emphasis is on freshness, in their seafood and other products. There are some on-board lecturer programs, as well as local speakers in some ports.

The emphasis on these two ships is on comfort, spaciousness, and great food, and their

These sternwheelers offer the plushest accommodations in the Pacific Northwest. All outside cabins have big windows, and TV/VCRs, and some have private balconies. There is a fine collection of photographs and paintings on display. Good standard food is served by a spirited young crew at a single open seating. An onboard historian gives talks, and when passengers are in port, bus drivers provide a commentary as they drive to natural sites of interest and interpretive centers.

The emphasis is very much on creature comforts and onboard entertainment, with nightly cabarets, big band sounds, and country-and-

small capacity makes them popular with school and museums groups.

American West Steamboat Company

The American West Steamboat Company (www.columbiarivercruise.com) operates two very similar, diesel-powered sternwheelers, the 163-passenger *Queen of the West* and the 235-passenger *Empress of the North*. They ply the Columbia and Snake rivers nearly year-round and the Inside Passage in the summer.

LEFT: passengers on a Cruise West trip can travel to Alaska or California.
ABOVE: the *Yorktown Clipper*.

western music. The line offers the most departures, but you must be prepared for very hot weather in July and August and wind and snow in the dead of winter.

Clipper Cruise Line

The 100-passenger *Nantucket Clipper* and 138-passenger *Yorktown Clipper* are similar ships, offering varied itineraries on both coasts, in Alaska and Baja (www.clippercruise.com).

Cabins are small outside ones, nicely furnished, and some open onto a side deck. A single lounge serves as the social center and venue for tour-guide talks. Dining is open seating style and the service staff are of college age.

The line's chefs come from the USA's best cooking schools, so fresh ingredients and preparation are highlights. The atmosphere is country club casual.

Cruise West

Cruise West (www.cruisewest.com) is an Alaska specialist that sends several of its shallow-draft ships – *Spirit of '98*, *Spirit of Alaska* and *Spirit of Discovery* – on one-week cruises along the Columbia and Snake rivers between late March and early May and again during September and October. The fleet also cruises the rivers of Alaska and California, and Baja.

Cruise West ships can carry around 70 to 90 passengers in all.

The coastal steamboat-styled *Spirit of '98* has an elevator and is more nicely fitted than her plainly-furnished running mates. All the cabins are small outside ones and most of them have windows. The *Spirit of '98* also has cabin TVs and windows that open. The food is good US fare, using fresh, local Pacific Northwest ingredients, and dinner entrees run to five choices, including a vegetarian option. Evenings are convivial social gatherings, generally without any planned entertainment.

The line has recently upgraded its onboard enrichment programs by offering better training for the expedition leader and assistant, so that more information is available, imparted in an accessible and interesting manner.

Delta Queen Steamboat Company

The Delta Queen Steamboat Company (www.deltaqueen.com) run a trio of steamboats, the 174-passenger *Delta Queen* (1926), which is a National Landmark; the 414-passenger *Mississippi Queen* (1976), and the 436-passenger *American Queen* (1995). The three sister boats ply the navigable portions of the entire Mississippi River system as well as the Gulf Coast Intracoastal Waterway.

The onboard style of the three steamboats differs significantly. The wooden *Delta Queen* is small and genuinely old-fashioned, and the other two are larger and elegantly ersatz. The *Delta Queen*'s cabins run from tight upper- and lower-berth ones to plush queen-size and twin-bedded doubles with stained-glass transoms. Two forward lounges provide comfortable seating, and there's also a bar offering cabaret entertainment, and an interior parlor lounge for reading and card games. The dining room doubles as the show lounge.

The *Mississippi Queen* and the *American Queen* offer more of a conventional cruise experience, with larger, plusher cabins, some with private verandahs, show lounges where riverboat-style entertainment is staged, and more public spaces. Traveling historians, known onboard as "riverlorians," relate the river's geography and history in an informative way on all three boats.

The Delta Queen Company dates back to 1890, which means that it qualifies as a genuine link with the steamboat era. It offers a celebration of quintessential Americana, with Dixieland jazz and big band music, Cajun, Southern and Middle American food, local history, and river lore. Well-presented theme cruises include one on the Civil War, antebellum home visits, the Kentucky Derby, and the Great Steamboat Race.

Lindblad Expeditions

Lindblad (www.expeditions.com) offers hands-on well-planned nature-oriented West Coast adventure itineraries from Baja to Alaska. The *Sea Bird* and *Sea Lion*, each with a capacity for 70 passengers, are the smallest in the Pacific Northwest fleet.

The cabins are very small – only 90 sq ft (8 sq meters) – and simple, and a few on the lowest decks are inside ones that can be claustrophobic. There is one lounge. The restaurant serves all meals in the only dining room, which is bright and cheerful. Ingredients are of high quality, the preparation is sophisticated, and the results are extremely tasty.

A team comprising an expedition leader and four naturalists covers a wide variety of subjects – history, anthropology, botany, geology, and zoology – in their onboard talks and zodiac excursions to wildlife refuges. Kayaks are also carried for passengers' use. Lindblad provides the most intellectually stimulating and physically active cruises of all the small steamboat lines, which means that they tend to be more expensive than some of the others.

Riverbarge Excursion Lines

The Riverbarge Line (www.riverbarge.com) runs the 198-passenger *River Explorer*, the most unusual conveyance on North America's waterways. It comprises two three-deck barges tied together and propeled by a towboat lashed to the stern, which plies the Mississippi River system and the Gulf Coast Intracoastal Waterway year round.

There are 99 roomy cabins housed on two decks on the DeSoto barge; they differ only in that the upper deck units have a balcony. Windows open in all cabins and in-cabin amenities include TV/VCR, a fridge, and bathrooms with full tubs and showers. The public rooms, in the LaSalle barge, include a forward-facing guest pilot house complete with river charts, a purser's lobby lounge, midships card room and library, a two-story show lounge where local musicians entertain, as well as storytelling, and bingo. There's a buffet-style breakfast and lunch (called dinner here) in the dining room, while dinner (called supper) is waiter-served and includes a choice of two entrees, with advance requests taken for special diets. The food reflects a Middle America restaurant.

The roominess, sophisticated cabin accommodation, and a moderate price that includes shore trips and all gratuities are among the strengths of the *River Explorer*.

LEFT: passengers enjoy the view from the deck on an American coastal and river cruise.
RIGHT: enrichment lectures can be fascinating.

St Lawrence Cruise Lines

A family-run, Canadian operation, St Lawrence Cruise Lines (www.stlawrencecruiselines.com) runs the 66-passenger *Canadian Empress*, an odd-looking re-creation of a river steamboat, which plies the St Lawrence and Ottawa rivers.

The boat's interior exudes genuine Victorian charm, with a turn-of-the-20th-century, pressed white-tin ceiling and colorful Axminster carpets. Of the 32 cabins, 28 are similar, being compact with twin beds that either convert to a sofa or fold up to allow more floor space. Pipe racks and hooks serve as the closet, and a curtain separates the shower from the toilet. The

Grand Saloon doubles as a lounge and restaurant, and the dinner menu usually features perch, roast pork, or roast beef, with lighter fare at lunch. The top deck runs the entire length of the boat, with covered and open sections and an enormous checker board where passengers can move the pieces with hooked poles. Evening entertainment includes a band, guest singers, and a sing-along.

St Lawrence Cruise Lines is a small, hands-on operation that is as smooth as can be. The company, based in Kingston, Ontario, knows what its balanced American and Canadian clientele are looking for and has its well-honed itineraries down to a fine art. ❑

THE UPPER MISSISSIPPI RIVER

The combination of attractive riverside scenery and towns, offering glimpses into the pioneering past, make a trip on the Upper Mississippi a memorable one

Map on page 228

Some aficionados of river travel consider the cruises between St Louis and St Paul to be the most interesting of all because of the combination of high bluffs flanking the water, pleasant farmlands alongside, locks to be negotiated, and small, Victorian-era towns to visit. In the fall, the foliage in Wisconsin rivals that of New England. The river is gentle and placid; although winds can create some choppiness on the long reservoir pools between dams, the slight motion will not be noticed for long by those traveling in a large riverboat. The sometimes dramatic wind and weather are more of a hazard to pleasure boats.

The upper Midwest's first inhabitants were the Plains Indians, the Sioux, and the Algonquin, and the Mississippi provided the primary north–south route. In the latter part of the 17th century, the French began to arrive from Canada and the Great Lakes, using the Mississippi to explore the region.

Learning from the Native Americans

The French settlers first made their living as fur traders, and soon learned from the Native Americans about the lead mines close to the river. Word spread, and prospectors began to arrive and settle in the area. With the US pushing its frontiers west, and the absorption of the Louisiana Purchase land in 1803, military men, prospectors, and pioneering farmers came in ever larger numbers, creating friction with Native American peoples, who were forced west. The Upper Midwest began to develop its lumber and mining industries, and to clear lands for agriculture.

Burgeoning manufacturing, trade, and transportation rapidly created numerous river towns and cities of considerable importance, from St Paul down to St Louis. Germans, Scandinavians, and Poles formed the bulk of the immigrant population, and tended to engage in the trades they brought with them. Many of these early communities, however, had relatively short heydays, and their roles declined markedly, leaving the Victorian-era urban cores that we see today on an Upper Mississippi cruise.

The evolving river scene

The river scene, too, has changed dramatically, from steamboats stacked so high with produce that the boat was barely visible, to today's huge tows carrying 20,000–40,000 tons in strings of barges. Instead of every town having a landing, the river trade is now concentrated in a few large-scale locations.

River commerce remains a substantial business and the largest volumes of products carried are petroleum, in the forms of gasoline, kerosene, fuel, and lubricating oils which come upstream from the Texas, Louisiana, and Gulf oil fields. Coal is another

LEFT: the Gateway Arch and the St Louis skyline at night.
BELOW: Karen "Toots" Maloy on the *Mississippi Queen*.

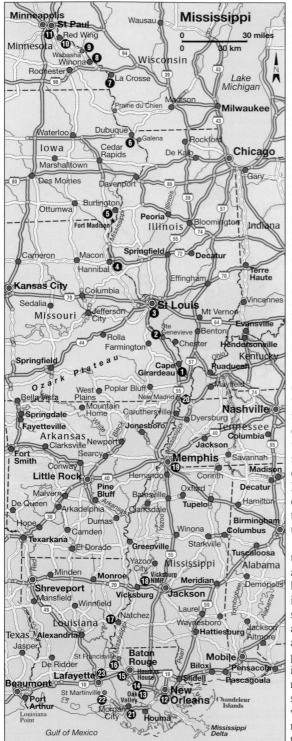

substantial commodity and grains such as corn, wheat, oats, barley, and rye are the principal downstream cargos moving from riverside grain elevators to barges, for trans-shipment at New Orleans. Other heavy items are scrap-iron, steel products, fertilizers, sulfur, cement, sugar, and molasses. Barges may be open for the carriage of coal, covered for grain transport, and in tanks for petroleum.

The Upper Mississippi connects directly to the Lower Mississippi, to the Ohio and to the Illinois Waterway leading to the Great Lakes, forming a continuous water highway of considerable commercial importance. When traffic is intense, there is a pecking order of priority to pass through a lock. The top of the list includes the US Coast Guard and the Army Corps of Engineers, then comes the *Delta Queen* before other scheduled passenger vessels. This is due to an archaic quirk: She is an official US Post Office and the mail contract gives her the edge. Towing vessels come next and, finally, small pleasure boats.

Passing through the locks

On a seven-day Upper Mississippi cruise, "locking through" will occur on average four times a day. When the light at the end of the lock turns green, the pilot moves the vessel forward into the chamber, which may possibly be shared with small private craft but never with a commercial tow. Barges are designed to completely fill a chamber, and the largest tows operating on the Lower Mississippi must split into two units to pass through.

Some locks are set up as tourist attractions with observation towers and parks alongside, and the calliope signals the boat's arrival (a calliope is a keyboard instrument with a series of whistles are sounded by steam or compressed air). In an age-old scene, passengers lining the rails and residents and visitors on land exchange pleasantries while the boat sinks or rises in the chamber. Once the new level is reached, the gates swing open and the lock signal light turns green. Slowly, the paddle-wheel begins to propel the boat into the main channel, passing tows waiting their turn to enter the chamber.

The Upper Mississippi officially begins at Mile 0, Cairo Point, Illinois, where the Ohio River converges, and ends 839 miles (1,350 km) to the north at Minneapolis/St Paul, Minnesota.

Map on page 228

Upper Mississippi river ports

The five states of Missouri, Illinois, Iowa, Wisconsin, and Minnesota contribute a collection of attractive river towns that had their heyday mostly in the 19th century. Their prosperity came from large-scale farming and mining, and the manufacturing and transportation industries that followed. The present-day lives of these towns may be a bit limp, but the history and architecture tell their varied stories. While cruising, you see a continuous US-heartland landscape of farms bracketed by woods, riverbanks rising to a line of high bluffs, and bridges linking towns on opposite shores.

Most Upper Mississippi cruises start or end at St Louis, although officially this stretch of river begins 180 miles (290 km) south at Cairo Point, Illinois, and includes the stops at Cape Girardeau, Chester, and Ste Genevieve.

Cotton fields covered a great deal of the south's farmland.

Cape Girardeau, Missouri

Located at Mile 52, **Cape Girardeau ❶** occupies the top of a flood plain in a rich agricultural district. Evolving from a French fur trading post, founded in 1733, to a permanent settlement, the town welcomed Lewis and Clark *(see page 21)* when they stepped onto Missouri soil here in November 1803 en route to St Louis to begin their intrepid westward exploration, immediately following the Louisiana Purchase. Cruise boats tie up below the levee. For those on a tour, there are a few sights within walking distance of the landing, but the Convention

BELOW: a view over Minnesota.

TIP

For full details of
opening hours and
contact information for
the sites and
museums mentioned
in this chapter,
see Travel Tips
page 340.

and Visitors' Bureau, housed a few blocks inland in a former city hall building at 100 Broadway, is a good place to start. The downtown and riverfront historic districts are primarily brick and wooden Victorians residences, gift shops, a few restaurants and some antiques and collectible stores.

Places to visit are the **Cape River Heritage Museum** (open Wed, Fri, Sat), about seven blocks away from the river, which focuses on the life of Native Americans and early settlers. **Old St Vincent's** church, inland a few blocks, was built in 1853 in homage to Italy's 15th-century Renaissance architecture.

Radio star Rush Limbaugh was born here in 1951, and grew up in the town. If you are a fan of his style, you can take a tour that includes the house where he lived, went to school, the barbershop where he shined shoes, and the radio station where he got his start (for the benefit of non-US readers, Limbaugh is a highly controversial radio talk show host).

The official cruise tour goes out to **Bollinger Mill State Historic Site** (grounds open daily), which offers an intriguing glimpse into a 19th-century way of life. Farmers brought their grain to the water-powered mill to have it ground into meal and flour. While they waited for their turn, whole families camped nearby and it became a seasonal, sociable event. Interpretation at the site includes an exhibit demonstrating how the mill was destroyed by Union forces in order to prevent its grain falling into rebel hands. The present mill, a four-story brick and stone affair, dates from 1867. Nearby stands a 140-ft (43-meter) covered bridge, one of only four in the state. It was built in 1868 of yellow poplar-tree wood, using a truss system of wooden compression members and vertical iron rods that was once common. A toll house used to stand at the east end of the bridge, but is long gone.

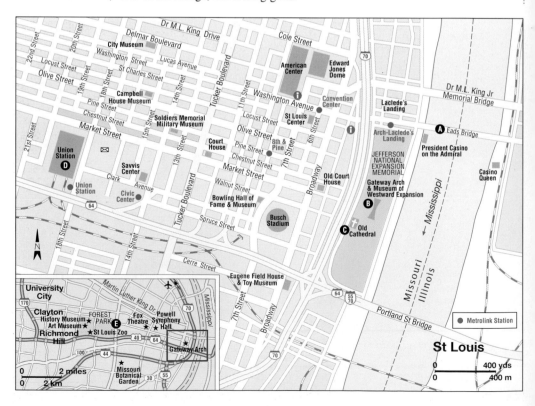

Chester, Illinois/Ste Genevieve, Missouri

The town of **Chester**, located on the east bank, was a once-important 19th-century steamboat stop, but is now a sleepy town used mainly as a landing to ferry passengers by bus across the river to **Ste Genevieve ❷**, Missouri, established in 1735 by French Canadians. It is well worth visiting, as it is the only remaining example of a French colonial town in the US. The ship's tour will visit several buildings, including the interpretive center where there's a film to watch, and allow time for a look at some other buildings, on foot and from the bus.

Bolduc House (open summer, daily), built in 1770, is of vertical log construction, and has a stockade fence surrounding it and an overhanging hip (sloping ends and sides) roof. It is maintained by the Missouri Society of the Colonial Dames of America and is considered to be one the best-restored Creole houses in the country, on a par with the Lower Mississippi's Laura Plantation.

The second visit on the tour is to the **Felix Valle State Historic Site** (open Mon–Sat and Sun pm), dating from 1818, shortly after the Louisiana Purchase. The one-and-a-half story house, with side gables, is built of limestone, and served as a combination store and family home.

St Louis, Missouri

Once the gateway to the West, **St Louis ❸** is a major embarkation and disembarkation port for cruises, and is worth extending your trip for a night or two before or after your cruise. For visitors traveling independently, Metrolink, the city's 34-mile (55-km) light rail line, with a one-day pass available, gives convenient and frequent access to many tourist destinations along the line between the riverfront landing and Lambert-St Louis International Airport.

Maps:
Area 228
City 230

BELOW: a view of Kiener Plaza and the Old Court House, in front of the Gateway Arch, St Louis.

It is said that St Louis, at the height of the steamboat era in 1843, handled more tonnage than the entire British Empire, and the Mississippi waterfront was packed solid with steamboats lined up side by side. When the railroads arrived, the city became the busiest transfer point in the US, both between trains and between trains and steamboats.

The fixed, multiple-span, steel-arched **Eads Bridge Ⓐ**, just to the north of the river landing, a marvel of its time when completed in 1874, became the first rail and road crossing of the Mississippi, eliminating the need for train and vehicle ferries. The bridge, engineered by James Buchanan Eads, has recently been fully restored, and the Metrolink uses it to cross the river into Illinois, so it is easy to take a ride over and back, although there is no reason to linger in East St Louis, one of the USA's most depressed cities. The former warehouse district at the bridge's western approach, **Laclede's Landing**, has been transformed into a trendy restaurant and nightclub district, while just below, gambling and restaurant boats are tied up.

Eero Saarinen's 630-ft (192-meter) **Gateway Arch Ⓑ**, completed in 1965, gave St Louis a much-needed icon as well as a monument of considerable beauty, especially when the stainless steel skin reflects the sun. While they are not for the claustrophobic, elevators whisk visitors to a small observation room at the top for a spectacular 30-mile (48-km) view over the city.

When the river is low, it is a climb across a vast expanse of levee up to the riverfront park where the arch is located. Here, too, the **Museum of Westward Expansion** (open daily; free) offers an overview of the Lewis and Clark Expedition, an authentic Indian *tipi* (tepee), and a collection of Native American peace medals. The **Old Cathedral Ⓒ**, the first dedicated west of the Mississippi in 1834, was originally the Basilica of St Louis, King of France, and is now a museum of religious artifacts. Walk to the right of the arch along Pine Street for five blocks for the Metrolink stop, and in the Lambert Airport direction, en route to Union Station, you pass Busch Stadium. St Louis **Union Station Ⓓ** was the country's largest when completed in 1894, and there are still a few tracks for private railroad cars within the great train shed. But the vast interior has been given over to stores, restaurants, and a Hyatt Regency Hotel. Its second-floor lobby, punctuated with skylights and lavishly decorated with Moorish and Egyptian motifs, is a splendid spot for a drink. For the best view of Union Station's neo-Romanesque frontage, cross Market Street to the Aloe Plaza and Milles Fountain.

Metrolink then continues on to Grand for theaters, concert halls, art galleries, and St Louis University, all located a few blocks north of the station. The train stops at Central West End for the city's poshest residential neighborhoods, then the line cuts along a corner of **Forest Park Ⓔ** and makes a stop at Forest Park station for the **History Museum** (open daily; free), **St Louis Art Museum** (closed Mon), and **St Louis Zoo** (open daily; free), all attractively laid out within the park. The last segment serves the University of Missouri-St Louis and the airport.

Leaving St Louis, and continuing north, the first lock is reached in just a few miles.

Hannibal, Missouri, was the boyhood home of great American writer and journalist, Mark Twain, also known as Samuel Clemens.

BELOW: river boats docked at Hannibal, Missouri.

Hannibal, Missouri

Hannibal ❹ reveals the world of Huckleberry Finn, Tom Sawyer, Becky Thatcher, and Injun Joe, characters created by Samuel Langhorne Clemens under the pen name for which he is famous – Mark Twain (1835–1910). A complex of museums, located within a few blocks of each other, contains the house where Clemens lived from 1844–53, Becky Thatcher's House, and an early drugstore, as well as a collection of Norman Rockwell paintings depicting Mark Twain stories. You can visit the cave that Tom Sawyer and Becky Thatcher explored, an intricate labyrinth of passages used by Native Americans, fur trappers, Jesse James, and slaves traveling the Underground Railroad. Twain wrote in *The Adventures of Tom Sawyer*, "It is said that one might wander days and nights through its intricate tangle of rifts and chasms and never find the end of the cave."

Lovers' Leap and a 300-ft (90-meter) high park overlooking the Mississippi gives great views of Hannibal, the steamboat, and the wide sluggish river. One of the ships' tours includes the site, but it is also possible to walk up independently from the landing.

Burlington, Iowa

Established by Zebulon Pike, who raised the Stars and Stripes there in 1805, the settlement of **Burlington** ❺ became an important river crossing after the Black Hawk War in 1832. By the mid-1850s, 600–700 wagons had crossed here by ferry, carrying families west. Then, in 1868, the Chicago, Burlington, and Quincy company built a single-track rail bridge to operate trains on a new east–west through-route from Chicago to Denver and the west. The city developed industrially around its road, rail, and steamboat transportation infrastructure.

Maps:
Area 228
City 230

BELOW: images of Mark Twain can be seen all over Hannibal, Missouri.

Wisconsin's rural road sign is in the shape of the state.

Ensuing prosperity produced what you can see at **Heritage Hill National Park**, with 160 structures listed on the National Register and executed in Gothic Revival, Victorian Greek, Italian Villa, Queen Anne, and Georgian styles. One, the Phelps Museum House, a Victorian dwelling built in 1851, has fine antiques from the 18th and 19th centuries. Its location is at the top end of Snake Alley, acclaimed by Ripley's, Believe It or Not! as the most crooked street in the world. On nearby high-ground locations, beautiful Mississippi River views can be enjoyed from Crapo Park and Mosquito Park.

The Burlington landing is also used for an excursion to **Fort Madison** (closed Mon–Tues), Iowa, which in 1803 established the first US military installation along the Upper Mississippi. The First Regiment US Infantry sought to protect the government trading post against Native American attacks and during peaceful periods they exchanged furs with the Sauk and Fox for blankets, iron tools, knives, and fishing hooks. Eventually, constant Native American harassment saw the fort abandoned and burned, so what we see today is a re-creation showing the frontier life of a soldier and his family in the very early 19th century.

The **Old Santa Fe Depot** near the riverfront park in Fort Madison, built by the rail company in 1909 in Spanish mission-style, is home to the North Lee County Historical Society, and exhibits Native American, pioneering, and railroad history, plus a section on the Shaeffer fountain pen.

Dubuque, Iowa

Named after a French fur trapper, Julien Dubuque, who settled here in the 1780s, the town of **Dubuque** ❻ is best known for the Lead Rush and the area's mining history. The Mesquakie tribe had mined lead for years before Europeans arrived, and because of its value for making lead shot, its use in paints and as window frames, Dubuque managed to negotiate control of the lead mines. When he died in 1810, the Native Americans took back their claims, until the US government moved in in 1822 and began to grant licenses to mine lead; by 1829 there were 4,000 claims. The Lead Rush was on, and the Midwest had its own version of the Wild West.

Riches before the Civil War produced a substantial town and many mansions. The steamboat tour visits **Mathias Ham House** (open daily), built by a prosperous lead miner in the 1850s on the site of a log cabin where he once lived. A similar double-log cabin, built in 1833, and the oldest building in the state, is on view to illustrate Ham's ascendancy from rags to riches. A film illustrates the history of the Lead Rush.

Dubuque has 57 churches, the number reflecting the religions of the many nationalities drawn here; they include St Luke's Methodist church, featuring some 100 Tiffany stained-glass windows. The local **Museum of Art** occupies the old jail, an unusual Egyptian Revival-style building.

A second excursion heads southeast to **Galena**, Illinois, where the Native Americans also mined lead ore before the French explorers discovered the mineral in the late 16th century. (Galena means lead sulfide, and it is usually found in cubes.) Congress established the

Upper Mississippi Land Mine District, and by the 1850s, Galena was the busiest river port between St Louis and St Paul. Prosperity before and after the Civil War resulted in a town rich in architecture – Federal, Italianate, Greek Revival, Queen Anne, Gothic Revival, Second Empire, and Romanesque Revival – with 85 percent of the homes on the National Register of Historic Places. A drive up to Eagle Point Park affords a terrific Mississippi River view.

Galena produced nine Union Army generals, including Ulysses S. Grant, and after the war Grant occasionally lived in an 1860 Italianate house given to him and his wife Julia, by grateful citizens. It is now the **Ulysses S. Grant Home State Historic Site**, furnished by the Grant family to reflect the period of his 1868 presidential campaign. Also included on the tour is the **Galena/Jo Davies County Historical Museum** (open daily), with a film dedicated to Galena's history and exhibits on subjects as diverse as lead mining, the Civil War, steamboats, clothing, and dolls.

La Crosse, Wisconsin

Three rivers converge here at **La Crosse ❼**, the site was a favorite for Sioux games, including lacrosse, played on the high bluffs. From atop the highest, some 600 ft (183 meters) above the Mississippi, views extend into three neighboring states – Minnesota, Wisconsin, and Iowa.

The **City Brewery** tour describes the beer-making process. The brewery was established here in 1858 as a family business and was once run by Johanna Heileman, one of the country's first female corporation presidents. The excursion includes a German beer hall, an 1870s home built by successful German immigrants, now the company headquarters, and a warehouse that can store an

Map on page 228

Historic sites can be found along the banks of the Mississippi River.

BELOW: a fall fishing trip for the family, Wisconsin.

unbelievable 40 million cans. Continuing the German heritage, the city celebrates *Oktoberfest* for a week each year.

The next three landings, Winona, Wabasha, and Red Wing, are all on the Minnesota side, opposite Wisconsin, and they appear on alternating itineraries. This is a very pretty section of bluffs; many were once Native American settlements and are now scenic overlooks. Between Wabasha and Red Wing the boat will cross the 3-mile (5-km) wide and 25-mile (40-km) long Lake Pepin, a natural body of water formed by a sandbar built up from the swifter Chippewa River waters entering the more sluggish Mississippi. Waterskiing got its start here in 1922. Today, Pepin is a very popular boating and sailing lake and wildlife refuge. Eagles and tundra swans are seen in the hundreds during spring and fall migration seasons. The vast expanse can become quite choppy and dangerous to small boats when the wind is strong.

Winona ❽, Minnesota, is named after the daughter of a Sioux Chief, and the town grew with the lumber industry and later became a grain market center; high-tech plastics now provide the mainstay industry. The actress Winona Ryder was born here in 1979. Polish immigrants working in the lumber and milling industries built St Stanislaus Kostka Catholic church, with its European-style dome and beautiful stained-glass windows. From 575 ft (175 meters) up at Garvin Heights, a scenic park, the view extends around 20–30 miles (32–48 km) up and downriver.

Wabasha ❾, Minnesota, named after a Dakota Native American family, qualifies as the state's oldest city, and the brick commercial center, a National Historic District, has changed little over the past century. The **Anderson House**, the state's oldest inn (1856) provides, at no extra charge, a choice of 12 resident cats as bed warmers when requested by guests. One of the cats, named Morris, was abducted by a young boy but the cat made such a fuss, it was discovered and rescued by hotel employees.

The main attraction is the toy collection from the **L.A.R.K Toy Company**, including lead soldiers, wind-up toys, hand puppets, puzzles, and dolls. A beautifully detailed, hand-carved carousel is available for rides, and adults without children need not be shy about having a turn. Another stop is **Arrowhead Bluffs Exhibit and Museum** (closed Sun), for a collection of Winchester guns sold between 1886 and 1982, plus sporting equipment and tools. A diorama, replicating a natural setting, displays Native American artifacts and wildlife.

Red Wing ❿, Minnesota's origin comes from a Sioux Chief, of that name, who wore red-dyed swans' wings in his headdress. Originally a Native American settlement, the present town, settled by Scandinavians and Swiss in the 1840s, became a major exporter of wheat, and was later headquarters for the Red Wing Shoe Company. The former pottery factory that housed the Union Stoneware Company is now a downtown shopping mall. Some of the original salt-glaze pottery is on display at the Goodhue County Historical Society. Main Street restoration is giving the center a rebirth, anchored by buildings such as the elegant St James Hotel (1875) and the active **T.B. Sheldon Auditorium Theater** (1904), where a daytime multimedia show covers early Red Wing history.

BELOW:
the architecture
of St Paul.

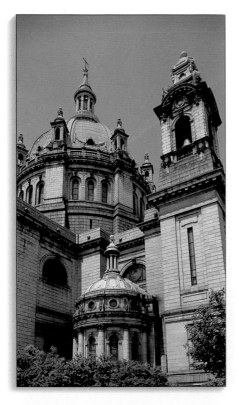

St Paul, Minnesota

St Paul ⓫ is the beginning or end of an Upper Mississippi cruise, and the more southerly of the Twin Cities, the other being Minneapolis. St Paul retains a compact center city where most of the great civic architecture is located. If you decide to spend an extra night here, you will find lots to do within walking distance of downtown. The 1905 **Minnesota State Capitol Building** (open daily), in beaux arts-style, by architect Cass Gilbert of New York's Woolworth Building fame, gives free tours at the end of each weekday. Visit the House, Senate, and Supreme Court chambers to view the stenciled ceilings, murals, and sculpture. In the basement, in true German style (Germans once made up the city's largest immigrant population), there's a restored Rathskeller Café, with delicately painted ceilings depicting mottoes from Minnesota's mid-19th-century days.

The **Minnesota Museum of American Art** (closed Mon–Wed), housed in the Landmark Center downtown, exhibits works by noted sculptors Louise Nevelson and Paul Manship, and mural paintings of everyday scenes of Midwestern life by Thomas Hart Benton (1889–1975), among others, which help interpret pioneering life and the coming of European sophistication to the region.

The top city attraction is the **James J. Hill House** (closed Mon–Tues and Sun am), an elaborate Romanesque mansion built in 1891 for the Great Northern Railway baron, representing the height of the Gilded Age. When finished, at a cost of nearly $1 million, it was Minnesota's largest mansion. The house's carved oak and mahogany interior, which Hill oversaw personally, contains no fewer than 13 bathrooms and 22 fireplaces. Hill amassed a huge fortune in railroads, ocean shipping, mining, milling, banking, finance, and agriculture, and lived here with his wife until his death in 1916. ❑

Map on page 228

LEFT: southern smiles.
BELOW: at the Minnesota Fair.

THE LOWER MISSISSIPPI RIVER PORTS

A river cruise to New Orleans is a trip to dream about, but the Lower Mississippi has much more to offer, including Memphis, birthplace of rock 'n' roll and the civil rights movement

The Mississippi River system consists of some 50 rivers and tributaries, half a dozen of which – the Atchafalaya, Arkansas, Ohio, Tennessee, Cumberland, Missouri, and Illinois – are navigable for considerable distances. They are known collectively as the Western Rivers, and the drainage basin covers an area of 1.2 million sq miles (3.2 million sq km), 41 percent of the contiguous 48 states, and includes all or parts of 31 states and two Canadian provinces. Only the Amazon and Congo watersheds surpass the Mississippi in size. The Lower Mississippi is defined as the 954 miles (1,528 km) between the mouth of the river just in from the Gulf of Mexico and the junction with the Ohio River. Mile 0 is called Head of Passes, Louisiana, and Mile 954 is Cairo Point, Illinois.

Very occasionally, a river cruise will make the 96-mile (152-km) journey from New Orleans through the delta to Mile 0. Once beyond the city, this stretch is characterized by low-lying land on which plantations and today's small communities were established, marshlands, numerous channels, some navigable, and the remains of early Spanish, French, and American forts, built to protect the growing inland empires. Large areas are protected animal and waterfowl refuges and are generally accessible only by boat.

River pilots are required by ocean-going ships – container vessels, bulk carriers, and tankers – from the pilot station at the mouth of the Mississippi along some 229 miles (368 km) past New Orleans to the Louisiana state capital at Baton Rouge. New Orleans is the principal embarkation port and terminus for most Lower Mississippi River cruises, operating year-round, with Memphis, Tennessee, 736 miles (1,176 km) upstream a secondary landing, mainly used for one-way trips south to New Orleans and northward into the Ohio, Cumberland, and Tennessee rivers. Boats generally stay south in the winter with increasingly fewer cruises from New Orleans as the hot summer approaches. Spring and fall are the best seasons, but rapid changes in the air temperatures can cause river fog which, especially when it rises late in the day, sends boats scurrying to the nearest safe landing, usually tying up to a tree until the visibility improves.

Sailing from New Orleans, the heavily commercial waterway extends for some hours but most departures are at night so the experience is mostly of bright lights and pungent smells. Container and bulk shipping gives way to the oil and chemical industries, and by morning the boat will be paddling through rural, mostly flat, southern Louisiana.

LEFT:
pretty balconies on Royal Street in the French Quarter of New Orleans.
BELOW:
life on the river.

You might spot some gator heads in New Orleans's French market.

The river, however, remains an important commercial artery used by the world's most impressive tows. As many as 30 or 40 barges may be strapped together to form a solid flotilla. Typical loads may be grain, salt, lime, coal, rocks, and petroleum products, and because of a tow's enormous size and lack of maneuverability when sailing with the current, a downriver load always has the right of way. The handsome towboats are hugely powerful machines, driving and guiding the tows at varying speeds, depending on the river's current and the direction in which they are sailing; 10 mph (16 kph) is a typical downriver speed, while upstream may be half that. Most are piloted with considerable skill, but occasionally, runaway barges are seen along the river banks. Crews live aboard for weeks at a time in considerable comfort, sometimes better than crew accommodations aboard cruise ships.

The Lower Mississippi has been tampered with more than the rest of the river system to improve navigation and flood control. While there are no locks on the lower river, there are long stretches of levees, embankments built to straighten out the river and to prevent periods of high water from spilling off into adjoining farmlands and flooding fields and towns, as so often happened in the past. Some levees are high enough to block the view inland.

It's the antebellum South, or the present-day interpretation of it, that most river cruisers come to see. The rural plantation homes and the stately mansions clustered in towns and cities exhibit rich examples of American architecture, some rebuilt after the Civil War and others that have undergone considerable restoration after periods of neglect to become an important draw for tourists and provide a new type of employment. Touring them brings out a past that is both romantic and tragic, and it is hoped that visitors will come away with a balanced

BELOW: a riverboat sails the Mississippi River, New Orleans.

view of the lives of the haves and have-nots, those caught in between, and the terrible war, like no other, that tore the country apart.

Most of the history beyond New Orleans is Cajun and Creole in the lower regions but increasingly, traveling northward, that of a growing new America, post-Louisiana Purchase. This emphasizes the rise of King Cotton, the poor rural south, slavery, the Civil War and its tumultuous aftermath, then the gradual industrialization of farming. Town centers that were once important have largely died as sprawl came to the South as to everywhere else. Nature is visible all around, and the Mississippi flyway is a hugely important corridor for birds, large ones like the Canada goose and small species such as warblers.

New Orleans, Louisiana

New Orleans ⑫ has both Spanish and French origins, and when the French took over a portion of North America from the Spanish, Napoleon counted on the city becoming the key entry point to his expanding empire in the New World. Events on the island of Hispaniola, where the French had established a colony at Cap Francais, were to change all this. The local slave uprising in 1791 threw out the French, and Haiti was eventually established on the western half of the island as the first independent state in the Western Hemisphere, after the US (by 1820 it had become a republic). Napoleon's troops, now fighting a major war against the British, were spread too thinly and to help pay for the continuing battles he decided to sell the bulk of the French North American territories (the Louisiana Purchase) to the US for $15 million. Papers were signed on April 30, 1803, and the US suddenly had an additional 800,000 sq miles (2 million sq km) that extended the westward frontier to the Rocky Mountains.

Maps:
Area 228
City 242

TIP

For full details of **opening hours** and contact information for the sites and museums mentioned in this chapter, see Travel Tips page 342.

BELOW: street musicians entertain.

The Vieux Carre bus runs through New Orleans.

The purchase had a major effect on the importance of the Mississippi River Valley and its tributaries as an artery for expansion in the West, Midwest, and the South. New Orleans would rapidly become the most important entreport, prompted by the development of reliable inland steamboat transportation.

Before the purchase, New Orleans' population was largely French, plus Spanish, Portuguese, and West Indians of African descent. The term Creole refers to the early French and their descendants born in the colony, but also to Spanish, and Portuguese, and the term Creole of Color was applied to those who were an intermarriage of the three. When the city joined the US, a large Anglo-Saxon influx arrived to cash in on the growing prosperity based on cotton, sugar, and shipping. Because they were not readily accepted by the Creole, this contingent established residences in what became the Garden District, upriver from the French Quarter. While the Quarter consisted of tightly-packed houses facing directly onto the streets, with wrought-iron fronts and private inner courtyards, the Garden District featured streets of mansions with impressive columned

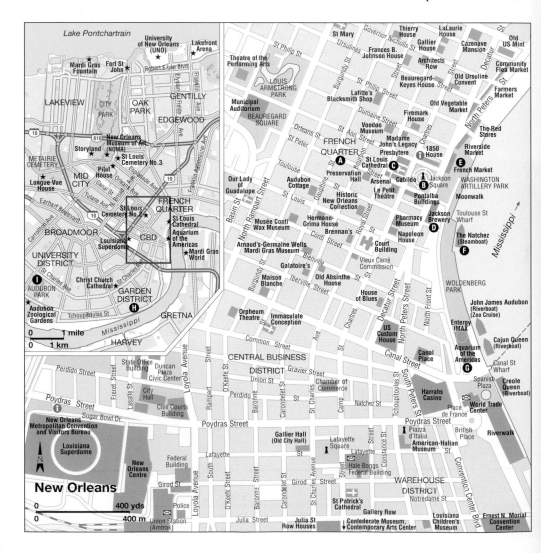

porticos and front gardens. The oldest date from the late 1830s, and while none are open to individual visitors, a few can be see on an organized tour.

The **French Quarter Ⓐ**, the most European section of any American city, a 12- by six-block rectangle, is the place to start, for its boutique and chain hotels, restaurants, some famous for many decades, modern and Dixieland jazz clubs, crafts, art and antiques stores, and the riverfront. During holidays and in the busy spring period, the streets become thronged with tourists, some out for a stroll and others wandering around in loud T-shirts, drinking from cans of beer. Sometimes the elegance of the setting is spoiled and but much of the tawdriness is confined to a few streets. At night, the choices of music venues are unparalleled. Jazz got its big boost here with the likes of Louis Armstrong, King Oliver, and Jelly Roll Morton, and Preservation Hall and the Palm Court Café are still very much in demand. But the variations also include rhythm and blues, gospel, Latin, Cajun, and zydeco (which uses an accordion and a corrugated rub board and various other instruments).

Jackson Square Ⓑ, the French Quarter's largest open space, facing onto the Mississippi, is rimmed by handsome buildings dating from the early to mid-19th century. Most notable is **St Louis Cathedral Ⓒ**, the principal church for the Roman Catholic Archdiocese of New Orleans. The cathedral gardens, courtyards, and antebellum row houses are well worth visiting on a walk around the immediate area. The former **Jackson Brewery Ⓓ**, on one corner of the square, is now filled with stores and restaurants, and the **French Market Ⓔ** has more shopping, crafts, bistros, and a farmers' produce market off the square's downriver end.

A popular offbeat activity is a visit to one of the **Cities of the Dead**, a cemetery where the tombs are built above ground because of New Orleans' high

Map on page 242

New Orleans has a host of pretty colonial-style homes.

BELOW: take a horse-and-buggy ride around Jackson Square.

The streets are crowded during Mardi Gras.

water table. The structures that rise above the burial chambers create a dense cityscape in miniature. For some, but not all, you need to take a cab or bus. St Louis Cemetery No. 2 has one section set aside for African-American Catholics, whose artisans fashioned its iron ornaments and tomb gates. The National Park Service operates daily tours.

Down by the riverside, the steamboat *Natchez* **F** sails from a landing opposite Jackson Square on daily Mississippi River cruises, and the Canal-Algiers Ferry makes short trips across the river from the end of Canal Street to Algiers Point, a 19th-century neighborhood listed on the National Register of Historic Places. Riverwalk, a relatively new pedestrian promenade, leads from Jackson Square, past the **Aquarium of the Americas** **G**, and the casino to the **Convention Center**. The 2-mile (3-km) riverfront streetcar line parallels the route and comes close enough to the cruise docks to be a useful way to get into the center.

One of the best ways to get an overview of uptown New Orleans, a repository of some 11,000 historic buildings, is to ride the 1920s streetcars of the St Charles Avenue Line, the oldest urban railway in the US, dating from 1835, which begins at Canal Street and runs for 13 miles (20 km). The first portion operates in a grassy median strip along an oak-lined boulevard through the **Garden District** **H** and **Audubon Park** **I**, which includes the New Orleans Zoo, and on past Loyola and Tulane Universities into working-class neighborhoods. During the spring blossom season, you can smell the flowers through the open windows of the cars, and near the far end the streetcar barn is open for visitors to view.

Mardi Gras is without a doubt the best-known annual event, and while the one in New Orleans is the largest by far, it has become very touristy. Some visitors make a point of avoiding the city then, and perhaps seeking out a more low-key

BELOW: Oak Alley Plantation.

Maps:
Area 228
City 242

version in Mobile or a smaller town in Cajun Country. The event takes place on the days leading up to Ash Wednesday, the beginning of Lent, a period of denial in the weeks before Easter (Mardi Gras means Fat Tuesday). The street parades, lead by Rex, King of Carnival, were initiated in 1872 and now involve a million people.

The steamboat and barge cruises leave from the long pier parallel to the river just beyond the convention center. Passengers arriving early or staying overnight on the boats have easy access to the principal tourist attractions via a short cab ride or by walking the few blocks and hopping on the Riverfront streetcar.

While Cajun Country cruises to the Atchafalaya Basin head a few miles downriver before turning west into the Intracoastal Waterway, all the others aim upriver. The route takes you past the main container piers, then under the sweeping Huey P. Long Highway and Railroad Bridge, past city suburbs and a long section connected to the oil and chemical industries. It's just short of 60 miles (96 km) to the first stop that steamboats often make at Laura Plantation.

The property that became **Laura Plantation** (open daily), located just upriver from Vacherie, Louisiana, was originally French owned but its most significant period dates from the antebellum era, when Creole families owned the vast sugar cane plantations. The main house (c. 1805), has a raised brick basement with the upper floors executed in Federal style. The front is characterized by a full-width covered porch and double staircase. Inside, the house exhibits original family clothing, toiletries, and slave business records. Also highly significant are six slave quarters and a collection of outbuildings that show how the sugar industry developed. The slave cabins are said to have produced the first recorded West African folktales similar to the English *Br'er Rabbit* stories.

Oak Alley, Louisiana

The steamboats tie up at a landing on the river side of the levee, and from there it is but a short walk up and over to the property. Built in 1837–9 as Bon Sejour, the name **Oak Alley** ⑬ caught on after the impressive growth of a double line of oaks that stretched from the river landing to the main Greek Revival-style house, characterized by 28 Doric columns. Oak Alley, built with all local materials except the marble, was just one of many stately mansions and its major restoration took place in the 1920s after years of deterioration. Its pink plaster columns and blue-green shutters date from that period.

If there is still time after the tour, consider taking a walk south along the levee overlooking farms, sugar cane fields, and small clusters of modest houses. You get a brief glimpse of the rural South today, here still moderately poor but with active church communities, small farms, and a sugar industry. During cane cutting season, loaded trucks will be traveling full in the downriver direction and returning empty.

Houmas House, Louisiana

For **Houmas House** ⑭ (open daily), boats simply slide up to the landing and tie up to posts set along the levee. Leaving via the landing stage, it's a climb up the slope to where, on the far side, sits the 1840 white-

BELOW:
a streetcar in the
Garden District.

TIP

If you want to strike out on your own it would be wise to stop by the Baton Rouge Convention and Visitors Bureau (730 North Boulevard, tel: 225-383-1825, closed Sat, Sun), for maps and tourist information.

pillared Greek Revival mansion at the end of a double line of equally old oak trees. It's a story-book colonnaded antebellum home with arched Federal dormers built by John and Caroline Smith Preston, and set on 20,000 acres (8,000 hectares) of sugar cane fields. The property was first bought in 1812 by Caroline's father, General Wade Hampton, a Revolutionary War hero from South Carolina. At one time it was the largest slave-holding plantation in the South, employing some 800 field and household slaves. Quite a few interior changes took place, especially in the 1940s, so all is not true to the original period of construction. Because of its classic exterior style, the house has been featured in several movies, including *Hush, Hush, Sweet Charlotte*, in which Bette Davis and Olivia de Haviland live an increasingly uneasy life as feuding sisters.

Baton Rouge, Louisiana

At **Baton Rouge** ⓰, the Louisiana State Capital, you land opposite the civic center, just upriver from a floating casino and the USS *Kidd*, a faithfully-restored World War II destroyer. Simply walk down the embankment for a visit to the ship, which is often hosted by a retired sailor, and highly informative for those who enjoy learning about military history from the era of sail-powered warships to today's sophisticated nuclear submarines. The *Kidd* received 12 battle stars and served in both World War II and the Korean War, suffering a kamikaze attack in the former that killed some 38 servicemen.

The glue that binds any visit to Baton Rouge is the Huey P. Long stories related by the guides, and none needs to be embellished. As Louisiana's governor from 1928 to 1931, "The Kingfish" ruled the state like a monarch from the governor's mansion he built in 1930, an architectural mirror of the Washington

BELOW: the state Capitol Building in Baton Rouge.

White House, including an Oval Office, East Room, and West Wing. It is said that Long wanted to be familiar with the layout of the real White House before he became president.

Within a short walk from the landing, you can visit the nation's tallest state **Capitol Building** (open daily; free), a 34-story art deco masterpiece constructed on orders from Long during the height of the Great Depression, with an Alabama-clad limestone exterior and marbled interior. Tours are conducted at regular intervals, and the tales you'll be told during the course of it include Long's assassination here in 1935 while he was a US senator. Afterward, take the elevator up for a splendid view of the otherwise low-rise city, the surrounding countryside and the mighty Mississippi. Long's gravesite is in the nearby gardens, and his memorial is a statue showing him holding a model of the monument. Baton Rouge has little downtown street life and virtually no shopping, a sad characteristic of many mid-size American cities, where the heart has been sapped by shopping centers built on the periphery.

Two excursions are made to sites outside the city, and during the bus trips you will hear additional Huey Long tales and pass by the Louisiana State University (LSU) campus. Notice a dormitory built into the sports stadium, and the wealthy, middle-class, and poor residential suburban neighborhoods.

Map on page 228

The Cajun Heritage tour, a Baton Rouge excursion, is a bit phoney, but at least you get some insights. The better tours take place in the Atchafalaya Basin on the Cajun and Creole cruises. Most of the tour consists of presentations of Cajun music using accordion, corrugated metal rub-board and more modern instruments, plus two-step dancing and snack food, which includes *cocodrie* (alligator), *boudin* (generally a French blood sausage but sometimes a white one made of chicken, pork, or veal), and *jambalaya* (a Creole mix of meat, chicken, shellfish, onions, tomatoes, peppers, rice, and spices). Visitors are encouraged to join the dancing, which some really enjoy and others try to avoid.

Much more enlightening is the experience gained at the LSU **Rural Life Museum**, which is arranged as if one had stepped out the back door of the "Big House" to see how the rest of the community lived their daily lives on an antebellum working plantation. The original 19th-century buildings include the overseer's house and kitchen, slave cabins, sick house, a one-room school house, blacksmith shop, Baptist church with painted windows instead of more expensive stained glass, and a barn filled with farm implements; there are also farm vehicles and fishing, hunting, and trapping equipment. Guides are on hand to answer questions, and photos and maps help tell the story of plantation life.

St Francisville, Louisiana

St Francisville ⑯, the once important, now sleepy town of about 1,700 residents used to be home to more millionaires than any other place in America, the wealth based on cotton, sugar cane, finance, and trading. The original settlement, first called New Valencia by the Spanish, then Bayou Sara (until 1860), used to be by the river and was once a major steamboat landing, but after too many floods, the population moved a couple of miles inland to the bluffs on higher ground.

The 140 structures listed on the National Register of Historic Places include the Georgian Revival courthouse, neo-Romanesque Revival Bank of Commerce & Trust, and French colonial, antebellum, neoclassical, gingerbread-Victorian, and dog-trot houses, the latter characterized by a covered breezeway dividing the house into two symmetrical sections. Walkers may want to head back to the landing on foot, passing swampy ponds where fishermen are out hoping to catch the next catfish meal.

An excellent bus tour includes two widely different examples of a Big House, the first a prison, the second an imposing mansion. The state of Louisiana is unusual – unique, in fact – in allowing visitors into a maximum security prison, the **Louisiana State Penitentiary** at Angola. The place name refers to the African country from where many of the slaves came. Once known as the bloodiest prison in the South because of inmate assaults, the place seems almost tranquil today. In a bend in the Mississippi River, the 18,000-acre (7,200-hectare) site is rich farmland tilled by the inmates. You learn about the various educational, social, and medical services provided, visit a museum that exhibits a primitive electric chair, contraband taken from the prisoners, guards' uniforms and weapons, and examples of criminal records.

BELOW: dancing and having fun Louisiana-style.

The steamboat Natchez *ferries passengers along the river.*

The second Big House is entirely different. **Greenwood Plantation** is an early 19th-century residence fronted with 28 Doric columns that the present owner, who may be on hand when you visit, rebuilt after a major fire in 1960. The story of the reconstruction is key to the tour. There's a copy of the original working kitchen, always kept separate from the main house because of the danger of fire, which had to produce an enormous number of meals to feed a small community. The house served as the setting for the movie *Sister, Sister,* and the *North and South* TV miniseries.

Another tour visits two more plantation houses. **Rosedown**, built with virtually unlimited funds in 1835, lies at the end of a double line of arcing trees. The 371-acre (150-hectare) property reveals considerable wealth in its collection of fine antiques from French Empire, Federal, and Victorian periods and paintings bought in Europe and America. The gardens, designed by the original owner's wife, are copied in part from the formal and wild gardens at Versailles, just outside Paris, France.

A visit to **The Myrtles** is more about ghosts than grandeur, but the story is intriguing. A servant named Chloe, because of harsh punishment received from her master, poisoned the owner's children, and then killed herself. Now she is said to haunt the house, which has furnishings, gilded mirrors, and Baccarat crystal chandeliers that once belonged to the Emperor Napoleon. The oldest section dates from 1796, while overall the house dates from the 1850s.

Natchez, Mississippi

BELOW: outside the Rosalie mansion.

Founded as a river settlement in 1716, **Natchez** ⓱ has always been an important landing, especially during the height of the steamboat era. The steamboats arrive at Under-the-Hill, the riverside landing beneath the town center. In former days, it was a rowdy sort of place, frequented by passengers and crew and the merchants, gamblers, and prostitutes who served and fleeced them. Today's buildings are a quiet reminder of a larger complex that once existed here.

The main event in Natchez is visiting a few of the antebellum houses. The town has 200 historic homes among more than 500 antebellum structures and up to three dozen are open to the public, depending on the time of year. You can choose to take the steamboat's tour or buy your own tickets locally – these allow you to visit up to four houses. For about five weeks in March and April, and another three in October, some 30 houses are open either in the morning or afternoon on a rotating basis.

The **Natchez Visitors' Center** is the place to start. While there, be sure to take in the free film *The History of Natchez* for its background information. For independent visitors, a continuous trolley-bus shuttle service runs between the houses and serves the steamboat landing. Good walkers can readily visit many of the town houses on foot.

Perhaps the most interesting combination of a house and a story is at **Longwood**, the largest octagon house ever built in the US. Designed like an Arabian palace, the interior was never finished. When the Civil War began, the owner slipped into poverty and died in

1864. His wife subsequently raised eight children there, living in the basement and surviving on meager war reparations.

With an impressive, white-columned portico affixed to a Georgian style-brick mansion, **Rosalie**, built in 1823, is set in attractive grounds overlooking the Mississippi. Besides having nearly all original furnishings, the house features several special exhibits such as 19th-century children's clothing, Victorian costumes, descriptions of customs relating to death and dying, a collection of family photographs, and a ship's bell from the battleship USS *Mississippi* that served the country between 1908 and 1914.

An excursion outside town visits **Dunleith** (1856), an antebellum mansion sitting on a knoll overlooking 40 acres (16 hectares) of woodland and bayous. Its chief characteristic is a colossal, four-sided colonnade considerably enlarging the appearance of the house. The ground floor, antebellum period rooms are open to the public and the upstairs bedrooms are used for bed-and-breakfast accommodations. Also open to the public are several outbuildings, such as the three-story service wing where the servants lived, poultry house, carriage house, and garden hothouse, while the former stable serves as an upscale restaurant.

Frogmore Plantation and Museum gives the best interpretation of cotton industry history, from the 18th century until today. Listed on the National Register of Historic Places, Frogmore consists of 18 restored antebellum structures, including furnished slave cabins and a steam-powered cotton gin. As in most places of historic interest, the guides are costumed and well informed about life on the plantation in the Big House, in the slave quarters and in the fields. The tour also visits the present 1,800 acres (728 hectares) of cotton fields and shows the operation of a cotton gin capable of assembling 900 bales a day.

The Forks of the Road market place at a busy intersection in Natchez was a 19th century slave market and later a refuge for emancipated slaves. The riverside landing at Natchez Under-the-Hill was also used to auction enslaved Africans.

BELOW: riverboats used to land at Natchez Under-the-Hill.

When commercial picking is not taking place, visitors can roam through the fields and pluck fluffy cotton balls for souvenirs.

Vicksburg, Mississippi

Vicksburg National Military Park ⓲ (open daily) is the principal destination and an organized tour is by far the best way to appreciate the battle's significance and the incredible suffering that occurred during the 42-day siege and the final capture of the city by Ulysses S. Grant on July 4, 1863. The river town's strategic location as "The Gibraltar of the South" is evident from the moment you leave the boat landing and begin the long climb. Whoever controlled Vicksburg's cannon and artillery could control the Mississippi's north–south traffic.

The battlefield, considered the best preserved in the US, maintains the land's natural contours, wooded sections, and small buildings. The **Gray and Blue Naval Museum** exhibits an impressive model collection of Civil War gunboats. The full-size *Cairo* is worth learning about, not only for its role in the war but for its surprise recovery. While it was recorded as sinking in the Mississippi, it was actually recovered up the tributary Yazoo River.

If there is time before returning to the cruise boat, visit Vicksburg's town center for the towering **Old Court House Museum** (closed Sun am), constructed by slaves in 1858. Inside, you get a glimpse at the life of Jefferson Davis, the Confederate South's president, a congressman, senator, and secretary of war. One courtroom was the scene of the trial of Captain Frederick Speed, who, at the end of the Civil War, commanded the overloaded steamboat *Sultana* that exploded, resulting in some 1,700 fatalities. In a room full of toys, you can see a teddy bear that Theodore (Teddy) Roosevelt gave to a Vicksburg child in 1907. It is said that the teddy bear concept originated just north of Vicksburg in 1902 when Roosevelt refused to shoot a bear cub.

The **Coca-Cola Museum** (closed Sun am), housed in an old pharmacy, reveals that Coke was first bottled here for a delivery run out to the countryside. The historic downtown district has a cluster of bed-and-breakfasts, a few elaborate inns, and some impressive public buildings, but most of it is a bit ramshackle.

Memphis, Tennessee

Memphis ⓳, a city that bills itself as Home of the Blues and Birthplace of Rock 'n' Roll, is usually an embarkation or disembarkation port for river cruisers. Boats dock at **Mud Island River Park**, a recreation and museum center worth a visit before boarding or while waiting for a shuttle to the airport.

Mud Island's centerpiece is the 18-gallery **Mississippi River Museum** (closed Mon) with exhibits on exploration and settlement, river transportation, the Civil War, engineering, and the people who worked on the river. The outdoor model of the Riverwalk demonstrates the geography and the important events that have occurred on the Lower Mississippi from Cairo, Illinois to New Orleans. Every 30 inches (76 cm) represents 1 mile (1.6 km) of river. Here you can rent canoes, kayaks, airboats, and pedal boats to explore the riverfront, and bicycles to do the same on land.

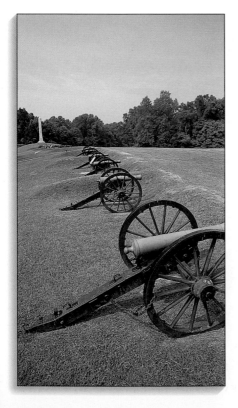

BELOW: cannon at Vicksburg National Military Park.

A useful Main Street trolley service links most of the downtown attractions. **Beale Street Entertainment District**, concentrated along a three-block stretch, features more than two dozen nightclubs, restaurants, and retail stores. Outdoor music events take place at adjacent **Handy Park**, named after pianist W.C. Handy (1873–1958), Father of the Blues.

The **National Civil Rights Museum** (closed Tues; free on Sun and Mon pm), also accessible by trolley, is housed in the former Lorraine Motel, where Martin Luther King Jr was shot dead in April 1968. Exhibits include a walk-in Montgomery Alabama city bus, where you can imagine Rosa Parks sitting in one of the whites-only front seats, as she did in 1955, precipitating the modern civil rights movement in the United States. A student sit-in is recreated at a restored dime-store lunch counter, with a backdrop of historic documentary footage. Expanded in 2002, the museum complex also includes the boarding house from where the fatal shot was fired at King.

The venerable Peabody Hotel, built in the mid-19th century, stages what was once a quirky event, known only to local people and hotel guests, but is now a true tourist show. Twice a day the resident ducks leave the lobby's fountain pool and pitter-patter wet-footed to the elevator for feeding time on the roof.

Outside town, **Graceland** (open daily), draws the largest crowds north of New Orleans. This was Elvis Presley's jazzed up Georgian-style home from 1957 until his death in 1977. Exhibits portray the multiple facets of his life. The Trophy Building displays his collection of gold records, and the automobile museum houses 22 of his vehicles, including the best known, his 1955 pink Cadillac. There is a collection of private jet aircraft, a Meditation Garden, and Elvis' burial site, located next to the swimming pool. You can eat in one of his

Map on page 228

BELOW: all kinds of souvenirs and memorabilia at Graceland.

Map on page 228

restaurants and spend oodles of money of an amazing array of Elvis souvenirs, from jewelry, clothing, books, videos/DVDs, to musical teddy bears.

New Madrid, Missouri

Located at a horseshoe bend in the river, **New Madrid** ⑳ was one of the first towns in what would become the state of Missouri. The name is derived from a failed 1789 plan by George Morgan, a maverick entrepreneur and Indian trader, to get a grant from Spain to establish a 15 million-acre (6 million-hectare) development to check American advancement into Spanish territory.

The Pony Express started in Missouri and Jesse James was gunned down here, in St Joseph, in 1882.

But the most interesting aspects of the town's history are, literally, earth-shaking. On December 16, 1811, and January 23 and February 7, 1812, the three largest recorded earthquakes in American history occurred here, all in excess of 8.0 on the Richter scale, with aftershocks continuing for a full year. The intensity was 10 times that of the great San Francisco earthquake of 1906. The New Madrid Fault sent shock waves as far as Canada to the north, the Gulf of Mexico to the south, and Boston and Washington in the east, and toppled chimneys in Cincinnati 375 miles (605 km) away. Up to 5,000 sq miles (13,000 sq km) of land was affected by fissures, landslides, upheavals, flooding, destruction of forests, creation of lakes, and the changing of the course of the Mississippi River. During the earthquake, witnesses saw the river running backwards, and the steamboat *New Orleans* that had tied up to an island during the night found terra firma had disappeared underwater by the morning. Many houses in New Madrid, which then had a population of about 3,000, were destroyed or damaged, but only two people died, which seems miraculous.

BELOW: bright flora in Missouri.
RIGHT: New Orleans.

Most of the town's attractions are within a short walk of the landing stage, adjoining a riverside park. Leaving the boat, turn right and walk upstream parallel to the river. You will soon come to the Chamber of Commerce and to the historical museum and one-room school house.

The **New Madrid Historical Museum** (open daily), is housed in a former saloon located near the riverfront at No. 1 Main Street. Exhibits include a seismograph to show continuing earthquake activity, Indian artifacts, Civil War history, some furnished period rooms, and a large collection of hand-made quilts. Up Main Street, visit the one-room, restored Higgerson School House that shows the 19th-century life of a school with eight grades and a single teacher. An attendant is on hand to show how the students were grouped for their lessons.

For the remaining 65 miles (105 km) to the confluence with the Ohio, the river is broad and the flow sluggish. The landscape is mostly rural farmland, peppered with small towns with Civil War connections. Several long, mid-stream islands divide the Mississippi into two channels, with markers to show safe passage. For the last couple of miles approaching Cairo Point, the waters may take on two quite different hues, depending on the relative strengths of the two currents, fed by the Upper Mississippi and the Ohio. Boats bound for Louisville, Nashville and Cincinnati turn right into the Ohio, while those bound for St Louis stay left. ❑

AN INTRODUCTION TO CAJUN AND CREOLE COUNTRY

The Cajun and Creole culture of Louisiana is a rich, colorful mixture, as is evident in the architecture, the music, and the food

Louisiana's Creole and Cajun country is a vibrant mélange of cultures, loaded with colonial history. Some have compared its ethnic and cultural diversity to that of Brazil. It was the Spanish who first landed here, in 1528,

a small group, led by Cabeza de Vaca, that had become separated from the main expedition sent from Spain the year before. The group was captured by native people, although Cabeza de Vaca escaped and in 1537 returned to Spain, where he was rewarded with the governorship of Río de la Plata (now largely Paraguay). By 1682, however, the French explorer René-Robert Cavelier, Sieur de La Salle, had traveled south from Canada, down the Mississippi River to the Gulf of Mexico. He claimed all the land drained by the great river and its tributaries for France, naming it Louisiana after Louis XIV, the Sun King.

The French and the Africans

As the first Europeans – mostly fur traders and missionaries – began to settle the area, present-day Mobile, Alabama, was established as the colonial capital, although capital status was allotted to New Orleans in 1723. At this time, enslaved Africans began to arrive, shipped in in the holds of galleons, to replace the Native American workers, most of whom either ran away or died in captivity, due to exposure to European diseases to which they had no immunity. The *Code Noir* formally institutionalized slavery, requiring slaves to be instructed as

---

LONGFELLOW'S EVANGELINE

"Beautiful is the land, with its prairies and forests of fruit trees; / Under the feet a garden of flowers, and the bluest of heavens / Bending above, and resting its dome on the walls of the forest. / They who dwell there have named it the Eden of Louisiana!"

Inspired by exile of the French Acadians from their homeland of Nova Scotia, Henry Wadsworth Longfellow composed *Evangeline* in 1847. Little did he know that his epic poem would spread across the country – absorbed as a schoolroom curriculum classic and bonding the tragedy of the Cajuns to the American romantic psyche. The poem begins with a young Acadian maiden named

Evangeline Bellefontaine and her lover, Gabriel, who are separated in Nova Scotia on their wedding day as the mass exodus begins. In search of her lost fiancé, she travels to Louisiana via the Mississippi River, only to learn that Gabriel has already departed for the north. The two lovers are reunited at last, but only on Gabriels's deathbed.

In tribute to their lost love and to the poem, an Evangeline statue was erected in the historic town of St Martinville on a spot marking the alleged burial place of Emmeline Labiche, the "real" Evangeline, despite evidence that Longfellow was somewhat creative in his interpretation of the facts.

Catholics, not as Protestants, in order to bolster the French missionary movement. As defined at this time, the status of slave passed through the mother, and the rights of those enslaved were rigidly limited.

However, the relationship between the French and the Africans became a major component in Creole culture, as the ruling class trained the slaves to speak their language, to prepare French cuisine, and to adopt French customs. The slaves improvised on those traditions, reinterpreted French as patois, and invested the European customs with vestiges of African culture. Some blurring between the groups became officially sanctioned. In New Orleans, Congo Square was designated as a semi-tolerant zone for African dance and religious worship. Taking mulatto, or mixed-raced, mistresses became an accepted practice for French gentleman.

The French–Indian War

Between 1755 and 1763, the French–Indian War was fought between the French (with Native American allies) and the British, at the same time that the two colonial powers were engaged in war in Europe. As the war drew to an end, the French secretly ceded much of the Louisiana territory to Spain, in order to avoiding handing it over to the victorious British under the terms of the Treaty of Paris (1763). French colonists despised the new Spanish rule and fought to retain their own language and customs. But the production of rice and sugar cane boomed under the Spaniards, and this led to something of a truce. Ironically, it was the Spanish who built many of the colonial structures that still stand in the so-called French Quarter of New Orleans.

The Spaniards and the British

In 1755, the Spanish government sheltered some 4,000 French-speaking Acadians who had been exiled from their Nova Scotia homeland by the British. Renamed Cajuns (a corruption of the original word Acadian), they settled in less populous, often Native Choctaw-settled areas along the Mississippi River and in the southern parts of the territory. Fishing and trapping provided income in the swamplands, while small family farms sprang up on the drier, more northerly plains.

A true melting pot

This mixture of Acadian, French, Spanish, African, and Native American peoples was well established by the time President Jefferson engineered the Louisiana Purchase in 1803, grafting the territory onto the United States of America. Waves of migrants in search of work have since contributed to the cultural mix. Remnants of 18th-century German settlements from the failed Company of the Indies have

been absorbed. In the 19th and 20th centuries, Yugoslavians came to harvest oysters on the Gulf Coast, and stayed on; Hungarian immigrants profited from strawberry cultivation, and Hispanic and Vietnamese refugees began to fish and farm in South Louisiana, where you'll now find restaurants serving crawfish egg rolls and crawfish *tamales*.

Today, the heart of Creole Country remains in New Orleans, although French traditions influence other areas of the state. For example, counties are known as parishes, and the Napoleonic Code (rather than Common Law) holds sway in courtrooms. Spanish is also spoken in some communities, such as the St

---

LEFT: Henry Wadsworth Longfellow wrote a tragic poem about an Acadian, Evangeline, in 1847.
RIGHT: the fiddle is essential to Cajun music.

Bernard Parish south of New Orleans. And African influences are certainly plentiful – in the naming of Congo Square in New Orleans, and in dishes such as gumbo, the African name for okra. Interestingly enough, Creole, once a word used to distinguish citizens of French descent from Native Americans and rural Cajun immigrants, has evolved to reflect the inclusion and mix of cultures.

Acadians-plus

In contrast, the Cajun community has remained more centralized. Cajun Country today lies in a 22-parish area that extends from the Louisiana coast and peaks near Alexandria in the central part of the state, with the unofficial capital located in Lafayette and an estimated population of 500,000. The Acadian culture was dominant in many parts of the area, and when elements of other cultures were cherry-picked or grafted onto it, a new variation, known as Cajun, was created. During the 1950s and 1960s, government reforms banned the use of Cajun (a variety of French) in schools and sought to blend the culture into mainstream society. More recently, however, Cajun culture has experienced something of a revival. The state now supports the language, via the Coun-

cil for the Development of French in Louisiana (CODOFIL). More influential have been the efforts of the Cajuns themselves, such as parents teaching their children traditional dances.

Fellow Americans also adore and idealize the Cajuns, which leads to somewhat misguided interpretations of them in films such as *The Big Easy* (where Dennis Quaid has a very odd accent) or culinary mistakes such as Pizza Hut's Cajun pizza. Purists within the community may cringe, but in light of the culture's melting-pot history, these aspects may end up being another ingredient that enhances the blend. ❏

ABOVE: the Cajun-style cuisine class at New Orleans School of Cooking can be fun.

MUSIC

One of the most authentic ways to experience Cajun culture is through its music, which is becoming increasingly popular outside the region. You'll find old men performing on town steps, ad-hoc performances in bars, even all-Cajun, all-French radio stations. Sometimes lively, always with strains of wistful melancholy, Cajun music blends African rhythms and French lyrics. The principal instruments are the fiddle, accordion, and triangle, though drums and guitars have been adopted. The best way to enjoy this music is to dance to it. Community dances called *faidodo* are held weekly in some Cajun towns, and nightclubs burst with music on the streets of Lafayette.

Cajun and Creole Food

Some cultures build pyramids. Others build roads. The Cajuns and Creoles build up an appetite. If they're not cooking, they're eating or planning what to eat next, which is just about the most satisfying aspect of visiting this area. Hunger is a physical impossibility.

Like the Acadian people who immigrated to Louisiana from Nova Scotia in the 18th century, Cajun dishes tend to be hardy. Made from a simple range of fresh, local ingredients from family farms and swamp lands, these were meals for hungry working people, cooked in a single, cast-iron pot over a fire. We're talking here about spicy bowls of *gumbo* (a rich stew thickened with *roux* and flavored with crab, sausages, and sometimes chicken), *jambalaya* (a rice dish similar to paella, but loaded with meat), *andouille* (smoked sausage), as well as the full range of fried fish, fried shrimp, fried oyster, fried-everything that appears on every menu in the state of Louisiana. Nowadays, most Cajuns also revere alligator steaks, and some 21st-century variations on the traditional cuisine have been introduced by Cajun celebrity chefs, such as Paul Prudome and Emeril.

Creole cuisine, on the other hand, is considered more refined – a legacy of the area's colonial ruling classes. Designed for the elegant tables of New Orleans and the wealthy plantation houses, these dishes were influenced by French and Spanish traditions, as well by the African slaves who prepared the European recipes and made subtle alterations. The most obvious characteristic is extravagant amounts of butter – once a great luxury only the rich could afford. Typical dishes are oysters Rockefeller (oysters baked in butter and spinach), shrimp *remoulade* (chilled gulf shrimp dipped in a creamy, cayenne cocktail sauce), crawfish *etouffee* (a velvety stew studded with crawfish, served with rice), Bananas Foster (bananas flambéed in liquor and brown sugar, served with ice cream).

Essential ingredients

Despite their differences, you'll notice Cajuns and Creoles rely on a tried and tested formula – basically, anything that utilises large quantities of

RIGHT: a colourful crawfish boil is cooked with lots of tasty southern ingredients.

seafood or meat, which is then well-spiced, and spooned over rice. *Roux* (flour cooked and thickened in butter) is used as a base for both Cajun and Creole food, along with what's known as "the holy trinity" – green pepper, onion, and celery.

The most interesting aspect of this whole family of food is that there are no official recipes. These dishes were developed in family kitchens, and passed on mother-to-daughter and neighbor-to-neighbor. Like the traditional music here, improvisation is not just encouraged, it's absolutely required, or, as they say in Cajun French, "*Cuire a la couleur de ton idees,*" – cook according to the color of your ideas. Consequently, a *gumbo* in one

kitchen will bear little or no resemblance to a *gumbo* in the next.

In fact, the only thing that remains consistent is portion size. Generosity is a Cajun and Creole tradition. Plates come heaped, mounded, and overflowing, and hospitality is spontaneous. Don't be surprised if a woman you meet on the sidewalk invites you over for a cup of chicory coffee and a hot, sugar-coated beignet doughnut.

The trick to eating happily in the region is to play by the local rules – arrive hungry, go with the flow, and have fun. So when a brown-paper sack of boiling-red crawfish is tipped out all over your table, roll up your sleeves, rip off their heads, suck out the meat, and enjoy it. ❑

CAJUN COUNTRY: THE ATCHAFALAYA BASIN

Steamy swamps, Cajun cooking, a garden in a lake and a reconstructed Acadian town are among the pleasures of the Atchafalaya Basin

Map on page 228

The landing places and excursion programs in Cajun Country vary a great deal, depending on which cruise you take. One itinerary, for example, utilises the Gulf Coast section of the Intracoastal Waterway through southern Louisiana into Texas, as far west as the Port of Galveston. This chapter, however, will concentrate on the landscape, towns, and sightseeing opportunities of popular itineraries that make a tight loop, using the Intracoastal Waterway as far west as Morgan City, then the Atchafalaya Basin route, to rejoin the Mississippi at Baton Rouge. Not all landings are included in any one cruise but the itineraries are tailored to ensure that passengers get a flavor of what the region has to offer.

The Intracoastal Waterway

A few miles downstream from New Orleans, riverboats turn into the Intracoastal Waterway via Algiers Lock, to begin heading roughly west into an intriguing, low-lying region of cypress swamps and intersecting bayous (creeks), fringed by lakes. The busy waterway, completed after World War II, crosses what is largely a pristine, natural wonderland, the air full of birds, slithering and sure-footed creatures on land, and aquatic ones in the dark waters.

LEFT: traveling south under sail.
BELOW: Louisiana veteran musicians.

One of the itineraries is called the **Route of Jean Lafitte**, named after a renegade Frenchman (a pirate, some would say) who commanded a naval force of some 1,000 privateers and 50 warships to help beat the British in the Battle of New Orleans in January 1815. Andrew Jackson offered him and his men citizenship in return for their help, especially their skilled use of cannon fire. Lafitte, a restless adventurer, moved on west into Texas while many of his men remained in and around southern Louisiana's Barataria swamp and established successful Louisiana Delta fishing and trapping communities that still carry the name of Jean Lafitte.

Abundant nature

Cruise operators usually offer small-boat trips into the surrounding bayous, fringed by cypress trees and hanging Spanish moss, to spot alligators, turtles, nutria – a kind of coypu, an aquatic, furry rodent – herons, egrets, and, if you look carefully, perhaps a water moccasin (a semi-aquatic, poisonous snake). After a long rural stretch of waterway, the landscape changes markedly as the boat approaches **Amelia** to reveal a fleet of laid-up towboats, some permanently out of action and others under repair before being returned to

An antique bedroom interior preserved by the Acadian Memorial Museum, St Martinville.

BELOW: a shrimp boat celebration and parade.
RIGHT: Evangeline Oak, the tree marks the spot.

duty. At the Atchafalaya Basin's major center, **Morgan City ㉑**, docks stretch along the north side. The cruise boat will probably have to tie up in a slightly out-of-the-way location, making independent touring rather difficult, so you should sign up for your boat's organized excursions.

Morgan City and St Martinville

One such excursion is an evening outing to a Cajun restaurant and dance hall where visitors get to mix with the local people, especially on the dance floor for the two-step, a popular dance. The atmosphere may sometimes be a bit strained at first, but soon warms up and becomes more festive, especially after a lavish Cajun dinner. A typical meal might consist of a spicy seafood *gumbo*, crawfish pie, crab cakes, *boudin* (pork sausage and rice), and perhaps an apple crumble for dessert. Music will be provided by the fiddle, accordion, and triangle, plus the modern additions of drums and guitar.

Morgan City is also the base for excursions to Cajun destinations such as **St Martinville ㉒**, between New Iberia and Lafayette, the latter a university city and official capital of the Acadians. St Martinville, the center established along Teche Bayou just north of the modern city of New Iberia, developed between 1755 and 1765 after the expelled Acadians came to settle on land granted by the French government. Their major crops were sugar cane and rice, and a visit to the **Konrico Rice Company**, Louisiana's oldest, reveals the legacy of that era. While sugar, rice, and fishing industries still exist, many Cajuns today work in the oil industry, which has a number of refineries in the region.

The town itself is now a tourist attraction: six historic blocks surrounding St Martin Square and **St Martinville de Tours** catholic church (closed Fri am), the

mother church for Acadians, established in 1765. Henry Wadsworth Long-fellow's 1847 poem *Evangeline* is said to parallel the story of a local girl called Emmeline Labiche *(see page 254)*, and the **Evangeline Statue** was donated by Dolores del Rio after she starred in the 1929 film based on the poem. St Martin-ville Cultural Heritage Center comprises two museums dedicated to two different groups of settlers. The **African American Museum** (open daily) tells the story of the Africans' arrival in southwest Louisiana in the mid-1700s; and the **Acadian Memorial Museum** (open daily), concentrates on the exile and arrival of the Acadians. This is depicted in a huge mural on the memorial, while a wall is inscribed with 13,000 names originating from ship manifests. The nearby **Petit Paris Museum** (open daily) exhibits Mardi Gras costumes.

Jefferson Island, Louisiana

At **Jefferson Island**, a few miles southwest, you can enjoy a multifaceted visit to a stately home and botanical gardens. A 19th-century actor and artist named Joseph Jefferson bought a piece of property called Orange Island, renamed it Jefferson Island, then built an elaborate house here in 1870. The botanical gardens he had designed were named **Rip Van Winkle Gardens**, after one of his best-known stage roles. Both the house, now containing a museum, and the 25-acre (10-hectare) semitropical gardens with magnolias, camellias, bromeliads, and irises, are open to the public, and a bizarre but true story is told during the course of the tour. The property is partly sited on an old salt dome in the shallow, 1,300-acre (526-hectare) Lake Peigneur. Texaco had the rights to drill for oil here, but on November 11, 1980, the drilling platform they had erected began to tilt alarmingly and a wide crater opened up. The drill had punctured the

Map on page 228

TIP

For full details of **opening hours** and contact information for the sites and museums mentioned in this chapter, see Travel Tips page 343.

BELOW: Rip Van Winkle Gardens, Jefferson Island.

Map on page 228

tunnel of an active salt mine and the lake began to drain into an ever widening whirlpool as the underground salt pillars started to dissolve. Two drilling rigs, a tug, 11 barges, 70 acres (28 hectares) of Jefferson Island and its botanical gardens, greenhouses, and trees were sucked down before the flooding stopped. The crater was eventually filled in, the botanical gardens restored, and the site restored to what we see today.

Vermillionville, Minnesota

Next comes a stop at **Vermillionville**, a section of present-day **Lafayette** ㉓. This is Cajun Country's version of Colonial Williamsburg, a collection of authentic and restored buildings and new construction that recreates the life of a small Cajun town over several decades in the 19th century. Vermillionville was founded here in 1822, but the name was changed in 1844 to Lafayette, to honor the French Marquis de Lafayette, who fought for the republic in the Revolutionary War. Today, the historic town of Vermillionville is a separate attraction from the modern city of Lafayette.

At the Visitors' Center, you can pick up a leaflet showing the route of a walking tour, and it's an easy one to do on your own. Many of the locations will have guides on hand to help interpret what you see.

Beau Bassin, an 1840s house in a blend of Creole and American Greek-Revival styles, uses colombage, a construction technique of half-timbered wall frames and a mixture of Spanish moss and mud. Spinning, quilting, and textile craftwork are usually demonstrated, using cotton instead of flax and wool as the Acadian women would have done in Canada. One curiosity is an upper room called a *garçonniere*, reserved for the boys in the family, and reached by a private outside staircase.

BELOW: iron working at Vermillionville.
RIGHT: river cruising in Cajun Country.

L'Academie is a re-creation of an 1890s schoolhouse. In the summer, local children come here to learn French folk songs and Acadian crafts and games. **La Maison Boucvalt**, built between 1860 and 1890, is a classic example of how an Acadian/Creole house adapted to the climate of South Louisiana. The design is symmetrical with a house-wide front porch, two front rooms and two in the rear. The chimney is smack in the center. Glass transoms let light in and hot air out, and the shutters are louvered and adjustable. The kitchen and bathroom date from a century ago, but remain to show how changes and improvements took place. Comparisons can be made with an older (1803–7) house, **La Maison Buller**, a French design brought to Canada and the Mississippi Valley. Small rear bedrooms, or *cabinets*, were designed for the daughters and connected to their parents' large bedroom. Another bedroom opens only onto the porch, reserved for strangers as a place to stay before commercial lodging arrived.

Other things to see in the historic town are a replica of an Acadian Catholic chapel; Le Presbytere, a cottage attached to the church; and a cemetery with above-ground tombs, a style imported from France and Spain and essential here because of the high water table. A trail of native and introduced 19th-century plants fringes the shores of Bayou Vermillion. ❏

OHIO-TENNESSEE-CUMBERLAND RIVERS

Cruising these rivers takes you back to a time when the west was opened up and the United States gained its independence and unity

A t the dawn of the New World, a great divide separated Colonial America from its destiny. This divide was the vast Appalachian mountain range, and what lay on the far side was wild, unexplored, and there for the taking.

The year was 1769 – six years before the Revolutionary War that would give America its independence – when Daniel Boone set out for the bluegrass of Kentucky. Among his discoveries was the Cumberland Gap – a pass at a height of 1,300 ft (396 meters), cutting through the Cumberland Mountains and forming a gate way through the southern Appalachians. From then on, America would always look west.

It is against this backdrop that cruises of the Ohio, Tennessee, and Cumberland rivers must be seen, and that makes them an historically authentic way to see the countryside. It often seems to visitors traveling these rivers that they are stepping back in time: Steamboats began sailing the "western" rivers in 1811, and their arrival fueled the development of an economy that began in the 1830s with the advent of the railroad, and developed into a nationwide system of trade and transportation.

The frontier days have long since passed, but a regional character remains, one that is thoroughly modern on the surface, but steeped in legend and still acutely in tune with the rhythms of the rivers.

The towns along the way reflect the eclectic influences that have converged in this region, in much the way the river system feeds one tributary into another. In these valleys, north meets south and east meets west, as the rivers meander through a five-state region encompassing parts of Ohio, West Virginia, Kentucky, Tennessee, and Alabama.

PRECEDING PAGES: onboard the *Mississippi Queen* as it sails the Tennessee River, near Chattanooga.
LEFT: fishing for bass on the Tennessee River.
RIGHT: frontiersman Daniel Boone.

Geology

While there are parts of the United States that were colonized earlier, few regions have a geological and archeological record that dates back as far as this one. Older than the Rocky Moun-

DANIEL BOONE

Daniel Boone was born in Pennsylvania in 1734 to a Quaker family, who moved to North Carolina when he was 15. His first adventure was in the French and Indian Wars, five years later, but it was not until the 1760s that he set out, with a companion, John Finley, on his great journey of exploration. The call of the wild was always strong, but Daniel was a devoted family man, father of ten children, who declared that the most important things in life were "a good gun, a good horse, and a good wife." He left Boonesboro in 1788, first for West Virginia, then Missouri. When asked why he was leaving Kentucky he replied simply "Too crowded."

tains, the Appalachians parallel almost the entire eastern US seaboard from Maine to Alabama. Along the southern stretch, the Cumberland plateau constitutes one of its major ranges and spawns several rivers. Among these are the 650-mile (1,050-km) Tennessee and the 690-mile (1,100-km) Cumberland. Both empty into the 980-mile (1,580-km) Ohio, which in turn feeds the mighty Mississippi.

Early inhabitants

The earliest known inhabitants of this region were the Cherokee, the Chickasaw, and the Shawnee, who left behind giant earthen

the revolution, the War of Independence and conflict with the Native Americans would preclude any serious efforts to populate Ohio, Kentucky, and Tennessee.

Among the earliest settlements in the region were Boonesboro, named after the intrepid explorer, and Nashborough, which was named in honor or General Francis Nash, a hero of the War of Independence. Today, we know this community by its modern name, Nashville. Another revolutionary hero, George Rogers Clark (1752–1818), founded Louisville, which is named after Louis XVI, who was king of France until he met his death on the guillotine

mounds that intrigue archeologists and anthropologists to this day. The builders of these mounds faded into obscurity around 1400 – some 300 years before the influx of outsiders. The first European settlers were French fur traders, who began filtering into the region during the early 1700s and were to make themselves a fine living.

Boone blazes a trail

Not until Daniel Boone arrived did a mass migration begin, however. In 1775, Boone marked a trail, which became known as the Wilderness Road, for settlers to follow. While the initial push over the mountains came before

in 1793, the most high-ranking victim of the French Revolution.

As the close of the 18th century drew nearer, the end of hostilities in the United States brought a flood of westward settlers. Kentucky became the 15th state on June 1, 1792. Tennessee followed as the 16th exactly four years later, and Ohio joined the Union as the 17th state on March 1, 1803.

North versus south

While the territories west of the Appalachians were becoming settled, organized, and integrated into the national economy, a new division was starting to take place by the middle of the 19th century: the north versus the south. The states of Kentucky and Tennessee were destined to be on the front line of this north–south divide.

When Civil War broke out in 1861, Kentucky remained in the Union, while Tennessee seceded to the Confederacy. Although it sided with the Union, Kentucky would remain a slave state for the duration of the war, and its slaves would not be freed until the adoption of the 13th Amendment in 1865 at the end of hostilities. Tennessee was to become a major battleground: during the four years of bloody conflict, there were more than 450 battles

manufacturing, and other light industries. Coal mining and tobacco farming were two other economic mainstays of these river valleys. Due to the topography, there were few grand plantations, which were mainly found in the cotton and sugar regions of the Deep South.

Social planning

Even so, the region remained largely rural, and modernization came slowly. In 1933, as part of the New Deal, Congress authorized the creation of the Tennessee Valley Authority. Considered one of the great achievements of the Roosevelt administration, the TVA was a broad

fought in the state of Tennessee – a number that was surpassed only by Virginia.

Industry and manufacturing

By the end of the war, manufacturing was well established in the river valleys' larger cities. At the outbreak of the conflict, Cincinnati was already recognized as the third-ranking industrial center in the nation, and the leading manufacturing center of the west. Chief among its industries were pork-packing plants, soap

LEFT: a rural view of the Ohio River near Marietta, by Henry Cheever Pratt (1803–80).
ABOVE: a replica of a wagon used on the Oregon Trail.

experiment in social planning. It built dams and hydroelectric plants, and fostered soil conservation, reforestation, and overall industrialization. Most significantly, it brought electrification to the entire region and is credited with greatly improving the standard of living for people in the valley.

The TVA left behind another enduring legacy: the Land Between the Lakes, a 170,000-acre (69,000-hectare) peninsula preserved for outdoor recreation and environmental education. Located below two dams on the Tennessee River, just north of the Tennessee-Kentucky border, this scenic area is featured on many cruises of the region (see page 282). ❏

THE OHIO-TENNESSEE-CUMBERLAND RIVER PORTS

On a journey through the Midwest to the southern states you will find the water flows by spectacular scenery, fast-paced urban centers of culture and high art, and historic Civil War sites

Map on page 272

The Ohio River is a scenic and varied waterway, with twists and turns below Pittsburgh, high bluffs, attractive agricultural landscapes, small riverside towns, rust-belt cities' active and abandoned industries, graceful bridges, occasional cross-river ferries, and impressive arrivals and departures at Pittsburgh and Cincinnati. The Ohio begins at the western Pennsylvanian junction of the Monongahela and Allegheny rivers at Fort Point, Pittsburgh. It is 982 miles (1,580 km) to Cairo Point, where the Ohio joins the Mississippi, and en route forms the borders of West Virginia, Ohio, Kentucky, Indiana, and Illinois. The Tennessee River's main navigable channel is 652 miles (1,050 km) long. It begins just above Knoxville, Tennessee, and empties into the Ohio River at Paducah, Kentucky. The Cumberland River is 687 miles (1,106 km) long, rising in the east of Kentucky and winding southwest to the Ohio River near Paducah.

River itineraries

There is not one single itinerary that calls at all the ports along the Ohio, Tennessee, and Cumberland rivers, but that is hardly a problem, as it's such a colorful, event-packed region that you may want to cruise along it more than once. Some cruises may have a theme – the Civil War, Native American culture, or fall foliage, for example – with special onboard lectures scheduled to enhance the experience.

Although the rivers flow through a number of major population centers, most of the communities are small and easily explored, although in many cases a ship's tour is beneficial. Some may be included in the price of your cruise, depending on the company you're sailing with, but others may be available at a nominal charge – shore excursions on river cruises are generally quite affordable.

Ports of call vary by itinerary, and are described here in geographical progression from east to west – a reflection of the historical migration of westward settlers. Certain cities serve both as ports of call and as points of embarkation, allowing visitors to spend additional time there if desired.

Pittsburgh, Pennsylvania

Geography has everything to do with Pittsburgh's development. First the site was an Iroquois camp, then strategic forts, Fort Duquesne (French) and Fort Pitt (British), were built where two rivers, the Monongahela and Allegheny, join. After the British took control in November 1758, following the French and Indian War, the permanent fort grew into a settlement and

LEFT: the Duquesne incline overlooking Pittsburgh.
BELOW: a view of Louisville, Kentucky, from the Ohio River.

USS Requin *stands at the water side next to the Carnegie Science Center, Pittsburgh.*

the most prominent landing place for traders and settlers heading west via the Ohio water highway. Steamboat trade mushroomed, then railroads arrived from all directions to form a major transportation hub.

Nearby, Pennsylvania coal mining built the steel industry. **Pittsburgh ❶** became an industrial powerhouse, and, because of its river valley setting, one of the smoggiest cities in America. In the early and mid-20th century drivers used their headlights at noon and streetlights were kept on all day. But all that has changed, and architecturally-rich downtown Pittsburgh, known as the **Golden Triangle**, is clean and clear and, with a compact center, is easy to navigate on foot. One of the many companies that maintain headquarters here, PPG (Pittsburgh Plate Glass) Industries, built the postmodern, green-glass-tinted One PPG Place in 1984, a striking, downtown icon featuring 231 spires and a winter garden.

Tourist steamboats lie along the Monongahela side of the Golden Triangle between Fort Point and the Smithfield Street Bridge. If you are staying over before or after your cruise, there is much to see and do. On the opposite bank, the South Shore, sits **Station Square**, the former Pittsburgh and Lake Erie Station. It's now a restaurant (Grand Concourse) and shopping complex where trains, all freight these days, pass through without stopping. A steep cliff rises behind the station and along the river, and two incline railways climb to the top, making a terrific outing.

The closest to Station Square is the Monongahela Incline, at the top of which is one of the city's smartest suburbs. You can walk along the ridge via Grandview Avenue to the Duquesne Incline, and take a great photograph of the three rivers coming together, the city's impressive skyline, and the steamboat, before returning to river level and walking across the Fort Pitt Bridge, or turning right back to the Smithfield Street Bridge.

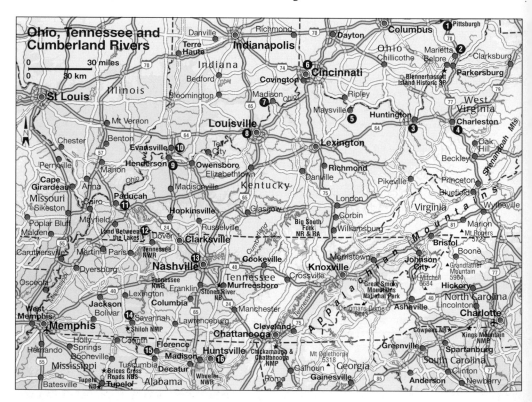

East of downtown

Just 2 miles (4 km) east of downtown and easily accessed by bus are the **Carnegie Museum of Art** and the **Carnegie Museum of Natural History** (both closed Mon and Sun am). Andrew Carnegie, a Scottish immigrant who, by 1901, had become a steel magnate, a philanthropist, and the richest man in the world, wanted to develop a contemporary art museum, so he began by purchasing works by Winslow Homer, James Whistler, and Camille Pissarro. This fledgling collection formed the basis of one that now spans the period from the mid-19th to the late 20th century. The **Hall of Architecture**, covering the same era, exhibits drawings, prints, and models to show the development of modern building. In the Natural History building, kids will head for the dinosaur hall and the interactive fossil dig, while parents with historical interests may gravitate to the natural history discoveries of the Lewis and Clark Expedition.

Henry Clay Frick, a partner of Andrew Carnegie, with whom he was often at loggerheads, developed a process for making coke out of coal that greatly advanced the Pennsylvania steel industry. With his money, he amassed an estate and collections that are housed on a 6-acre (2.5-hectare) site in the **Frick Art and Historical Center** (closed Mon and Sun am), about 20 minutes from the Carnegie site. It comprises Frick's mansion, an art gallery, a carriage museum, a greenhouse, and children's playhouse. The main house, purchased by Frick in 1882, was transformed and enlarged from an Italianate villa into a château-style mansion.

In 1905 he left Pittsburgh and moved to Fifth Avenue, New York, where his home now holds the Frick Collection. Happily for Pittsburgh, 95 percent of the contents of the house, including furniture and art, stayed behind, nicely

Map on page 272

TIP

For full details of **opening hours** and contact information for the sites and museums mentioned in this chapter, see Travel Tips page 344.

BELOW: Pittsburgh's Golden Triangle at night.

balancing the contents of the New York complex. The Car and Carriage House includes Frick's 1914 Rolls-Royce Silver Ghost among the 20 vintage cars.

Leaving Pittsburgh, the boat passes Fort Point and Three Rivers Stadium, and soon leaves the city behind to enter an increasingly rural stretch of river for the overnight trip to the first stop. The first lock and dam come within 6 miles (10 km) and several more will be passed through during the course of the night. The 172 miles (277 km) to Marietta form one of the loveliest rural stretches of river in the country. High banks define the stream, and where the woods part, agricultural land stretches right down to the water, while small river towns provide a warm welcome with their neat clusters of stone and brick buildings, and residents often come out to wave to passing steamboat passengers.

Marietta, Ohio

Marietta ❷, the oldest town in Ohio, is a quintessential riverfront community and steamboats dock adjacent to a lovely park. The city, founded in 1787 by the land speculators, Ohio Company and Associates, is named after Queen Marie Antoinette, as a tribute to French help during the American Revolution. Because of its prime location along the Ohio River, the town grew as a trading center for the Northwest Territory. Banks were established and agricultural produce from the rich surrounding land was brought here for shipment. Later, shipbuilding took hold and the city prospered. For a photograph of your ship, walk south to the bridge spanning the Ohio and climb the steps to the footpath. If you keep walking, you'll be able to catch the steamboat set against the city park, its gazebo, the imposing brick Lafayette Hotel, and an attractive row of Victorian houses.

While there are excursions to the area's attractions, it is also worth spending an independent day here. The **Ohio River Museum** (closed Mon–Tues and Sun am), minutes on foot from the landing, displays steamboat history in models, photographs, and an excellent film. The cabins and quarters of the *W.P. Snyder, Jr*, the last steam-powered, stern-wheel towboat, can be explored. In the same building, which is on the site of the fort built to protect early settlers and to serve as the seat of government, sits the **Campus Martius Museum** (hours as above), an interpretive center for the history of settlement and migration in Ohio. The center can be visited as part of an organized tour, but it can be explored easily on your own, as well. A shuttle service is sometimes provided to and from the pier. This is true in many ports along the rivers where passengers may want to explore independently; check with your cruise line to see where such services are offered.

Out of town excursions include the **Lee Middleton Original Dolls** factory, at **Belpre**, America's largest doll-making operation, where artisans mold, hand-paint, and assemble high-quality models. The second stop, the **Children's Toy and Doll Museum** (open Sat pm and by appointment) at Harmar Village, exhibits a collection of dolls, dolls' houses, teddy bears, antique metal cash machines, and games that once entertained and educated generations of children.

The next stretch of the Ohio is marked by wooded bluffs and the river makes lots of twists and turns,

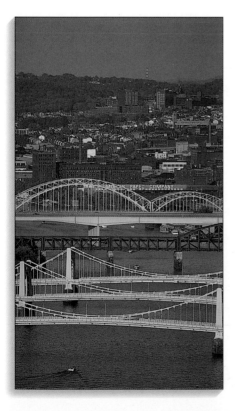

BELOW: Pittsburgh's 6th, 7th, and 8th Street bridges are known as the Three Sisters.

often blocking out any sign of habitation. Then, around the next bend, a Victorian river town will appear and the boat signals a greeting with a burst of tunes from the calliope. An island appears in midstream just a mile downriver from Parkersburg, West Virginia and the boat ties up at a landing.

Map on page 272

Blennerhassett, Huntington, and Charleston

On **Blennerhassett Island**, Parkersburg, an Irish aristocrat built a Palladian-style mansion in the early 1800s, but lost his reputation when he teamed up with maverick statesman Aaron Burr (1756–1836), who tried to raise a force to conquer Texas and establish a republic. Like Burr, he was tried for treason in 1807, but acquitted. Imprisoned for a time, he subsequently lost his fortune. The present house is a reconstruction, started in 1973, as the first one burned down in 1811, and it is considered to be one of the finest estates west of the Allegheny Mountains.

About 120 miles (193 km) downriver boats tie up alongside a riverside park adjacent to **Huntington ❸**, West Virginia's second largest city. From the landing, the boat's excursion visits the **Huntington Museum of Art** (closed Mon and Sun am), which exhibits 19th- and 20th-century American and European paintings and sculpture, Georgian silver, and a glass collection. Huntington is also a great shopping port, with a downtown antiques and curio store area. It's also a glass-manufacturing center, you can see stained glass being produced at **Blenko Glass**, and after a tour of the factory and museum, there will be time for the gift shop. Purchases made here can be shipped directly to your home address.

The capital of West Virginia, **Charleston ❹**, offers the chance to explore the **State Capitol Complex**. Designed in Italian Renaissance style, the exterior of the dome is resplendent. Inside, the main rotunda is crowned with a

BELOW: the palmetto-lined Battery faces Charleston Harbor.

Visitors to Charleston can explore the historic district by horse-and-carriage.

BELOW: the gardens at Drayton Hall, Charleston.

chandelier composed of more than 10,000 pieces. In the grounds are statues of Stonewall Jackson, Booker T. Washington, and Abraham Lincoln. The complex can be toured independently or as part of an organized excursion.

Maysville, Kentucky

Once a manufacturing city, incorporated in 1796 and rising to importance by the 1830s, **Maysville ❺** is the oldest landing place on the Ohio. It once fired bricks and made wrought-iron fences and gates and ornamental street furnishings such as clocks, lamp posts, benches, and signs. Daniel Boone, explorer of unmapped spaces and responsible for the settlement of Kentucky, once ran a tavern in the town. The town's prosperity is revealed in a 24-block, 160-building historic district, which is on the National Register. It features brick streets and neo-Romanesque, Georgian, and Victorian styles, all walkable from the steamboat landing. Ships organize walking tours of Maysville, and they are a good idea as they are led by local escorts who can point out places of particular interest, and will no doubt also tell you that, along with its reputation for manufacturing, the town also became renowned as a center of educational enlightenment.

The graceful suspension bridge spanning the Ohio, constructed in 1931, was the prototype for San Francisco's Golden Gate Bridge and leads to **Ripley**, Ohio, once an important stop on the slaves' Underground Railroad. It also served as the setting for Eliza's escape in Harriet Beecher Stowe's classic novel, *Uncle Tom's Cabin*.

The primary visit on the steamboat excursion is to the **Ohio Tobacco Museum** (open Apr–Dec, Sat–Sun), which displays agricultural tools and demonstrates farming procedures and the vital role the river played in shipping produce to

market. The museum, housed in an 1850 Federal/Georgian-style home, is located next to the tobacco warehouses. With more tobacco growers selling directly to the manufacturers, the tobacco auctions have declined by 50 percent in recent years, while tourism is rising in importance in the local economy.

Map on page 272

Cincinnati, Ohio

No river city provides a more exciting steamboat arrival than Cincinnati, with the city and the smaller towns of Newport and Covington opposite, all fronting directly onto the Ohio. Founded in 1788, **Cincinnati ❻** was a riverboat city from the start. In the 1800s, it was one of the area's busiest river ports, with hundreds of steamboats leaving daily. Many, in fact, were built here. The steamboats drop their passengers at the Public Landing opposite the **Great American Ballpark**, home for the Cincinnati Reds and the stadium for the Cincinnati Bengals. The location is between the **Roebling Suspension Bridge**, once the world's longest such bridge and the 1868 prototype for the Brooklyn Bridge, and the **Taylor Southgate Bridge** carrying US Highway 27.

Just up from the landing, about a 10-minute walk, downtown Cincinnati, anchored by **Fountain Square**, is the heart of the city. The combination of offices, hotels, and restaurants generates a lot of pedestrian traffic. Make for the 1931 art deco **Carew Tower** for the view from the 48th story, and be sure to look inside the **Hilton Cincinnati Netherland Plaza**, a National Historic Landmark. The French-style art deco building features a beautiful lobby and a Palm Court restaurant executed in a colorful Egyptian art deco style.

Bus Route No. 1 leaves from Fifth and Walnut (Fountain Square) and passes the 1888 Richardson neo-Romanesque **City Hall** en route to the magnificent art

BELOW: a barge on the Ohio River.

First time visitors to Cincinnati may prefer to take the boat's tour for an overview of the city, including attractions such as Fountain Square, the Cincinnati Art Museum and the Krohn Conservatory. But it is easy enough to get around on your own.

deco **Cincinnati Union Terminal**, built in 1933, and its broad boulevard approach. While Amtrak intercity trains still call here, most of the building houses the **Cincinnati Museum Center** (open daily), which includes a history museum, a children's museum, a natural history and science museum, plus an OMNIMAX theater. In the central Rotunda, a mural covers the dome, and the *Tom Greene*, one of the Greene Line steamboats (which was *Delta Queen*'s predecessor company) is right up there among the city's icons.

Mount Adams, a short taxi ride up one of Cincinnati's seven hills, is a trendy residential neighborhood with restaurants, including an atmospheric bistro in a former pottery kiln. Also here are leafy Eden Park, where the **Cincinnati Art Museum** (closed Mon; free) is located, and a wonderful Ohio River overlook. Another point of interest is the **Krohn Conservatory** (open daily; free), where you'll be transported to environments far removed from the American Midwest. Its major collections depict rain forest, desert, and tropical landscapes.

Because many river cruises begin in Cincinnati, it may be possible to spend additional time here before or after a cruise. Packages are often available, and may include transfers, hotel accommodations, dinner, and sightseeing to a choice of local attractions. Passengers spending the night can visit the **Aronoff Center for the Arts**, which presents traveling Broadway-style shows.

Madison, Indiana

This river town, listed on the National Register of Historic Places, is a repository of 19th-century residential architecture and bills itself as the most beautiful town in the Midwest. Built in the early steamboat era, **Madison ❼**, on a bend of the Ohio River, prospered as a river and railroad town well into the 20th century

BELOW: Cincinnati's landing is close to the heart of the city.

before falling into a long slumber. In the 1960s, the preservation movement started and you can now enjoy a superbly maintained residential district on your own or on the steamboat's walking tour. The town's principal shopping street was chosen by the National Trust for Historic Preservation as a Main Street pilot project.

The imposing, two-story, 1844 Greek Revival **Lanier Mansion**, constructed of brick on a raised stone foundation, was built for the railroad financier and magnate James F.D. Lanier and the gardens reflect a 19th-century formality.

Louisville, Kentucky

The next major city along the river is **Louisville ❽**, the largest population center in Kentucky. Founded in 1778, the city grew rapidly after the arrival of steamboats in the 1820s and prospered as a river port. The city's icon is the 1914 steamboat *Belle of Louisville*, the oldest river steamer in the USA and a National Landmark. Previously named *Idlewild* and *Avalon*, she plied all the Midwest's rivers carrying passengers, vehicles, and freight until finally coming here as an excursion boat. Since 1963, she has mostly challenged the 1926 *Delta Queen* in an annual late April race that is more about steam, smoke, and calliope than it is about high speeds – although the boats may reach 10 miles (16 km) per hour with the currents' help. It is a great civic event watched from aboard a fleet of boats and from the shore.

A shore excursion is advisable in Louisville if you're a first-time visitor, since there is so much to see. The city has contributed a great deal to the US scene – including the cheeseburger, which was first served in here in 1934. Even better would be a hotel package for travelers whose cruise begins or ends in Louisville, since the city is definitely worth a couple of days exploration.

Map on page 272

Louisville is the birthplace of former World Heavyweight Boxing champion and activist, Muhammad Ali. There are plans to build a multi-million dollar center in Ali's honor, in downtown Louisville.

BELOW: Cincinnati Union Terminal.

The restored 19th-century Lanier Mansion is located at 601 W. First Street in Madison, Indiana. Guided tours are available April to mid-Dec, Tues–Sat 9am–4pm and Sunday 1–4pm; closed Mon, tel: 812-265 3526.

BELOW: Lanier Mansion, Indiana, is a National Historic Landmark.

Downtown is within a stone's throw of the landing site at Waterfront Park, and Main Street is where you'll want to head after disembarking, to see the largest collection of iron-facade buildings outside of New York's SoHo district. Along Main Street are several attractions, all within walking distance of each other, including the **Louisville Slugger Museum** (open daily). This is the home of the Hillerich & Bradsby Company, makers of the Louisville Slugger baseball bat since 1884. Tours include a film, exhibits, and a walk through the factory. Just a few blocks away lies the **Louisville Science Center** (closed Sun am), complete with hands-on exhibits and an IMAX theater. Those with an interest in armaments may enjoy a visit to the Frazier Historical Arms Museum, which features a permanent exhibit drawn in part from the Royal Armoury in London.

One block over from Main is Market Street, where **Glassworks** has studios, galleries, and daily tours. The facility is said to be the only one of its kind in the US. Up the block is the **Kentucky International Convention Center**, which incorporates a visitor information center.

Louisville is best known as the home of **Churchill Downs** and the Kentucky Derby, a thoroughbred race held the first Saturday of May since 1875, when the track was built. The Derby began as a 1½-mile (2.4-km) race for three-year-old thoroughbreds and was later shortened to 1¼ miles (2 km). The first horse to win was Aristides, and subsequent winners have included Exterminator (1918), Whirlaway (1941), Secretariat (1973) and Funny Cide (2003).

A tour of a local thoroughbred training center provides a view of the scenic bluegrass country and a first-hand look at the breeding of championship race horses. Some cruise departures are scheduled to arrive at Louisville in time for the "Run for the Roses," and include tickets to the race as well as an expert guide for on-board lectures. At other times, excursions visit the **Kentucky Derby Museum** (closed Sun am), where you can retrace the history of what's been called "the greatest two minutes in sports," with a multimedia film about the race, and hands-on displays for children. A tour of the track includes the grandstands, the Winner's Circle, the paddock, and stables.

Kentucky bourbon and the distilling process can be seen at several locations in and around Louisville, such as the **Jim Beam American Outpost** and the **Labrot & Graham Distillery**. There are free samples to taste and a store where you can stock up.

Henderson, Kentucky

The main attraction in **Henderson** ❾ is a WPA (Works Progress Administration, begun in 1935 by President Roosevelt, to alleviate poverty during the Depression) project that created a turreted, slate-roofed, French-style country inn to house the **James J. Audubon Museum** (open daily), dedicated to the wildlife of the area and to Audubon's visits and nearby residency. Audubon, the first artist to depict life-size birds and animals in natural settings, lived and worked in Henderson from 1810–18, choosing the location because it was on the Mississippi flyway. This, the largest gathering of Audubon memorabilia, includes his original drawings, paintings, and watercolors, a complete collection of his publications, and belongings such as family heirlooms, correspondence, journals, and ledgers. A glass-enclosed observation room looks out into the forest, a 692-acre (280-hectare) state park with miles of trails to explore. Among the main attractions are the 20 species of warblers that arrive in the spring.

Map on page 272

Five miles (8 km) across the river in **Evansville ⑩**, Indiana, the **Reitz Home Museum** (open Wed–Sun pm), the crown jewel of the Riverside Historic District, exhibits the lifestyle of a Prussian couple who met in the US and established a lumber empire. Their house, built in 1871 in French Second Empire style, is Victorian within, as their son, Francis Joseph, redecorated the interior in the 1890s. There are original pieces of furniture, stained-glass windows, watercolor-on-canvas ceilings, Tiffany mantels, damask wall coverings, and crystal chandeliers.

Paducah, Kentucky

Located at the junction of the Tennessee and Ohio rivers, **Paducah ⑪** looks, from the river, like a busy place, with all the barge and tow traffic tied up out front. From here, tens of thousands of Union soldiers boarded 185 transports bound for Shiloh *(see page 283)*. The boat lands at the base of a substantial levee that is attractively landscaped at the top. Once inside the flood wall, look at the set of attractive murals running along it, reflecting the town's connection to the river and its railroad history.

Directly ahead as you leave the landing stage is Broadway, the main street, lined with small-town storefronts that cater to the collectibles trade. The **Market House Museum** (closed Mon and Sun am), and a golden-age movie palace, easily recognized by its terracotta facade, are the main sites. With its old-fashioned streetlamps, tree-lined sidewalks, and redbrick buildings, Paducah could have been the setting for a Norman Rockwell painting.

BELOW:
Funny Cide leads
the Kentucky Derby.

The Museum of the American Quilters' Society in Paducah displays spectacular quilts that are works of art.

BELOW: a Civil War battle reenactment in Shiloh, Savannah.

One block left, the **Seaman's Church Institute of New York**, an arm of the Episcopal Church, operates an important training center for inland river pilots and crews. Conducting courses in navigation, the key ingredient is a simulator that replicates a specific stretch of river, with currents and wind added, to test and upgrade navigational skills.

A few blocks in and to the right is the **Museum of the American Quilters' Society** (closed Sun), a non-profit organization dedicated to the art, history, and heritage of hand-sewn and machine-made quilts. The museum, established in 1991, has a collection of 200 antique and contemporary quilts on rotating display hanging in one large gallery and two rooms showing others that have been loaned to the museum. Museum staff give *Delta Queen* passengers a special welcome and a reduced rate, and they conduct tours and workshops.

You could also join a ship-organized tour, led by a resident artist, to the galleries in the **Lowertown** fine arts district, to view work in a broad range of media, from paint to print, and sculpture to photography.

Sailing the Cumberland River Route

On the Cumberland River, Dover, just below Paducah, is the jumping-off point for excursions to the **Land Between the Lakes ⑫**, an attractive 40-mile (64-km) strip of land between two man-made lakes. This can only be explored on a ship-organized tour, which takes passengers back to the lifestyle of the 1800s. At the **Homeplace Living History Farm**, interpreters in period costume re-create common tasks, including harvesting tobacco, caring for livestock, and performing household chores. Another stop at the **Great Western Furnace** offers a glimpse of an industry once central to the local economy.

Map on page 272

From Paducah it's 30 miles (48 km) to Barkley Lock on the Cumberland River, which raises boats up to **Lake Barkley** and the picturesque lakes region. Next stop is **Clarksville**, Tennessee, and then its upriver through Cheatham Lock and on to the state capital of **Nashville** ⓮, Tennessee, rich in history and music that has brought it fame. The city has art galleries, museums, and entertainment venues of all kinds, from large amphitheaters to small, out-of-the-way places where famous entertainers sometimes appear. The original settlement was founded in 1779, when James Robertson crossed the Cumberland River and made camp on the overlooking bluffs, where they built Fort Nashborough. Nashville's early growth came from the westward expansion of the original colonies, and its key position on the Cumberland River. The river served as a highway, bringing goods and new residents, and transforming the small fort into a full-scale city. Nashville has been called "the Athens of the South," for its institutions of higher learning, and "Music City, USA," for the many recording studios, the headquarters of Gibson and Epiphone guitars, and the **Grand Ole Opry**.

Casting off from Paducah, the steamboat has just 47 miles (76 km) to go to the meeting of the waters of the Ohio and Mississippi at Cairo Point. Depending on the itinerary, the boat may make a hard right for an upriver sail to St Louis or go gently left (south) downriver to Memphis. Alternatively, your itinerary may take you southward on the Tennessee River.

Southward on the Tennessee

Traveling south brings us to **Savannah** ⓯, where riverboats and barges make landfall for excursions to **Shiloh**, one of the most important crossroads of the Civil War. A visit to a Civil War battleground can be a reflective and moving

The Cumberland River flows from east Kentucky to the Ohio River, near Paducah. The Tennessee Valley Authority built a series of locks and dams making 381 miles (613 km) of the river navigable and bringing electricity to the Cumberland hill communities (see page 269.)

BELOW: a shuttle at the US Space and Rocket Center in Huntsville.

Map on page 272

The Tennessee River-park, Chatanooga, extends through Downtown to the Tennessee River Gorge, and Blount Mansion (closed Sun, open Sat in summer only) is in Knoxville.

BELOW: the Alabama Music Hall of Fame.
RIGHT: a view from the *Mississippi Queen* over the Tennessee River.

experience, even for those with only a passing interest in military history. The National Park Service does an excellent job of preservation and interpretation, providing visitors with an experience that is tasteful and informative.

About 9 miles (14 km) south of Savannah, on the west bank of the Tennessee River, lies the **Shiloh National Military Park**. Established on December 27, 1894, the park preserves the site where 65,000 Union men met 44,000 Confederate soldiers in the first major battle of the western theater of the Civil War. At stake were the Confederacy's western railroads, and military control of the lower Mississippi River Valley. In two days, 23,746 men were killed, wounded, or declared missing in action, including General Albert Sidney Johnston, the highest ranking American ever killed in combat. The results were a decisive Union victory, which allowed federal forces to achieve their strategic objective of taking the railroad system. In the grounds of the park there are monuments, cannon, and more than 450 historic tablets, all set on 4,000 acres (1,620 hectares) overlooking the Tennessee River. Also within its boundaries is the **Shiloh National Cemetery**, as well as carefully-preserved prehistoric Native American mounds, which are listed as historic landmarks.

Delta Queen's themed Civil War cruise is a six-day trip, from Chattanooga to Memphis, which gives passengers an in-depth look at the Shiloh battlefields, informed by the onboard historians specialising in this period of American history. This particular trip also visits New Madrid, Missouri *(see page 252)*, where the most powerful earthquake ever to hit America was centered, in 1811.

Florence and Huntsville, Alabama

A short way downriver, **Florence ⓰** presents an unusual congregation of attractions. Here you'll find Alabama's only example of Frank Lloyd Wright's architecture, the **Rosenbaum House**, built in 1940 and still occupied by members of the family for whom it was designed, plus the largest Native American mound in the Tennessee Valley and the birthplace of W.C. Handy, "The Father of the Blues." The log cabin where he was born and brought up has been restored and is now open as a small museum, and there's a statue to him in Wilson Park. Florence is rightly proud of Handy, although he is often associated in the public mind with Memphis, where he moved in 1909 and set up his headquarters at Beale Street. Ships organize tours, by road, that take in these sights and more – including the **Alabama Music Hall of Fame**, just outside town at Tuscumbia, which pays tribute to renowned Alabamians such as Hank Williams, Tammy Wynette, and Nat King Cole.

Not far away, Decatur is the port city for nearby **Huntsville ⓰**, the destination of several excursions. One popular option is a visit to the **US Space and Rocket Center** (open daily), the largest space museum in the world. On site are a giant OMNIMAX theater showing films related to space travel, and hardware from the mission of Apollo 16, the penultimate manned mission to the moon, as well as an aviation museum. The tour to the Space Center may sometimes be combined with a look at historic Huntsville, including the antebellum railroad depot. ❑

TO THE PACIFIC NORTHWEST: THE COLUMBIA AND SNAKE RIVERS

A journey along the Columbia and Snake rivers is a journey through the history of this fascinating region

The Columbia and Snake rivers have served for centuries as the primary artery for east–west travel in the Pacific Northwest, used by the Native American Nez Perce, and by explorers, fur traders, settlers, the military, and missionaries. Canoes were joined by cargo rafts and keelboats, then steamboats and now barges carrying lumber, grain, and fuels. The river valleys created a natural path for railroads to be laid, and later for the expanding federal and interstate highway systems.

The Columbia-Snake system is second only to the Mississippi-Missouri in area drained. The Columbia flows 1,200 miles (1,930 km) from the Canadian Rockies in Southeast British Columbia into Washington, then forms the border with Oregon on its way to the Pacific Ocean. Ten major tributaries feed it, with the Snake the most important, supplying 20 percent of the Columbia's water. The 1,000-mile (1,610-km) long Snake rises in Yellowstone National Park and flows through Idaho into eastern Washington to join the Columbia at the cities of Pasco, Richland, and Kennewick.

Varied landscapes

Today, the Columbia-Snake corridor provides a fascinating trip into more varied landscapes than can be found along any North American river. Beginning at the Pacific Ocean breakers, the river mouth near Astoria starts as a broad bay, narrows upriver to a more natural stream, then dramatically squeezes through the deep Columbia Gorge. Thickly forested slopes rise to high cliffs and melting snow cascades into pencil-thin waterfalls. The river's surface is turbulent and the winds strong, before a series of dams, the first started during the Great Depression, tames the flow into a series of separate pools. Navigation locks lift the boats and barges, and parallel fish ladders provide a

LEFT: Crown Point, in the Columbia River Gorge.
RIGHT: at Fort Clatsop National Memorial, near Astoria.

bypass for salmon heading upstream to spawn and the young returning to reach the Pacific.

Beyond the gorge, the land becomes drier, and with good soil and an ideal climate, vineyards have burgeoned in both Washington and

Oregon to create the largest wine producing region after California. Wildlife, seen and unseen, is abundant, including hundreds of thousands of birds that come to roost and nest, especially in the Umatilla National Wildlife Refuge. By the time the Snake River is reached, the land on either side shows few signs of habitation and boats sail between layers of basalt, laid down millions of years ago to form multi-colored buttes and mesas.

Finally, after passing through four Snake River locks and dams, boats reach the end of deep-water navigation along Washington's border with Idaho, 465 miles (750 km) upriver from the Pacific Ocean. To continue along the

Snake River, passengers take to jet-boats for an exhilarating ride up through the rapids into Hells Canyon, one that is even deeper than the Grand Canyon in Colorado.

The Nez Perce and the explorers

Before European and Americans arrived, the Pacific Northwest was home to the native Nez Perce, a designation for the largest congregation of distinct tribes living together in the western United States, primarily in what is now Washington, Oregon, and Idaho. The name Nez Perce was coined during the Lewis and Clark Expedition to mean "those with pierced noses."

These Native Americans did not, in fact, engage in this practice, although ceremonial piercing was practiced by another, more southerly, tribe. The real tribal name is Nee-Me-Poo but the term Nez Perce has stuck, to this day. During the hunting season, the Native Americans traveled over the Rockies eastward into the Great Plains. In the Pacific Northwest, the bighorn sheep provided most of life's necessities, meat for food, hide for clothing and horn for utensils such as spoons and knives, as well as for bows.

Captain James Cook came this way in 1778 looking for the Northwest Passage, and then Captain George Vancouver, who had sailed with Cook, returned to explore further, only to learn that there was no Northwest Passage after all, but a very large continent that blocked the route. His voyages coincided with Spain's determination to reassert claims to the land north of Spanish California.

Captain Vancouver is now remembered by three locations bearing his name – Vancouver, British Columbia, Vancouver Island, BC, and the lesser-known, Vancouver, Washington across the Columbia from Portland, Oregon.

The Captain unfortunately missed the mouth of the Columbia River, thinking that the mud and debris he saw there was of no importance. In 1792, Captain Robert Gray, an American engaged in trade, found the mouth of the Columbia, and named it after his ship. Vancouver, having met Gray and heard of the discovery, sent Lt Boughton to investigate. He sailed into the mouth just south of Cape Disappointment, where he transferred to a small boat to continue inland for 100 miles (160 km) to the barrier of the Columbia Gorge rapids. He claimed the river and the coast for King George III of England and this claim would be a bone of contention for the next several decades.

The fur trade

In the wake of a message from Thomas Jefferson to Congress in 1803, just after the Louisiana Purchase, a US government appropriation funded an expedition that would establish relations with the Native Americans, foster trade, and explore and document new territories that extended to the Pacific Ocean. After the Lewis and Clark Expedition in 1803–6 more fur trappers, traders, settlers, and missionaries arrived. Many made a good living from trapping and trading. One entrepreneur was John Jacob Astor, a German immigrant who had arrived in New York in 1774. In 1810 he established the Pacific Fur Company, a small business that grew into one of the most profitable ventures in early American history.

The trade in sea otter and beaver furs reached its height between 1787 and 1812, with constant friction between the British and Americans. Most European traders came by sea via the tip of South America and the Pacific coast. The items they used for trading included tools, weapons, cloth, buttons, mirrors, combs, and liquor. Initially, the fur traders and the Native American tribes traded together without conflict, but this was not to last.

Devastation of tribal lands

The tribal lands once extended over 17 million acres (7 million hectares), but European and American penetration soon began to unbalance, then devastate, the Native Americans' way of life. The first tensions arose with the coming of the fur trappers in the late 18th century, and were exacerbated by the influx of settlers in the first half of the 19th century. When the United States government stepped in to control the unrest, wholesale land confiscation became codified in a series of so-called treaties. The Union army made sure that the new order was enforced, and the Nez Perce's tribal lands

The treaty generated a huge influx of settlers along the Oregon Trail, which stretched northwest through what would become eastern Oregon then followed the Columbia River from Fort Walla Walla in eastern Washington to Fort William, the site of present-day Portland.

Settlers came in increasing numbers in the years after the treaty, then by the thousands, until Oregon gained statehood, as the 33rd state, in 1859. Most settled in the Willamette Valley, south of Portland, the center of population today. Washington, once part of Oregon, was organized as a separate territory in 1853 but did not become the 42nd state until 1889.

rapidly diminished to the miniscule 138,000 acres (56,000 hectares) they occupy today.

War, treaty, and statehood

During the 19th century, the British and Americans continued to fight over rights to the land, especially during the War of 1812, and it was not until 1846, with the signing of the Oregon Treaty, that the British gave up claims to the lands south of the 49th parallel – today the western border between the USA and Canada.

LEFT: Lewis and Clark opened up new territory in North America.
ABOVE: welcome to the Cascades of the Columbia.

Preserving the culture

Cruise boats visit reservation land in eastern Washington, and in a few short hours, passengers are exposed to some Native American culture and customs, and learn how tribe members cope today in partial isolation, and in the wider world. In the meantime, the older Nez Perce people attempt to keep their traditions alive – costumes, dances, crafts, language, and storytelling – in their cultural centers and schools, although many younger people are attracted to a more Americanized way of life.

The more recent history of the Columbia and Snake rivers is covered in the subsequent chapter *(see pages 291–300).* ❑

COLUMBIA AND SNAKE RIVER PORTS

Maps:
Area 294
City 292

Starting with the graceful architecture of Portland and ending in Hell's Canyon, a cruise on the Columbia and Snake rivers can offer history, adventure, and stunning landscapes

Most Columbia and Snake river cruises cover the entire navigable portion of the rivers between Astoria, Oregon, at the mouth of the Columbia just inland from the Pacific, and Lewiston, a deepwater port 465 miles (750 km) upstream in the state of Idaho. Jet-boat excursions continue for another 25 miles (40 km) up the Snake, and deep into Hells Canyon.

Portland is the embarkation city for all Columbia-Snake cruises; some trips head immediately upriver and others first sail overnight to Astoria. To appreciate the full impact of the rapidly changing landscape during the week a cruise usually lasts, this chapter will cover the landings and sightseeing destinations en route, beginning at the mouth of the Columbia, after the section on Portland.

Arriving in Portland, Oregon

Portland ❶, with a population of just over half a million, provides one of the most welcoming arrivals of any city in North America. The airport is connected directly to the downtown area by Metropolitan Area Express (MAX), the light-rail system. Fares are reasonable and a day pass is available.

Portland Union Station Ⓐ (1889), at the north end of downtown adjacent to the Willamette River, represents Victorian railroad architecture at its very best. Trains arrive from Chicago in the east, California stations in the south, and Seattle and Vancouver to the north, at a handsome, brick and stone structure topped by a clock tower. The marble interior, coffered ceiling, and slowly-turning ceiling fans lend a tropical atmosphere, yet Portland is nowhere near the equator. The station's forecourt is landscaped with roses and shrubbery, and its graceful, curved facade has an overhanging roof, old-fashioned awnings, and an iron canopy. If only all arrivals were so stylish.

The city has kept its human scale better than most. It has maintained a vibrant downtown and much of its traditional architecture, and prevented major expressways from slicing through its heart. Known as the City of Roses, Portland has 250 parks, gardens, and greenways. Since 1907 it has celebrated the annual **Portland Rose Festival** in a big way for several weeks in June, with an extravagant floral parade, music, car and boat races, and naval ship visits.

Seeing the sights

The city's core is **Pioneer Courthouse Square Ⓑ**, anchored by Nordstrom's department store, and the center has a prosperous feel. MAX, the streetcar line, offers a free-ride area downtown and passes through

LEFT: Multnomah Falls, Columbia River Gorge.
BELOW: cherry blossom in Portland.

TIP

For full details of **opening hours** and contact information for the sites and museums mentioned in this chapter, see Travel Tips page 346.

the square on two sides, SW Morrison and SW Yamhill streets. Edging on the north side of the square, the **Glazed Terra-Cotta Historic District ⊙** is a cluster of commercial buildings constructed between 1890 and 1910. Terracotta was once widely used as it was an economical material easily crafted into decorative shapes. To the east, the six-block-square **Yamhill National Historic District ⊙** is a handsome repository of 19th-century cast-iron architecture, a structural facade design that permitted large, open, interior spaces. The neighborhood fronts onto **Waterfront Park** fringing the Willamette River, and a 3-mile (5-km) path makes an interesting loop on both sides, connected by two bridge crossings.

On Saturday and Sunday, the so-called **Saturday Market**, is a huge draw for its open-air handicraft, clothing, and jewelry stands. Its location draws you to the **Skidmore District ⊙** or Old Town, where Portland first developed. Once more like a skid row, the vastly improved 20-block-square area includes **Chinatown District**, the **Japanese-American Historical Plaza**, and the **Oregon Maritime Center and Museum ⊙** (open Fri–Sun), although the

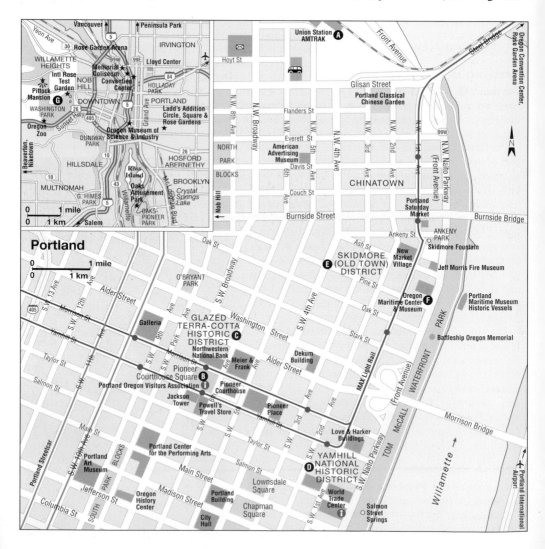

museum's collection, featuring models of ships that plied the rivers and photographs of Portland's substantial shipbuilding and repair docks, recently moved out of its building and into the sternwheel tugboat *Portland* docked across the street. Built in 1947, the steam-powered vessel is the last of its type in the United States to remain operational.

The port of Portland stretches for many miles along the Columbia and Willamette rivers and includes container berths, oil terminals, and piers handling lumber and imported autos. High up to the west of downtown, **Washington Park**'s ⑥ terraced gardens display 400 varieties of roses, at their blooming peak during June and July and again in September and October. On a clear day, the site offers views across the downtown skyline to Mount Hood, 50 miles (80 km) away. The park's Japanese Gardens has a ceremonial teahouse, oriental pavilion, and sand-and-stone garden. **Oregon Zoo** (open daily), established in 1887, houses African animals and reptiles – elephants, hippos, rhinos, zebras, and pythons. At the penguin enclosure during feeding time, visitors view the action from an underwater chamber. The foot-weary can board a narrow-gauge train that links all the park sights via a 4-mile (6-km) loop.

Leaving Portland

On leaving Portland in the evening, week-long cruises usually begin by following the Willamette River through the heart of the city, past the glowing skyline, under the bridges, and as far as the Willamette Falls at Oregon City before heading into the Columbia for the overnight sail to the Pacific Ocean.

At dawn, the boat will be in a completely different world, where the widening Columbia meets the Pacific Ocean at the Columbia River Bar. Hundreds of

Map on page 292

There are daily tours of the submarine USS Blueback, *at the Oregon Museum of Science and Industry, 1945 SE Water Avenue, Portland. Tel: 503-797 4000 for more information.*

BELOW: USS *Blueback* at the Oregon Museum of Science and Industry.

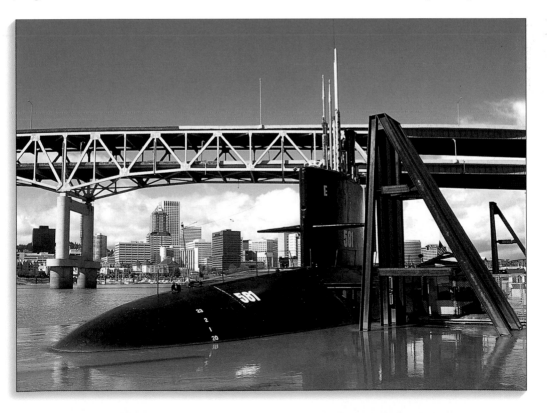

ships have come to grief here, where powerful river currents collide with ocean breakers at a shallow sandbar. When the weather closed in, many early explorers passing this way missed the existence of a river altogether *(see page 288)*, and it was not until the very end of the 18th century that the Columbia was found and named. After that, developments happened very quickly.

On display at the Columbia River Maritime Museum, Astoria.

Astoria, Oregon

First established as a fort, serving both British and American interests, it was the fur trade, in sea otter and then beaver pelts, in the period 1787–1812, that created the permanent settlement of **Astoria ❷**. Founded in 1811, it was named for John Jacob Astor, who financed the original fur-trading colony. The lumber industry followed later in the century and made the town a rich center for shipping and trade.

Cruise boats tie up at a pier that houses the **Columbia River Maritime Museum** (open daily), part of the pier complex. It covers the history of Columbia River trade, with model ships and photos, and presents a chart documenting the location of the myriad shipwrecks littering the coast. A dramatic film shows the grounding of the Japanese tanker *New Clarissa* in February 1999, the attempts to pull her off-shore, and the fire set to burn the cargo of heavy tar bunker oil before it could contaminate the marine and bird life and the beaches.

Astoria's commercial center has seen much better days, but just a few blocks inland, 71 buildings, mostly residential, are listed on the National Register. One mansion, **Flavel House** (open daily), is well worth visiting. Built in 1884 by Captain George Flavel, a Columbia Bar pilot who also owned successful businesses, the grand, Queen Anne-style house continued to be occupied after his death, well into the 20th century, by two unmarried daughters. The fourth-level cupola was designed for viewing the river, much like the widows' walk atop Nantucket houses, so the daughters could watch for their father's return. Inside, the paneling and door frames are of beautiful Douglas fir, and the furnishings, while of the period, are not the original ones that were in the house. The entry fee to Flavel House also gives access to the **Heritage Museum** (open Wed–Sat), outlining the history of Astoria with maps, photographs, and furnishings in a sort of grandma's attic display.

It's a 20-minute walk up Coxcomb Hill to **Astoria Column**, which dominates the landscape. Built in 1926, it has colorful murals surrounding the base, showing the city's settlement, and 164 spiral steps lead up to a wonderful view of the river meeting the Pacific breakers, and, like a layered Chinese painting, the folds of Cascade Range, woodland, and farms. Visitors are encouraged to buy a little balsawood model airplane and hurl it from the viewing platform.

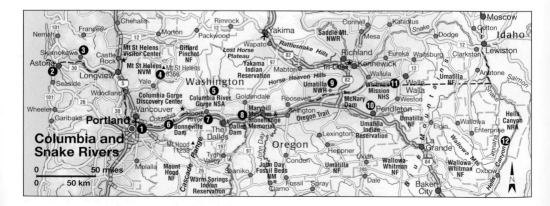

Map on page 294

The organized excursions head downriver to **Fort Clatsop** (open daily), a reconstructed stockade showing where Lewis and Clark spent four wet winter months in 1805–6 that was rebuilt according to William Clark's detailed journals. Costumed park rangers demonstrate how to make fire with flint and steel, and relate tales of how miserable the men were, especially as their clothes never completely dried out. If the day is damp, you are likely to get the picture, but if it's hot, it is much harder to imagine their misery in so beautiful a setting.

On the coast, the seaside resort of **Cannon Beach** is a big draw for its wooden, weathered-cedar shopping district with craft-type boutiques. The place gets packed in the summer and is best enjoyed off-season. The principal geographic feature is **Haystack Rock**, a 235-ft (72-meter) monolith. The base is accessible during low tide, but it is unwise to climb it, because high tides will prevent you returning to shore for hours.

Climbing the Columbia River

Leaving Astoria, the boat begins climbing the Columbia via eight locks to inland Idaho, providing a wonderfully varied passage. When the Columbia begins to narrow, you may stop at **Skamokawa** ❸, one of the few remaining, intact fishing villages on the river. The site of a Native American encampment for 2,000 years, it became a trading post in 1844 and a settlement 20 years later. The main occupations then were commercial salmon fishing and logging, which peaked from 1890 to 1910. **Redmen Hall**, built as a school in 1894, looms large over a cluster of wooden houses facing the river. The imposing wooden building houses a photographic collection showing the area's activities between 1850 and 1930, and a climb up to its bell tower provides a great view of the river. The town – now a National Historic District – remained isolated until the north shore road arrived in the 1920s, and it still maintains a certain sense of solitude.

Longview, Washington, a lumber port, is used as a landing to transfer passengers by bus inland and up to **Mount St Helens** ❹. In a matter of minutes, on May 18, 1980, a volcanic eruption reduced the mountain's height by about 1,000 ft (300 meters) – from the state's fifth-highest peak to its 24th. Following an interpretive center film showing the explosion, the drive uphill winds through increasingly scarred hillsides covered in lava, ash, and mud and 150 sq miles (390 sq km) of forest destroyed in six minutes. A higher elevation interpretive center overlooks the cloud- enshrouded mountain top and enables you to peer into the deep wasteland of a valley. The waters of Spirit Lake down below rose in a huge wave created by rockslide debris, and stripped trees as far as 850 ft (260 meters) up the slopes.

Next comes the passage through the dramatic **Columbia Gorge** ❺, leaving the tidal river behind. The flanking slopes are steep, the current fast, and the winds strong as they funnel through the narrow cleavage in the north–south Cascade Range. To feel, hear, and see the full effect, be sure to stand on the forward deck. About a dozen waterfalls cluster along this stretch; **Multnomah Falls** is the highest. Narrow and delicate, it is better appreciated close up – or even

BELOW: kite sailing, Hood River.

The Spirit of '98
sails through the
Bonneville Lock.

BELOW:
the *Spirit of '98* on
the Columbia River.

from underneath it. If time permits, climb a short way through the thick woods to the next level to experience the majesty of the forest. Another natural wonder looming over the river is Beacon Rock, the world's second largest stone monolith after Gibraltar.

Bonneville Dam and Columbia Gorge

Bonneville Dam ❻ signaled the first major WPA undertaking by the US Army Corps of Engineers to create a safe passage through the Cascade Rapids for diesel oil shipments upriver, and grain and timber downriver. (The WPA was the Works Progress Administration, begun in 1935 by President Franklin Delano Roosevelt, to alleviate poverty during the Depression.) The dam created Lake Bonneville, and its hydroelectric plants generated power sufficient to light 40,000 homes. The boat enters the lock chamber and ties up to floating bollards for the 60-ft (18-meter) rise. The Visitors' Center, just steps from where the boat docks, screens a slide film showing the dam under construction and the mesh protectors being installed to keep fish from being sucked into the turbines.

The visit includes the powerhouse and the fish ladders, created to allow salmon to swim from the Pacific to the spawning waters upriver. A visit to the counting room may reveal fish, including coho, sockeye, Chinook, steelhead or rainbow trout, shad, and eels, swimming by the window. During the migrating season, there will be someone on hand making the tallies and recording them on a public counter. The numbers of fish peaked at between 10 and 16 million salmon but then fell to about 2 million in 1989. With the numbers declining, the Army Corps established fish hatcheries for fingerling salmon, rainbow trout, and sturgeon, and the goal is to attain 5 million.

Map
on page
294

The Columbia Gorge Discovery Center (open daily) covers the area's history and geology in a film that reveals how the Columbia Gorge was formed by violent volcanic upheavals and raging floods. Another film shows the building of the Columbia River Scenic Highway that leads to Multnomah Falls. The displays include a working model of a stationary steam engine, steamboat models, black-and-white photos showing industries along the river, people at work on boats, log jams, and Native Americans fishing, An exhibit on the Lewis and Clark Expedition illustrates how Lewis divided his equipment needs into seven distinct categories: arms and accoutrements, camp equipment and provisions, clothing, medicines, mathematical instruments, transportation, and gifts, the latter to be brought to meetings with the Native Americans for procurement of guides, food, and horses.

Hood River ❼, Oregon, benefited from the lake that the Bonneville Dam created. Windsurfing was invented here in the 1930s, by attaching a sail to a surfboard and using the strong easterly winds that funnel through Columbia Gorge. The sport is now a major tourist activity.

Some boat operators use the **Mount Hood Railroad**, built in 1906–10 to carry lumber and apples and pears. Today, freight handling is a thing of the past, and the line runs as an excursion service. Its famous switchbacks, where a train uses a Z-track configuration, moving ahead on the lowest track then backing up to the next level, then moving ahead again, are the only ones west of the Mississippi.

On the slopes of Mount Hood, at the 6,000-ft (1,830-meter) level, stands Timberline Lodge, a timber and stone WPA hotel project, built in 1932. The construction was notable for its use of a lot of recycled materials for the carved

BELOW: fishing at Bonneville Dam.

woodwork, iron railings, and irons in the huge stone fireplaces. There's a view north to Mount Adams, part of a line of volcano-formed mountains that include Mount St Helens and Mount Rainier.

At the **Dalles Lock and Dam**, an excursion crosses the river to **Maryhill Museum and Stonehenge Memorial** ❽ (open summer, daily), in Washington. A Midwesterner named Sam Hill, son-in-law of James J. Hill of the Great Northern Railroad, also made money in railroads and came west to live. He first established the Washington State Good Roads Association in 1901 to improve automobile travel. This led ultimately to the creation of the Pacific Coast Highway, US 101 in Washington, Oregon, and northern California, and State 1 south from there, and also to scenic local roads in Washington.

In 1907, Sam Hill bought land on a site overlooking the Columbia River and began building a mansion for his wife, Mary, but she died suddenly and the place was never occupied. Instead, he created the **Museum of Art and Artifacts** here, and had Queen Marie of Romania dedicate the museum in 1926, before anything was installed. She agreed to do so because of the financial help Hill had offered Romania after World War I. After Hill died, the Spreckels, a wealthy San Francisco sugar-cane family who had built the Palace of the Legion of Honor, took on the museum as their project and it finally opened in 1940.

The building houses Queen Marie's royal regalia, including her coronation gown, crown, silverware, gilt furniture, and rock crystal and gold jewelry. There's also memorabilia, Russian Orthodox icons, including many with elaborate metal and enamel insets with semi-precious stones, Rodin sculptures, a collection of 250 chess sets, fashion costumes in miniature on stage sets, and Native American costumes, baskets, and weapons. Nearby stands a folly called Stonehenge, a copy of the real thing in Wiltshire, England that Hill, a Quaker, built as a peace memorial to those who served in World War I.

BELOW: bighorn sheep graze on the bank of the Snake River.

Upriver landscapes

During the continuing passage upriver, the landscape begins to change markedly from the lush vegetation and well-watered forests to which you will have become accustomed, to drier, semi-arid land, some of which is ideal for growing grapes. Washington is the largest US producer of wines after California, thanks to the warm, sunny days and cool nights, the right soil, and dry conditions where the moisture can be controlled during the crucial growing season. Cruise passengers usually visit one of the wineries on an organized excursion.

Just short of the McNary Lock and Dam, the **Umatilla National Wildlife Refuge** ❾, straddling both sides of the river, covers 29,370 acres (11,890 hectares) of marshes, sloughs, open water, cropland, and sage-brush uplands, which form a superb habitat and nesting area for white pelicans, great blue herons, red-tail and marsh hawk, green-winged terns, bald eagles, long-billed curlews, Canada Geese, mallards, and pintails. Mammals include the elusive coyote and the more often seen mule deer feeding by the water which in turn is home to walleye, steelhead, salmon, sturgeon, crappie, and bass.

Map on page 294

Pendleton, Oregon

The town of **Pendleton ❿** is usually a scheduled stop on riverboat tours, in particular the **Pendleton Roundup Grounds**. The main events are in mid-September, but, depending on when you visit, you may see authentic Native American war dances, bareback riding, bucking broncos, calf roping, or steer wrestling.

In town, **Underground Pendleton** is a tour that shows how Chinese laborers were reduced to living in a warren of rooms and passages under the streets and not permitted out after dark. The tour visits rooms where they slept, gambled, and smoked opium. Back on the street, you can visit the former hotel for "working girls", a bordello that is now a Victorian-style bed-and-breakfast renamed the W.G. Hotel. Pendleton may be best known for its **woolen mills**, established in 1895 to make blankets and robes for Native Americans. Later, the mills, using wool from the local sheep ranches, started weaving men's utility shirts, then in 1924 branched out with virgin wool shirts, and in 1949 started making clothes for women. A factory tour ends in the Pendleton stores.

The **Tamastslikt Cultural Institute** (open daily) presents a variety of Native American traditions. You may see dancing to drums and hear storytelling that explains life before the Europeans arrived, the initial peaceful trading period, and ultimate defeat and banishment. Exhibits include horse regalia, war bonnets, bows, and saddle making. Activities can be touristy, but the storytelling is powerful.

Shortly after boats leave the Columbia for the Snake, a landing at Ice Harbor and Dam gives access to the **Whitman Mission ⓫** (open daily) in southeast Washington. In 1836, a small group of Presbyterian missionaries accompanied a fur-trappers' caravan into what was then known as Oregon Territory. Marcus and Narcissa Whitman and Eliza Spaulding were among them, the two women

BELOW: the *Spirit of Columbia* on the Snake River.

Map on page 294

The region's rivers have some of the best fishing.

BELOW: windsurfing in the Columbia River Gorge.
RIGHT: Bonneville Lock and Dam.

being the first white females to travel across the continent. The mission they established near present-day Walla Walla became an important stop on the newly established Oregon Trail, but tensions arose because of cultural differences between the local Cayuse people and the missionaries, and increasingly so with the subsequent white immigrants. In 1847 a measles outbreak killed half the Cayuse; blaming the Whitmans, the survivors massacred them and 11 others, and some 60 people were taken hostage. Eventually, five Cayuse were tried and hung, and many fled east into the isolated Blue Mountains of southeast Washington. The response of Congress was to establish Oregon as a US territory. Many of the frightened settlers remained, but the Oregon Trail was moved further south. The Whitman Mission site tells the story thoughtfully in its interpretive center, where there is a collection of farm buildings and the grave site where burials were recorded, including those of the Whitmans.

Nearby, **Fort Walla Walla** (open summer, daily) exhibits a collection of carefully restored and recreated buildings that include a schoolhouse, doctor's office, train station, and one- and two-story houses arranged in a closed compound. Other buildings house farm equipment and a fire engine that was drawn by a team of 33 mules. During a visit, you may find a retired local doctor dressed up as a 19th-century rural physician, describing what life was like in those days.

The journey up the **Snake River** now begins. The river banks are made of layers of basaltic lava formed by magma issuing from fissures between 10 and 17 million years ago. After taking decades to cool, the distinct layers became the multitoned buttes and mesas between which the boat now travels. One particularly beautiful section lies at the mouth of the Palouse River, and some operators sail a short way up the navigable portion for a stop, allowing passengers to go kayaking or climb the buttes while the crew prepares a riverside barbecue.

The Snake has four locks and dams to control the river en route to Lewiston, Idaho, and Clarkston, Washington, the twin towns located on opposite banks that were named to honor Lewis and Clark, who camped here at the confluence of the Snake and Clearwater rivers. A jet-boat ride into **Hells Canyon** ⑫, Idaho, in the designated Hells Canyon National Recreation Area, is an all-day excursion. The river starts out sluggishly, then becomes extremely fast-flowing. Paddle steamers used cables to get up the river, and today whitewater rafting is a big draw.

Jet-boat passengers are likely to see bighorn sheep on rocky ledges, deer down by the water, and eagles and osprey, but the river otters and black bear are more elusive. The boats will nose up to Nez Perce petroglyphs inscribed on the flat rock surfaces. Lots of fishermen in small boats are likely to be around, angling after small-mouth bass, rainbow trout, and steelhead. If a white sturgeon, North America's largest freshwater fish, is caught, it must be released.

Most trips go up about 25 miles (40 km) and turn at, or just above the junction with Salmon River. Continue on ahead and you would eventually reach Yellowstone National Park, the river's source, but you would need to transfer to a sturdy canoe and use considerable muscle power. ❑

SAILING THE GREAT LAKES

Map on page 304

Rugged wilderness, romantic old towns, birdlife, and breweries are among Great Lakes highlights – and the small, comfortable boats that cruise the waters are a pleasure in themselves

The wild beauty of the Great Lakes was created when the glaciers melted, some 10,000 years ago. Lakes Superior, Michigan, Huron, Erie, and Ontario and their connecting channels form the largest fresh surface-water system on earth. Visible from space, the familiar shapes and locations of the Lakes cover more than 94,000 sq miles (244,000 sq km) and hold an estimated 6 quadrillion US gallons (23 quadrillion liters) of water, about one-fifth of the entire world's freshwater supply and nine-tenths of the water supply of the United States of America.

The channels that connect the Great Lakes offer rugged wilderness shorelines and are a highlight of any cruise in this region. The popular route through the 35-mile (56-km) Niagara River links lakes Erie and Ontario, and is the source of the cascading water flowing over Niagara Falls; the Welland Canal provides a detour around the falls and also links the two lakes. From Lake Ontario access to the Atlantic Ocean through the St Lawrence River, about 1,000 miles (1,600 km) away, is a popular cruise route in itself. Access from Lake Superior to Lake Huron is via St Mary's River, a 60-mile (96 km) waterway where rapids are a factor to be reckoned with. The Soo Locks bypass the rough waters, providing safe passage for ships. The St Clair and Detroit rivers, a trek of almost 90 miles (145 km), connect Lake Huron and Lake Erie.

The Great Lakes is not a year-round cruise region due to the icy-cold winters. Cruises operate from May through mid-October, with the highlight being the fall foliage cruises and the warmer summer adventures. Forget gambling and the Vegas-style acts offered on most big boats – all passenger cruise vessels in the region are forbidden to offer gambling on board. Entertainment on the Great Lakes ships is far more subdued; passengers mostly dine early, then listen to a lecture about the next port, or a regional band performing in the lounge.

Ships that cruise the lakes

Sailing on the Great Lakes is all done on small ships, because locks and canals do not have the capacity to cope with large ones. Small vessels can also cruise close to shore to give passengers views of wildlife and nature. A handful of cruise vessels, including sleek mega-yachts, stop at a variety of Great Lakes ports of call in Canada and the United States. Among the most popular ships to sail the Great Lakes region is the Bahamian-flagged *Orion*. This is the newest ship in the area, a very upscale vessel that carries 106 passengers and sails between Montréal and Milwaukee. While its technical features enable it to explore some of the world's most remote regions, it

LEFT: sailboats on the lake.
BELOW: a Montréal smile.

For full details of **opening hours** and contact information for the sites and museums mentioned in this chapter, see Travel Tips page 347.

is *Orion*'s accommodations that set it apart, as guests are all housed in large staterooms and suites. The vessel is also wheelchair accessible. All staterooms and suites are exterior ones and feature a sitting area or living room, direct Internet access, a mini-refrigerator, a private bathroom with marble fitments, ample closet space, and large windows affording excellent views of the passing scenery and ports of call.

The US-flagged *Nantucket Clipper*, with its all-American crew, is an extremely popular and less expensive alternative. The ship sails along the St Lawrence River and Seaway into the Great Lakes from late June through September, on various itineraries. Accommodations are snug, but the spacious observation lounge serves as the main meeting place for informal briefings and social gatherings. The window-lined dining room accommodates all guests in one leisurely open seating plan. Healthy, regionally-influenced American-style food is served, with every dish individually prepared to order. Outside, you'll find ample deck space and a promenade for viewing the passing scenery. Onboard naturalists and historians will explain and recap each day's events in informal talk on topics ranging from the natural northern wilderness to the role the lakes have played in fur trading.

Le Levant, a French-flagged mega-yacht, staffed by a 50-strong French crew, is another alternative. It is built for adventure travel while providing comfort and elegance. It accommodates 90 guests in 45 spacious, outside staterooms, each fitted out with inlaid wood and a color TV/VCR, a refrigerator, generous storage space, and a large picture window for views of the surroundings. Public areas include the Grand Salon where lectures are held, a verandah restaurant for breakfast and lunch with both indoor and outdoor seating, a dining room, a

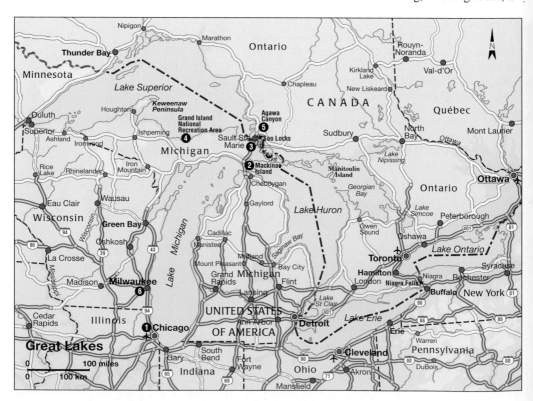

wood-paneled library filled with a selection of books on *Le Levant*'s destinations, a gymnasium, a boutique, a beauty salon, and an outdoor pool and bar.

Cruise passengers can begin their journey through the Great Lakes in Chicago, Port Huron, Michigan, or Windsor, Ontario, just across the bridge from Detroit, but the most popular itinerary sails from Toronto to Chicago and cruises through all five of the Great Lakes. Ships make port calls in the major cities as well as small towns and regions with interesting history and scenery. **Chicago ❶** is definitely worth some attention if you have the time to spare, or plan to extend your trip. From the Chicago Water Tower and Pumping Station to Sears Tower, the tallest building in America, the city's skyline was built to impress.

Mackinac, Michigan

Some 390 miles (628 km) from Chicago, **Mackinac Island ❷** (pronounced Mackinaw) is the most popular port in the region. Here, bicycles and horse-drawn carriages are the only modes of transportation. Except for the tourists, the town looks much as it did in 1875, when Congress designated 80 percent of the island a national park, and the buildings have all the elegance and charm of the Victorian era. On the island, the highlight is a visit to the exclusive Grand Hotel. Many cruise lines arrange either afternoon teas with a lecture and stroll along the 660-ft (200-meter) porch, the world's longest, or a luncheon package. Don't miss a taste of a Grand Pecan Ball, the hotel's most popular dessert. If you visit the hotel on your own there is a $10 per person entrance fee, but it's worth it for a peek at this exclusive hotel.

Mackinac has been a popular summer resort since the 1870s and was the setting for the 1949 movie *This Time for Keeps*, with Esther Williams and Jimmy

Map on page 304

There is much to see and do in Chicago: the architecture is stunning and there is a great lakeshore, with beaches, parks and some of America's finest cultural institutions. Visitors can get around easily by a light railway known as the El, for "elevated".

BELOW: a ship passing through Chicago.

Map on page 304

Durante, and 30 years later *Somewhere in Time*, starring Christopher Reeve, Jane Seymour, and Christopher Plummer, about a man who time-traveled back to the early 1900s, was filmed here. Anyone interested in history will enjoy a visit to Fort Mackinac, while romantics can stroll the grounds of the hotel or take a horse-drawn carriage tour around the island.

Sault Sainte Marie ❸ and **Soo Locks** make a popular trip from Michigan's Upper Pennisula port, and include a visit to the Upper and Lower Taquamenon Falls – the upper one the second largest east of the Mississippi River, and both of them are an amazing sight. You can explore the ancient paintings and rock formations on Lake Superior's cliffs, and at Whitefish Point visit the fascinating **Great Lakes Shipwreck Museum** (open May–Oct, daily), which tell the story of sailors and ships who braved the waters of Lake Superior. Here, too, is the oldest active lighthouse on Lake Superior, with guided tours of the lightkeeper's quarters. At the nearby **Whitefish Point Bird Observatory** (visitor center closed Wed and Nov–Mar) you can see falcons, hawks, and migrating owls in spring, as well as a host of waterfowl.

The **Hiawatha National Forest** covers 1,375 sq miles (3,560 sq km), spread over four distinctly different Great Lakes islands. The largest and most visited of these is the **Grand Island National Recreation Area ❹**, where you can bike and hike or rent a sea kayak and take to the water. Here, too, you can see the shores of "Gitchee Gummee," made famous in Longfellow's *Song of Hiawatha*, published in 1855.

Just over the International Bridge to Canada, passengers can take a train ride into the Laurentian wilderness area and to **Agawa Canyon ❺** where pristine lakes, granite mounds, and – at the right time of year – incredible fall colors greet you at every turn of the tracks. For those who may have missed not being able to gamble while onboard, there are several Vegas-style casinos in the region. You could spend a whole day on the waterfront at Bay Mills Casino about 20 miles (32 km) outside town. Right at the head of Lake Superior lie the twin ports of Duluth and Superior. Once the gateways for immigrant people, they now handle the produce of the farming heartland of America.

Milwaukee breweries

Milwaukee ❻ is positioned in the center of the Midwest, in the southeast corner of Wisconsin, on Lake Michigan's western shore. Covering nearly 96 sq miles (248 sq km), this is a city with lots to see and do. The brewing industry was established here in the mid-19th century, and Milwaukee was known for a long time as the beer capital of the world. The industry still flourishes, and brewery tours, usually organized by the ship, are popular. You can visit the master brewer, the Miller Brewing Company, and enjoy sampling the product, or take a trip to Milwaukee's original microbrewery, Sprechers, where European-style beers (lagers) and gourmet sodas are on hand. A local favorite is Lakefront Brewery, a producer of award-winning beers. For a glimpse of the city's beer-related history, visit the Frederick Pabst Mansion – home of the 19th-century founder of Pabst Brewery. ❑

BELOW: a picnic by Lake Michigan. **RIGHT:** the ferris wheel and the carousel at Navy Pier, Chicago.

THE ST LAWRENCE SEAWAY

Constructing the St Lawrence Seaway was no easy matter, but cruise passengers today are beneficiaries of this engineering feat

The mighty St Lawrence is a chain of lakes and rivers that has served, over the centuries, as a waterway for Canadian fur traders, North American explorers, cargo freighters, and luxury riverboats and their passengers. This deep waterway, consisting of lakes, rivers, and locks, extends from the

Atlantic Ocean to the western slopes of Lake Superior, straddles two countries – Canada and the US – and ultimately extends 2,340 miles (3,766 km) from the Atlantic to the head of the Great Lakes. Officially, however, the seaway portion of the St Lawrence only applies to the section that runs from Montréal to Lake Ontario.

The French move in

French explorer Jacques Cartier was the first European to discover the St Lawrence. In 1534 he sailed into the Gulf of St Lawrence and claimed the Québec region for France. He was the first to enter Pillage Bay, on the river's north shore, and christened it St Laurens after the treasurer of the Christian church, who had died a martyr at the hands of the Romans in AD258.

The St Lawrence cruising season runs from May to late September or early October. The Seaway handles some 4,000 commercial ships annually and is considered a mechanical and technological marvel. The waters rise from 22 ft (7 meters) above sea level in Montréal to 246 ft (75 meters) at Kingston, on Lake Ontario. Cultivating the St Lawrence as a navigable body of water was a huge project that was first attempted in stages. Dollier de Casson, superior of Montréal's Sulpician Seminary, was the first to try, in 1680. He began building a 5-ft (2-meter) deep canal, to help ships bypass the Lachine Rapids between Montréal and Lake St Louis. The project wasn't completed until 1824. During the 19th century, improvements included the Lachine Canal, linking Montréal with Lake St Louis, and the Welland Canal in Ontario's Niagara region. Other canals were created at Cornwall and Beauharnois.

The first step to a modern seaway

In 1895, the importance of this waterway was acknowledged by the formation of the joint United States and Canadian Deep Waterways Commission. The commission made little progress, though improvements continued. The completion of the fourth Welland Canal in 1932 meant that eight locks could raise ships some 326 ft (100 meters), representing the first step in creating a modern seaway.

But by 1949, increasing public interest as well as trade pressures led Canada and the US to develop another joint commission. This time, it was effective. The resulting St Lawrence Seaway Authority Act and the International Rapids Power Development Act (1951), permitted Canadians to begin navigation work on their side of the river – from Montréal to Lake Ontario and in the Welland Canal. The US began work on the Wiley-Dondero Canal, which would ultimately re-route ships around the International Rapids.

Even more progress was made in 1954 when Canada's St Lawrence Seaway Authority was established. It allowed developers to acquire land, and construct, operate, and maintain a deep-draft waterway between Montréal and Lake Erie, and to build bridges that spanned the US and Canada. At the same time, the US passed the Wiley-Dondero Act (or Seaway Act) creating the US Saint Lawrence Seaway Development Corporation. The agreement between the two countries involved the construction of the seaway. The cost of the project was estimated at $470.3 million (Canada paid $336.5 million), and work began.

Unpopular changes

Key projects included digging new channels and dredging existing ones. Wholly separate, however, was the need to acquire 100 sq miles (260 sq km) of land in order to create new waterways. This project meant relocating entire communities, expropriating land, and moving homes, schools, churches, and stores. It was a controversial approach, particularly for generations of families who were forced to move to new villages, such as Ontario's Long Sault, Ingleside, and Iroquois.

The modern day St Lawrence Seaway was completed in 1959 when the icebreaker *D'Iberville* began the first through-transit. The seaway was officially opened by Queen Elizabeth and President Eisenhower on the Canadian side, and, the next day, by the queen and Vice-President Richard M. Nixon on the US side.

The pleasures of the seaway

One of the nicest aspects of a cruise along the St Lawrence is the scenery, in many places untouched by industry, with miles of forests and farms. Aside from the occasional (and generally massive) power plants, this is gentle, rolling, pastoral country. But it is the locks themselves that are the big attraction. As riverboats travel through the seaway between Montréal and Kingston, ships go through seven locks. On entering the lock's chamber, the vessel is safely moored by the linesman. Huge steel gates close and operators push valves that fill or empty the chamber (depending whether

---

PRECEDING PAGES: Québec City.
LEFT: the St Lawrence Seaway under construction.
RIGHT: Princess Margaret at the opening ceremony.

the ship is traveling east to west or vice-versa). Twenty million gallons (75.7 million liters) of water are required when a ship uses a lock.

Operators like St Lawrence Cruise Lines, whose *Canadian Empress* holds just 66 passengers, say that most of their passengers are primarily intrigued by the locks, but also interested in the villages and the bucolic landscapes that are an integral part of the river.

What you will see

A trip along the St Lawrence is a wonderful experience. Sightseeing highlights include the cosmopolitan city of **Montréal** – the world's

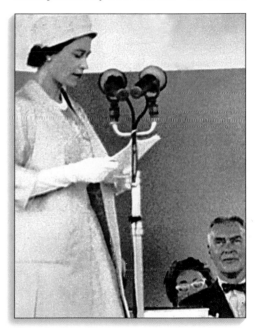

second-largest French-speaking city; and **Québec City**, North America's only walled city (although it's not technically part of the official seaway). Then there are smaller places, such as the **Fort Wellington** historic site at Prescott, Ontario; **Clayton**, New York, home of the **Antique Boat Museum**; and the gorgeous **Thousand Islands** area, where a castle and mansions occupy the lovely terrain.

Wildlife is abundant in and around the St Lawrence and the valley. Fish species include bass, trout, perch, and eels. The river attracts ducks, geese, loons, and gulls; and forests alongside grow spruce, birch, elm, hemlock, maple, and oak trees. ❑

ST LAWRENCE SEAWAY PORTS OF CALL

Maps:
Area 316
City 314

As well as enjoying the wonders of the seaway itself, you can visit North America's only walled town and sample the sophisticated pleasures of Montréal

St Lawrence River cruises follow a variety of itineraries. Most of them include visits to Montréal and Kingston. Québec City may be on the route, too; it lies on the St Lawrence River, although it is not technically part of the seaway. But anyone who is specifically interested in the engineering wonders of the St Lawrence Seaway System will find the choice limited to smaller ships. While major cruise lines such as Holland America Line and Princess Cruises regularly travel the St Lawrence River on "fall foliage" voyages, their itineraries begin in Montréal and end before they get to the seaway portion, because the ships are simply too long and too wide.

The Kingston-based St Lawrence Cruise Lines launched *Canadian Empress* in 1981 and from May to September runs six-night voyages that cruise between Québec City and Kingston. Other options for experiencing the Seaway include Clipper Cruise Lines, which offers itineraries that also call at Toronto, Buffalo (for Niagara Falls), Halifax in Nova Scotia, and Charlottetown, Prince Edward Island. Le Levant, another small-ship operator, offers some cursory stops along the St Lawrence Seaway, such as Montréal and the Thousand Islands.

LEFT: the Old City, Québec.
BELOW: Parc du Mont-Royal, Belvedere du Chalet in Montréal.

Québec City

The oldest city in Canada, **Québec City ❶** is the only walled city in North America, and has an interesting pedigree. Its strong French influence is due to its foundation, in the 17th century, as a base for France's colonial empire in North America. Along with its provincial counterpart, Montréal, it was part of New France for 150 years, until its ultimate conquest by the British during the Seven Years' War (1756–63).

When visitors dream of Québec City, they are most likely to imagine the romantic, historic, old town. This lies along the banks of the St Lawrence, and comprises two distinct sections. The Lower Town (Basse-Ville), adjacent to the port, has been totally restored, and is attractive, if over-gentrified. Its ancient buildings now house boutiques, museums, galleries, and sidewalk cafés. Highlights are the **Maison Chevalier**, which displays 18th-century decorative arts, silverware, and furniture, and is linked to the modern **Musée de la Civilisation** (closed Mon), which showcase life in old Québec, and history through the ages.

The Upper Town (Haute-Ville) is accessible from the Lower Town by a steep flight of steps (or, for those who don't like exercise, there's a funicular). Up here there are official buildings, like the **Hôtel de Ville** (City Hall), a wildly elaborate cathedral, the **Basilique Notre-Dame-de-Québec**, which dates from

Try to make time for lunch or a drink in Montréal's old town.

1647, and pleasant squares with plants and greenery. **Rue de Tresor** is a little alleyway chock-a-block with artists displaying etchings, watercolors, photographs, and oil paintings. **Rue St-Jean** is the heart of the old city's shopping district, and you'll also find cafés and cozy pubs. The **Musée du Fort** stages shows that replicate Québec's battles. **Château Frontenac**, a copper-roofed landmark that soars above the cruise ship pier from its lofty perch, is an historic hotel in the grand tradition and is well worth a look; there's a lovely bar with a fireplace and beautiful, panoramic views. The **Musée d'Art Inuit Brousseau** (closed Mon) offers an important collection of art created by the people whose ancestors occupied this land prior to colonization.

Montréal

Montréal ② is the world's second-largest French-speaking city, yet this metropolis of some 3.4 million people has at least 80 different ethnic groups. Communities include people of Italian, Jewish, Muslim, Greek, and Chinese heritage.

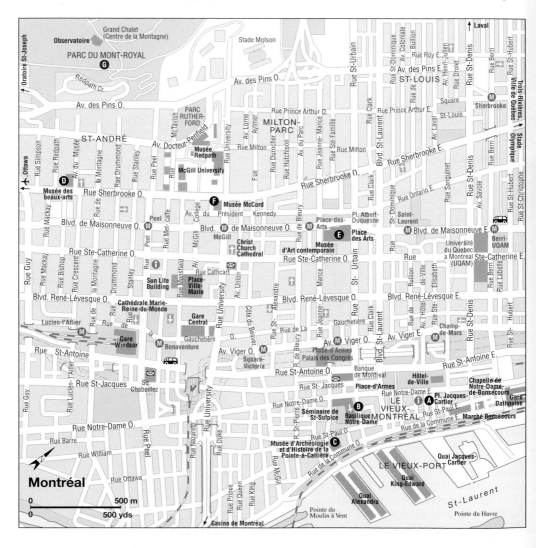

Montréal

The bustling riverfront of the St Laurent (Lawrence) and the imposing dome of Mont Royal, which at one time was an active volcano, contrast mightily with the city's urban splendors. These range from downtown's elegant skyline to the chi-chi boutiques of **Rue Sherbrooke** and the sleek **Casino de Montréal**.

Montréal really consists of two cities. first, there's Vieux Montréal, the old city, which borders the St Lawrence and is exquisitely restored. The old town was home to the first European settlers who arrived in the mid-17th century.

The French explorer Jacques Cartier first came here in 1535, drawn to the area by Mont Royal (Royal Mountain). Settlement didn't begin to take hold until nearly 100 years later, but by 1642 the colony of Montréal had begun to prosper as a military and trading center. In 1760, however, war intervened and Montréal, then called "New France," was officially ceded to Great Britain. Tensions arising from the conflicting British and French heritage continue among residents of this dual-language city to this day.

Vieux-Montréal still evokes the atmosphere of an old French village. The center of activity is **Place Jacques-Cartier** Ⓐ, a cobbled pedestrian street lined with sidewalk cafés and peppered with street musicians and artists. Adjoining the old city is the **Vieux-Port** – once a seedy section of Montréal – which has been vibrantly transformed and is a hub for everything from a fabulous flea market to riverside roller-blading on its promenade.

Other diversions in Vieux Montréal include shopping – its tiny, winding streets are chock full of art galleries, unusual boutiques, and trinket stores. Old Montréal also possesses some interesting museums and churches, including the 19th-century **Basilique Notre-Dame-de-Montréal** Ⓑ, known for its twin towers, North America's biggest bell, and an organ with more than 7,000 pipes; the **Musée**

For full details of **opening hours** and contact information for the sites and museums mentioned in this chapter, see Travel Tips page 348.

BELOW: a view of Montréal from Clock Tower Pier.

d'Archéologie et d'Histoire de la Pointe-à-Callière **C** (closed Mon), is housed in a contemporary building, but its exhibits feature artifacts dating from the 17th century, along with new interactive displays, and virtual characters.

In contrast to the romantic allure of Vieux Montréal, the city's downtown area is a vibrant contemporary metropolis with all the urban advantages, such as culture, arts, restaurants, and shopping, and all the disadvantages – such as crime and poverty.

A ship approaches Thousand Island Bridge on the St Lawrence Seaway.

Montréal is compact and easy to explore. The downtown core, lying between the old city and Mont Royal, contains high-rise blocks, department stores, and restaurants. Certainly worth visiting are the **Musée des Beaux-Arts** **D** (closed Mon), known for its Impressionist and Modernist collections; and the **Musée d'Art Contemporain de Montréal** **E** (closed Mon), which is Canada's only institution devoted entirely to showcasing modern works. And any traveler with an interest in Canadian history should check out the eccentric **Musée McCord** **F** (McCord Museum of Canadian History; open daily; closed Mon in winter), located at the prestigious McGill University and featuring costumes, artifacts, and photographs.

One of Montréal's distinctions is that its urban neighborhoods are fabulous pockets of ethnicity. The city makes it incredibly easy to get around these – ranging from **Chinatown** to the **Quartier Latin** – with its underground metro system and access to the **Underground City**, a vast area of pedestrian walkways with shops, bars, restaurants, hotels and offices. It's a great hideout during Montréal's traditionally cold winters, and also incorporates a number of metro stations. One of the city's most important playgrounds is the **Parc du Mont-Royal** **G**, named for the hill – and now-dormant volcano – that rises at its center. You can hike up to the top for marvelous vistas, and on a clear day, you can see as far as New York State's Adirondacks and the Green Mountains of Vermont.

Upper Canada Village

No site along the St Lawrence Seaway is more poignant – or relevant – to this itinerary than is **Upper Canada Village Heritage Park** **3** (open summer, daily), which evolved out of the seaway's huge land requisition project. In the 1950s, seaway developers needed 20,000 acres (8,100 hectares) of land that could be flooded as part of a joint Canadian-US hydro-dam project, being developed in conjunction with the system of locks. As a result, five communities were uprooted. Ultimately, more than 500 structures – homes, churches, barns, mills, and stores – were moved. Some were used to establish new communities along the banks of the St Lawrence, but the most historic ones – along

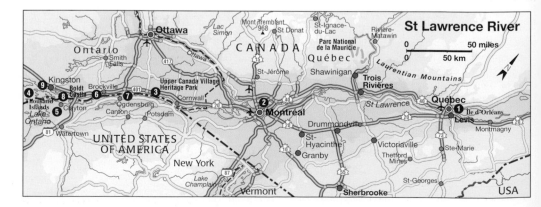

with other important buildings from eastern Ontario – were donated to the Upper Canada Village Heritage Park, which operates as if it were entrenched in the 1860s. More than just a collection of historic structures, the village hums with activity as costumed interpreters provide oral histories, and artisans and craftspeople make articles, from brooms and quilts to shoes and bread, in their old-world surroundings. The community mixes its genuinely historic structures, which include Asseltine's Woolen Mill, the blacksmith shop, Christ Church, Cook's Tavern, Willard's Hotel, and Bellamy's Grist Mill, with a handful that have been re-created using mid-19th century building techniques. The latter include the Cheese Factory, the Bakery, and the school.

While museum stores are often appealing, the sprawling gift shop in Upper Canada Village is unusual in that it sells products made on the site, ranging from fresh-baked bread from the bakery (local people line up daily to buy loaves) to cheese and handicrafts.

The Thousand Islands

Easily the most attractive resort area along the St Lawrence River, the **Thousand Islands ❹** region – comprising 1,800 isles – straddles the US and Canada. The islands are surrounded by the St Lawrence River, Lake Ontario, and the Adirondack Mountains. Some are mere rocks while others extend to several square miles. On some islands there are towns and villages; on others, modern mansions and even a castle.

For cruise travelers, a voyage in and around the Thousand Islands can result in an unusual day's itinerary. Ships bounce back and forth like ping-pong balls from village to island, and from New York State to Canada. Calls at ports here may only last for an hour or two – just long enough for passengers to experience the highlights of the village before they re-board and head off to the next spot, which is likely to be only an hour away.

Part of the appeal of cruising among the Thousand Islands is the abundant wildlife and natural landscapes. Beyond its history as a resort destination, the area today is best known as a magnet for sport fishing; species that can be found in these waters include salmon, trout, bass, pike, musky, and steelhead.

Below are some Thousand Islands stops often included on a St Lawrence Seaway itinerary.

Clayton, New York

Clayton ❺, an attractive village, is best known as the home of the **Antique Boat Museum** (closed Sun). It was established in the 1970s as the Thousand Islands Shipyard Museum, and its mission – and its growing collection – was spurred by a desire to preserve the islands' nautical history. Its founders acquired a run-down boat works in 1971, and three years later added an old lumberyard. Soon, families in the region began donating their own antique boats and river memorabilia. Beyond the permanent collections, which primarily focus on old boats, the museum offers a changing array of exhibits; one delightful show traced the region's tourist history, with artifacts from the grand old hotels that once dotted these shores. If

Maps:
Area 316
City 314

Craftsmen working at Upper Canada Village Heritage Park make the goods sold in the gift shop.

BELOW: daily life in the Upper Canada Village Heritage Park.

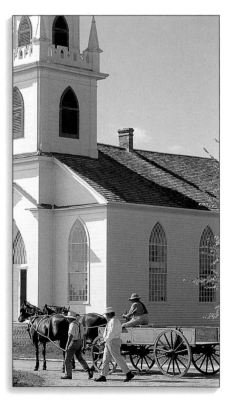

there's time, take advantage of another feature of the Antique Boat Museum – during the summer months it offers trips in boats that range from fast racing vessels to oh-so-slow self-piloted canoes.

Brockville, Ontario

Founded in 1785 by United Empire Loyalists, the village of **Brockville ❻**, Ontario – whose main claim to fame is its grand, Victorian-era town square – is named for the Canadian general who was killed near Niagara Falls during the War of 1812. Today, the 22,000-resident town is better known as a jumping-off point for the Thousand Islands. Brockville is also distinguished as one of Canada's oldest Loyalist settlements. (Loyalists, also known as royalists, had fled the US after the American Revolution in 1776, seeking protection in Canada under the British flag.) The government rewarded their loyalty to the Crown with land grants. One of the most prominent was William Buell of Connecticut; he was granted 505 acres (200 hectares) and wound up donating land for a jail, a courthouse, and the three churches that flank the town square.

Ogdensburg, New York

In **Ogdensburg ❼**, New York, the main attraction for cruise travelers is a visit to the renowned **Frederic Remington Art Museum** (closed Sun am and Mon–Tues in winter). Remington, who was best known for his odes to the western cowboy through bronze sculptures and oil paintings, also painted numerous landscapes of the Thousand Islands, which he loved. Remington and his family spent many summers in a cottage outside Ogdensburg.

BELOW: take a cruise on an antique boat.

Interestingly, it is the setting that distinguishes a visit to the Frederic Remington Art Museum. The house itself, where Remington's wife Eva lived after his death, has a homey atmosphere, with Remington's own possessions ranging from his book collection to sketchbooks to the very narrow bed the couple slept in. His art, of course, is the main event and is housed in a contemporary gallery adjacent to the house that showcases a wide range of his oils and bronzes.

Heart Island's Boldt Castle

One place that must be seen in the Thousand Islands is **Boldt Castle ❽**. Just after the turn of the 20th century, George C. Boldt, a millionaire who created New York City's prestigious Waldorf Astoria Hotel, decided to build a castle, designed after those in the German Rhineland, as a tribute to his wife. It was intended as a summer home.

Boldt was the son of poor parents from Prussia, who emigrated to the USA in the 1860s. He became a classic American success story, working his way from the bottom to become a hotel magnate. In addition to the Waldorf Astoria, Boldt was also proprietor of Philadelphia's famous Bellevue Stratford Hotel.

A man of great appetite and enthusiasm, he set out to design and build the "ultimate" summer residence: a six-story castle with 120 rooms on an island that also contained underground tunnels, Italian gardens, its own power house, and a mini-castle called the

Map on page 316

Alster Tower, intended to be used as a play house. Work began on the castle in 1900 and continued for the next four years until disaster struck. His beloved wife Louise died suddenly, and Boldt, at the time living in New York City, telegraphed the workers to halt construction immediately. The broken-hearted magnate never again returned to the island.

Today, the castle is an eerie, but gorgeous, not-quite-finished site, left as it was in 1904, when work abruptly ceased. While the permanent structure, the walls and roof, were already finished, work on the interior was still in progress. The castle, which had been left to disintegrate, was eventually purchased in 1977 by the Thousand Islands Bridge Authority, which has begun its completion.

Kingston, Ontario

Kingston ❾ lies at the confluence of the St Lawrence River, Lake Ontario, and the Rideau Canal, and has a lovely harbor. It's the oldest city in Ontario, founded by United Empire Loyalists in 1783, and served as Canada's original capital city between 1841 and 1843. It prospered during the War of 1812 as the British naval base for operations against the Americans, and is proud of its long maritime history. Fort Henry, built during the War of 1812, is now a museum. Kingston is the seat of Queen's University, founded in 1841, and is home to Canada's Royal Military College.

Among its attractions is a complex comprising the **Pump House Steam Museum** (open summer, daily), an old pump house that now exhibits a collection of antique steam engines, and the **Marine Museum of the Great Lakes** (open summer, daily; winter Mon–Fri), where displays feature marine artifacts and historical information on all the Great Lakes. ❑

BELOW: *Canadian Empress* sails near Heart Island.

INSIGHT GUIDES

The classic series that puts you in the picture

Alaska
Amazon Wildlife
American Southwest
Amsterdam
Argentina
Arizona & Grand Canyon
Asia's Best Hotels
& Resorts
Asia, East
Asia, Southeast
Australia
Austria
Bahamas
Bali
Baltic States
Bangkok
Barbados
Barcelona
Beijing
Belgium
Belize
Berlin
Bermuda
Boston
Brazil
Brittany
Brussels
Buenos Aires
Burgundy
Burma (Myanmar)
Cairo
California
California, Southern
Canada
Caribbean
Caribbean Cruises
Channel Islands
Chicago
Chile
China
Continental Europe
Corsica
Costa Rica
Crete
Croatia
Cuba
Cyprus
Czech & Slovak Republic
Delhi, Jaipur & Agra

Denmark
Dominican Rep. & Haiti
Dublin
East African Wildlife
Eastern Europe
Ecuador
Edinburgh
Egypt
England
Finland
Florence
Florida
France
France, Southwest
French Riviera
Gambia & Senegal
Germany
Glasgow
Gran Canaria
Great Britain
Great Gardens of Britain
& Ireland
Great Railway Journeys
of Europe
Greece
Greek Islands
Guatemala, Belize
& Yucatán
Hawaii
Hong Kong
Hungary
Iceland
India
India, South
Indonesia
Ireland
Israel
Istanbul
Italy
Italy, Northern
Italy, Southern
Jamaica
Japan
Jerusalem
Jordan
Kenya
Korea
Laos & Cambodia
Las Vegas

Lisbon
London
Los Angeles
Madeira
Madrid
Malaysia
Mallorca & Ibiza
Malta
Mauritius Réunion
& Seychelles
Melbourne
Mexico
Miami
Montreal
Morocco
Moscow
Namibia
Nepal
Netherlands
New England
New Orleans
New York City
New York State
New Zealand
Nile
Normandy
Norway
Oman & The UAE
Oxford
Pacific Northwest
Pakistan
Paris
Peru
Philadelphia
Philippines
Poland
Portugal
Prague
Provence
Puerto Rico
Rajasthan
Rio de Janeiro

Rome
Russia
St Petersburg
San Francisco
Sardinia
Scandinavia
Scotland
Seattle
Shanghai
Sicily
Singapore
South Africa
South America
Spain
Spain, Northern
Spain, Southern
Sri Lanka
Sweden
Switzerland
Sydney
Syria & Lebanon
Taiwan
Tanzania & Zanzibar
Tenerife
Texas
Thailand
Tokyo
Trinidad & Tobago
Tunisia
Turkey
Tuscany
Umbria
USA: On The Road
USA: Western States
US National Parks: West
Venezuela
Venice
Vienna
Vietnam
Wales
Walt Disney World/Orlando

INSIGHT GUIDES

The world's largest collection of visual travel guides & maps

CONTENTS

Getting Acquainted

Topography

Topography

MAINLAND USA

Mainland USA borders Mexico, with the Gulf of Mexico to the south, Canada to the north, the Pacific Ocean to the west, and the Atlantic Ocean to the east. Alaska and Hawaii (2,000 miles/3,200 km west of California's coast), both US states, are discrete.

The topography is massively diverse. Broadly speaking, there is a vast, central plain with lofty mountain ranges to the west and east. The west coast is prone to earthquake activity.

Land in the east ranges from the mountains and forests of New England in the north, through the open grasslands scattered with bushes and trees further south, to sub-tropical Florida.

Mountain ranges are in evidence in many of the central states, and there are huge plains around the Mississippi/Missouri river basin.

Scrub and desert are features of the southwest, while high plateaus and temperate forests abound in the northwest.

ALASKA

Alaska, which is bordered to the north by the Arctic Ocean, to the west by the Bering Strait, to the south by the Gulf of Alaska, and to the east by Canada, has both Pacific and Arctic mountain systems, broad river valleys, and a central plateau. Alaska has more than 40 active volcanoes, many of which have erupted violently and repeatedly over the past 200 years.

HAWAII

Hawaii is a group of 20 volcanic islands. They have a rugged, verdant topography. Contrary to popular belief, Hawaii is not in the South Pacific. (It is, however, part of Polynesia, most of which *is* in the South Pacific.)

CANADA

Canada borders the North Atlantic Ocean to the east, the North Pacific Ocean to the west, the Arctic Ocean to the north, and the United States of America to the south. It is the second-largest country in the world (after Russia) and covers two-fifths of North America.

Canada is divided into seven regions, each with a discrete landscape, ranging from coastal mountains, inland plateaus and fertile prairies towards the west coast to lowlands further east.

Climate

MAINLAND USA

The USA is mainly temperate, with continental conditions in the interior. Hawaii and Florida are tropical and semi-tropical respectively, and Alaska is arctic. The great plains to the west of the Mississippi are semi-arid, and the Great Basin of the southwest is arid.

ALASKA

In the southeast of Alaska it is wet and mild. The southcentral region sees considerably less rainfall the further inland you go.

In the northwest and on the Arctic coast high winds are common, and average temperatures are too low to permit trees to grow. Summer temperatures are in the high 30s °F (3°C) and 40s °F (4°C). This is also an extremely dry area, receiving only minimal amounts of moisture every year.

The southwest and the Aleutian Islands have high winds *(williwaws)*, which can reach speeds of 100 mph (165 kph). Heavy fog is common, as are rain and cool temperatures. The southwestern mainland is the meeting point for Aleutian weather and Interior weather, and often experiences unsettled conditions, frequently accompanied by high winds.

HAWAII

Most of Hawaii experiences balmy weather from April through October, and cooler, wetter weather from November through March. Rarely does the mercury drop below 60°F (15°C), nor go higher than about 90°F (32°C).

Hawaii has strong sunlight. The surrounding sea and northeasterly trade winds are a natural air-conditioning system. However, when the trade winds stop, and less frequent southerly winds take over, the result is often sticky and humid weather.

Certain areas on each island – usually on the windward side of mountains – receive more rainfall than others. One of the wettest spots on earth is Mount Wai'ale'ale on Kauai, which has been drenched by as much as 486 inches (1,234 cm) of rain in a year.

CANADA

Temperatures in Canada are between 68 and 90°F (20 and 32°C) in summer. Winter temperatures average 10°F–25°F (-5°C–10°C) from the Maritimes through southern Ontario. It gets colder and windier from northern Québec through the Rockies. In the Yukon, Northwest Territories, and Nunavut the mercury can drop to as low as -40°F (-40°C). On the southern coast of British Columbia (BC), however, warm Pacific currents generally keep the temperature above freezing during the winter.

Planning the Trip

Health

A doctor and nurse come as standard as lifeboats on cruise ships. Their facilities may vary, but, for a consultation fee, ship-board doctors can treat most medical problems. When they can't handle a complaint, they'll either stabilize you or have you airlifted to a hospital. Don't forget to bring your own prescription medication – beyond sea-sickness tablets, which they often give out for free, doctors carry little prescription medication.

SUN PROTECTION

Always apply high-factor sunscreen before going on deck or land. If you've been shut up indoors for a while before the cruise, protect yourself gradually. Try to go out only in the morning and late afternoon at first. This way, you'll build a tan that will protect you better against the more intense early afternoon rays (though you should continue to apply sunscreen). A hat with a brim will also help save your skin on lengthy hikes, when sightseeing, or lounging on deck.

IMMUNIZATION

You won't need any specific immunization for travel throughout the continental US, Alaska and Hawaii. Neither are you likely to need immunizations if you plan on entering Canada or Mexico, but it can't hurt to consult the Centers for Disease Control and Prevention (www.cdc.gov) in the USA for medical updates about locations on your itinerary. UK visitors can contact the Foreign and Commonwealth Office (www.fco.gov.uk) for comprehensive travel advice.

Time Zones

The continental US spans four time zones, which are:
- **Eastern Standard Time** (Greenwich Mean Time minus five hours)
- **Central Standard Time** (Greenwich Mean Time minus six hours)
- **Mountain Standard Time** (Greenwich Mean Time minus seven hours)
- **Pacific Standard Time** (Greenwich mean Time minus eight hours).

Canada has six time zones, the same four as the US, plus:
- **Atlantic Standard Time** (Greenwich Mean Time minus four hours)
- **Newfoundland Standard Time** (Greenwich Mean Time minus three and a half hours)

Alaskan clocks are set to **Alaska Standard Time** (Greenwich Mean Time minus nine hours).

Hawaii-Aleutian Standard Time (Greenwich Mean Time minus 10 hours) prevails in Hawaii.

Most of Mexico observes Central Standard Time, though the Baja region follows Pacific Standard Time. Both Canada and Mexico observe daylight savings time.

DAYLIGHT SAVINGS TIME

This begins each year at 2am on the first Sunday in April when clocks are advanced one hour, and ends on the last Sunday in October. Hawaii, Arizona and Indiana do not observe Daylight Savings Time.

Electricity

Electricity on a cruise liner comes as standard in the same way as in any hotel room. Cabins contain the 110 AC outlets that are standard in the US.

Canada and Mexico use the same system, though in the latter country you'll want to use low power settings on your hairdryer and other appliances so they don't overheat from the slower-cycling current. Likewise, when going to Mexico, you should bring along a three-prong plug adapter, as many old hotels still use the two-plug outlets that may not work for three-pronged appliances.

Public Holidays

As with other countries, the US has gradually shifted most of its public holidays to the Monday closest to the actual dates, thus creating a number of three-day weekends throughout the year.

Keep in mind that during public holidays, post offices, banks, government offices and many private businesses are closed.

- **January 1** New Year's Day
- **July 4** Independence Day
- **November 11** Veterans' Day
- **December 25** Christmas Day
Other holidays are:
- **Third Monday in January** Martin Luther King Jr Day
- **Third Monday in February** Presidents' Day
- **March/April** Good Friday, Easter Monday
- **Last Monday in May** Memorial Day
- **First Monday in September** Labor Day
- **Second Monday in October** Columbus Day
- **Last Thursday in November** Thanksgiving

Money Matters

American cruise liners carry the US dollar as the primary currency for all drinks, gambling and other services. Though the boats come equipped with ATMs, you may balk at the fees the machines charge. Use more reasonably-priced ATMs on shore when you can.

When coming ashore at Canadian and Mexican ports, you'll need the local currency. Remember to always shop around before making a currency conversion. You'll almost always get a better deal if you exchange money before the trip with your local bank. If you need to change more money while on the trip, banks in port will yield better exchange rates than any you can get on a ship.

Some ports may give you the option of spending in US dollars or the local currency. In this situation, compare the prices in both currencies and see which one gives you a better deal.

American visitors

One way around exchange rate anxiety is to just use a **credit card** or travelers check whenever possible. Credit cards are accepted almost everywhere on dry land, although not all cards at all places. Most hotels, restaurants and shops take the major ones such as American Express, Diners Club, MasterCard and Visa. Along with out-of-state or overseas bank cards, they can also be used to withdraw money at ATMs. **Travelers checks** are widely accepted, although you may have to provide proof of identification when cashing them at banks (this is not usually required at stores).

Overseas visitors

Travelers from other countries cruising in North America will probably want to make their currency conversions at home. Travelers checks in US dollars are much more widely accepted than those in other currencies. The best rates of exchange for them are in banks. Take along your passport if you want to cash checks. You can also use a major credit card issued by American Express, MasterCard or Visa, or, in most cases, your bank debit card to make purchases. But check what your bank charges to make international transactions.

Entry Regulations

PASSPORTS AND VISAS

While you won't need your passport to travel from state to state, you should bring it or a birth certificate anyway as a backup to supplement your other IDs. Overseas visitors will need a passport and possibly a visa to gain entry to the United States and Canada, check with the US Embassy in your home country for current regulations. International law doesn't require US citizens to carry a passport for entry into Canada, but it's a good idea to bring one, especially with tightened security since September 11, 2001. All travelers, US residents and non-US residents will need a passport or some other photo ID or proof of citizenship when visiting Mexico. However, if your trip takes you to Baja, US citizens won't need a passport for the dip into Mexico, so long as the visit is for no more than 72 hours. For any time longer than that, a passport and a Mexican Tourist Permit (FMT) is required, which is free of charge and can be issued for up to 180 days. US residents don't need a visa to enter Canada or Mexico.

When you disembark, you shouldn't leave without your cruise ship ID card. This card, given out by most ships these days, functions as both your room key and as a way for the ship to keep tabs on you. You swipe it as you leave the ship and board it, letting the crew know you're present before the ship leaves port.

Taxes

If you see a fare that sounds too good to be true, it probably doesn't include the port charges that you'll have to pay. These fees, charged in the US, Canada and Mexico, can add a sizable amount to the overall cost of the trip (depending on how many stops you make), so be sure to read the fine print before buying your ticket.

When staying ashore in the US, Canada and Mexico, hotels charge room taxes that add up to varying percentages of the bill. Additionally, Canada's 7 percent goods and service tax (GST) or the 15 percent harmonized sales tax (HST) of the provinces are calculated either in the nightly rate or added to the bill separately. Canada's hotels and duty-free shops offer applications to get full rebates on GST and HST taxes with the submission of receipts on anything except car rentals and restaurant meals.

Most regions of Mexico apply a 15 percent IVA (value-added) tax on goods and services in the posted price. In addition, Mexico charges an $18 exit tax on every visitor leaving the country.

Travel Insurance

More people book insurance for cruises than for any other form of travel. That's because the all-inclusive cruising fees mean you have more to lose if something goes wrong. Cruise lines have begun offering their own travel insurance, but you are likely to get a better rate with an independent company. Ask your travel agent for advice or your own insurance company for recommendations, and shop around for the best deal. You'll want a comprehensive insurance package that covers emergency medical care, repatriation by air ambulance (essential for international travelers), accidental death, baggage and document loss, and trip cancellation.

Cruise Lines

There are many cruise lines that travel the waters of North America and Eastern Canada. It's up to you whether you choose a big ship or a small one, if you sail the ocean or along the nation's rivers, lakes, and canals. A list of cruise lines and their contact information follows:

American Canadian Caribbean Line
461 Water Street, PO Box 368, Warren, RI 02885, Rhode Island, USA
Tel: 800-556 7450; (401) 247 0955
www.accl-smallships.com

American Cruise Lines
1 Marine Park, Haddam,
CT 06438, Connecticut, USA
Tel: 800-814 6880; (860) 345 3311
www.americancruiselines.com

The American West Steamboat Company
2101 4th Avenue, Suite 1150,
Seattle, WA 98121,
Washington, USA
Tel: 800-434 1232; (206) 621 0913
www.columbiarivercruise.com

Carnival Cruise Line
3655 NW 87th Avenue, Miami,
FL 33178, Florida, USA
Tel: 800-438 6744; (305) 599 2600
www.carnival.com

Celebrity Cruises
1050 Caribbean Way, Miami,
FL 33132, Florida, USA
Tel: 800-722 5941; (305) 539 6000
www.celebrity.com

Clipper Cruise Line
11969 Westline Industrial Drive,
St Louis, Missouri 63146 3220, USA
Tel: 800-325 0010; (314) 655 6700
www.clippercruise.com

Cruise West
2401 4th Avenue, Suite 700,
Seattle, WA 98121-1438,
Washington, USA
Tel: 888-851 8133
www.cruisewest.com

Crystal Cruises
2049 Century Park East,
Suite 1400, Los Angeles,
CA 90067, California, USA
Tel: 800-804 1500; (310) 785 9300
www.crystalcruises.com

The Delta Queen Steamboat Company
Robin Street Wharf, 1380 Port of
New Orleans Place, New Orleans,
Louisiana 70130-1890, USA
Tel: 800-543 1949; (504) 586 0631
www.deltaqueen.com

Holland America Line
300 Elliott Avenue West, Seattle,
WA 98119, Washington, USA
Tel: 877-SAIL-HAL; (206) 281 3535
www.hollandamerica.com

Lindblad Expeditions
720 5th Avenue, Floor 6, New York,
NY 10019, USA
Tel: 800-EXPEDITIONS (397 3348);
(212) 765 7740
www.expeditions.com

Norwegian Cruise Line
7665 Corporate Center Drive,
Miami, FL 33126, Florida, USA
Tel: 800-327 7030; (305) 436 4000
www.ncl.com

Princess Cruises
24844 Avenue Rockefeller, Santa
Clarita, CA 91355, California, USA
Tel: 800-PRINCESS; (661) 753 0000
www.princesscruises.com

Radisson Seven Seas Cruises
600 Corporate Drive, Suite 410,
Fort Lauderdale, FL 33334,
Florida, USA
Tel: 800-477 7500; (954) 776 6123
www.rssc.com

RiverBarge Excursion Lines
201 Opelousas Avenue,
New Orleans, LA 70114,
Louisiana, USA
Tel: 888-GO-BARGE (888-462 2743)
www.riverbarge.com

Royal Caribbean International
1080 Caribbean Way, Miami,
FL 33132, Florida, USA
Tel: 800-327 6700; (305) 539 6000
www.royalcaribbean.com

St Lawrence Cruise Lines
253 Ontario Street, Kingston,
Ontario K7L2Z4, Canada
Tel: 800-267 7868; (613) 549 8091
www.stlawrencecruiselines.com

Silversea Cruises
110 East Broward Boulevard,
Fort Lauderdale, FL 33301,
Florida, USA
Tel: 800-722 9955; (954) 522 4477
www.silversea.com

Yachts of Seabourn
6100 Blue Lagoon Drive, Suite 400,
Miami, FL 33126, Florida, USA
Tel: 800-929-9391; (305) 463 3000
www.seabourn.com

Practical Tips

Telephone, Fax and Internet

Making a telephone call via a ship's satellite system can be extremely expensive. North American travelers should be able to save by using their own cellular phones in port, but European visitors with mobile phones will need at least a tri-band handset and network availability with a roaming agreement to make calls from the US.

On dry land, public coin-operated telephones can be found around the port areas and in the main commercial districts. To call long-distance, dial 1+area code+local number. Have plenty of change with you to deposit when the operator prompts you to do so.

Residents of the US and Canada can use AT&T USA Direct public phones with a charge card. Some public phones also allow holders of a European charge card, such as a BT Chargecard, or a major credit card to access the home operator.

Toll-free Calls

When in the US, make use of toll-free numbers. They usually start with 800, 1-800, 888 or 877.

FAXES & EMAIL

Western Union (tel: 800-325 6000) takes telegram and telex messages, plus orders to wire money over the phone. Calls and faxes may be sent from public calling and fax centres. This is a popular and cost effective way to keep in touch with home, for passengers and crew.

A growing number of locations

have internet cafés. Almost all ships, too, offer internet access although charges vary enormously. The cheapest way to stay in touch via email on board is to use a free web-based service like Yahoo, Hotmail or Fastmail. With these, you only incur a cost for time online. Actually sending and receiving email on a ship via the ship's email address may be charged per email or per kilobyte, and incoming mail is likely to be delivered under your door as a hard copy several hours after it arrives – hardly conducive to speed or privacy.

Traveling with Children

Despite its image as an old people's vacation, cruising can be perfect for families

Some ships are more suitable than others for families. Princess, Royal Caribbean, Norwegian Cruise Line and Holland America all have good children's facilities and entertainment (see page 40).

Anyone who does not want to spend their vacation with children would be advised to avoid a big ship in the school holidays.

Facilities for Disabled Travelers

Generally speaking, cruising can be an ideal vacation for someone with mobility difficulties or in a wheelchair, as most ships provide a relaxing, sociable setting while visiting numerous destinations with minimal hassle. Take the advice of a specialist cruise travel agent before booking and make sure they provide specific information about the facilities onboard the ship and the cabin itself. Some of the larger ships have better facilities for physically challenged passengers but bear in mind that even though there will be more space to maneuver on a large ship there will also be more ground to cover to get from point A to point B. Cruise ships do not generally provide special facilities for those with hearing difficulties, although two of Crystal's

Hot Tips for Cruisers

Don't feel you have to tip people like the maître d' unless they have performed a special service for you, but, of course, they always appreciate it if you do.

● If the service is poor, raise the issue with the hotel manager onboard.

● It is good practice to tip your cabin steward extra if you leave your cabin in disarray.

● On some ships, it is forbidden for staff to accept cash tips. If you do give them cash, don't hand it over conspicuously.

● If tips are automatically added to your onboard account, you are perfectly entitled to adjust the amount.

● If you want to do more than tip, a genuine "Thank you" and a letter to the employee's immediate superior is a thoughtful gesture.

ships, and some of the Celebrity fleet have special headsets for the hard of hearing in their cinemas. Newer ships have some signage in Braille for the blind.

The quality of cabins for the disabled, however, varies. If specially fitted cabins are not available, choose as large a cabin as possible, close to the elevator, if you're on a big ship. When arranging mealtimes, make sure the maître d' allocates you a table with space for a wheelchair.

Weights & Measures

The US operates on the imperial system of weights and measures. Metric is rarely used. Below is a conversion chart:
1 inch = 2.54 centimeters
1 foot = 30.48 centimeters
1 mile = 1.609 kilometers
1 quart = 1.136 liters
1 ounce = 28.40 grams
1 pound = 0.453 kilograms
1 yard = 0.9144 meters

Getting Around

Shore Excursions

Passengers are encouraged to book shore excursions in advance, which can be done online with some cruise lines. Popular excursions do sell out, but don't feel pressurized to book everything before boarding the ship; a couple of days off at sea may be welcome on a cruise with an intensive itinerary. A shore excursion will provide an overview of a new place, or greater detail on a specific site; it may be an opportunity to try a new sport, like kayaking or mountain biking, in a group. If you want to linger in a museum or gallery, or spend the day shopping, or take a long lunch, go it alone. Shore tours do have free time built-in, but not much.

TOURING INDEPENDENTLY

While your ship may offer onshore tours of ports, independent bus or walking tours are often cheaper and more colorful. If you forget to call ahead to reserve a spot on such a tour, the cruise ship purser or customer relations staff can do it for you, for a small fee.

Research your destination thoroughly before you arrive, and take a good map. Always check that train, bus and ferry times coincide with the ship's arrival and departure. Make reservations for special lunch venues and check that museums and galleries are open on the day you will be visiting (see pages 328–49 for details of major museums).

Remember that it is your responsibility to get back to the ship on time and, if you miss it, to catch up with it at the next port.

Car Rental

For those ports with easy-to-navigate streets, and where you will have time to explore independently, renting a car for the day, or even a few hours, can be an unbeatable way to see the local sites. It's cheapest to book a car, up to a day ahead of time, over the phone or over the web. But if the whim to drive suddenly strikes you, the ship's purser can arrange to have a rental vehicle waiting for you at the port, for a small fee, and this will save valuable time. Most rental companies require drivers to be over 21 years old (sometimes 25 or more) and you will need to show a valid driver's license and pay for the car rental (and deposit) with a major credit card. You'll also need insurance, purchased from the company. Be sure to check the fine print on the insurance document; US drivers may already be covered by their own auto insurance, while international drivers may need additional cover.

DRIVING IN NORTH AMERICA

In the US, Canada and Mexico you drive on the right, usually in a left-hand-drive vehicle. The rules of the road vary from state to state so be vigilant, and invest in a good map so that you can be sure to reach your destination and get back to the ship in good time.

Remember that Mexican drivers take an "anything goes" approach to driving.

Motor Homes

If you are planning to extend your stay to tour Alaska or another region, you could rent an RV (recreational vehicle), also called a motor home *(see page 102)*. No special license is necessary to operate an RV, but a rental package will not be cheap, so you may find it more cost effective to join an organized tour or to rent a car and stay in motels, hotels, lodges or campsites. Keep in mind that the vehicles are large and slow and can be difficult to handle on narrow roads, even with automatic transmission and power steering.

Taxis

Most cruise lines should warn you if the immediate port area is less than safe. For those occasions, skip the walk to town, if you are not joining an organized shore excursion, and take a taxi to the area you want to see. Taxis are the most common means for cruise line passengers to get around. Their fixed and published rates are usually not too costly, and the drivers almost always know where you want to go – and can recommend destinations and offer other local knowledge as well. You can often find printed or posted information on rates at points of entry, or from taxi drivers and tourist offices. If you are relying on a taxi to get you to an attraction and back again always agree on a rate with the driver before getting into the vehicle, and never pay the whole fare until you return to the ship. Also, only use official cabs that frequent the ports or have been called in advance by your hotel, if you are staying on.

Buses

Navigating the local bus system may prove more of a headache than it's worth, especially if you're just going to be ashore for a few hours. But for extended stays, the cheap rates of buses make them great bargains. Hotels, tourist offices and police stations can provide bus maps and rates.

Staying On

Extending Your Stay

Travelers can extend their vacation by adding a land-based stay to their cruise itinerary. Stays can amount to an extra day or two pre- or post-cruise, or up to a week to explore a region or city. One of the most popular options is to combine an itinerary-packed Alaskan cruise with a more leisurely week-long tour inland to the national parks and Native Alaskan villages *(see pages 93–102)*. Princess Cruise Lines offers good-quality cruise tours in Alaska. Alternatively, cruise passengers might like to tag on a few days to explore the galleries, museums and nightlife of a main cruise gateway city, such as San Francisco, Chicago, New York, Boston, New Orleans or Charleston.

The cruise lines can help passengers organize a vacation extension, and many offer good deals on land-based accommodation and advice about transportation and guided tours. Passengers arriving from Europe and elsewhere outside the US will usually incur an overnight stay anyway, so adding extra nights in the hotel, before or after the cruise, should be simple and not too costly.

Directory of Ports

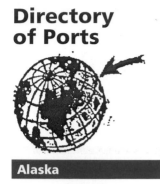

SEATTLE

More than the sum of its coffee houses, Seattle dining is studded with the celebrity chefs and fancy restaurants you'd expect from a city this size. Local menus include salmon, shellfish, sweet onions, mushrooms, stone fruits, berries, and asparagus, and the city's location along the Pacific means it is influenced by fine Asian cooking.

In terms of lodging, Seattle is full of eclectic hotels providing an alternative to the many chains also present. There is also plenty to see and do if you plan to overnight here, or stay on in the city for a day or two, or longer.

Tourist Information
Seattle Visitor Information Center
Washington State Convention and Trade Center, 800 Convention Place, Galleria Level
Tel: (206) 461 5840
www.seeseattle.org

Where to Stay
The Claremont Hotel
2000 Fourth Avenue
Tel: 877-448 8600
www.claremonthotel.com
A blast from the 1920s, this Belltown hotel preserves the Jazz

Hotel Price Guide

Price categories are based on the average cost of a double room per night.
$ = $50 or less
$$ = $50–150
$$$ = $150–250

Age elegance in its hand-carved Italian chandeliers, vintage tiled floors, and hand-made glass items. Located just a block away is the restored Cinerama movie theater, one of the few remaining movie houses with a curved screen. **$$**
MarQueen Hotel
600 Queen Avenue North
Tel: 1-888-445 3076
www.marqueen.com
This elegant and historic 1918 building in Queen Hill has retained its terrazzo floors, marble accents, high ceilings with cove moldings, mahogany wainscoting and grand staircase. **$$$**

Eating Out
Palisade
2601 West Marina Place
Tel: (206) 285 1000
This waterfront restaurant, with its indoor, fish-stocked pond and great views of the Sound and Olympic Mountains, has a menu to match its ambience. The almondine buttered lobster tails, prawns and crème brûlée sampler for dessert are among the finer selections. **$$$$**
Red Mill Burgers
316 North 67th Street
Tel: (206) 783 6362
Straightforward as its no-nonsense name suggests, this small diner serves up some of Seattle's best burgers and onion rings – or at least the biggest and messiest. The beef patties come flame-broiled, the chicken patties are marinated in lemon-honey, and the fancier toppings include crumbled bleu cheese, caramelized red onion and pepper bacon. **$**

Culture and Attractions
Experience Music Project
325 5th Avenue North
Tel: (206) 770 2702; 367 5483
www.emplive.com
Designed by architect Frank Gehry with lots of swoops and bulges inspired by guitars, this museum explores American music through interactive exhibits. Open Mon–Sat 10am–5pm; until 9pm Fri–Sat, but times can vary seasonally. Entrance fee.

Pacific Science Center
200 Second Avenue North
Tel: (206) 443 2001
www.pacsci.org
Located near the Space Needle, the Science Center has permanent and visiting interactive exhibits, a planetarium and IMAX cinemas. Open Mon–Fri 10am–5pm, Sat–Sun 10am–6pm. Entrance fee.
Pike Place Market
Pike Place and Western Avenue
www.pikeplacemarket.org
Market tours available for a fee. Open Mon–Sat 9am–6pm, Sun 11am–5pm.

VANCOUVER

For a city so close to the wild, Vancouver offers a surprising variety of options for dining and accommodations. Having shaken the confines of its British heritage long ago, the dining scene specializes in seafood, fusion and a variety of ethnic foods. Likewise, its hotels span the simplest dives to the most chic boutiques.

Tourist Information
Vancouver Tourist Information Center
Plaza Level, 200 Burrard Street
Tel: (604) 683 2000
www.tourism-vancouver.org

Where to Stay
Le Soleil Hotel and Suites
567 Hornby Street
Tel: 877-632 3030
www.lesoleilhotel.com
The lobby of this old-world charmer says it all – fluted columns, a 30-ft (9-meter) ceiling, Italian marble, crystal chandeliers. The French château atmosphere carries through in the rooms, decorated with Louis XV furniture, satin-covered sofas, and marble in the bathrooms. **$$$**
Opus Hotel
322 Davie Street
Tel: (604) 642 6787
www.opushotel.com
This boutique hotel in trendy Yaletown was converted from an old warehouse. The rooms are decorated

in five styles spanning minimalist to eclectic modern. Somehow, they all fit with the belle époque look of Elixir, the attached French brasserie. **$$**

Eating Out
Rooster's Quarters
836 Denman Street
Tel: (604) 689 8023
Canadian comfort food in a crowded but congenial setting. The place serves barbecue with Québec-style maple sauce and poutine (French fries in melted cheese curd and gravy) along with burgers and other standard North American fare. **$**
The Teahouse Restaurant
1583 Coal Harbour Quay
Tel: (604) 669 3281
For a taste of Vancouver's famous outdoors along with some fine local seafood and French country cuisine, try this restaurant in Stanley Park. Its tree-shrouded patio offers great views of English Bay, and its menu provides such fare as pepper garlic prawns and ravioli stuffed with wild mushroom. **$$$**

Culture and Attractions
Aquarium Marine Science Centre
845 Avison Way
Tel: (604) 659 3474
www.vanaqua.org
Located west of Downtown in Stanley Park. Open daily 10am–5.30pm (winter), July–Aug 9.30am–7.30pm. Entrance fee.
Museum of Anthropology at the University of British Columbia
6393 NW Marine Drive
Tel: (604) 822 5087
Open daily 10am–5pm, Tues until 9pm (summer); Tues–Sat 11am–5pm, Tues until 9pm (winter). Entrance fee. Wheelchair accessible.
Stanley Park
Entrances: west end of Beach Avenue, Nelson Street, or Georgia Street
www.seestanleypark.com
This busy 1,000-acre (405-hectare) park in the city has the carved Haida Indian statues to fulfill your totem pole fix (practically a requirement in this totem-filled

town) as well as plenty of gardens, beaches and trails to stroll. Open daily 10am–6pm (summer); Tues–Sun 10am–4.30pm (winter). Entrance fee to the Chinese Garden.

KETCHIKAN

As a self-dubbed "Gateway City," Ketchikan has retained a fair number of quaint old hotels, inns and lodges from the days before it became a tourist stop. Expect typical Alaskan fare in the restaurants, namely, superb seafood offerings.

Tourist Information
Ketchikan Visitors' Bureau
131 Front Street
Tel: (907) 225 6166
www.visit-ketchikan.com

Where to Stay
Blueberry Hill
500 Front Street
Tel: (907) 247 2583
www.blueberryhillbb.com
An attractively restored historic home in downtown Ketchikan with views of the Tongass Narrows and Deer Mountain. Rooms come with hardwood floors, hand-made quilts, four-poster beds and other cozy décor. **$$**
Gilmore Hotel
326 Front Street
Tel: 800-275 9423
www.gilmorehotel.com
This landmark on the National Historic Register is located downtown right across from the cruise ship dock, its front rooms overlooking the Tongas Narrows waterfront. Built in 1927, the hotel has a tasteful combination of furnishings evocative of both modern times and frontier Alaska. **$$**

Eating Out
Annabelle's Famous Keg and Chowder House
326 Front Street
Tel: (907) 225 9423
There's a 19-century Gold Rush feel to the décor (wall-sized murals, a massive mahogany bar) and

general informal atmosphere in this steak and seafood house just off the lobby of the Gilmore Hotel. The sourdough pancakes, steamer seafood basket and cannery bread are all delicious. **$**
Burger Queen
518 Water Street
Tel: (907) 225 6060
Just like the name says, this unassuming, cramped diner serves up what are widely considered to be the best burgers in town. **$**

Culture and Attractions
Dolly's House
24 Creek Street
Tel: (907) 225 2279/6329
In the Creek Street Historic District sits this 1919 former house of ill repute. Now the base of Madam Dolly Arthur's business – filled with antiques and secret cubbyholes – is open again as a museum. Open daily in the summer when cruise ships are in town. Entrance fee.
Southeast Alaska Discovery Center
50 Main Street
Tel: (907) 228 6220
An information center with Native Alaskan art displays. Open daily 8am–5pm (summer); Tues–Sat 10am–4.30pm (winter).
Totem Heritage Center
601 Deermount Street
Tel: (907) 225 5900
www.city.ketchikan.ak.us
The museum exhibits priceless totem poles, and the center also preserves and promotes the traditional art of the Tlingit, Haida, and Tsimshian Native Alaskans. Open daily 8am–5pm (summer); Mon–Fri 1–5pm (winter). Entrance fee.

JUNEAU

Independently-run hotels are sparse in Alaska's capital, making B&Bs and lodges (or at least hotels that look like lodges) outside town the best bet for more personal stays. Along with seafood, Juneau also specializes in coffee. Heritage Coffee makes its home here, and all the self-respecting restaurants serve a fine pot of some brew or another.

Tourist Information
Davis Log Cabin Visitor Information Center
101 Egan Drive
Tel: 888-581 2201
www.traveljuneau.com

Where to Stay
Blueberry Lodge
9436 North Douglas Highway
Tel: (907) 463 5886
www.blueberrylodge.com
Blueberry Lodge offers the best of mountain-man living with a lot less work and much better food (like sourdough Belgian waffles with spruce-tip syrup). This hand-crafted log cabin features five bedrooms, a view of an occupied eagle's nest out the window, and easy access to the alpine trails and beaches of the surrounding tidelands. **$$**

Hotel Price Guide

Price categories are based on the average cost of a double room per night.
$ = $50 or less
$$ = $50–150
$$$ = $150–250

Pearsons Pond Luxury Inn and Adventure Spa
4541 Sawa Circle
Tel: (907) 789 3772
www.pearsonspond.com
Though it feels like a getaway, this waterfront property is actually conveniently located near downtown and Glacier Bay. Within the inn's rainforest setting you'll find a pond with fountains and rowboats, trails, a northern lights viewing station, and views of Mendenhall Glacier. **$$**

Eating Out
Buzz's Paradise Lunch and Bakery
245 Marine Way
Tel: (907) 586 2253
This small maritime hangout across from the cruise ship dock specializes in takeout lunches for cruise ship passengers. The chicken and lime soup and paradise sausage soup with black olives and zucchini are especially good for a picnic in the nearby park. **$**

The Summit Restaurant
455 South Franklin Street
Tel: (907) 586 2050
Overlooking the cruise ship dock, this elegant restaurant – the most acclaimed in Juneau – changes its menu often, featuring king crab legs with Thai chili drawn butter and grilled filet of beef with demi-glaze and gorgonzola butter. **$$$**

Culture and Attractions
Alaska State Museum
395 Whittier Street
Tel: (907) 465 2901
www.museums.state.ak.us
Exhibits on Native Americans, Russian America, and natural history, including an "eagle tree" diorama. Open daily 8.30am–5.30pm (summer); Tues–Sat 10am–4pm (winter).

Mendenhall Glacier
8465 Old Dairy Road
Tel: (907) 789 0097
On Mendenhall Lake, this big ice cube is 1.5 miles (2 km) wide and 12 miles (19 km) long, one of the loveliest drive-up geological wonders. Entrance fee.

Sitka
Alaska Raptor Center
1000 Raptor Way
Tel: (907) 747 8662/6281
www.alaskaraptor.org
The center is located on 17 acres (7 hectares) of land near the Tongass National Forest, and the Indian River in Sitka. Open daily 8am–5pm (summer); tours May to Sept; Mon–Fri 8am–4pm (winter).

Sheldon Jackson Museum
104 College Drive
Tel: (907) 747 8981
www.museums.state.ak.us
An extensive collection of Native

Alaskan art, and interactive demonstrations. Open daily 9am–5pm (summer); Tues–Sat 10am–4pm (winter). Closed holidays. Entrance fee.

Skagway
Klondike Gold Rush National Historic Park
Second and Broadway
Tel: (907) 983 2921
Historic district with guided walking tours and hiking trails nearby. Open daily 8am–6pm (summer); Mon–Fri (winter). Fee charged for tours.

Haines
Chilkat Bald Eagle Preserve
Tel: (907) 766 3094 (Ranger station)
www.dnr.state.ak.us
Open daily 9am–6pm (summer) when cruise ships are in port; call for hours in winter.

Hammer Museum
Main Street
Tel: (907) 766 2374
Hammers through the ages on display. Open Mon–Fri 10am–5pm (summer only).

Sheldon Museum and Cultural Center
11 Main Street
Tel: (907) 766 2366
The history of the Tlingit in the Chilkat Valley, and the pioneer settlers. Open year-round, Mon–Fri 11am–6pm, Sat–Sun 2–6pm (summer); Mon–Fri 1–4pm (winter).

ANCHORAGE AND SEWARD

Alaska's largest city offers the state's widest selection of restaurants and accommodations. Naturally, seafood reigns here, particularly when it comes to dishes involving local fish like salmon, halibut and shellfish. Locally-brewed beers in pubs are also popular. Smoking in public places is banned.

Tourist Information
Anchorage Convention and Visitors' Bureau
524 West Fourth Avenue
Tel: (907) 276 4118
www.anchorage.net

Where to Stay

Diamond Center Hotel
700 East Diamond Boulevard
Tel: (866) 770 5002
www.diamondcenterhotel.com
A boutique hotel, offering some of
the finest views of the Chugach
mountain range you're likely to see.
The thoroughly modern décor
compliments the environment
outside, with furnishings done in
crisp, cool colors and northern
hardwoods, as well as a life-size
Wooly Mammoth in the wildflower
courtyard. **$$**

Historic Anchorage Hotel
330 East Street
Tel: (907) 272 4553
www.historicanchoragehotel.com
The only Anchorage hotel listed on
the National Register of Historic
Places, this restored property has
been a downtown staple since
1916. The building is stuffed with
Queen Anne style furniture, and with
Aromae Botanicals toiletries in its
bathrooms. **$$**

Eating Out

Humpy's Great Alaskan Ale House
610 West Sixth Avenue
Tel: (907) 276 2337
www.humpys.com
Along with the 36 beers on tap,
this classic Anchorage pub has
a menu of good ale-house
food tailored to the region, such
as halibut burgers, halibut tacos,
and smoked salmon scallops.
$$

Simon & Seaforts Saloon & Grill
420 L Street
Tel: (907) 274 3502
Serving up such dishes as
sizzled seafood stew, king crab,
and desserts like Simon's burnt
cream, this popular steak and
seafood grill has been outfitted

Restaurant Prices

Price categories are based on
the average cost of a meal for
two, excluding drinks, tax and tip.
$ = $20 or less
$$ = $20–40
$$$ = $40–60
$$$$ = $60 and up

with turn-of-the-century saloon
furnishings. Those cutesy additions
pale next to the view of Cook
Inlet through the large windows.
$$$

Culture and Attractions

Alaska Native Heritage Center
8800 Heritage Center Drive
At the North Muldoon exit, off Glenn
Highway
Tel: 800-315 6608; Tel: (907) 330
8000
www.alaskanative.net
Built and run by Alaska Natives,
this center offers interaction
with storytellers, artisans and
dancers, along with galleries of
cultural displays and exhibits.
Open daily 9am–6pm (summer);
Mon–Fri noon–5pm (winter).
Entrance fee.

Alaska SeaLife Center
301 Railway Avenue, Seward
Tel: (907) 224 6300
Educational and research facility
with some interesting marine
exhibits. Open daily 8am–8pm
(summer); 10am–5pm (winter).
Entrance fee.

**Anchorage Museum of History
and Art**
Corner of Seventh Avenue and
C Street
Tel: (907) 343 4326
www.anchoragemuseum.org
Displays of art, history and cultural
exhibits. Open daily 9am–6pm,
Thur until 9pm (summer); Wed–Sat
10am–6pm, Sun noon–5pm (winter).
Entrance fee.

**The Imaginarium Science
Discovery Center**
737 West Fifth Avenue
Tel: (907) 276 3179
www.imaginarium.org
A hands-on science activity center
in downtown Anchorage. Open
Mon–Sat 10am–6pm, Sun
noon–5pm. Entrance fee.

Oscar Anderson House Museum
420 M Street
Tel: (907) 274 2336
Museum in an old property built
in 1915. Guided tours of the
historic district also start here.
Open Tues–Sat 11am–4pm
(summer); by appointment only in
winter.

New England and the East Coast

NEW YORK

When it comes to food and hotels,
the city truly has it all. The difficulty
is in the choosing. You can dine at
any hour on foods as simple as a
slice of pizza on a loud city street to
a multi-course meal in a quiet SoHo
bistro. The range in lodging options
is just as wide, from posh to
Bohemian. One way to narrow your
decision-making is to look for the
good deals, of which there are more
than you'd think.

Tourist Information

nycvisit.com
810 Seventh Avenue
Tel: 800-692 8474; (212) 484 1222
www.visitnewyork.com

Where to Stay

Gershwin Hotel
7 East 27th Street
Tel: (212) 545 8000
www.gershwinhotel.com
Located a few blocks from the
Empire State Building in the Flatiron
district, this hotel has turned itself
into a veritable gallery space, with
Pop Art lining the lobby (including
an original Andy Warhol Campbell's
Soup Can print) and original art
installations on all 13 floors. The
attached **Living Room** hosts music,
comedy and theater acts. **$$**

The Time Hotel
224 West 49th Street
Tel: 877-846 3692
A perfect compliment to the
Museum of Modern Art, a few
blocks away, this super-modern
hotel has been carefully designed,
from the minimalist glass and
metal furnishings to the startling
color schemes to the "color-
inspired" scents pumped into the
air. The attached **Time Lounge**
makes tasty martinis. **$$$**

Eating Out

Carnegie Deli
854 Seventh Avenue
Tel: 800-334 5606
www.carnegiedeli.com
The quintessential New York deli,

Restaurant Prices

Price categories are based on the average cost of a meal for two, excluding drinks, tax and tip.
$ = $20 or less
$$ = $20–40
$$$ = $40–60
$$$$ = $60 and up

with gruff old waiters in white shirts and ties serving vast platters of food beneath the autographed publicity portraits of celebrities past their prime. The sandwiches are veritable mountains of corned beef, pastrami, and almost any meat product you could desire between two slabs of bread. **$–$$**

Time Café
380 Lafayette Street
Tel: (212) 533 7000
www.timecafenyc.com
Nouveau American cuisine in the Village. Seafood gets much of the attention here from the chef and the patrons alike, particularly the black sesame-crusted salmon and the grilled yellowfin tuna with piquillo pepper coulis. Seating in the cozy interior or on the busy sidewalk assures some great people watching. **$$$**

Culture and Attractions

American Museum of Natural History
Central Park West and 79th Street
Tel: (212) 769 5100
www.amnh.org
This world famous collection of dinosaur bones and taxidermic creatures from the four corners of the earth improved with the remodeling of the attached **Hayden Planetarium**. Tom Hanks, Harrison Ford and other celebrities narrate various shows about the universe in the state-of-the-art facility. Museum open daily 10am–5.45pm. Entrance fee.

Empire State Building
350 Fifth Avenue, at 34th Street
www.esbnyc.com
Opened in 1931, this is one of New York City's most famous landmarks, with stunning panoramic views over the city and beyond for 80 miles

(128 km), on a clear day. Take the elevator to observation decks on the 86th and 102nd floors. Open 365 days a year 10am–midnight, 9.30am–midnight (Sat–Sun). Last elevator at 11.15pm. Entrance fee.

Metropolitan Museum of Art
1000 Fifth Avenue, at 82nd Street
Tel: (212) 535 7710
www.metmuseum.org
A sprawling, neo-Gothic building, begun in 1874, is the country's largest art museum, with an unmatchable series of galleries, period rooms and gardens. Open Sun, Tues–Thur 9.30am–5.30pm; Fri–Sat 9.30am–9pm. Closed Mon (except Thanksgiving, Christmas Day and New Year's Day). Entrance fee.

Rockefeller Center
Fifth Avenue, at 50th Street
Tel: (212) 632 3975; (212) 664 3700 (for NBC studio tours)
www.rockefellercenter.com
Art Deco buildings containing a large business and entertainment complex, spanning several blocks, and winter ice skating rink. Art and architecture tours; home of NBC Studios, with guided tours from the 49th Street entrance. Fee for tours.

Solomon R. Guggenheim Museum
1071 Fifth Avenue, at 89th Street
Tel: (212) 423 3500
www.guggenheim.org
A Frank Lloyd Wright white funnel structure that has caused controversy since its opening in 1959. Changing exhibitions. Open Sat–Wed 10am–5.45pm; Fri 10am–8pm.

BOSTON

Boston is a town that hasn't forgotten its culinary roots. Along with all the haute cuisine you'd expect from a major city are numerous restaurants still serving up traditional New England food. Naturally, seafood abounds as well. Lodging choices run the gamut throughout the city, from historic inns to modern landmarks with executive suites.

Tourist Information

Boston Visitors' Center
Tremont Street, at the edge of Boston Common
Tel: 1-888-SEE BOSTON
www.bostonusa.com

Where to Stay

Clarendon Square Inn
198 West Brookline Street
Tel: (617) 536 2229
www.clarendonsquare.com
The wood molding, hardwood and limestone floors and other sumptuous features of this South End townhouse have been lovingly restored to their 1860s splendor. Tastefully chic modern furniture in every room compliments the Victorian shell. **$$**

Tremont Boston
275 Tremont Street
Tel: (617) 426 1400
A deluxe hotel in Boston's theater district that's maintained the same jazz age appeal since it was built in 1925. Decked out with ornate furniture, imported rugs, marble pillars and dark-wood trim. **$$$**

Hotel Price Guide

Price categories are based on the average cost of a double room per night.
$ = $50 or less
$$ = $50–150
$$$ = $150–250

Eating Out

The Dish
253 Shawmut Avenue
Tel: (617) 426 7866
www.southenddish.com
A South End neighborhood bistro that fuses American fare with Asian and Mediterranean influences without getting too fussy about it. Items like Cajun meatloaf with ricotta mashed potatoes, pork tenderloin with pistachio goat cheese crust and lots of gourmet wood-oven pizzas may be glorified staple dishes, but they're tasty glorified staple dishes. **$$$**

Durgin Park
340 North Market Street
Tel: (617) 227 2038
A Boston classic, serving traditional

New England food and attitude since 1827. The waiters maintain a whimsically-grumpy demeanor as they serve up the restaurant's famous baked beans, prime rib and Indian pudding (cornmeal and molasses). **$$**

Culture and Attractions

Faneuil Hall
Clinton, Chatham and Commercial streets, Downtown Boston
The market place is on the first floor, while on the second floor National Park Service Rangers present historical talks every half hour (9.30am–4.30pm), unless the hall is in use. Open daily 9am–5pm.

Freedom Trail
Starting points all over Boston
Guided tours from 15 State Street
Tel: (617) 227 8800
www.thefreedomtrail.org
From Boston Common to The Bunker Hill Monument and 14 other historic sites in between, this red-brick line connects all the historic sites in town that commemorate the American rebellion.

Old State House
206 Washington Street
Tel: (617) 720 1713
www.bostonhistory.org
Open daily 9.30am–5pm.
Entrance fee.

Paul Revere House
19 North Square
Tel: (617) 523 2338
www.paulreverehouse.org
A national historic landmark. Open daily 9.30am–5.15pm (summer); 9.30am–4.15pm (winter). Closed Mon Jan–Mar. Entrance fee.

BEYOND BOSTON

Culture and Attractions

Abee Museum
26 Mount Desert Street, Bar Harbor, Maine
Tel: (207) 288 3519
www.abbemuseum.org
A museum celebrating Native American culture. Open Sun–Wed 10am–5pm, Thur–Sat 10am–9pm (July–Aug); Thur–Sun 10am–5pm (Sept–mid-Oct). Closed Jan.

The Breakers and The Elms
Newport, Rhode Island
Tel: (401) 847 1000
www.newportmansions.org
Newport Mansions in scenic Newport, Rhode Island, managed by the Preservation Society of Newport County. Opening hours vary so call in advance of a visit. Entrance fee.

Hadwen House
96 Main Street, at Pleasant Street
Nantucket
Tel: (568) 228 1894 (group tours)
Fee charged for walking tours.

Lizzie Borden Museum
92 Second Street, Fall River
Tel: (508) 675 7333
www.lizzie-borden.com
A historical Greek Revival property that is both a museum, exploring the Lizzie Borden story, and a bed and breakfast place. Daily tours July–Aug, on the half hour 11am–2.30pm; May–June tours Sat–Sun only.

Maine Lobster Museum and Hatchery, at Mount Desert Oceanarium
Thomas Bay, Bar Harbor, Maine
Tel: (207) 288 5005
Open daily 9am–5pm (summer), except Sun in mid-May to late Oct. Entrance fee.

Marine Museum
70 Water Street, Fall River
Tel: (508) 674 3533
www.marinemuseum.org
Marine artifacts and a photographic collection. Open Mon–Fri 9am–5pm; Sat noon–5pm; Sun noon–4pm.

Mashantucket Pequot Museum
110 Pequot Trail
Mashantucket, Connecticut
Tel: 1-800-411 9671
www.pequotmuseum.org
Modern building housing what claims to be the largest and most comprehensive Native American museum in the world. Open daily 9am–5pm, last admission 4pm. Entrance fee.

Mystic Seaport
Mystic, Connecticut
Tel: (203) 572 0711
www.mysticseaport.org
A large maritime museum along the waterfront on a 17-acre (7-hectare) property that contains several

replica ships and historic buildings. Open daily 9am–5pm (summer); 10am–4pm (winter). Entrance fee.

New Bedford Whaling Museum
18 Johnny Cake Hill, New Bedford
Tel: (508) 997 0046
www.whalingmuseum.org
Open daily 9am–5pm, until 9pm on second Thur of the month. Entrance fee.

Peabody Essex Museum
East India Square, Salem
Tel: (978) 745 9500; (866) 745 1876
www.pem.org
The oldest museum in the US was expanded and revamped in 2003. Open daily 10am–5pm. Entrance fee.

Submarine Force Museum
Groton, Connecticut
Tel: 1-800-343 0079; (860) 694 3174
www.ussnautilus.org
A comprehensive collection of submarine artifacts including the USS *Nautilus* (SSN 571). Open daily 9am–5pm, closed first full week in May (summer); Wed–Mon 9am–4pm (winter). Entrance fee.

Vineyard Museum
Corner of Cooke and School streets
Edgartown, Martha's Vineyard
Tel: (508) 627 4441
www.marthasvineyardhistory.org
Run by the Martha's Vineyard Historical Society at Pease House. Exhibits include the Thomas Cooke House, the Francis Foster Maritime Gallery and the Carriage Shed. Open Tues–Sat 10am–4pm (summer); Wed–Fri 1–4pm, Sat 10am–4pm (winter). Entrance fee in summer.

Miami, Florida

The restaurants and hotels of the de facto Latin capital of the United States have attracted worldwide attention, and justifiably so. Restaurants specializing in Latin American and Asian foods serve some of the best Nicaraguan, Peruvian, Colombian, Puerto Rican and Vietnamese food in America. The colorful accommodations of South Beach have set a new standard for the boutique trend in US hotels, and, along with Miami's restaurants, become an intrinsic part of the city's nightlife.

Tourist Information
Miami Visitors' Bureau
701 Brickell Avenue 2700
Tel: 800-933 8448; (305) 539 3000
www.gmcvb.com

Where to Stay
Hotel Chelsea
944 Washington Avenue
Tel: (305) 534 4069
www.thehotelchelsea.com
A three-story 1936 art deco building decked out in Japanese-style "floating" furniture and bamboo flooring, as well as bathrooms of slate tile, and glass-enclosed showers. A mere two blocks from South Beach, and a popular hangout for cocktails to boot. **$$**
The Mercury Hotel
100 Collins Avenue
Tel: (305) 398 3000
www.mercuryresort.com
This sleek, Mediterranean Revival-style edifice sits in a quiet section of the art deco district in South Beach, sporting Italian furnishings, Belgian linens, and a stream-lined style that is 100 percent Miami. **$$$**

Hotel Price Guide

Price categories are based on the average cost of a double room per night.
$ = $50 or less
$$ = $50–150
$$$ = $150–250

Eating Out
Tantra
1445 Pennsylvania Avenue
Tel: (305) 672 4765
Specializing in "aphrodisiac cuisine," this exotic restaurant sets a romantic mood with a dark and cozy setting featuring a grass floor and a water wall. The menu stays just as intimate, with offerings like the Tantra Plate (assorted oysters, grilled eel and lobster *wontons*), silken-seared *foie gras*, and that ultimate dessert of love, the Goddess Cake, a flourless confection of dark chocolate *ganache* and *crème anglaise*. **$$$**
Versailles
3555 Southwest Eighth Street
Tel: (305) 444 0240
A popular Little Havana diner with wall-to-wall mirrors and a friendly atmosphere that appeals as much to families as late-night clubbers. Of the Cuban sandwiches on the menu, the *media noche* (ham, pork and cheese) stands out, and you can't go wrong with the *arroz con pollo* (chicken with yellow rice). **$**

Culture and Attractions
St-Bernard de Clairvaux
16711 West Dixie Highway
Tel: (304) 945 1461
www.spanishmonastery.co
This 10th-century monastery was shipped here in pieces from Spain at the behest of newspaper magnate William Randolph Hearst. Now anyone can tour the beautiful cloistered structure in a setting that evokes a simpler millennia.
Miami Metro Zoo
12400 SW 152nd Street
Tel: (305) 251 0400
Open year-round, daily 10am–5pm. Entrance fee.
Miami Seaquarium
4400 Rickenbecker Causeway, Key Biscayne
Tel: (305) 361 5705
All the wonders of the deep. Open year-round, daily 9.30am–5pm. Entrance fee.

Southeastern Ports

CHARLESTON

Charleston draws on more of its past than just the Civil War. Many chefs in town have preserved and evolved the local tradition of low country cooking, a hearty cuisine that mixes seafood and rice with Carolina, Caribbean, French, English, and Spanish ingredients. Likewise, the lodging industry has maintained a number of old buildings as hotels.

Tourist Information
Charleston Visitor Information Center
375 Meeting Street
Tel: (843) 853 8000
www.charlestoncvb.com

Where to Stay
Andrew Pinckney Inn
40 Pinckney Street
Tel: (843) 937 8800
www.andrewpinckneyinn.com
Cleaned up quite a bit since its days as an 18th-century stable, this charming inn is the only place in town that offers a three-story atrium, a courtyard and meals on a rooftop terrace overlooking the homes and churches of the historic district. **$$**
Francis Marion Hotel
387 King Street
Tel: (843) 722 0600
This 1924 hotel had its neo-classical features (notably a knock-out lobby that resembles a Greek temple) restored with a multi-million-dollar award from the National Trust for Historic Preservation. Rooms have European-style bed linens and marble bathrooms, offer great views of downtown's Marion Square and Charleston's South Harbor. **$$$**

Eating Out
Peninsula Grill
112 North Market Street
Tel: (843) 722 2345
Done up with chandeliers, oil paintings and velvet-padded walls, and a courtyard for an entrance, this enchanting spot gives low country cuisine the high-end

treatment. Dishes like country oyster stew with wild mushroom grits, Carolina quail stuffed with pecan cornbread and a widely-praised coconut cake have made the restaurant one of Charleston's best. **$$$$**

Sticky Fingers Restaurant
235 Meeting Street
Tel: (843) 853 7427
A favorite barbecue joint that serves its ribs in five different styles. But you'll want to try the local way: Carolina Sweet, served South Carolina style with a mustard-based sauce. **$$**

Culture and Attractions
The Charleston Museum
360 Meeting Street
Tel: (843) 722 2996
www.charlestonmuseum.org
Across the road from the Charleston Visitor Center. Open Mon–Sat 9am–5pm; Sun 1–5pm. Entrance fee.
The museum also manages two historic houses: the **Joseph Manigault House** and the **Heyward-Washington House**. Open Mon–Sat 10am–5pm (last tour 4.30pm); Sun 1–5pm. Entrance fee.

The Citadel Museum
171 Moultrie Street
Tel: (843) 953 6846
Archives and artifacts from the Military College of South Carolina, which was founded in 1842. Open Sun–Fri 2–5pm; Sat noon–5pm. The archives are open Mon–Fri 8.30am–5pm.

Edmonston-Alston House
21 East Battery
Tel: (843) 722 7171
Open Tues–Sun 10am–4.30pm; Sun–Mon 1.30–4.30pm.

Fort Sumter National Monument
1214 Middle Street, Sullivan's Island, Charleston Harbor
Tel: (843) 883 3123
www.nps.gov/fosu
A National Park preserving the spot where the first shot of the Civil War rang out on April 12, 1861 (the fort itself was reduced to rubble after four years of fighting). Open daily 10am–5.30pm (Apr–Labor Day); 10am–4pm (Mar, Sept–Nov). Ferries for the fort depart from **Fort**

Sumter Visitor's Center on the mainland at Liberty Square, Charleston Harbor.

Historic Charleston Foundation
Tel: (843) 723 1623
www.historiccharleston.org
A collection of historic and cultural landmarks of the antebellum owned, managed and preserved by the Historic Charleston Foundation. Properties include: **Aiken-Rhett House**, 48 Elizabeth Street; **Nathaniel Russell House**, 51 Meeting Street. Open Mon–Sat 10am–5pm, Sun 2–5pm. Entrance fee.

The Slave Mart Museum
6 Chalmers Street
Tel: (843) 724 7395
Museum of African-American history, arts, artifacts and crafts. Open Mon–Sat 10am–5pm; Sun 2–5pm.

South Carolina Aquarium
100 Aquarium Wharf
Tel: (843) 720 1990
www.scaquarium.org
The city's most visited attraction on the waterfront. Open Mon–Sat 9am–6pm, Sun noon–6pm, last ticket 5pm (summer); Mon–Sat 9am–6pm, Sun noon–5pm, last ticket 4pm (fall/winter). Closed Thanksgiving and Christmas.

NORFOLK

In Norfolk, the best hotels aren't on the beach, just as the best food isn't necessarily from the ocean. The city has preserved enough of its history to offer some historically-rich lodging and dining options.

Tourist Information
Norfolk Visitors' Center
232 East Main Street
Tel: (757) 664 6620
www.norfolkcvb.com

Where to Stay
Page House Inn
323 Fairfax Avenue
Tel: (757) 625 5033
www.pagehouseinn.com
Built as a mansion over a century ago, this Georgian Revival beauty in the Ghent Historic District has operated as an inn since 1990.

Suite names like Master Percy's Room and Missy Hulda's Room heighten the Victoriana already evident in the décor. **$$**

The Tazewell Hotel & Suites
245 Granby Street
Tel: (757) 623 6200
The subject of a $7-million renovation, this seven-story, early 20th-century building is stuffed with tasteful furnishings and a lot of history. Built in 1906 atop the stump of the locally-famous Wishing Oak, the hotel was the first building in the area with air conditioning and elevators. **$$**

Eating Out
Doumar's Diner & Curb Service
1919 Monticello Avenue
Tel: (757) 627 4163
www.doumars.com
A classic 1950s drive-in (though it's been running since 1907) that gave birth to the ice cream cone. The place still makes cones from its original machine, along with hot dogs, hamburgers and North Carolina barbecues from more modern appliances. **$**

Freemason Abbey Restaurant
209 West Freemason Street
Tel: (757) 622 3966
www.freemasonabbey.com
This restaurant sticks to the traditional side of the American menu as it serves up fresh lobster, seafood, prime ribs and other staples in a Victorian church. **$$$**

Restaurant Prices

Price categories are based on the average cost of a meal for two, excluding drinks, tax and tip.
$ = **$20** or less
$$ = **$20–40**
$$$ = **$40–60**
$$$$ = **$60** and up

Culture and Attractions
Chrysler Museum of Art
245 West Olney Road
Tel: (757) 664 6200
US and European masterpieces, plus decorative arts. Open Thur–Sat 10am–5pm, Wed 10am–9pm, Sun 1–5pm. Entrance fee.

Nauticus National Maritime Center
One Waterside Drive
Tel: (757) 664 1000
www.nauticus.org
No, it's not the submarine Captain
Nemo took 20,000 leagues under
the sea, it's a huge hands-on
museum that features the
battleship *Wisconsin* and several
exhibits on the ocean. Also home to
the **Tugboat Museum**, tel: (757)
627 4884. Both open daily 11am–
5pm (Memorial Day to Labor Day);
Tues–Sun (winter). Entrance fee.

WASHINGTON DC

The nation's capital has much to
offer in the form of dining,
accommodations, historical
monuments and world-class
museums – more than enough to
justify a prolonged visit to the city,
either before or after a cruise.

Tourist Information
**DC Chamber of Commerce Visitor
Information Center**
1300 Pennsylvania Avenue NW, in
the Ronald Reagan Building and
International Trade Center
Tel: 1-866-324 7386; 1-800-422
8644
www.dcvisit.com
www.washington.org

Where to Stay
The Mansion on O Street
2020 O Street, NW
Tel: (202) 496 2000
Fax: (202) 659 0547
Email: hotel@omansion.com
www.omansion.com
Eclectic decoration and furnishings
– a mixture of Victoriana, avant-
garde, art deco and modern-day
decoration that reflects the
personality of the original owner.
The mansion is actually two
converted townhouses.
Reservations by fax or email only.
$$$+
Swann House B&B
1808 New Hampshire Avenue, NW
Tel: (202) 265 4414
www.swannhouse.com
Top rate B&B near to Dupont Circle.
Neo-Romanesque architecture,

some rooms with a fireplace and
Jacuzzi, and furnished with both
antique and contemporary décor.
There is also a rooftop deck and
pool. **$–$$$+**

Eating Out
Sam and Harry's
1200 19th Street NW
Tel: (202) 296 4333
One of the best steak houses in the
US, it will not disappoint. The décor
features mahogany and stained
glass, while the menu includes
prime beef, fresh seafood and good
American wine. **$$$$**
Taberna del Alabardero
1776 I Street NW, at 18th Street
Tel: (202) 429 220
Consistently rated among
Washington DC's best restaurants,
this is the place to go for authentic
Spanish cuisine. **$$$$**

Culture and Attractions
National Gallery of Art
National Mall, between Third and
Ninth streets, at Constitution
Avenue NW
Tel: (202) 737 4215
www.nga.gov
Open year-round Mon–Sat
10am–5pm; Sun 11–6pm.
Lincoln Memorial Museum
900 Ohio Drive SW
Tel: (202) 426 6841
www.nps.gov
Built to resemble a Greek temple
the Memorial is a tribute to
President Abraham Lincoln.
Managed by the National Park
Service. Open year-round daily
8am–11.30pm.
Smithsonian Institution
1000 Jefferson Drive SW
www.si.edu
Fourteen museums on the National
Mall, including the **National Air and
Space Museum** at Sixth and
Independence Avenue SW, and
the **Hirshorn Museum** at the corner
of 7th Street SW, and
Independence Avenue. Open daily
10am–5.30pm.
Thomas Jefferson Memorial
900 Ohio Drive SW
Tel: (202) 426 6841
www.nps.gov
Run by the National Park Service.

Open year-round daily 8am–
11.30pm.
Washington Monument
15th Street SW
Open year-round daily 9am–5pm.

BALTIMORE

The city's food and lodging are as
eclectic as the city itself, but most
people come here for the seafood
joints and the old hotels. In both
regards, Baltimore rarely
disappoints its visitors.

Tourist Information
Baltimore Visitor Center
Constellation Pier in Inner Harbor
Tel: 800-282 6632; (410) 837 4636

Where to Stay
The Admiral Fell Inn
888 South Broadway
Tel: 800-292 4667
www.admiralfell.com
This stately brick Federal
style building, a former vinegar
factory dating back to the
19th century, gets its name from
the seafaring Baltimorian for whom
the neighborhood, Fell's Point, is
also named. A cozy pub and
Hamilton's Restaurant are on site.
$$$

Hotel Price Guide

Price categories are based on
the average cost of a double
room per night.
$** = **$50 or less
$$** = **$50–150
$$$** = **$150–250

Peabody Court
612 Cathedral Street
Tel: (410) 234 0550
www.peabodycourt.snbhotels.com
A stand-out in the Mount Vernon
Square neighborhood, this
Renaissance Revival-style hotel
has been around since 1928,
and its 6-ft (1.8-meter) Baccarat
chandelier, paneled library,
and period furnishings retain
a 1920s' sense of classiness.
$$

Eating Out

Legal Seafoods
100 East Pratt Street
Tel: (410) 332 7360
This Inner Harbor landmark serves almost every fish in the seven seas in a semi-cafeteria setting with a delightfully cheesy nautical theme. The place is touristy, but for a good reason: the quality of the seafood and the selection of seafood-inspired pasta dishes. **$$**

Pierpoint
1822 Alice Anna Street
Tel: (410) 675 2080
www.pierpointrestaurant.com
The glaring yellow walls and green booths shouldn't distract you from some of the city's best seafood. Crab cakes, served traditional and smoked, star on a menu of exceptional dishes like walnut-crusted red snapper and the paella like *cioppino*. **$$$$**

Culture and Attractions

American Visionary Art Museum
800 Key Highway
Tel: (410) 244 1900
www.avam.org
The four-story, 55-ft (17-meter) tall wind-powered sculpture of spinning junk called the Giant Whirligig outside the entrance is just the beginning of the weird and wacky creations you'll encounter at this fun fringe art museum. Open Tues–Sun 10am–6pm. Entrance fee.

Babe Ruth Birthplace and Baltimore Orioles Museum
216 Emory Street
Tel: (410) 727 1539
www.baberuthmuseum.com
Open Mon–Sun 10am–5pm, until 7pm on Orioles home game days (summer); 10am–4pm (winter). Entrance fee.

Baltimore Maritime Museum
802 South Caroline Street
Tel: (410) 396 3453
www.baltomaritimemuseum.org
A collection of ships that are also national landmarks. Open daily 10am–6pm (summer); Fri–Sun 10am–5pm (winter). Chesapeake Lighthouse: daily 10am–6pm (summer); *Torsk* submarine: 10am–8.30pm (summer); *Taney*: 10am–5pm (summer).

Maryland Science Center
601 Light Street
Tel: (410) 685 5225
www.mdsci.org
Open Tues–Fri 10am–5pm; Sat 10am–6pm; Sun noon–5pm (Sept–May). Entrance fee.

National Aquarium
501 East Pratt Street
Tel: (410) 576 3800
www.aqua.org
Open year-round daily, but times change according to the season so call ahead for hours. Entrance fee.

Peabody Institute
1 East Mount Vernon Place
Tel: (410) 724 0009
www.peabody.jhu.edu
On the campus of the Johns Hopkins University the institute was included in the $26-million campus development. Call ahead for opening hours.

The Walters Art Museum
600 North Charles Street
Tel: (410) 547 9000
www.thewalters.org
Open Wed–Sun 10am–5pm. Entrance fee.

PHILADELPHIA

The city may have popularized the cheese-steak (and more power to it for doing so), but you'll find greater culinary choices than meat and dairy concoctions in this town. There's also a great variety of hotels, both old and new, to choose from.

Tourist Information

Philadelphia Visitor Center
JFK Plaza
Tel: (215) 636 1666
www.gophila.com

Where to Stay

Antique Row Bed & Breakfast
341 South 12th Street
Tel: (215) 592 7802
www.antiquerowbnb.com
The wholesale antique dealers of Antique Row in the Center City neighborhood have gone, but beautiful 18th-century buildings like this one remain. The B&B exudes comfortable Victorian charm from

the tiled fireplace to the eclectic period furniture. **$$**

Latham Hotel
135 South 17th Street
Tel: 877-528 4261
www.lathamhotel.com
Victorian-style accommodation in a beautiful building filled with European furnishings and lots of deep-red and green fabrics. Bay windows overlooking shops and restaurants. **$$$**

Eating Out

City Tavern
138 South 2nd Street
Tel: (215) 413 1443
www.citytavern.com
This restaurant dates back to Colonial times – Paul Revere stopped here once with news that the British had closed Boston Harbor. Did he stay for the mallard duck sausage or paillard of salmon? If he didn't, he missed out. **$$$$**

Restaurant Prices

Price categories are based on the average cost of a meal for two, excluding drinks, tax and tip.
$ = $20 or less
$$ = $20–40
$$$ = $40–60
$$$$ = $60 and up

Silk City Diner
425 Spring Garden Street
Tel: (215) 592 8838
A 1950s diner done up in pink and green Formica, a jukebox and lots of stainless steel. Plus all the burgers, pancakes, shakes and other comfort food you'd expect, with specialties like chocolate bread pudding thrown in for good measure. **$**

Culture and Attractions

Independence National Historical Park
143 South Third Street
Tel: 800-967 2283
www.nps.gov/inde/home.htm
This history-rich area encompasses the Liberty Bell and Independence Hall, where the Declaration of Independence and the US Constitution were haggled over and

signed. The Liberty Bell occupies a pavilion that opened in Fall of 2003. Open year-round daily 9am–5pm. Entrance fee.

Philadelphia City Hall
1400 John F. Kennedy Boulevard
National Historic Landmark. Tours
Mon–Fri 12.30pm; tours to the tower every 15 minutes
9.30am–4.30pm.

The West Coast

LOS CABOS, BAJA

Ships on Mexican Riviera itineraries use Los Cabos as a port of call, while those cruising the Sea of Cortéz typically embark in La Paz, four hours north. Developed by the Mexican government as a tourism destination in the 1970s, Los Cabos resembles Southern California or Hawaii rather than its Mexican counterparts. Golf courses and extravagant resort hotels are the norm; sportfishing is one of the main attractions. Development of the region seems never ending. It's the most expensive destination in Mexico, with astronomical hotel room rates and Southern California restaurant prices. The unit of currency is the peso, but US dollars are readily accepted. There are no official tourist information offices in Los Cabos. Timeshare hustlers at the airport and on the sidewalks are quick to offer advice in exchange for several hours of your time. If you plan to extend your stay before or after a cruise then your cruise line or hotel activity desks are the best source of information.

Where to Stay

Moderately priced hotels are hard to find in this region, where most places charge upwards of $200 a night for a double in high season, and rates of $500 a night are common. None of the resort hotels cost under $200 a night.

Casa Natalia
Boulevard Mijares 4
San José del Cabo
Tel: (624) 142 5100
www.casanatalia.com
This architecturally stunning

boutique hotel is both comfortable and chic. The rooms are artfully decorated with Mexican folk art; suites have large terraces with hot tubs and hammocks. The restaurant is innovative and intimate; its popularity among locals and visitors makes reservations essential in high season. **$$$+**

Solmar Suites
Avenue Solmar at Boulevard
Marina, Cabo San Lucas
Tel: (624) 143 3535
www.solmar.com
A longtime favorite with rooms built into the rock walls of the cliffs at land's end, a broad beach with thundering waves, and a good Mexican restaurant. Many of the guests and staff members have been around for decades; their camaraderie gives the hotel a *mi casa es su casa* ("my home is your home") ambiance. **$$–$$$**

Eating Out

Damiana
Boulevard Mijares 8
Tel: (624) 142 0499
All the charm of San José is evident in this restored house with trees and bougainvillea shading the candlelit courtyard. The signature shrimp steak is exceptional, especially when accompanied by a *margarita* made with *damiana (see the Shopping box on page 339).* **$–$$$**

Marisquería Mazatlán
Mendoza at 16 Septiembre, Cabo
San Lucas
Tel: (624) 143 8565.
You'll find more locals than tourists feasting on seafood cocktails, marinated octopus, and fried fish at this busy restaurant. The décor is basic plastic and Formica, but the food is outstanding. **$–$$$**

Restaurant Prices

Price categories are based on the average cost of a meal for two, excluding drinks, tax and tip.
$ = $20 or less
$$ = $20–40
$$$ = $40–60
$$$$ = $60 and up

Attractions

The Glass Factory
Off Highway 19, Cabo San Lucas
Tel: (624) 143 0255
Master glassblowers create platters, vases, and stemware at huge blazing ovens. Visitors can try blowing a glass creation, and shop for hand-crafted glassware.

Beaches

Playa Santa María
Highway 1, Km 12
One of the best swimming and snorkeling beaches in Los Cabos, with a clean curve of sand and clear water. Snorkel gear and umbrellas are sometimes available for rent.

LA PAZ, BAJA

La Paz is the commercial and civic capital of Baja California Sur, a place where nearly everyone who lives in the state eventually comes to shop and take care of government business. Tourism is a secondary concern here, and visitors are quickly absorbed into the stream of activity on the city streets and the beaches.

Tourist Information

Baja Sur State Tourist Office
Malecón, at Avenida de Septiembre
Tel: (612) 124 0199
www.vivalapaz.com

Where to Stay

El Angel Azul
Independencia 518, Downtown
Tel: (612) 125 5130
www.elangelazul.com
An enchanting B&B in a restored historic courthouse near the main plaza, filled with art and handcrafted furnishings. The courtyard is a cool respite from the city, and guests feel at home in the cozy lounge. **$–$$**

La Concha Beach Resort
Carretera a Pichilingue, Km 5
between Downtown and Pichilingue
Tel: (612) 121 6344
www.laconcha.com
The closest La Paz comes to a full-blown beach resort is this sprawling compound a few minutes from downtown. Basic rooms and well-equipped condos, the water

Shopping in Baja

Some shops along the Malecón sell a limited selection of crafts from Baja's ranch settlements, locally handcrafted pottery, and folk art from mainland Mexico. Look for ironwood carvings of whales, dolphins, and marlin, lamps and sculptures made from cardón cacti, and Damiana liqueur from a desert plant, believed to be an aphrodisiac.

sports center and dive shop line a decent beach on the bay. **$$–$$$**

Eating Out
El Bismark II
Degollado at Altamirano, Downtown
Tel: (612) 122 4854
Fresh *ceviche*, fried whole red snapper, and grilled lobster are served in a somewhat lackadaisical manner in a neighborhood institution. The TV over the bar sometimes receives more attention than the customers, but the food is worth the wait. **$–$$$**
La Pazta
Allende 36, Downtown
Tel: (612) 125 1195
Pastas, pizzas, fresh salads, and imported cheeses and wines are served stylishly in a trendy black-and-white trattoria. The small hotel beside the restaurant is popular with European travelers and residents of Los Cabos on shopping excursions. **$–$$$**

Culture and Attractions
Museo de Antropología
Corner Altamirano and 5 de Mayo
Tel: (805) 683 3036 (information)
www.folklorico.com/lugares/museo-la-paz
An excellent overview of Baja's history, plus fossils and whale skeletons. Open Tues–Sun 9am–7pm. Entrance fee.
Museo de los Misiones (Museum of Anthropology and History)
Calle Salvatierra, Loreto
Tel: (805) 683 3036
www.folklorico.com/lugares/museo-la-paz
Exhibits include religious relics and agricultural tools. Open Tues–Sun. Entrance fee.

SAN FRANCISCO, CALIFORNIA

There's no single San Francisco cuisine, but the city does Mexican, Japanese and Chinese particularly well, along with American "fusion." Several chefs of late have also taken advantage of such local food resources as organic dairies, wine makers, olive-oil producers, bakeries, and fishmongers. As for hotels, the fog-drenched sky's the limit, from the ritziest historic stalwart to the hippest boutique to the coziest Victorian inn.

Tourist Information
San Francisco Visitor Information Center
900 Market Street
Tel: (415) 391 2000
www.sfvisitor.org

Where to Stay
The Beresford Arms Hotel
701 Post Street
Tel: 1-800-533 6533
www.beresford.com/arms
Listed on the National Register of Historic Places, this Victorian classic has been housing visitors in the Nob Hill district since 1910. Three blocks from Union Square, the hotel is also home to The White Horse, an English-style restaurant. **$$–$$$**
Seal Rock Inn
545 Point Lobos Avenue
Tel: 888-732 5762
www.sealrockinn.com
Out in the northwest tip of the city, where the ocean roils, this is *the* place to stay, and not just because pickings are otherwise slim in this part of town. San Francisco's only ocean-front hotel is done up in a funky 1970s style, offering spacious rooms, some equipped

Hotel Price Guide

Price categories are based on the average cost of a double room per night.
$ = $50 or less
$$ = $50–150
$$$ = $150–250

with fireplaces to fight off the cold when the fog rolls in. **$$$**

Eating Out
Chava's
3248 18th Street
Tel: (415) 552 9387
This laid-back mission eatery serves inexpensive Mexican food to a loyal clientele. The cheap *burritos* are always favorites, but the *birria* (goat stew), the *carne asada* (roast meat), and slow-cooked chicken *mole* are stand-outs. **$**
Cliff House
1090 Point Lobos Avenue
Tel: (415) 386 3330
Located just below the Seal Rock Inn, this 1909 neo-classic landmark serves seafood in an unbeatable setting overlooking the Seal Rocks, the Marin Headlands, and the ocean. Crab Louis may well be the most popular dish, but if you just want to take in the view, you can pick up a sandwich at one of the two bars. **$$$**

Culture and Attractions
Alcatraz Island
From Pier 39
Tel: (415) 773 1188; 705 5555
www.pier39.com
Daily departures year-round; advance booking essential.
Guinness Book of World Records Museum
235 Jefferson Street
Tel: (415) 771 9890
Open Sun–Thur 11am–10pm, Fri–Sat 10am–midnight. Entrance fee.
Musée Mecanique
Pier 45 at end of Taylor Street, Fisherman's Wharf
Tel: (415) 346 2000
www.museemecanique.citysearch.com
While perusing the 160 antique, coin-operated machines in this restored penny arcade, be sure to drop a coin into Laughing Sal, the formidable "fat lady" who's been scaring kids for 60 years. Open daily.
Ripley's Believe It or Not!
175 Jefferson Street
Tel: (415) 771 6188
www.ripleysf.com
Entertainment complex with inter-active displays and galleries. Open

daily, Sun–Thur 10am–10pm, Fri–Sat 10am–midnight. Entrance fee.

Wax Museum
Fisherman's Wharf
Tel: 800-439 4305
www.waxmuseum.com
Open Mon–Fri 10am–9pm, Sat–Sun 9am–11pm. Entrance fee.

Hawaii

HONOLULU, OAHU

To stay right on the beach in Oahu, visitors generally have to check into a resort – which means paying high prices. Staying at a less expensive hotel or inn a few blocks away from the beach is the more practical option. The island's restaurants produce a wide variety of ethnic foods, but a local specialty worth trying is the plate lunch. Served from lunch counters and lunch wagons, these fast and inexpensive home-cooked meals serve up entrees like beef *teriyaki*, *mahi mahi* and *shoyu* chicken with rice and macaroni salad and rich gravy.

Tourist Information
Oahu Visitors' Bureau
Pauahi Tower, Suite 47
1001 Bishop Street
Tel: 877-525 6248
www.visit-oahu.com

Where to Stay
Aston Waikiki Beach Hotel
2570 Kalakaua Avenue
Tel: (808) 926 6400
Following a $30-million refurbishment, this hotel makes you feel as if you are stepping onto the set of a 1960s Elvis movie. The rooms are decked out in aloha-print bedspreads, bamboo curtains painted with hula dancers, and Indonesian teak furnishings, while the lobby, halls and pool area are lined with surfboards, *tikis*, and traditional *tapa* prints. In the morning, a ukulele player entertains on the terrace. **$$$**
New Otani Kaimana Beach Hotel
2863 Kalakaua Avenue
Tel: (808) 923 1555
www.kaimana.com
One of the few reasonably-priced

hotels on the beach (Sans Souci), it was built in 1964 sits across from Kapiolani Park. All the rooms, decorated in a minimalist Asian design aesthetic imported by the Japanese owners, have balconies overlooking either Diamond Head Crater, the park, or the ocean. **$$**

Eating Out
Café Haleiwa
66–460 Kamehameha Highway
Tel: (808) 637 5516
A popular surfer hangout serving sandwiches and acclaimed breakfast food to people bound for the beach. You can't go wrong with any of the omelets. **$**
Hau Tree Lanai
2863 Kalakaua Avenue
Tel: (808) 921 7066
A restaurant on Sans Souci Beach serving Pacific Rim delicacies under the limbs of an ancient banyan tree that once shaded Robert Louis Stevenson. *Poi* pancakes, moonfish, and *opakapaka* (Hawaiian pink snapper) rank high among the specialties. **$$$$**

Restaurant Prices

Price categories are based on the average cost of a meal for two, excluding drinks, tax and tip.
$ = $20 or less
$$ = $20–40
$$$ = $40–60
$$$$ = $60 and up

Culture and Attractions
Bishops Museum
1525 Bernice Street
Tel: (808) 847 3511
www.bishopmuseum.org
The museum is close to Halona Point in Waikiki. Open year-round daily 9am–5pm. Entrance fee.
Polynesian Cultural Center
55 Kamehameha Highway, Laie
Tel: (808) 367 7060; (808) 293 3333
www.polynesia.com
A 42-acre (17-hectare) park filled with recreated villages scattered around an artificial lagoon traversed by canoe. Costumed performers enact the songs and dances of the

Pacific islands and somehow inject an air of dignity into proceedings that would be cheesy in less capable hands. Open year-round Mon–Sat 12.30–6pm. Entrance fee.
USS *Arizona* Memorial
1 Arizona Memorial Place
Tel: (808) 422 0561
www.arizonamemorial.org
Hawaii's most visited site. Visitor center open year-round daily 7.30am–5pm.

Upper Mississippi River Route

ST LOUIS, MISSOURI

Though filled with a broad range of dining options, the city that invented iced tea and popularized hot dogs and hamburgers at the 1904 World's Fair still does Midwestern-style comfort food best. More recently, St Louis has discovered such culinary creations as toasted ravioli, frozen custard "concrete" and gooey butter coffee cake. Like those offbeat dishes, a handful of unusual hotels stand out amid more conventional offerings.

Tourist Information
St Louis Visitors' Center
Kiener Plaza at Sixth and Chestnut
Tel: 800-325 7962
www.explorestlouis.com

Where to Stay
Cheshire Inn & Lodge
6300 Clayton Road
Tel: 888-860 2966
www.cheshirelodge.com
This Tudor-style hotel slathers on the British charm with its own double-decker bus, Victorian furniture, suites with names like "The Treehouse at Sherwood Forest," and a lovely old tavern. **$$**
Napoleon's Retreat Bed & Breakfast
1815 Lafayette Avenue
Tel: (314) 772 6979
www.napoleonsretreat.com
In the Lafayette Square neighborhood, one of the best collections of Victorian homes in the nation, this 1880 French Second Empire Victorian stands out. With a double set of 12-ft (3½-meter) doors, period

furniture and plenty of art and antiques scattered about, it captures the look and feel of 19th-century St Louis. **$$**

Eating Out

Duff's Restaurant
392 North Euclid Avenue
Tel: (314) 361 0522
This Central West End bistro serves international nouveau cuisine such as *coronettas de pollo* (chicken enchiladas) and spinach feta strudel. **$$$$**

Rigazzi's
4945 Daget Boulevard
Tel: (314) 772 4900
A local favorite for Italian cooking, with a big menu and big dishes like toasted ravioli and veal Parmiciano (veal covered with cheese and baked in meat sauce). **$$**

Ted Drewes Frozen Custard
6726 Chippewa
Tel: (314) 481 2652
A Mecca for lovers of that thick dairy product called "concrete" since it opened on this stretch of old Route 66 in 1929. Vanilla remains the only flavor after all these years, but that hardly matters given the seemingly endless choice of toppings – fresh roasted pecans, hot fudge, butterscotch, macadamia nuts, and a secret chocolate sauce.

Culture and Attractions

Missouri History Museum
Lindell and DeBaliviere streets
Tel: (314) 747 4599
www.mohistory.org
Open daily 10am–6pm.

Museum of Westward Expansion
11 N. Fourth Street
Tel: (314) 655 1700
Good overview of the Lewis and Clark expedition. Open daily 8am–10pm (summer); 9am–6pm (winter).

St Louis Art Museum
3750 Washington Boulevard
Tel: (314) 535 4660
www.slfp.com
An excellent collection of contemporary art. Open Tues–Sun 10am–5pm, Fri until 9pm. Free, except for the Shoemberg Collection. No charge on Fri.

St Louis Zoo
1 Government Drive
Tel: (314) 781 0900
www.concierge.com
Open daily 8am–7pm (summer); 9am–5pm (winter). Free.

ST PAUL, MINNESOTA

In the ongoing sibling struggle of the Twin Cities, Minneapolis' restaurants and hotels typically get all the attention. But like any ignored little brother, St Paul has its very own special gifts to offer the visitor.

Tourist Information

St Paul Convention and Visitors Bureau
175 West Kellogg Boulevard, Suite 502
Tel: 800-627 6101

Where to Stay

Covington Inn Bed & Breakfast
Pier 1, Harriet Island
Tel: (651) 292 1411
www.covingtoninn.com
Its fixtures have been salvaged, its antiques and art all bear a nautical theme, and mahogany, brass and bronze line its walls from stem to stern. This may be the only inn you'll find housed in a restored 1946 towboat, moored in the reflection of downtown St Paul. **$$$**

The St Paul Hotel
350 Market Street
Tel: 800-292 9292
www.stpaulhotel.com
Around since 1910, this is the city's only historic hotel, but lack of competition hasn't made it go soft. Its early 20th-century trimmings and traditions like High Tea continually win it four-star ratings. **$$$**

Hotel Price Guide

Price categories are based on the average cost of a double room per night.
$ = $50 or less
$$ = $50–150
$$$ = $150–250

Eating Out

Cossetta's Italian Market and Pizzeria
211 West Seventh Street
Tel: (651) 222 3476
Known around St Paul for some of the finest pizza in the city, this combination grocery-cafeteria has been baking, frying and twirling Italian food since 1911. **$**

St Paul Grill
350 Market Street
Tel: (651) 224 7455
www.stpaulgrill.com
As fancy and immaculate as the St Paul Hotel, which houses it, the Grill serves some of the city's finest fare, including pan-fried walleye fillet and cracked black-pepper sirloin, as well as turtle tart and root beer float for dessert. Many a local power broker can be spotted between the tinted glass partitions. **$$$$**

Culture and Attractions

Cathedral of St Paul
239 Selby Street
Tel: (651) 228 1766
Built between 1906 and 1915 with Italian marble, and bronze grills, the fourth largest cathedral in the United States underwent a $35-million refurbishment to replace the copper roof and clean the outer walls.

James J. Hill House
240 Summit Avenue
Tel: (651) 297 2555
www.mnhs.org/places
Splendid neo-Romanesque mansion with 13 bathrooms. Open Wed–Sat 10am–3.30pm; Sun 1–3.30pm. Entrance fee.

Minnesota Museum
120 West Kellogg Boulevard
Tel: (651) 221 9444
www.smm.org/pvisitorinfo
Excellent science museum. Open Thur 11–8pm; Fri–Sat 11am–4pm; Sun 1–5pm. Entrance fee.

Minnesota State Capitol Building
75 Martin Luther King Boulevard
Tel: (651) 296 2881
www.mnhs.org/places
Open Mon–Fri 9am–4pm; Sat 10am–3pm; Sun 1–4pm. Entrance fee.

More Upper Mississippi Attractions
Fort Madison
811 Avenue E, Fort Madison
Burlington, Iowa
Tel: (319) 372 6318
www.oldfortmadison.com
Open Wed–Sun 9.30am–5pm
(summer); Mon–Fri 9.30am–5pm
(May and Sept). Entrance fee.
Galena/Jo Davies County Historical Museum
211 S. Bench Street
Galena, Illinois
Tel: (815) 777 9129.
Diverse exhibits, from steamboats
to lead mining and the Civil War.
Open daily 9am–4.30pm.
Entrance fee.
Mathias Ham House
2241 Lincoln Avenue
Dubuque, Iowa
Tel: (319) 557 9545
www.dubuque365.com
Opulent antebellum mansion with
an old log cabin on site. Open daily
10am–4.30pm. Entrance fee.

Lower Mississippi River Route

NEW ORLEANS

Get ready for a fascinating city
overflowing with spicy food, spicy
music, and a vibrant and varied
history.

Tourist Information
New Orleans Convention and Visitors' Bureau
1520 Sugar Bowls Drive
New Orleans, LA 70112
Tel: 1-800-672 6124
www.nawlins.com

Where to Stay
The Hotel Monteleone
214 Rue Royale
Tel: 800-535 9595
A historic, landmark hotel, right in
the French Quarter, with 600
rooms, roof-top pool and health
club, plus the famous Carousel
Lounge. **$$$**
Hotel Royal
1006 Rue Royal
Tel: 800-776 3901
Small French Quarter hotel with

Hotel Price Guide

Price categories are based on
the average cost of a double
room per night.
$ = $50 or less
$$ = $50–150
$$$ = $150–250

private brick courtyard and
splashing fountain, individually
decorated rooms, and buckets of
antique charm. **$$–$$$**

Eating Out
Don't miss Cajun and Creole
specialties such as crawfish
etouffee, *gumbo*, and *jambalya*.
There's a strong Italian-American
influence too, and seafood,
seafood, seafood.
Acme Oyster House
724 Iberville Street
Tel: (504) 522 5973
A French Quarter legend for just-
shucked oysters, draft beer, and
huge fried po-boy sandwiches. Dig
in. **$$–$$$**
Antoine's Restaurant
713–17 Rue Saint Louis
Tel: (504) 581 442
The traditional big-night-out
restaurant where the menus are
written in French; operated by the
same family for more than 150
years, and known for its rich
seafood Creole dishes. Male diners
require a jacket. **$$$–$$$$**

Shore Activities
Excursions
Walking tours of the French Quarter
and Garden districts, antique-
shopping on Royal and Magazine
streets, the New Orleans Museum
of Art and its sculpture garden,
coffee at Café du Monde, Jackson
Square, the French Market.

Music, Music, Music
New Orleans is a city steeped in
jazz, blues, *zydeco*, cajun, rock, you
name it. Each club attracts a
different crowd, so find your own
place in the city's favorite scene.
Famous clubs include **Preservation
Hall** (726 St Peter Street, tel: 504-
522 2841) for traditional New

Orleans jazz; **Tipitina's** (two
locations, 501 Napoleon Avenue or
235 North Peters, tel: 504-895
8477) for blues and local bands;
Snug Harbor (626 Frenchman
Street, tel: 504-949 0696) for jazz
greats from all over the country.
Frenchman Street is part of the
Faubourg District, where locals
wander from club to club all night,
sampling a range of musical flavors.

Culture and Attractions
Audubon Aquarium of the Americas
1 Canal Street
Tel: 800-774 7394
www.auduboninstitute.org
Open daily 9.30am–6pm.
Entrance fee.
St Louis Cathedral
Jackson Square
Tel: (314) 533 0544 for tours
Open daily 6am–5pm; tours Mon–Fri
10am–3pm.

MEMPHIS, TENNESSEE

Memphis has plenty of Southern
cooking, but not a lot of locally-
owned Southern hospitality. Finding
a non-chain hotel for under $200 a
night takes some doing, but it can
be done.

Tourist Information
Tennessee State Welcome Center
119 North Riverside Drive
Tel: (901) 543 5333
www.memphistravel.com

Where to Stay
Elvis Presley's Heartbreak Hotel
3734 Elvis Presley Boulevard
Tel: (901) 332 1000
www.elvis.com/epheartbreakhotel
Taking design cues from Graceland,
across the street, this hotel has
animal prints, retro furniture, garish
colors, and an old TV in the lobby
that plays only Elvis movies. **$$**
French Quarter Hotel
2149 Madison Avenue
Tel: 866-260 0402
A luxury Southern chateau in
midtown Memphis' historic Overton
Square.With classical French décor
and all-important ceiling fans, it's a
pastel-colored nonpareil. **$$**

Eating Out

The Arcade
540 South Main Street
Tel: (901) 526 5757
This classic diner has been serving up a mean all-day Southern breakfast and tasty pizzas since 1919. **$**

Charlie Vergo's Rendezvous
52 South Second Street
Tel: (901) 523 2746
Ribs are what you want to try during your stay, and this is the place to try them. This relaxed downtown restaurant has been cooking up some of Memphis' most acclaimed pork since 1948. **$$–$$$**

Restaurant Prices

Price categories are based on the average cost of a meal for two, excluding drinks, tax and tip.
$ = $20 or less
$$ = $20–40
$$$ = $40–60
$$$$ = $60 and up

Culture and Attractions

Graceland
Elvis Presley Boulevard
Tel: (901) 332 3322
www.elvis.com
Grounds open year-round daily 10am–6pm except public holidays; mansion closed Tues in winter. Entrance fee.

Mississippi River Museum
125 N. Front Street
Tel: (901) 576 7241
www.muddisland.com
Open daily 10am–8pm (summer); Tues–Sun 10am–5pm (spring and fall). Entrance fee.

National Civil Rights Museum
450 Mulberry Street
Tel: (901) 521 9699.
Open Wed–Sat and Mon 9am–5pm, Sun 1–5pm. Entrance fee, but free Mon 3–6pm.

Sun Studio
706 Union Avenue
Tel: (901) 521 0664
Tour the recording studio that claims to be "the birthplace of rock 'n roll" and see where Elvis, Johnny Cash, Jerry Lee Lewis and Carl Perkins recorded their pioneering music (as well as hear original recordings with great acoustics). Open Mon–Sat 10am–6pm. Entrance fee.

More Lower Mississippi Attractions

Capitol Building
Baton Rouge
www.crt.state.la.us
Open daily 8am–4.30pm. Free.

Coca-Cola Museum
1107 Washington Street
Vicksburg
Tel: (601) 638 6514
www.preservevicksburg.com
Open Mon–Sat 9am–5pm, Sun 1.30–4.30pm except public holidays. Entrance fee.

Houmas House
40136 Highway 942
Darrow
Tel: (504) 891 9494
www.houmashouse.com
Open daily 9am–5pm. Entrance fee.

Laura Plantation
2247 Highway 18
Vacherie
Tel: 800-799 7690
www.lauraplantation.com
Open daily year-round 9.30am–5pm, except public holidays. Entrance fee.

New Madrid Historical Museum
1 Main Street
New Madrid
Tel: (573) 748 5944
Open daily 10am–5pm. Entrance fee.

Old Court House Museum
1008 Cherry Street
Court Square
Vicksburg
Tel: (601) 636 0741
www.oldcourthouse.org
Open Mon–Sat 8.30am–4.30pm, Sun 1.30–4.30pm. Entrance fee.

Vicksburg National Military Park
3201 Clay Street
Vicksburg
Tel: (601) 636 0583
www.gov/vick/home
Open daily 8am–5pm. Entrance fee.

The Atchafalaya Basin

ST MARTINVILLE AND LAFAYETTE

The towns in the region known as Cajun Country are not only popular cruise ports, but are also historic centers of Acadian culture.

Tourist Information

St Martinville Information Center
215 Evangeline Boulevard
Tel: (337) 394 2230

Where to Stay

Bienvenue House
421 N. Main Street
St Martinville
Tel: (337) 394 9100
www.bienvenuehouse.com
Antebellum home with porch swings and gourmet breakfast, within walking distance of center. **$$**

Bois des Chênes
338 N. Sterling Drive
Lafayette
Tel: (337) 233 7816
Lovingly converted plantation carriage house close to the center. **$$**

Country French Bed & Breakfast
616 General Mouton
Lafayette
Tel: (337) 234 2866
Located within a country French antiques shop and furnished accordingly. **$$**

La Maison Louie B&B
517 E. Bridge Street
St Martinville
Tel: (337) 394 1872
Open weekends only, there's a friendly welcome for guests to this French colonial house. **$$**

The Old Castillo Hotel
220 Evangeline Boulevard
St Martinville
Tel: 800-880 7050; (337) 394-4010
Beautiful historic inn with excellent restaurant on Bayou Teche. **$$**

Eating Out

Acadiana Catfish Shack
5818 Johnston Street
Lafayette
Tel: (337) 988 2200
www.catfishshack.com
Excellent seafood, buffet style. **$**

Maison de Ville Restaurant
100 N. Main Street
St Martinville
Tel: (337) 394 5700
Serves fine regional cuisine,
and there's an interesting bar.
$$
La Place D'Evangeline
Restaurant
220 Evangeline Boulevard
St Martinville
Tel: (337) 394 4010
French cuisine, located in the
Historic District. **$**
Poor Boy's Riverside Inn
US Highway 90 East
Lafayette
Tel: (337) 235 8559
Cajun seafood and steaks
served in a casual atmosphere, and
a beautiful setting overlooking the
river. **$**
Prejean's
3480 1-49 North
Lafayette
Tel: (337) 896 3247
Famous for its live Cajun music and
award-winning *gumbos*, often busy,
and even more so, when tour
groups visit. **$**

Culture and Attractions
Acadian Memorial Museum
121 South New Market Street
St Martinville
Tel: (337) 394 2258
www.acadianmemorial.org
Open daily 10am–4pm.
Entrance fee.
African American Museum
123 South New Market Street
St Martinville
Tel: (337) 394 4562
www.acadianmemorial.org
Open daily 10am–4pm.
Entrance fee.
Petit Paris Museum
103 South Main Street
St Martinville
Tel: (337) 394 7334
www.acadianmemorial.org
Open daily 9.30am–4.30pm.
Entrance fee.
Rip Van Winkle Gardens
5505 Rip Van Winkle Road
New Iberia
Tel: (318) 365 3332
Open daily 10am–4pm.
Entrance fee.

Ohio-Tennessee-Cumberland Ports

PITTSBURGH, PENNSYLVANIA

The city's industrial roots have
infused its restaurant scene with
plenty of meat-and-potato "working
man" joints, but its ethnic diversity
has kept eating options more
diverse. The city's hotels include
several gorgeous reminders of the
gilded age, as well as other options.

Tourist Information
Pittsburgh Visitors' Bureau
Downtown at Liberty Avenue,
adjacent to Gateway Center
Tel: 800-366-0093; (412) 281 7711
www.pittsburgh-cvb.org

Where to Stay
The Priory
614 Pressley Street
Tel: 866-814 4406
This former hostelry for Benedictine
priests passing through town has
added quite a few creature
comforts since its days of
abstinence. Victorian trimmings
enhance the beautiful garden and
sense of peace about the place. **$$**

Hotel Price Guide

Price categories are based on
the average cost of a double
room per night.
$ = $50 or less
$$ = $50–150
$$$ = $150–250

Renaissance Pittsburgh Hotel
107 Sixth Street
Tel: (412) 562 1200
The sort of sturdy edifice you'd
expect from a Pittsburgh hotel – a
granite and brick exterior, a copper
rotunda dome; marble and mosaic
tiles are all elements in the build-
ing's Renaissance Revival style. **$$$**

Eating Out
Mallorca Restaurant
2228 East Carson Street
Tel: (412) 488 1818
Spanish-style food and décor, from

the paella and rabbit with Marsala
sauce to the painted tiles on the
walls and the outdoor terrace. You'll
feel like you've touched down in
1930s Madrid. **$$$–$$$$**
Wholey's Fish Market
1711 Penn Avenue
Tel: (412) 391 2884
The market portion of this local
institution sells all manner of meats
under its extensive red awning, but
the restaurant section specializes
in the freshest fish in town. Chief
on its menu of fried and broiled
delights is the famous fish
sandwich (called just that,
"Famous Fish Sandwich") and
delicious crab cakes. **$**

Culture and Attractions
Andy Warhol Museum
117 Sandusky Street
Tel: (412) 237 8300
www.warhol.org
The artist may have been the
quintessential New Yorker, but he
was born here, and that's where the
Andy Warhol Foundation chose to
honor him with a seven-floor museum
filled with over 4,000 pieces of art
and other odds and ends. Open
Tues–Sun 10am–5pm. Entrance fee.
Carnegie Museum of Art
Carnegie Museum of Natural
History
4400 Forbes Avenue
Tel: (412) 622 3131
www.carnegiemuseums.org
Open Tues–Sat 10am–5pm, Sun
1–5pm. Entrance fee; combined
ticket available.
Frick Art and Historical Center
7227 Reynolds Street
Tel: (412) 371 0600
Open Tues–Sat 10am–5pm, Sun
noon–5pm; Gallery/museum free;
fee for house visits and tours.

CINCINNATI, OHIO

This Ohio River town has more
gourmet and ethnic food
(particularly French and German)
than you'd expect of a place whose
great contribution to the world of
food is Cincinnati-style chili. Thanks
to its rich history as a major port
town, Cincinnatians of yore built

enough art deco hotels to leave a few survivors alongside the modern accommodations rising high on the skyline.

Tourist Information
The Cincinnati Visitor Center
Fifth Third Center, Fifth and Walnut
Tel: 1-800-CINCY-USA

Where to Stay
Cincinnatian Hotel
601 Vine Street
Tel: 800-942 9000
www.cincinnatianhotel.com
Conceived as a "Grand Hotel" when built in 1882, the eight-story Cincinnatian Hotel was the tallest building in the city (and certainly the biggest one in the French Second Empire style). Skyscrapers may dwarf it these days, but it's still got style: rooms with balconies, robes, Roman tubs, fireplaces and elegant modern furniture. **$$$**
Gaslight Bed & Breakfast
3652 Middleton Avenue
Tel: (513) 861 5222
Up on a hill in Clifton, the historic gaslight district, this 1909 four-story house beckons travelers to rest in its overstuffed furniture or sip iced tea on its shady porch. The sturdy inn, with its stained glass, high ceilings and windows and hardwood floors, survived a fire. **$$**

Eating Out
Lenhardt's & Christy's
151 West McMillan Avenue
Tel: (513) 281 3600
Inexpensive food in a lovely house built in the 1880s. The Yugoslavian owners have represented their homeland well with *sauerbraten* and *spaetzle*, Hungarian *goulasch* and *goetta dogs* sharing space on the menu with jalapeno hot peppers and burgers. **$–$$**
Maisonette
114 East Sixth Street
Tel: (513) 721 2260
This French bistro has a reputation as the finest in the city. The tuna tartare with caviar and the veal chop *grandmère* are highlights, but there is a distinct absence of vegetarian options on the menu.
$$$$

Restaurant Prices

Price categories are based on the average cost of a meal for two, excluding drinks, tax and tip.
$ = $20 or less
$$ = $20–40
$$$ = $40–60
$$$$ = $60 and up

Culture and Attractions
Cincinnati Art Museum
953 Eden Park Drive
Tel: 877-472 4CAM; (513) 639 2995
www.cincinnatiartmuseum.org
Open Tues–Sun 11am–5pm, until 9pm on Wed.
Cincinnati Museum Center
1301 Western Avenue
Tel: (513) 287 7000
www.cincymuseum.org
Three in one – history, natural science and children's museums. Open Mon–Sat 10am–5pm, Sun 11am–6pm. Entrance fee.
Krohn Conservatory
1501 Eden Park Drive
Tel: (513) 421 5707
Open daily 10am–5pm.
Taft Museum of Art
316 Pike Street
Tel: (513) 241 0343
www.taftmuseum.org
This National Historic Landmark, with a collection focused on European old masters and 19th-century American painters, unveiled a new look in 2004 – a renovation that doubled its size with more rooms and parking, a performance space and tea rooms. Open Tues–Sat 10am–5pm, until 8pm Thur, Sun noon–5pm. Entrance fee.

More Ohio & Tennessee rivers Attractions
Campus Martius Museum
601 Second Street, Marietta
Tel: 800-860 0145; (740) 373 3750
www.ohiohistory.org
Open Wed–Sat 9.30am–5pm, Sun noon–5pm. Disabled access. Entrance fee.
Children's Toy and Doll Museum
206 Gilman Street, Huntington
Tel: (740) 373 5900
Open Sat 1–4pm and by appointment. Entrance fee.

Huntington Museum of Art
2033 McCoy Road, Huntington
Tel: (304) 529 2701
www.hmoa.org
Open Tues–Sat 10am–5pm, until 9pm on Tues, Sun noon–5pm. Entrance fee.
James Audubon Museum
3100 Highway 41, Henderson
Tel: (502) 827 1893
Open daily 10am–5pm. Entrance fee.
Kentucky Derby Museum
700 Central Avenue, Louisville
Tel: (502) 637 7097
www.derbymuseum.org
Open Mon–Sat 9am–5pm, Sun noon–5pm. Entrance fee.
Louisville Science Center
727 West Main Street, Louisville
Tel: (502) 561 6100
www.louisvillescience.org
Open Mon–Thur 9.30am–5pm, Fri–Sat 9.30am–9pm, Sun noon–6pm. Entrance fee.
Louisville Slugger Museum
800 West Main Street, Louisville
Tel: (502) 588 7228
www.sluggermuseum.org
Open daily for tours; last tour 4pm. Entrance fee.
Market House Museum
121 Market House Square, Paducah
Tel: (270) 443 7759
Open Tues–Sat noon–4pm, Sun 1–4pm. Entrance fee.
Museum of American Quilters
215 Jefferson Street, Paducah
Tel: (270) 442 8856
www.quiltmuseum.org
Open Mon–Sat 10am–5pm, plus Sun 1–5pm in summer. Entrance fee.
Ohio River Museum
601 Second Street, Marietta
Tel: 800-860 0145; (740) 373 3717
www.ohiohistory.org
Open Wed–Sat 9.30am–5pm, Sun noon–5pm. Entrance fee.
Ohio Tobacco Museum
703 South Second Street, Ripley
Tel: (937) 392 9410
Open Apr–Dec, Sat 10am–4pm, Sun 1–4pm, or by appointment.
Reitz Home Museum
224 Southeast First Street, Evansville
Tel: (812) 426 1871
www.reitzhome.evansville.net
Open Feb–Dec, Wed–Sun 1–4pm.

Shiloh National Military Park
1055 Pittsburg Landing Road, Shiloh
Tel: (731) 689 5696
Open daily 8am to dusk. Call ahead
for information. Entrance fee.
US Space & Rocket Center
1 Tranquility Base, Huntsville
Tel: (256) 837 3400
www.spacecamp.com
Open daily 9am–6pm (summer);
9am–5pm (winter). Entrance fee;
combination ticket for the museum,
Rocket Park and one movie in the
Spacedome IMAX theater.

The Columbia & Snake Rivers

PORTLAND, OREGON

When it comes to dining in "The City
of Roses," seafood is just the
beginning. Portland sits in a valley
that some people have compared to
the Normandy region of France,
bursting with mushrooms, horse
radish, peppermint, berries,
cherries, hazelnuts and pears, all
ripe for the pan of a clever chef.
Downtown Portland has a number
of historic gems, as well as wacky
boutique hotels and hotel chains.

Tourist Information
**Visitor Information and Services
Center**
Pioneer Courthouse Square
Tel: 1-877-678 5263; (503) 275
8355
www.pova.com

Where to Stay
Benson
309 South West Broadway
Tel: (503) 228 2000
Built in 1912, this elegant hotel
blends age-old traditions like
afternoon tea with Internet for
guests' use. An extensive

Hotel Price Guide

Price categories are based on
the average cost of a double
room per night.
$ = $50 or less
$$ = $50–150
$$$ = $150–250

renovation helped its Italian marble
floors, Circassian walnut walls and
antique Austrian crystal chandeliers
achieve maximum opulence. **$$**
The Mallory Hotel
729 Southwest 15th Avenue
Tel: (503) 223 6311
A boutique hotel before the term
existed, The Mallory has offered
reasonably-priced luxury since
1912. That luxury includes a
mirrored lobby, leaded chandeliers,
a grandfather clock, floral-print bed
spreads and oak furniture. **$$**

Eating Out
Alexis
215 West Burnside Street
Tel: (503) 224 8577
If you couldn't identify this as a
Greek taverna by the white walls,
blue-and-white check vinyl
tablecloths and belly dancers, the
sumptuous aroma of *souvlaki* will
do it. Try the Alexis sample platter
of assorted Greek and Middle
Eastern food and the moussaka
(lamb and eggplant casserole).
$$–$$$
Jakes Famous Crawfish
401 Southwest 12th Avenue
Tel: (503) 226 1419
The mahogany walls of this century-
old local favorite are imbued with the
pleasant scents of meals past and
present: chowder, salmon, halibut,
clams, oysters, bouillabaisse and
other fresh seafood staples, along
with fine Caesar salads. **$$$**

Culture and Attractions
**Oregon Maritime Center and
Museum**
113 SW Naito Parkway
Tel: (503) 224 7724
Open Wed–Sun 11am–4pm
(summer); Fri–Sun 11am–4pm
(winter). Entrance fee.
Oregon Zoo
4001 SW Canyon Road
Tel: (503) 226 1561
www.zooregon.org
Open daily 9am–6pm (summer);
9am–4pm (winter). Entrance fee.
Powell's City of Books
701 Southwest 6th Avenue
Tel: (503) 223 1613
www.powells.com
Portland is a city of many

bookstores and, since this one
claims to be "the world's largest
bookstore," Powell's will fulfill most
bibliophilic needs.

More Columbia & Snake rivers Attractions
Columbia Gorge Discovery Center
5000 Discovery Drive, The Dalles
Tel: (541) 296 8600
www.gorgediscovery.org
Open daily except public holidays
9am–5pm. Also includes the Wasco
County Historical Museum.
Entrance fee.
Columbia River Maritime Museum
1792 Marine Drive, Astoria
Tel: (503) 325 2323
www.crmm.org
Interactive exhibits. Open daily
9.30am–5pm. Entrance fee.
Flavel House
441 Eighth Street, Astoria
Tel: (503) 325 2563
Open daily 10am–5pm.
Entrance fee.
Fort Clatsop
92343 Clatsop Road, Astoria
Tel: (503) 861 2471
www.oldoregon.com
Operated by the National Park
Service. Open daily 9am–7pm
(summer); 9am–5pm (fall). Timed
tickets. Entrance fee.
Fort Walla Walla
755 Myra Road, Walla Walla
Tel: (509) 525 7703
www.fortwallawallamuseum.org
Open summer only, daily 10am–
5pm. Entrance fee.
Heritage Museum
1618 Exchange Street, Astoria
Tel: (503) 325 2203
Open Wed–Sat 1–5pm, Thur–Fri
1–4pm. Donations welcome.
**Maryhill Museum of Art and
Stonehenge Monument**
335 Maryhill Museum Drive,
Goldendale
Tel: (509) 773 3733
www.maryhillmuseum.org
Open summer only, daily 9am–5pm.
Entrance fee.
Tamastslikt Cultural Institute
72789 Highway 331, Pendleton
Tel: (541) 966 9748
www.tamastslikt.com
Open daily except public holidays
9am–5pm. Entrance fee.

Whitman Mission
328 Whitman Mission Road
Walla Walla
Tel: (509) 529 2761
www.whitmanmission.areaparks.com
The Mission is in southeast
Washington, seven miles west of
Walla Walla. Open daily 8am–6pm
(summer); 8am–4.30pm (winter).

The Great Lakes Ports

CHICAGO, ILLINOIS

You could content yourself with
Chicago classics such as deep-dish
pizza and Polish food, not to
mention cheesecake, Italian beef
sandwiches and Chicken Vesuvio.
But the city also has many world-
class restaurants serving all sorts
of gourmet delights. Likewise,
Chicago hotels span the ultra-
sophisticated to the small boutique.

Tourist Information
Chicago Water Works Visitor Center
163 East Pearson Street at
Michigan Avenue
Tel: (312) 744 2400
www.ci.chi.il.us/Tourism

Where to Stay
Hotel Burnham
1 West Washington
Tel: 877-294 9712
www.burnhamhotel.com
This boutique hotel in the century-
old Reliance Building features
terrazzo floors, marble ceilings and
glass and terracotta facade,
restored to their "Chicago Style"
glory. All rooms contain rich gold
and blue fabrics, and dramatic
views of the city's skyline. **$$$**
The Raphael Chicago
201 East Delaware Place
Tel: (312) 943 5000
www.raphaelchicago.com
Built in the 1920s as a nurses'
dormitory, this red-brick hotel is
located near the John Hancock
Center and Michigan Avenue stores.
Rooms feature arched entryways,
and wood-beamed ceilings. **$$**
Silversmith Crowne Plaza
10 South Wabash Avenue
Tel: (312) 372 7696
A Chicago classic. Registered as a

historic landmark, this 1897 hotel
is designed in the style of local
architect, Frank Lloyd Wright, its
rooms accented with wood. **$$$**

Eating Out
Billy Goat Tavern
430 North Michigan Avenue
Tel: (312) 222 1525
Made famous by John Belushi's
"cheeseborger" skit on Saturday
Night Live in the 1970s, this
basement-level greasy spoon has
been serving comfort food to
Chicago Tribune reporters and other
regulars for decades. **$**
The Rosebud
1500 West Taylor Street
Tel: (312) 942 1117
An institution of Chicago's Little
Italy, tucked away in a veritable
living room locale with wood
paneling, bookshelves and a
portrait of Frank Sinatra on the wall.
Try the homemade *cavatelli* and the
baked lasagna, and polish them off
with the triple chocolate cake. **$$$**

Restaurant Prices

Price categories are based on
the average cost of a meal for
two, excluding drinks, tax and tip.
$ = $20 or less
$$ = $20–40
$$$ = $40–60
$$$$ = $60 and up

Culture and Attractions
The Art Institute of Chicago
111 South Michigan Avenue
Tel: (312) 443 3600
www.artic.edu
A top-notch art museum, crammed
with items dating as far back as
3,000 BC. Specializes in French
Impressionist paintings and fine
and decorative arts from America,
Europe, Africa, Asia and Latin
America. Open Mon–Fri
10am–4.30pm, until 8pm on Tues,
Sat–Sun 10am–5pm. Entrance fee.
Museum of Science and Industry
57th Street at Lake Shore Drive
Tel: (773) 684 1414
www.msichicago.org
Wild West and wildlife exhibits as
well as fascinating interactive

science and industry displays.
Open Mon–Sat 9.30am–5.30pm,
Sun 11am–5.30pm (summer); until
9.30am–4pm (winter). Entrance fee

ALBANY, NEW YORK

Among the hotel chains that
dominate this town's lodging scene,
there are a few gems. You'll find
more locally-owned variety in
Albany's restaurants, mostly
serving American and ethnic
options. Despite its landlocked
location the city restaurants also
have good seafood, perhaps a
holdover from its heyday as an Erie
Canal stop.

Tourist Information
**Albany Heritage Area Visitors
Center**
25 Quackenbush Square.
Tel: (518) 434 0405.
www.albany.org

Where to Stay
Mansion Hill Inn and Restaurant
115 Philip Street.
Tel: (518) 465 2038.
www.mansionhill.com
A cozy downtown bed and
breakfast, with a landscaped
courtyard, and a restaurant with
an upscale menu. **$$**
The Morgan State House
393 State Street
Tel: 888-427 6063
www.statehouse.com
A Capital District townhouse
mansion restored to its original
late 19th-century glamour. Rich
woods line the halls and stairs,
and elegant modern décor in the
guest rooms. **$$$**

Eating Out
River Street Cafe
429 River Street
Tel: (518) 273 2740
This restaurant serves fusion cuisine
in an upstairs dining room with
great views of the Hudson River.
The menu uses local ingredients
such as beet-stuffed Portobello
and "honey-crisp duck two ways"
in a sauce of port, balsamic vinegar
and blackberries. **$$$**

Tollgate Ice Cream & Coffee Shop
1569 New Scotland Road.
Tel: 518-439-9824.
Albany's resident dairy stop,
serving homemade ice cream and
local favorites like the Eight-Inch
Super Sundae. Also burgers,
seafood platters and steaks. **$**

Culture and Attractions
Historic Cherry Hill
523 1/2 South Pearl Street
Tel: (518) 434 4791
www.historiccherryhill.org
A beautiful mansion built in 1787,
overlooking the Hudson River, that's
filled with antiques and other
artifacts. Entrance fee.

St Lawrence Seaway

QUÉBEC

Québec is big on ciders, cheese
(100 varieties), and local delicacies
like lobster from the Îles-de-la-
Madeleine, apples, blueberries
and numerous treats and entrées
that use syrup from the annual
"Sugar Shack" maple harvest as the
prime ingredient. The city's strong
French heritage touches nearly all its
restaurants, as well as its hotels.

Tourist Information
Centre Infotouriste
12 rue Sainte Anne
Tel: 1-877-266 5687;
(418) 641 6290
www.bonjourquebec.com

Where to Stay
The Château Bonne Entente
3400 Chemin Sainte-Foy
Tel: (418) 653 5221
Though only 10 minutes from Old
Québec and five minutes from the
airport, the château's 11 acres
(4.5 hectares) of Canadian
countryside feel a world away. Built
in 1950, there are three terraces,
gardens, a pool, spa, and ball
courts. Fine French dining in its two
restaurants. **$$$**
Fairmont Le Château Frontenac
1 ruc des Carrières
Tel: 800-828 7447; (418) 692
3861
More than a century old, this French

Hotel Price Guide

Price categories are based on
the average cost of a double
room per night.
$ = $50 or less
$$ = $50–150
$$$ = $150–250

castle in Old Québec affords
magnificent views of Lévis, the
Island of Orleans, and the St
Lawrence River. Facilities include a
ballroom and modern amenities
such as a health spa and in-room
video game console. Still the hotel
preserves 19th-century Québec. **$$$**
Le Saint-Paul
229 rue Saint-Paul
Tel: (418) 266 2165
www.quebecweb.com
This hotel is housed in an unusual
1854 building that suits the
architecture of the nearby railroad
station and Québec's old
fortifications. The Victorian interior
has exposed brick and wood beams
and floor-to-ceiling windows. **$$**

Eating Out
Chez Ashton
640 Grande Allée Est
Tel: (418) 522 3449
This fast food chain serves local
delicacies like *poutines* (fries
topped with cheese curd and brown
gravy) with the burgers and other
standard fare. This particular
branch is worth noting because of
its popular terrace overlooking one
of Québec's busy, scenic streets. **$**
L'Echaudé
73 rue Sault-au-Matelot
Tel: (418) 692 1299
A casual bistro in the Vieux-Port
area with art deco décor and a
terrace over a pedestrianized
street. The menu sticks to the
classics of nouvelle French cuisine
like steak frites and *confit de
canard*. **$$$$**

Culture and Attractions
Basilique-Cathédrale Notre-Dame
20 rue De Buade
Tel: (418) 694 0665
Built in 1647, this basilica – full of
baroque details and Christian

treasures – relates history in the
multi-media show, "Feux Sacrés."
Tours are free but there is an
entrance fee to the cathedral.
Musée d'Art Inuit Brousseau
39 rue St-Louis
Tel: (418) 694 1828
Open Tues–Sun 10am–5pm.
Entrance fee.
Musée de la Civilisation
85 rue Dalhousie
Tel: (418) 643 2158
Open Tues–Sun 10am–5pm.
Entrance fee.

MONTRÉAL

When dining at one of Montréal's
restaurants, represented by over 75
ethnic groups, consider ordering the
table d'hôte, a two- to four-course
menu that is usually less expensive
than ordering à la carte. As in
Québec, menus are bilingual, and
some are French only, which can
make ordering even the simplest
plate of *stimés* (steamed hot dogs)
a challenge if you're not prepared.
The local hotel scene is much more
straightforward, a mix of cozy inns,
B&Bs and historic hotels, as well as
popular chains.

Tourist Information
Centre Infotouriste
1001 rue du Square-Dorchester
Tel: 877-266 5687; (514) 873 2015
www.tourisme-montreal.org

Where to Stay
Château Versailles Hotel
1659 rue Sherbrooke Ouest
Tel: (514) 933 3611
This four-story mansion, built in
1919, has Edwardian comforts.
With custom-made wood furniture
and bold color schemes, some of
the rooms have fireplaces. **$$**
La Maison Pierre du Calvet
405 rue Bonsecours
Tel: 866-544 1725
www.pierreducalvet.ca
It was good enough for Benjamin
Franklin. He stayed here during the
French rule of Canada. The thick
stone walls, high, beamed ceilings
and huge chimneys of this 1725
house have withstood the tests of

time on a cobblestoned, gas-lit street in Old Montréal. $$$

The Ritz-Carlton Montréal
1228 Rue Sherbrooke Ouest
Tel: 800-363 0366
www.ritzcarlton.com/hotels/montreal
The rooms of this 1913 building have been done up in a fancy Edwardian style with Louis XV-style furniture and bed linen of Egyptian cotton. Even if you don't stay here, swing through the lobby, decorated with engraved mirrors and oil paintings. $$$

Eating Out
Chez Schwartz Charcuterie
3895 Boulevard St-Laurent
Tel: (514) 842 4813
This is a deli, plain and simple, but one that serves some of best smoked meat in the city. Long lines of local people wait to sit at the lunch counter of this cramped space to get a fix of this Canadian treat, usually served in great piles between slices of rye bread. $–$$

Restaurant Prices

Price categories are based on the average cost of a meal for two, excluding drinks, tax and tip.
$ = $20 or less
$$ = $20–40
$$$ = $40–60
$$$$ = $60 and up

Les Halles
1450 Crescent Street
Tel: (514) 844 2328
A well-respected downtown restaurant with over 30 years experience, serving traditional French cooking with a contemporary flourish. The menu includes such dishes as lobster in herb butter, red wine-marinated caribou and gateau Josephine (chocolate cake). $$$

Culture and Attractions
Biodôme de Montréal
4777 Pierre-de-Coubertin Avenue
Tel: (514) 868 3000
www.biodome.qc.ca
A leftover from the 1976 Olympics, next to Montréal's Botanical Garden, it houses re-creations of a

rainforest, the Laurentian forest, the St Lawrence marine system, and a polar environment, with over 6,000 fauna and 210 flora (as well as 4,000 trees) between them.

Musée d'Archéologie et d'Histoire de la Pointe-à-Calliere
350 Place Royale
Tel: (514) 872 9150
Open Tues–Fri 10am–5pm, Sat–Sun 11am–5pm. Entrance fee.

Musée d'Art Contemporain
185 rue Ste-Catherine Ouest
Tel: (514) 847 6226
Open Tues–Sun 11am–6pm, until 9pm on Wed. Entrance fee.

Musée des Beaux Arts
1380 rue Sherbrooke Ouest
Tel: (514) 285 2000
Open Tues–Sun 11am–5pm. Entrance fee.

Musée McCord
690 rue Sherbrooke Ouest
Tel: (514) 398 7100
Open Tues–Fri 10am–6pm, Sat–Sun 10am–5pm, and Mon in summer.

More St Lawrence Attractions
Antique Boat Museum
750 Mary Street, Clayton
Tel: (315) 686 4104
www.abm.org
Open Mon–Sat 9am–5pm. Entrance fee.

Frederic Remington Art Museum
303 Washington Street, Ogdensburg
Tel: (315) 393 2425
www.fredericremington.org
Open Mon–Sat 10am–5pm, Sun 1–5pm (summer); Wed–Sat 11am–5pm, Sun 1–5pm (winter). Entrance fee.

Marine Museum of the Great Lakes and **Pump House Steam Museum**
55 Ontario Street, Kingston
Tel: (613) 542 2261
www.marmus.ca
Open daily 10am–5pm (summer); Mon–Fri 10am–4pm (winter). Pump House open daily 10am–4pm (summer only). Entrance fee.

Upper Canada Village Heritage Park
County Road 2, Morrisburg
Tel: (613) 543 4328
www.uppercanadavillage.com
Open daily 9.30am– 5pm (summer only). Entrance fee.

Language

The majority of people in mainland US, much of Alaska, Hawaii, and Canada speak English. Spanish is spoken by a sizable minority of people in the southern states of the USA, and French is spoken in parts of Canada. Hawaii does have its own language and many native peoples speak their own languages in Canada and Alaska.

Canadian French

Pronunciation is key to French; people really will not understand if you get it very wrong. Remember to emphasize each syllable, not to pronounce the last consonant of a word as a rule (this includes the plural "s"), and always to drop your "h"s. Whether to use "*vous*" or "*tu*" is a vexed question; increasingly the familiar form of "*tu*" is used by many people. However, it is better to be too formal, and use "*vous*" if in doubt. It is important to be polite; always address people as Madame or Monsieur, and address them by their surnames until you are confident first names are acceptable.

Learning the pronunciation of the French alphabet is a good idea and, in particular, learn to spell your name.

Montréal is the second-largest French-speaking city in the world, after Paris. Some 65 percent of the city's residents and 70 percent of those in the metropolitan area are French-speakers (francophones), with 12 percent and 15 percent English-speakers (anglophones) respectively. Despite nationalistic insistence, the province's French has never been pure. After 300 years of separation from the motherland, how could it be? Over the past decades, as Montréalers acknowledge differences and gain confidence, this is amusing rather than disconcerting.

Unique to Montréal is joual, a patois whose name is garbled French for horse: *cheval*. The earthy dialect flourishes among the city's working class and in the work of playwright Michel Tremblay.

Pronunciation of mainstream French also differs. Accents distinguish French in Québec from French in Paris or Marseilles. Québec's francophones form sounds deep in the throat, lisp slightly, voice toward diphthongs, and bend single vowels into exotic shapes. It has also incorporated some English words, such as "chum," as in *mon chum* or *ma chumme*, and blonde, for girlfriend, while *le fun* is a good time.

Even if you don't speak much French, starting a conversation with "Bonjour," is likely to evoke a positive response. Some shopkeepers hedge, with an all-purpose "*Hi-bonjour.*"

Hawaiian

The Hawaiian language has acquired several interesting grammatical complications, as well as a pronunciation system known for its complex vowel combinations and small number of consonants.

The consonant symbol ' – called the *'okina* – represents a glottal stop, which indicates a stop-start pronunciation. If you would like more *kokua* (help) with Hawaiian language, refer to three excellent books on the subject: *Spoken Hawaiian*, by Samuel Elbert; *Let's Speak Hawaiian*, by Dorothy Kahananui and A. Anthony; and *The Hawaiian Dictionary*, by Samuel Elbert and Mary Kawena Pukui.

Canadian Inuit

There is little available literature on the Inuktitut Inuit language, largely because the Inuits don't want their language to be taken away. The best guide to the language and culture is *The Inuit of Canada*, published by The Inuit of Taparitsat, 170 Laurier Avenue W, Ste 150, Ottawa, Ontario K1P 5V5. Tel: (613) 238 8181.

Further Reading

History, Economics and Culture

Undaunted Courage, by Stephen Ambrose, Simon & Schuster. A detailed account of the Lewis and Clark expedition.
Shoal of Time, by Gavan Daws, University of Hawaii Press. A history of Hawaii emphasizing its politics and culture.

Fiction

Moby Dick, by Herman Melville, Bantam Classics. Part classic novel, part primer on American whaling as practiced in its heyday.
Hawaii, by James Michener, Bt Bound. A sweeping saga based strongly on Hawaiian history.
The House of the Seven Gables, by Nathaniel Hawthorne, Bantam Classics. A New England tale based in colonial-era Salem, Massachusetts.
The Shipping News, by E. Annie Proulx, Scribner. The tale of a journalist who rebuilds his shattered life in Newfoundland.
Show Boat, by Edna Ferber, Lightyear Pr. A fun, somewhat trashy read about a floating theater that conveys much detail about river life of the post-Civil War era.

Travelogues and Non-fiction

The Perfect Storm, by Sebastian Junger, W.W. Norton & Co. An account of the "storm of the [20th] century" that gives insight into fishing life on the eastern seaboard.
Life on the Mississippi, by Mark Twain, Library of America. The classic memoir/travelogue of the Mississippi River as it was in the era of steamships.
Old Glory, An American Voyage, by Jonathan Raban, Harperperennial

Library. A life on the Mississippi for the 21st century, as the writer chronicles his motor boat trip down the river.
Travels in Alaska, by John Muir, Mariner Books. A beloved classic of the great naturalist's journey through Alaska and discovery of Glacier Bay.
The Log from the Sea of Cortéz, by John Steinbeck, Penguin. A day-by-day account of Steinbeck's 1940 trip into the Gulf of California with his pal, biologist Ed Ricketts.

Cruise Guides

Complete Guide to Ocean Cruising & Cruise Ships by Douglas Ward, Berlitz (2004).The industry's bible, it contains detailed, candid reviews of 254 ships, plus impeccable advice.

Other Insight Guides

Insight Guides publishes a comprehensive range of titles.

Companion titles to *Insight Guide North American and Alaskan Cruises* include many guides in the North American series such as: **Western United States, American Southwest, Arizona and the Grand Canyon, Boston, California, Canada, Southern California, Chicago, Florida, Hawaii, Las Vegas, Los Angeles, Miami, Montréal, New England, New Orleans, New York City, New York City Museums, New York State, The New South, Orlando, Pacific Northwest, Philadelphia, San Francisco, Seattle, Texas, USA On The Road, Vancouver,** and **Washington DC**. Thematic titles include **Caribbean Cruises** and **Mediterranean Cruises**.

In addition, there are related titles in the **Insight Pocket Guide** and **Insight Compact Guide** series, and also **Insight Maps**.

ART & PHOTO CREDITS

Cartographic Editor **Zoë Goodwin**
Production **Linton Donaldson**
Design Director **Klaus Geisler**
Picture Research **Hilary Genin**

Map Production
Polyglott Kartographie, Berndtson & Berndtson Publications
© 2004 Apa Publications GmbH & Co. Verlag KG
(Singapore Branch)

Index

Numbers in italics refer to photographs

A
B
C
D
F
G
H
I
J
a
b
c
d
e
f
h
i
j
k
l